Property, Freedom, & Society

Essays in Honor of
Hans-Hermann Hoppe

Property, Freedom, & Society

Essays in Honor of
Hans-Hermann Hoppe

Edited by
Jörg Guido Hülsmann
and Stephan Kinsella

LvMI
MISES INSTITUTE

Ludwig von Mises Institute
518 West Magnolia Avenue
Auburn, Alabama 36832
mises.org

ISBN: 978-1-535150-68-2

Hans-Hermann Hoppe

Contents

PART FIVE: ECONOMICS

Introduction

Hans-Hermann Hoppe is one of the most important scholars of our time. He has made pioneering contributions to sociology, economics, philosophy, and history. He is the dean of the present-day Austrian School of economics, and is famous as a libertarian philosopher. He and his writings have inspired scholars all over the world to follow in his footsteps and to provide a scientific foundation for individual freedom and a free society. The following pages are a modest attempt to honor the occasion of Professor Hoppe's 60th birthday. The contributors are former students, colleagues, and collaborators, united in admiration for, and friendship with, the laureate.

Hans-Hermann Hoppe was born in the German town of Peine on September 2, 1949. In the late 1960s and early 1970s he studied history, sociology, and philosophy at the universities of Saarbrücken and Frankfurt am Main. His 1974 doctoral dissertation, published in 1976, dealt with the praxeological foundations of epistemology. Its central thesis was that all cognitive processes, and thus the sciences, are but special forms of human action. It followed that the laws of action were also the basic laws of epistemology. Hoppe would soon discover that, a few years before him, the Austrian economist Ludwig von Mises had come to essentially the same conclusion. This was his first contact with Austro-Libertarianism and it was the beginning of a process in the course of which young Hoppe, at the time a left-leaning statist, came to revise his political beliefs. The process accelerated when he started reading Murray Rothbard and discovered that Misesian "subjectivist" economics could be combined with objective political philosophy. But he first continued his philosophical studies, developing a new epistemology and methodology of the social sciences, based on the insights he had received from Mises and Rothbard.

Eventually, Hoppe turned into a full-blown Austrian when, in the early 1980s, he went to the United States on a prestigious Heisenberg fellowship. This time his research project concerned political philosophy, but it was again squarely built on Austrian economics. In 1986, he became Rothbard's colleague at the University of Nevada, Las Vegas (UNLV), where he would teach for the next 21 years. After Rothbard's untimely death in 1995, Professor Hoppe assumed a place of uncontested leadership among Austro-libertarian scholars, becoming the editor of the *Journal of Libertarian Studies*, a co-editor of the *Review of Austrian Economics*, and then a co-editor of the *Quarterly Journal of Austrian Economics*. Professor Hoppe, now Professor Emeritus of Economics at UNLV and Distinguished Fellow with the Ludwig von Mises Institute, also serves on on the editorial board of *Libertarian Papers*. In addition to authoring numerous scholarly articles, his important books include *Handeln und Erkennen* (1976), *Kritik der Kausalwissenschaftlichen Sozialforschung* (1983), *Eigentum, Anarchie, und Staat* (1987), *A Theory of Socialism and Capitalism* (1989), *The Economics and Ethics of Private Property* (1993, enlarged 2nd edition 2006), *Democracy – The God that Failed* (2001), and *The Myth of National Defense* (editor, 2003). His works have been translated into at least 21 languages, not counting English.[1]

Among Professor Hoppe's many achievements we should stress in particular his brilliant critique of positivist methodology as applied to the social sciences, a new praxeological approach to political philosophy, an encompassing comparative analysis of socialism and capitalism, and a theory of secession as a means of

---

[1]Professors Hoppe's publications, including links to translations and a detailed bibliography, are available at his website, www.hanshoppe.com.

political reform. Most importantly, in his book *Democracy – The God that Failed*, Professor Hoppe has delivered a profound critique of democracy, as well as an original reinterpretation of Western history in the twentieth century, both of which have stirred international debate in academia and among the wider public. Other influential works from his pen have dealt with the role of migrations within a free society, and with the role of public intellectuals in political transformation processes. Moreover, he has excelled as an historian of thought and made path-breaking contributions to other areas such as monopoly theory; the theory of public goods; the sociology of taxation; the positive methodology of the social sciences; the theory of risk; the production of security; the transformation of formerly socialist countries; and the evolution of monetary institutions and their impact on international relations. And Professor Hoppe's work is ongoing: he is currently working on a major book project that will restate and elaborate on his previous work in the fields of epistemology and ethics — more generally, the nature of human rationality. The goal of the book is to provide "a systematic and interdisciplinary reconstruction of human history (pre-history, hunter-gatherer societies, agricultural societies, industrial societies)."[2]

The preceding list reveals that Professor Hoppe is not only an academic and scholar, but also a public intellectual of the first order. He has tackled important and controversial subjects even where this was likely to bring him into conflict with colleagues, politicians, businessmen, and conventional wisdom. He has not shied away from advancing provocative ideas, but has done so in a thoughtful and clear-cut manner that, more often than not, has garnered enthusiastic acclaim in lecture halls and among readers all over the world. His competent verve has inspired students and colleagues, such as those who have contributed to the present volume.

---

[2]"Hans-Hermann Hoppe: Potret Intelektual Anti-Intelektual" ["Interview with Hans-Hermann Hoppe, an Anti-Intellectual Intellectual"], interview by Sukasah Syahdan, *Akal dan Kehendak* (Indonesia) (Apr. 28, 2008) (English translation available at www.hanshoppe.com/publications).

Finally Professor Hoppe has shown leadership not only in the realm of ideas, but also through the practical promotion of scientific enquiry and open debate. Most notably, in August 2005, he initiated the foundation of the international Property and Freedom Society, which eventually held its inaugural meeting in May, 2006, and elected him president.

The purpose of the Property and Freedom Society is to promote the scientific debate of the politically relevant questions of our time without regard to the concerns of party politics. It acknowledges the expediency of intransigent libertarian radicalism, which, in the long run, is the surest path to a free society. It therefore seeks to promote Austro-libertarianism, which ties back to the nineteenth century French economists Frédéric Bastiat and Gustave de Molinari. It stands

> for justly acquired private property, freedom of contract, freedom of association—which logically implies the right to not associate with, or to discriminate against—anyone in one's personal and business relations—and unconditional free trade. It condemns imperialism and militarism and their fomenters, and champions peace. It rejects positivism, relativism, and egalitarianism in any form, whether of "outcome" or "opportunity," and it has an outspoken distaste for politics and politicians.[3]

The present *liber amicorum* is testimony to the fact that these ideals have a universal appeal and inspire scholars from all over the world. It is therefore fitting that the name of Hoppe's beloved Property and Freedom Society inspire the title of the present volume.

The editors wish to express their appreciation for the enthusiastic cooperation of all who have helped with this project. Our special thanks go to the contributors, as well as to Mr. Llewellyn Rockwell

---

[3]"Principles of the Property and Freedom Society," available at www.propertyandfreedom.org (quoting the Opening Declaration from the Inaugural Meeting: Bodrum, Turkey, May 2006).

for his unflagging support in producing and publishing the present beautiful volume. We also gratefully acknowledge the efficient editorial assistance from Mrs. Judy Thommesen and Mrs. Kathy White, both at the Mises Institute, and translation assistance from Mrs. Arlene Oost-Zinner.

Jörg Guido Hülsmann
Angers, France

Stephan Kinsella
Houston, Texas

May 2009

Part One

Grato Animo Beneficiique
Memores

A Life of Ideas

Llewellyn H. Rockwell, Jr.

My first full exposure to the brilliance of Hans-Hermann Hoppe came at an early Mises University in which he gave the main lecture on methodology. Here he offered a new take on Mises's Kantian method. Hoppe explained Kant's typology of propositions, and showed how Mises had appropriated them but with a new twist.

Instead of categories of thinking and categories of the mind, Mises went further than Kant to delineate categories of action, which is the foundation of economic reasoning. In this lecture, we all discovered something about Mises we had not known, something bigger and grander than we knew, and it caused us to think differently about a subject that we thought we knew well.

This same Hoppean effect—that sense of having been profoundly enlightened by a completely new way of understanding something—has happened many times over the years. He has made contributions to ethics, to international political economy, to the theory of the origin of the state, to comparative systems, to culture and its economic relation, to anthropology and the theory and practice of war. Even on a subject that everyone thinks about but

Llewellyn H. Rockwell, Jr., is founder and chairman of the board of the Ludwig von Mises Institute in Auburn, Alabama, and editor of LewRockwell.com.

no one really seems to understand – the system of democracy – he clarified matters in a way that helps you see the functioning of the world in a completely new light.

There aren't that many thinkers who have this kind of effect. Mises was one. Rothbard was another. Hoppe certainly fits in that line. He is the kind of thinker who reminds you that ideas are real things that shape how we understand the world around us. I dare say that no one can read works like *Democracy – The God that Failed, A Theory of Socialism and Capitalism*, and *The Economics and Ethics of Private Property* and come away unchanged.[1]

Often times when you first hear a point he makes, you resist it. I recall when he spoke at a conference we held on American history, and gave a paper on the U.S. Constitution. You might not think that a German economist could add anything to our knowledge on this topic. He argued that it represented a vast increase in government power and that this was its true purpose. It created a powerful central government, with the cover of liberty as an excuse. He used it as a case in point, and went further to argue that all constitutions are of the same type. In the name of limiting government – which they purportedly do – they invariably appear in periods of history when the elites are regrouping to emerge from what they consider to be near anarchy. The Constitution, then, represents the assertion of power.

When he finished, you could hear a pin drop. I'm not sure that anyone was instantly persuaded. He had challenged everything we thought we knew about ourselves. The applause was polite, but not enthusiastic. Yet his points stuck. Over time, I think all of us there travelled some intellectual distance. The Constitution was preceded by the Articles of Confederation, which Rothbard had described as near anarchist in effect. Who were these guys who cobbled together this Constitution? They were the leftovers from the war: military leaders, financiers, and other mucky mucks – a

---

[1]Hans-Hermann Hoppe, *Democracy – The God that Failed: The Economics and Politics of Monarchy, Democracy, and Natural Order* (New Brunswick, N.J.: Transaction Publishers, 2001); idem, *A Theory of Socialism and Capitalism* (Boston-Dordrecht-London: Kluwer, 1989); idem, *The Economics and Ethics of Private Property: Studies in Political Economy and Philosophy* (Boston: Kluwer, 1993).

very different crew from the people who signed the Declaration of Independence. Jefferson was out of the country when the Constitution was passed. And what was the effect of the Constitution? To restrain government? No. It was precisely the opposite, just as Hoppe said. It created a new and more powerful government that not only failed to restrain itself (what government has ever done that?), but grew and grew into the monstrosity we have today. It required a wholesale rethinking of the history, but what Hoppe had said that shocked everyone turns out to be precisely right—and this is only one example among many.

I'm speaking for multitudes when I say that he helped me understand democracy as a form of nationalization of the citizenry. We all became the government: or, we all became public property. And what happens to public property? It is overutilized and wasted because it is unowned by any one person or group of people in particular. Thus did the citizens become war fodder. We are taxed without limit. We have no way to restrain the state since no one in particular is made responsible for our plight. Our leaders are mere managers—not owners, like the monarchs—who are encouraged to loot and leave. They are there as covers for the real state, which is a faceless apparatus that is permanent and cares nothing for the value of the commonwealth. He contrasted this with monarchy, not because he favors monarchy but rather to help us understand. The monarch is the owner. He has the incentive to preserve value. He can hand it on to an heir. Heirs were raised and trained for governance, and in turn to hand it on to their heirs. So we might expect them to be relatively more civilized as compared with democratic rulers.

History bears this out. Hoppe dates the onset of modern democracy to World War I and following, and he has scandalized many by calling the U.S., the Soviet Union, and Nazi Germany all democracies, but he means this in his special sense: the people neither own themselves nor are owned by anyone. The citizens are public property and are said to all participate in their own governance understood as an elected executive state. This was a modern form of government that displaced the old form—and it goes a long way towards explaining the advent of total war and the total state.

There are many other issues for which he has done this—his *Economics and Ethics of Private Property* helped people to imagine society without a state as never before. On the issue of immigration, he showed how modern states use immigration as a means of state expansion. He has taken on the issue of property covenants and their relationship to private property. There is so much more. We have all suspected for some time that this will culminate in a sweeping treatment of socio-economics, an integrated master treatise along the lines of the great books of Austrians past. Its time is coming.

Hoppe is an original thinker, but he is glad to grant his debts to Mises, to Rothbard, to Eric von Kuehnelt-Leddihn, and to the postmodernists of his German education. He stands on the shoulders of giants, and has reached beyond them, as Murray often acknowledged. There aren't many thinkers we can name who have been so generous with their insights, and given so much to help us understand the world around us more clearly.

Let me finally mention that Hans has something else in common with his predecessors. He is a man of courage and conviction. He had plenty of opportunities to sell out for preferment's sake, but he has stayed the course, committed to truth and to freedom and to the free marketplace of ideas. He is a tough and relentless fighter that we can all admire. He fears no truth. All this is why I can confidently predict that he will always emerge from battle as a champion. ❧

Hans-Hermann Hoppe and the Political Equivalent of Nuclear Fusion

Sean Gabb

I have been invited to contribute a chapter to this book of appreciations of Hans-Hermann Hoppe. Now, he is a person of forbidding achievements. He has made important contributions to economics, to political theory, to law, and to epistemology, among much else. He is also a person of much organizational ability, and the conferences he runs at Bodrum for his Property and Freedom Society have rapidly established themselves as one of the high points in the libertarian calendar.

This makes it difficult to know where to start when it comes to writing a single chapter about his achievements. What I have decided to do, however, is to try and show how what he might regard as one of his minor achievements is contributing to a new and potentially significant consensus within the libertarian and conservative movements.

Sean Gabb (sean@libertarian.co.uk), an English libertarian and conservative, is the director of the Libertarian Alliance, a British free market and civil liberties think-tank.

THE END OF THE COLD WAR:
A VICTORY DENIED

In the ideological sense, the Cold War was fought between the defenders of liberty and tradition and their most open and comprehensive enemies. Yet, in the settlement that followed the defeat of Communism, the main losers have been libertarians and conservatives.

Those who still regard this defeat as one for the enemies of liberty and tradition have failed to see beneath the surface of things to the underlying reality. Orthodox Marxism-Leninism, together with its numerous heresies, was mostly important, not in its own terms, but as an excuse. In every generation, there are people who want to live at the expense of others, or to make them unhappy, or both. Unless they are able to be predators by act of conquest — the Assyrians, for example, or the Mongols — these people always need arguments to persuade their victims that being robbed or murdered will make the world a better place. Most of them need themselves to believe these arguments.

Long before the Berlin Wall came down, Marxism had become an embarrassment. Its historical and economic underpinnings had crumbled. Its predictions had all been falsified. Its promises were all broken. Its body count and the poverty of its survivors could no longer be denied. It no longer served to justify the actions or the existence of the Soviet state. Its disestablishment after 1989 was less a defeat for the enemies of liberty and tradition than a release.

The accelerated rise of politically correct multiculturalism since then, and the rise, from almost nothing, of environmentalism, should not, therefore, be seen as ideologies of asylum for dispossessed Marxists. Rather, they are ideologies of transformation and control more in keeping with the spirit of the present age. Just as Marxism once did, each provides a shared narrative, a shared terminology, and shared feeling of doing good for those whose objects are anything but good.

They are, moreover, better than Marxism, so far as they are less threatening to the powers that be in the West. Diversity and sustainability requirements raise up bureaucracies that allow a cartelization of costs that privilege established wealth against the competition of new entrants. They otherwise provide jobs and status in organizations that look reassuringly like conventional businesses.

THE NEW WORLD ORDER

The result has been the emergence, since 1989, of a new order in which broadly liberal and democratic institutions are being transformed into the agencies of a police state, and in which traditional ways of life and real diversities are being swept aside in favor of centrally-directed homogeneity.

There is nothing unusual about what is happening. There is nothing that should not have been at least dimly perceived back in 1989. At the end of every real war, the winning alliance tends to break up, as the often radically different interest groups that comprised it find that what brought them together no longer exists to hold them together. New alliances then form between interest groups on the winning and losing sides.

This happened at the end of the Napoleonic wars, when Britain and France found themselves increasingly on the same side against the Central European powers. It happened again at the end of the Second World War, when the Americans and Russians fell out, and both recruited their zones of occupied Germany as allies in the new struggle. It has now happened with the new ideological settlement that emerged at the end of the Cold War.

Whether or not this was to be expected, libertarians and conservatives have reason to feel aggrieved. They were perhaps the two most prominent ideological groups in the battle against Communism. Libertarian economists provided the most devastating weapons of attack. Conservatives did most to articulate the revulsion that ordinary people felt when confronted with the kleptocracy and mass-murder at the heart of Communism. They are now jointly surplus to requirements in a world where ex-Trotskyites and even former Communist Party members have put on suits and become government ministers, and now sit happily at dinner with the heads of global corporations.

There are three possible responses to this state of affairs. Libertarians and conservatives can whine piteously about the unfairness of things. Or they can carry on, as if nothing had changed after 1989, addressing arguments to the same allies and against the same enemies. Or they can recognize that the world has changed, and that promoting the same values requires differences of approach.

New Times, New Ways

Let me now drop the impersonal tone. I will not speak directly for the conservatives. But I will speak for the general libertarian movement. There is no orthodoxy here. Libertarians disagree with each other almost as much as we disagree with our various opponents. Even so, it is possible to see an emerging consensus — first, that there is need of a new approach, and second, about its nature.

In explaining this, the logical place to start is with our thoughts on the free market.

Limited Liability:
The Worm in the Free Market Bud

Everyone knows that libertarians believe in free markets. Something we have not always made sufficiently plain — something that we may not always have been clear about ourselves — is that when we talk about free markets, what we mean is markets of free people. It does not mean that we endorse markets simply because they are efficient, or even because they are creative. In particular, we have no affection for big business.

Though there can be no doubt they have enriched the world, companies like Microsoft and General Motors and ICI are not natural institutions. They are creatures of the State. They came into being and are sustained by incorporation laws. These laws permit individuals and groups of individuals to act, not as themselves, but as servants of a fictitious entity. The directors and shareholders are not legally responsible for the debts of the entity. Nor need they feel morally responsible for their actions or inaction on its behalf.

Because of limited liability, business corporations can attract large amounts of investment. Because they are not natural persons, they need not follow the cycle of growth and decline normal to unincorporated businesses. Instead, one generation of directors and shareholders can give way to another. These devices allow business corporations to grow much larger than unincorporated businesses.

It might be argued that incorporation laws are similar to marriage laws—that is, that they gather what would otherwise be a number of complex agreements into a single act. If there were no state, people would still cohabit. Each partner could still make the other next of kin. There would be agreements or customary rules to regulate the management of common property and the rearing of children.

But this is not the case with incorporation. Certainly, the owners of any business could agree with their suppliers and customers that they are servants of a fictitious entity, and that their liability for debt is limited to their investment in the entity. But they could not contract out of liability in tort. This fact alone would put off any investor who was not able to buy a controlling interest. I and countless millions of people like me own shares in companies of which I know nothing. If we knew that we were to be regarded, in the event of a large award of damages, as jointly and severally liable for payment, hardly any of us would risk being shareholders.

Now, except for anarchists, to say that something could not exist without the state does not, in itself, make it illegitimate. But it is a reasonable presumption that whatever cannot exist naturally needs a strong justification in terms of utility. It is not enough to point to the achievements of big business. Libertarians have faced similar arguments for centuries now about the state. In most countries, the state provides education. In my country, the state provides most healthcare. Obviously, this does not mean that education and healthcare would not be provided without the state. It is the same with business corporations. All pharmaceuticals and most computer software have been developed by big business corporations. But there is no reason to suppose they cannot be otherwise provided.

And even if it could be shown that there would be fewer of these things in a world without incorporation, the costs of incorporation must be weighed against the benefits.

CRONY CAPITALISM

When the number and size of business corporations grows beyond a certain limit, they tend to become part of the ruling class. To create a new business and make it grow large requires entrepreneurship, which is most often a quality of outsiders. To administer what is already established and make it bigger requires skills similar to those required by politics and state administration. Between the state and the larger business corporations, therefore, there will be an overlap or a continual exchange of personnel.

This will make it possible for business corporations to externalize some of their costs of growth. They will, as political insiders, press for state involvement in the building of roads and railways and other transport infrastructure that allows them to enjoy greater economies of scale than would otherwise be possible. They will press for the political control of foreign markets. They will be best placed for securing government contracts – often to provide things that they themselves insist are necessary.

Given an ideological climate favorable to active intervention, they will fashion the tax and regulatory system to the disadvantage of smaller competitors.

There are then the cultural costs. Anyone who works for any length of time in a large business corporation tends to become just another "human resource" – all his important life decisions made for him by others, and encouraged into political and cultural passivity. To do well there, he needs to become a receiver and transmitter of orders, to accept authority and avoid arguments with superiors, and to regard success in terms of steady income punctuated by steady advances. He must essentially be a bureaucrat. He will know nothing of how real business is transacted. He will care nothing about laws and taxes that stop others from transacting real business. He will not be inclined to resist paternalism in the political arrangements of his country.

AN END TO COMPROMISE

As said, this rejection of what may be called "actually existing capitalism" is only an emerging consensus. There are still many libertarians who see nothing wrong with business corporations in themselves, and, until quite recently, people like me were on the fringe of the libertarian movement. But, then, until recently, it was not unreasonable for libertarians to look favorably on business corporations.

Until 1989, all politics were shaped by the great ideological tug of war over socialism. We had little choice about joining that tug of war, and none in which direction we would be pulling—and none about with whom we would be pulling. The Communists wanted to destroy business corporations as well as market freedom. Even corrupted markets are better than no markets, and it should never be forgotten that "actually existing capitalism" works. It may constrain both markets and the human spirit, but it has been better than any other system of economic organization offered in the last hundred years. It has been fantastically productive. It has raised, and is raising, billions from poverty to prosperity. A libertarian world of small and unprivileged business units would be better. But what we have had was pretty good, and was to be defended against all its mainstream rivals.

But times are altered. Business corporations have become increasingly global since the end of the Cold War. They have been moving steadily out of their entrepreneurial phase into the bureaucratic. They are increasingly demanding naked privilege. They are demanding intellectual property rights laws that go far beyond what any ordinary person might think reasonable. Through what are called "free trade" agreements, they are promoting regulatory cartelization at the world level. Nobody of consequence wants to nationalize the corporations. They work happily with governments of every apparent persuasion. Their leading personnel are, more than ever, members of the ruling class.

The more libertarians doubt the legitimacy of the business corporation, more we reconnect or connect with other traditions of resistance to state power. There is nothing anti-libertarian about strong, working class organizations. So long as there is no grant of legal privilege, libertarians can have no objection to trade unions, or cooperatives, or other institutions. We might have nothing against the break up of large landed estates—country and town.

Big business no longer needs or deserves our support. We can now safely emphasize the radical elements of our ideology. We are no longer in danger of supporting alternative institutions that may turn out to be Communist front organizations.[1]

---

[1]None of the above should be regarded as original. There is a large, though mostly American, literature on this point. See, for example, Murray Rothbard:

> Every element in the New Deal program: central planning, creation of a network of compulsory cartels for industry and agriculture, inflation and credit expansion, artificial raising of wage rates and promotion of unions within the overall monopoly structure, government regulation and ownership, all this had been anticipated and adumbrated during the previous two decades. And this program, with its privileging of various big business interests at the top of the collectivist heap, was in no sense reminiscent of socialism or leftism; there was nothing smacking of the egalitarian or the proletarian here. No, the kinship of this burgeoning collectivism was not at all with socialism-communism but with fascism, or socialism-of-the-right, a kinship which many big businessmen of the twenties expressed openly in their yearning for abandonment of a quasi-*laissez-faire* system for a collectivism which they could control.... Both left and right have been persistently misled by the notion that intervention by the government is *ipso facto* leftish and antibusiness.

Murray N. Rothbard, "Left and Right: The Prospects for Liberty," *Left & Right* 1, no. 1 (Spring 1965).

For further discussions, see: Gabriel S. Kolko, *Railroads and Regulation, 1877–1916* (Princeton, N.J.: Princeton University Press, 1965) and idem, *The Triumph of Conservatism: A Reinterpretation of American History, 1900–1916* (New York: Free Press, 1965); Murray N. Rothbard, "War Collectivism in World War I," in Ronald Radosh and Murray N. Rothbard, eds., *A New History of Leviathan* (New York: Dutton, 1972); Robert Higgs, *Crisis and Leviathan: Critical Episodes in the Growth of American Government* (Oxford and New York: Oxford University Press, 1987); Paul Weaver, *The Suicidal Corporation: How Big Business Fails America* (New York: Simon & Schuster, 1988); Butler Shaffer, *In Restraint of Trade: The Business Campaign Against Competition, 1918–1938* (Lewisburg, Penn.: Bucknell University Press, 1997); John T. Flynn, *As We Go*

OUTREACH TO CONSERVATIVES:
OLD FRIENDS IN NEW TIMES

So much for the first part of our emerging strategy of resistance. But there is now the matter of our relationship with the conservatives. I do not mean by this the neo-conservatives. Generally speaking, the prefix "neo" has a negative meaning, and these people are less interested in tradition than in keeping up a military-industrial complex that *may* have been necessary to face down Soviet Communism, but which now is simply a standing danger to freedom at home and peace abroad.

No — what I mean is real conservatives in the English-speaking sense. Their defense of tradition is necessarily a defense of limited government, of due process, of civil liberty, and of market freedom. They were natural allies in the past. There is no reason why they should not continue to be in the future.

The problem, so far, has been that there are certain differences between libertarians and conservatives that have prevented full-hearted cooperation. Even now, it is not commonly accepted that there is a new threat just as deadly and just as much in need of co-ordinated resistance.

The main difference is one of vision. The libertarian utopia is one of maximum choice in a world of rapid technological progress. What we ultimately want is an order not wholly based on this planet, in which people live for at least a very long time. We are not very interested in keeping up old ways of life simply because they are old.

Marching (New York: Free Life, 1973); Roy Childs, *Big Business and the Rise of American Statism* (unnamed publisher, 1971); Joseph Stromberg, "Political Economy of Liberal Corporatism" (New York, Center for Libertarian Studies: 1978) and idem, "The Role of State Monopoly Capitalism in the American Empire" (New York, Center for Libertarian Studies: 1978); Kevin A. Carson, *The Iron Fist Behind the Invisible Hand: Corporate Capitalism as a System of State-Guaranteed Privilege* (Montreal: Red Lion Press, 2001); idem, "Austrian and Marxist Theories of Monopoly-Capital: A Mutualist Synthesis," *Economic Notes* 102 (London: The Libertarian Alliance, 2004).

I particularly commend the works of Kevin Carson.

Conservatives, of course, *are* interested in keeping up these old ways. They hated socialism as an attack on their ideal order. They sometimes regard libertarianism as barely less of an attack. In particular, they do not believe in mass immigration, which they perceive as a threat to their organic nation-state, and they are dubious about a freedom of trade that may prevent their country from feeding itself or from producing its own manufactures.

Here, we come at last to what I see as the main achievement of Hans-Hermann Hoppe. I am not qualified to assess his economic work. Because my own philosophical outlook is bounded by the Greek skeptics and by Epicurus and the British empiricists, his epistemology does not really answer any of the questions that I have ever asked. Nor will I claim that he agrees with my own dislike of business corporations. But his clarification of what a libertarian order might be is something that I can appreciate, and it is this that I think his greatest contribution to the joint cause of liberty and tradition.

The Problem of Immigration

Let us consider his work on immigration. Until the end of the twentieth century, there was a libertarian consensus over immigration that had emerged during earlier concerns about the entry of Jews and Irish Catholics into England or of the southern and eastern peoples of Europe into America. Libertarians insisted, and gained agreement over time, that the problems raised by these immigrations were either imaginary or short term; and that policies of benign neglect would turn strangers into citizens.

With the rise of mass immigration from outside the European world, this opinion has had to come under review. If every Jew in Eastern Europe had moved to England before 1906, it would have raised the population by perhaps three million. If every Slovak in Europe had moved to America before 1920, it would have raised the population also by three million. These were peoples whose appearance and values were reasonably similar to those of the native population, and who could be expected, in time, to become largely indistinguishable from the native population.

It may be different with non-European immigrants. They look different. Their values are often radically different, and even hostile.

There are potentially vast numbers of them. Their simple presence seems likely to displace cultural patterns that have long been vaguely favorable to freedom, and to place a strong downward pressure on the incomes of the poor. They are, moreover, being used as an excuse to create an order in which freedom of speech and contract and in which democratic accountability are being set aside in the supposed interests of public order.

The mainstream libertarian response has been to deny that there is in itself any problem at all, and that the experience of past immigrations will simply be repeated. Their only policy recommendations are to raise louder objections to the multicultural police-state that was already growing before the quickening of non-European immigration. They also point out that much dispute between newcomers and natives takes place within areas controlled or influenced by the state. Let there be no state education, and there need be no argument over whether some schools should allow teachers to wear veils and others should teach the inerrancy of the Bible or the non-existence of God. Let there be no welfare state, and there need be no argument over taxes on natives to maintain the children of strangers or over taxes on strangers to pay the pensions of natives.

As for the argument over falling wage rates, this is countered by the observation that greater market freedom would, after a while, check or even reverse this trend, or by denying the legitimacy of any state concern with the living standards of the poor.

What Professor Hoppe does is to ignore the polarity of the debate as it has been set up. Those who want an anarchist order have so far had to accept the legitimacy of mass immigration. Those who have been worried about mass immigration have had to accept the need of a state to control the border. Professor Hoppe walks straight through this debate.

THE STATE; NOT GUARDIAN BUT TRAITOR AT THE GATE

He regards the mass immigration of the past half-century into western countries as an instance, not of libertarian open borders, but of "forced integration." It is different from free trade in goods and services so far as it is not a free choice of individuals to associate as they please. Instead, it is a product of anti-discrimination laws and state welfare policies.

In a democracy, politicians will have an interest in importing those most likely to vote for big government, or those most likely to lend themselves to an electoral balkanization that puts an end to the accountability of rulers to ruled. Given enough pressure by the majority, these politicians will make immigration laws that look tough. But these will lead at best to random acts of oppression against the sorts of immigrant who, in any rational order, might be welcomed. The policies of indiscriminate welfare that attract paupers into the country, and of political correctness and multiculturalism that prevent the majority from resisting, will continue unchecked.

But let us imagine a society in which there is no state. Obviously, there would be no welfare provided by the tax payers. Nor would it be possible to frighten the natives into passivity. Nor, though, would there be unchecked immigration.

Professor Hoppe says:

> [L]et us . . . assume an anarcho-capitalist society. . . . All land is privately owned, including all streets, rivers, airports, harbors, etc. With respect to some pieces of land, the property title may be unrestricted; that is, the owner is permitted to do with his property whatever he pleases as long as he does not physically damage the property owned by others. With respect to other territories, the property title may be more or less severely restricted. As is currently the case in some housing developments, the owner may be bound by contractual limitations on what he can do with his property (voluntary zoning), which might include residential vs. commercial use, no buildings more than four stories high, no sale or rent to Jews, Germans, Catholics, homosexuals, Haitians, families with or without children, or smokers, for example.
>
> Clearly, under this scenario there exists no such thing as freedom of immigration. Rather, there exists the freedom of many independent private property owners to admit or exclude others from their own property in accordance with their own unrestricted or restricted property titles. Admission to some territories might be easy, while to others it might be nearly impossible. In any case, however, admission to the property of the

admitting person does not imply a "freedom to move around," unless other property owners consent to such movements. There will be as much immigration or non-immigration, inclusivity or exclusivity, desegregation or segregation, non-discrimination or discrimination based on racial, ethnic, linguistic, religious, cultural or whatever other grounds as individual owners or associations of individual owners allow.

Note that none of this, not even the most exclusive form of segregationism, has anything to do with a rejection of free trade and the adoption of protectionism. From the fact that one does not want to associate with or live in the neighborhood of Blacks, Turks, Catholics or Hindus, etc., it does not follow that one does not want to trade with them from a distance. To the contrary, it is precisely the absolute voluntariness of human association and separation—the absence of any form of forced integration—that makes peaceful relationships—free trade—between culturally, racially, ethnically, or religiously distinct people possible.[2]

Indeed, he does not stop with immigration. He argues that a libertarian world would have room for highly traditional communities in which conservative views of morality would be the norm.

Now, I repeat, this may be a theoretical contribution that Professor Hoppe rates lower than his work on Austrian economic theory. For me, and for anyone else who wants a fusion of libertarian and conservative movements, it is a contribution of first class importance.

Resisting the New World Order: The End of the Beginning?

Conservatives might not be wholly pleased by such a world. Their organic ideal has room for a powerful state. But the answer to this at the moment—and for some time to come—is that any state able to intervene in matters of personal morality will necessarily be run by the kind of people who now run the state that we

---

[2] Hans-Hermann Hoppe, "On Free Immigration and Forced Integration," LewRockwell.com (1999).

have. This will not be a conservative state. Therefore, libertarianism must, for the foreseeable future, be a strategy for conservatives.

We are talking here about a debate that is taking place between a few hundred people, and that is ignored by almost everyone else. There is no chance, either in England or in America, of a libertarian or even of a really conservative electoral victory.

But, if regrettable, this is not necessarily important. What is important is that two groups of intellectuals should arrive at the truth and agree between themselves on that truth and how it should be promoted. If what they decide is the truth, it will eventually have its effect.

I have said that those who enjoy living at the expense of others hardly ever argue honestly about what they want. They hardly ever admit to themselves what they want. Instead, they operate from behind the most presently convenient ideology of legitimization. Attack these ideologies hard enough, and they will crumble. That may provoke the oppressed to stand up and demand their rights. More likely, it will confuse and weaken those who benefit from such ideologies so that they eventually give in to less violent demands.

Libertarians and conservatives may have lost the Cold War. But the battle continues, and, thanks, in part, to the work of Hans-Hermann Hoppe, what just a few years ago might have seemed a futile last stand may be the prelude to a dazzling counter-attack. ❧

The Power of Argument
in a Crazy World

Remigijus Šimašius

W e should not be very surprised that the world is crazy. Human nature leads to individual pursuit of goals, which leads to conflicts, power, and abuse of power. The world, however, is even more than crazy nowadays. Instead of looking for the solutions as to how to deal with the dark side of human nature, the world's political and opinion leaders are busy ignoring the problem or making it much bigger. There are constant attacks on market economics and personal responsibility. Regulation, education, subsidies—everything is employed in the service of these attacks.

There are any number of strategies for dealing with this crazy world. You may go in line with it, rationalize its craziness, and earn

Remigijus Šimašius (Remigijus@lrinka.lt) is Minister of Justice of the Republic of Lithuania. Prior to his appointment to this position in December 2008, he was President of the Lithuanian Free Market Institute.

a living by serving those whose interests are to keep the public ignorant. Or, you may analyze the world around you, showing what is wrong with it and how things really are. Hans Hoppe is one of those people who always looks for the truth, digs deeper than others, and does not hesitate to expose his ideas to others.

Let's take some examples. Time preference is an essential issue when we speak about the creation of wealth. Hoppe explains that you may accumulate capital only if you are ready to postpone the pleasures of today for the sake of tomorrow. Saving, learning, and working mean the postponing of leisure and consumption.[1] But, if we look to the policies and sentiments dominant in the world today, we see that quite opposite virtues are being promoted: spending is treated as good, while saving is treated as bad, as is it hampers consumption today. Attacking the skilled, the talented, and the educated, not only with taxation, but with "progressive" taxation is treated as moral. Education is regarded as a benefit to the individual and society only for studies of things that do not bring financial gain. Working is discouraged by taxes, while not working is encouraged by subsidies. Hans Hoppe's arguments demonstrate that you get exactly what you encourage and subsidize. If you subsidize laziness, you get laziness. If you subsidize poverty, you get poverty. As he writes,

> As a result of subsidizing the malingerers, the neurotics, the careless, the alcoholics, the drug addicts, the AIDs-infected, and the physically and mentally "challenged" through insurance regulation and compulsory health insurance, there will be more illness, malingering, neuroticism, carelessness, alcoholism, drug addiction, AIDs infection, and physical and mental retardation.[2]

The economic crisis of 2008 (and the artificial boom preceding it) is another example of how crazy the world is. Everyone is in

---

[1] Hans-Hermann Hoppe, "On Time Preference, Government, and the Process of De-Civilization—From Monarchy to Democracy," in *Democracy—The God that Failed: The Economics and Politics of Monarchy, Democracy, and Natural Order* (New Brunswick, N.J.: Transaction Publishers, 2001); previously published in *Journal des Economistes et des Etudes Humaines* 5, no. 2 (1994).

[2] Idem, *Democracy*, p. 99.

panic, everyone is desperately looking for solution, and most turn to the government for a rescue plan. But what about the credit expansion as the ultimate precondition to the crisis? The Austrian theory of the business cycle was ignored before the crisis because there was no crisis. Now the theory is ignored because it explains that the government is the source of the crisis, and because it counsels that we need patiently to wait while the market consummates the malinvestment which has been encouraged for years. Hoppe explains that if you want to address the crisis, you must change the monetary system and abolish state-imposed fiduciary media.[3]

Hoppe's axiom of private property is also of crucial importance. If you debate about ethical issues, it means that you presuppose your own right, as well as the right of other people, to debate the issue.[4] This acceptance implies that you do respect the rights of others people involved in the debate to control their own bodies. And the conclusion is crucial: if you even begin debating what is right and what is wrong, it means that you already have acknowledged that private property is necessary and inescapable for any moral judgment. This applies even to those who try to argue against private property. The ethical ground for private property has never been so strong and deep before.

There are also many other fields where Hans Hoppe has pushed the limits of political and economic science. Monarchy is not as bad as democracy, he argues.[5] This was and still is unacceptable to many intellectuals, and most people have followed the lead of the intellectuals because they have had no good arguments to the contrary. A simple reference to the "strong hand" of a dictator was not

---

[3]Idem, *Democracy*, ch. 1 *et pass.*; idem, "How is Fiat Money Possible? — or, The Devolution of Money and Credit," *Review of Austrian Economics* 7 no. 2 (1994): 49–74; Hans-Hermann Hoppe, Jörg Guido Hülsmann & Walter Block, "Against Fiduciary Media," *Quarterly Journal of Austrian Economics* 1, no. 1 (1998): 19–50.

[4]Hans-Hermann Hoppe, *A Theory of Socialism and Capitalism: Economics, Politics, and Ethics* (Boston: Kluwer Academic Publishers, 1989), chs. 2 & 7; idem, *The Economics and Ethics of Private Property: Studies in Political Economy and Philosophy*, 2nd ed. (Auburn, Ala.: Ludwig von Mises Institute, 2006 [1993]), chs. 11–13, 15, and "Appendix: Four Critical Replies."

[5]Idem, *Democracy*.

only politically incorrect and old fashioned, but also contrary to the goals and the image of society most people actually have. Hoppe provides a clear explanation to sort through this intellectual mess. The absence of democracy in public decision-making does not necessarily mean dictatorship and the most terrible exploitation of the people. On the contrary: democracy is the system which leads to dictatorship, exploitation of others, ignorance, and vulgarity.

The private provision of security is another topic which has benefitted from Hoppe's insights.[6] Every decent person often feels that the police are actually not providing adequate protection. But what is the alternative? Better this than nothing, or so many of those unsatisfied with government tend to conclude. An army of intellectuals is ready to help them reach this conclusion. Hoppe provides sound arguments and explains the economics of the private production of defense. No serious scholar can ignore Hoppe's important arguments. Those who claim that there will be no security without government are simply mistaken. Now, you can direct them to Hans Hoppe's works.

Immigration, democracy, regulation—so many bad ideas abound concerning all of these issues, and Hoppe addresses them so well in his writings and speeches.[7]

Hans Hoppe is not, however, just a scholar who presents good arguments and defends them competently and passionately. He is like an argument himself. Meeting Hans is quite an event for many. He is a person who possesses a natural authority; it is impossible not to notice him in any group of people. I do not mean that Hans speaks loud, tells jokes, or acts in some kind of bizarre or excited manner. On the contrary, he respects manners, and is self-confident enough not to need to show that he is "not like others." It is just these good, old-fashioned manners, combined with

---

[6]Idem, "Government and the Private Production of Defense," in idem, ed., *The Myth of National Defense: Essays on the Theory and History of Security Production* (Auburn, Ala.: Ludwig von Mises Institute, 2003).

[7]On immigration, see Hans-Hermann Hoppe, "The Case for Free Trade and Restricted Immigration," *Journal of Libertarian Studies* 13, no. 2 (Summer 1998): 221–33; idem, "Natural Order, the State, and the Immigration Problem," *Journal of Libertarian Studies* 16, no. 1 (Winter 2002): 75–97.

huge intellect and knowledge which he never tries to hide from others, that make him a natural leader.

Hans knows how to present an argument in a way which is very understandable, even to a man of average intellectual capacities. His examples are sometimes so unexpected and direct that they really help or even force you to rethink what you have thought about the world before. It appears very natural for him, for example, to put a footnote in a book with a short explanation why public slavery is even worse than private slavery.[8] It does not mean that Hans tries to be simple. He is just very straightforward. He does not hesitate to criticize even free-market advocates who are not consistent in their argumentation. If you say something absurd or make flawed arguments, he usually will not hide the fact from you. Perhaps for this reason, some people even seem to be intimidated by Hans Hoppe. Understandably, it is not always pleasant to have your arguments smashed in public.

I met Hans first when he was giving one of his brilliant lectures. I traveled the whole day from Vilnius to Krakow to hear that lecture. It was a complete satisfaction. It is not only Hoppe's written texts which are so clear and appealing, but also his speeches. Subsequently, I have listened to his lectures, including on the same topics, several times. The strange thing is that they do not get boring, even the third or fourth time. The way he puts arguments in order to address the topic properly may be called an intellectual story. Accuracy comes together with intellectual elegance, and "elegant" is precisely the world to describe his speeches. They have nothing special — no fancy slides or funny stories — just the precision, strength, and the elegance of the argument.

Hans does not present himself as a big scholar. On the contrary, his ambition is not very great when he speaks about the role of the scholar (including himself) in society. It is not his ambition to invent some completely new theory or find a terra incognito. On the contrary, Hoppe claims that the role of a decent scholar is, first of all, to preserve what is already found, explained, and discovered. Not to waste the knowledge of the mankind, but to preserve

---

[8]Idem, "On Time Preference, Government, and the Process of De-Civilization," p. 24, n. 25.

and explain it in modern language to new generations, is to him an already ambitious task. He does it perfectly. Contrary to many of those who are happy with their ambitious and often fallacious new theories, or with "philosophical razzle-dazzle,"[9] he is always stressing the role of his teachers and predecessors, Rothbard and Mises.

Courage is another thing which goes well with Hans Hoppe's name. Political correctness is not a good principle to hold to when you are looking for the truth, and while many people pay lip service to the importance of truth, not everyone will defend it even when his own career and name are at stake. But when liberty and the truth are at the stake, Hans Hoppe will never give up. The well-known controversy surrounding an example given about the different time preferences among different groups of people perfectly illustrates this courage.[10]

Our world has become crazy, but there is hope. Hans Hoppe and his works are an essential part of this hope. ❧

---

[9]Cf. Hoppe's discussion of Robert Nozick's "disparate or loosely jointed arguments, conjectures, puzzles, counterexamples, experiments, paradoxes, surprising turns, startling twists, intellectual flashes, and philosophical razzle-dazzle," in "Murray N. Rothbard and the *Ethics of Liberty*," Introduction to Murray N. Rothbard, *The Ethics of Liberty*, 2nd ed. (New York and London: New York University Press, 1998), pp. xxiv.

[10]Stephan Kinsella & Jeffrey Tucker, "The Ordeal of Hoppe," *The Free Market* 26, no. 4 (April 2005).

4

Hans-Hermann Hoppe and the Libertarian Right

Paul Gottfried

To most of his colleagues in the libertarian movement here and in Europe, Hans-Hermann Hoppe is known to be an intellectually energetic companion in arms. This reputation seems entirely deserved for anyone who looks at Hans's numerous writings presenting libertarian views from a recognizably Austrian School perspective. Whether his subject is the welfare state's effect on economic growth, the Federal Reserve System, the possibility of privatizing most modern government functions, business cycles, or public consumer protection agencies, Hans has come down invariably against the "State." Although debate may occur about the details of these positions, Hans can always be found on policy questions among the advocates of the least possible government. Those who do not take such a stand would presumably not qualify as libertarians.

But beyond this area of consensus, there is an obvious gulf between left- and right-libertarians. This area of disagreement can be seen in a wide range of cultural, social, and historical issues, and

Paul Gottfried (gottfrpe@etown.edu) is Horace Raffensperger Professor of Humanities at Elizabethtown College and author of *Multiculturalism and the Politics of Guilt, The Strange Death of Marxism*, and *Conservatism in America: Making Sense of the American Right*, and his newly published autobiography, *Encounters: My Life with Nixon, Marcuse, and Other Friends and Teachers*.

the dividing line among self-described libertarians may be even more important than the consensus duly noted above. Although not the only illustration of a left-libertarian stance, a book by Stephen Moore and Julian Simon, *It's Getting Better All The Time*, contrasting the U.S. in 1900 and in 2000, exemplifies the left-libertarian worldview – which is presumably that of Cato Institute, the foundation with which Moore is closely associated. For almost 300 pages, Moore and Simon dwell on the political, social, economic, and moral progress that the U.S. underwent between 1900 and 2000.[1] This book is written against the "gloom and doom industry"; Lawrence Kudlow, in a breathlessly ecstatic endorsement, thanks Moore and Simon for "dismantling the doomsday pessimism that's still so commonplace in academia and the media."[2]

Examining what they see as convincing data for the preceding one-hundred-year period with a view toward increased life expectancy; continuing technological advances; the availability of public education for the majority of American youth – including college degrees for half of our high-school graduates; the acquisition of civil rights for blacks, women, and gays; a successful national crusade against xenophobia; and a vast increase in per capita wealth, Moore and Simon argue that the U.S. "is a vastly better place today than it was a hundred years ago." In contrast to those who complain about social disintegration and other signs of national decline, Moore and Simon see improvement in every aspect of human life.

Much of the evidence offered that "the human condition has improved dramatically" relates to a cluster of technological and medical advances that have been going on for centuries. Such developments deserve to be noted but also need to be treated in historic context. For example, infant mortality has been steadily

---

[1]Stephen Moore and Julian L. Simon, *It's Getting Better All the Time: 100 Greatest Trends of the Last 100 Years* (Washington, D.C.: Cato Institute, 2000), p. 1.

[2]Kudlow's blurb can be found on the Amazon.Com advertisement for *It's Getting Better All the Time*. Attention should also be paid to the critical assessment of the book's figures for GDP growth between 1900 and 2000 in Brendan Nyan and Ben Fritz, "The deceptive advocacy of Stephen Moore," *Spinsanity* blog (September 22, 2003) <www.spinsanity.org/columns/20030922.html> (visited Jan. 12, 2009).

declining because of medical discoveries that were made partly in the nineteenth century, and the effect of this in the twentieth century was that fewer infants and mothers died during childbirth or shortly thereafter. This has caused a dramatic rise in median life expectancy. Nonetheless, it is misleading to suggest that 47 year old people were dropping dead all over the U.S. in 1900, when what was really happening was that a higher proportion of infants did not survive their first year of life.

Moore's and Simon's comments on education verge on the ludicrous, a judgment that my forty years in academia would amply confirm. The authors should have looked at the by now proliferating studies showing the plummeting standards of literacy, mathematical knowledge, and cultural knowledge among American youth;[3] and the particularly meager results yielded by the heavy public investment in bringing up standards for minorities and the underclass. In their celebration of progress, the authors are also not particularly sensitive to the drastic reductions of academic freedom in the U.S. and in Europe as a result of the triumph of the multicultural Left. Public discourse on a variety of issues has been reduced to the recitation of PC platitudes about designated victims and the dangers of racism, sexism, and homophobia.

But my point here is less to challenge this book-length expression of heady optimism about human improvement than to stress the obvious. The authors do not object to massive governmental efforts to impose equality and end discrimination; this, in fact, is what much of their book is celebrating. Their argument, with due respect to the blurbers who praise this book as a hymn to freedom and free enterprise, is not a call for amelioration by getting government out of our faces. Quite the opposite conclusion might be drawn by anyone who reads the supposed good news from cover to cover. The rise of the most powerful states in modern history in the "democratic West" is not only not seen as a problem; it is made to appear to be the real means for advancing what our left-libertarian authors

---

[3]See, e.g., Chris Hedges, "America the Illiterate," *Truthdig* (Nov. 10, 2008); Robert Roy Britt, "14 Percent of U.S. Adults Can't Read," LiveScience.com (January 10, 2009)

truly value. The consequence of the enormous consolidation of administrative power between 1900 and 2000 has been the entirely acceptable price for promoting human equality.[4]

Left-libertarians have a special thing for equality. They see it as foundational for a foreign policy as well as domestic commitment, which is the bringing of equality to as much of the human race as they can manage to extend it to. One may agree or disagree with this value-preference, but the plain fact is that equality shapes the left-libertarian understanding of history and human affairs to a degree that its representatives may not even recognize. Thus, an argument one typically encounters among them is that it is silly to talk about liberty while blacks, women, gays, and so on have not yet been granted the same amount of this good as white males. And, even if we have achieved a reasonable amount of freedom for ourselves, we should value the natural right held by all human beings to have the same blessing made available to them.

Whence the willingness of the left-libertarian Virginia Postrel to entertain the idea of wars fought to spread "democracy" and whence the morbid sensitivity of all left-libertarians to any theory that would make minorities feel uncomfortable by suggesting the existence of inherited cognitive inequalities? Although modern libertarians may talk about "equal rights," among left-libertarians as much as socialists, the stress is on the "equal" distribution of the rights being privileged. This emphasis is what renders left-libertarians totally inoffensive to the big-government Left and the neoconservatives. Give or take some possible disagreements about particular regulations or drug laws, their views of history and the human good are largely indistinguishable.

It is hard to imagine, on the other hand, anyone who personifies more fully the right-libertarian stance than Hans. Indeed, his work *Democracy — The God that Failed* is a treasure trove of right-libertarian statements about life and history. In contrast to Moore and Simon, Hans observes that

---

[4]See *It's Getting Better All the Time*, especially pp. 241–60; also Paul Edward Gottfried, *After Liberalism: Mass Democracy and the Managerial State* (Princeton, N.J.: Princeton University, 1999); and Robert Higgs, *Crisis and Leviathan: Critical Episodes in the Growth of Government* (New York: Oxford University Press, 1987).

> [i]n comparison to the nineteenth century, the cognitive
> capacities of political and intellectual elites and the qual-
> ity of public education have declined. And the rates of
> crime, structural unemployment, welfare dependency,
> parasitism, negligence, recklessness, incivility, psy-
> chopathy, and hedonism have increased.[5]

Such assertions, which pervade his *magnum opus*, would obviously
upset the statistical researchers Moore and Simon or the editors of
the *Wall Street Journal*. Supposedly, they have demonstrated to our
satisfaction the continuous unfolding of human Progress, whereas
Hoppe has the temerity to propose exactly the opposite view.[6]

In point of fact, his cultural and political assertions are at least
as demonstrable as theirs. But unlike them, he has no special
regard for the principle of equality. From his point of view, equality and the democratic form of government that the advocates of
that ideal enshrine is a "decivilizing force." It generates a constantly expanding public administration that interferes in social
institutions, particularly the family, and confiscates wealth, in the
name of "social justice" and the "public good." Administered
democracy may also seem to require, for the sake of doctrinal consistency, the overrunning of one's country by immigrants. At the
very least, such a practice would offset the inertia that Postrel condemns in her book *The Future and Its Enemies*, in which she calls for
"a world of constant creation, discovery, and competition."[7] In her
hatred of "stasis," Postrel is annoyed that people prefer custom to
change: "*I like my neighborhood the way it is.* That is the all-too-
understandable sentiment that motivates stasist policy."[8] The
alternative to "keeping things as they are" is, for Postrel, among

---

[5]Hans-Hermann Hoppe, *Democracy – The God that Failed: The Economics
and Politics of Monarchy, Democracy, and Natural Order* (New Brunswick, N.J.:
Transaction Publishers, 2001), p. 42–43.

[6]See also ibid., p. 69: "The Whig theory of history, according to which
mankind marches continually forward toward ever higher levels of progress,
is incorrect."

[7]Virginia Postrel, *The Future and Its Enemies* (New York: Free Press, 1998),
p. xiv; see also David Gordon's penetrating review of Postrel's book, "Ask a
Silly Question," *Mises Review* 5, no. 1 (Spring 1999).

[8]Postrel, *The Future and Its Enemies*, p. 204.

other things, favoring a continuing transformation of one's culture and environment.

If the subject were the aggregate effects and distributed costs of our present immigration policy, Hoppe would have a stronger argument than the late Julian Simon. The social costs of our passion for diversity and undocumented, cheap labor are at least as great as Hoppe suggests. But it must be kept in mind that he and the left-libertarians are coming from entirely different value directions. Unlike them, he does not believe it is the duty of civil society to advance equal opportunities for the rest of the world, or even less, that the modern administrative state is a fitting instrument to carry out such a task. Nor does he have any patience with other characteristic assumptions of the left-libertarians, e.g., that democracy and liberal immigration policies expand the amount of ordered liberty in a country, that the more people we encourage to vote, the more "just" our society becomes, or that the quality of a civilization can be raised by increasing the extent of minimal literacy. Hoppe engages all of these sticky points — and other ones as well.

There is also much in his thought that is typically libertarian, such as his defense of Austrian economics and his model of civil society drawn at least partly from John Locke. For Hans the ideal society is a collection of property-owning individuals, who are left free to accumulate and spend wealth. They may also act collectively, on the basis of agreements, to restrict the membership of their property-holding community — or else to allow others to come in if they see fit. In this "anarcho-capitalist" vision, which was developed by Hans's mentor Murray Rothbard, individual property-holders should be free to conclude protective pacts, including agreements for raising their own military forces. They should also be authorized to bar from their communities unwanted immigrants who did not receive permission to settle there. Least of all should they be forced to provide for those with whom they did not elect to share their property assets. In this view, the state has co-opted activities that could be done more efficiently, or does not have to be done at all, by consenting property-holders. And these other arrangements would be possible if the state were not around.[9]

---

[9]Hoppe, *Democracy*; and Murray N. Rothbard, *Power and Market* (Kansas City: Sheed, Andrews and McMeel, 1977).

But because of the present impossibility of junking this parasitic institution, Hans suggests (perhaps not entirely tongue-in-cheek) a return to an already tried political alternative, namely, monarchy. Much of *Democracy – The God that Failed* deals with this other model and with showing that it is less predatory than a democratic regime. Monarchs have the advantage over democratic rulers that they view the realm that they control as a hereditary possession, albeit one with restrictions on what they could do to others. Their hereditary right to their position, however, renders monarchs less inclined to plunder than democratic officeholders, who have only limited tenures and who therefore feel impelled to take as much as they can from taxes and public properties before they retire from office.

Moreover, democratically selected rulers are usually emboldened by their popular mandate to enrich themselves *ad libitum*, whereas monarchs have been surrounded by jealous aristocrats and churchmen who have imposed limits on their appetites. Although Hans may overstate both the countervailing forces in monarchies and the lack of controls in democracies, his larger point – that everything being equal, monarchies are not as oppressive as democracies can be and have been – is probably correct. Both the elevation of democratic government to godlike status and the preoccupation of this form of government with equality have increased the potential of modern democratic regimes for destroying property rights and communal rights. Such regimes practice a form of interventionism that was not available to most monarchies – and certainly not to the Western-type monarchies that existed in the nineteenth century.

Significantly, Hans does not hold back in criticizing monarchies for doing in a quite primitive way what democratic administrations have succeeded in accomplishing with less fallout, which is monopolizing power. Like democrats, kings tried to marginalize their opposition by declaring all political authority to be a prerogative of the centralized state. Monarchical sovereignty was a prelude to democratic sovereignty, and it was based the same "original sin," "the *monopolization* of the function of judge and peacemaker."[10] The best form of authority for Hans is, in fact, "the natural order," one

---

[10]Hoppe, *Democracy*, p. 72.

that is "[t]he natural outcome of the voluntary transactions between various private property owners" and which is "decidedly nonegalitarian, hierarchical, and elitist."[11] Any effort to bring this about in our democratic, late modernity is hailed as a positive step: "Thus, in addition to advocating the abdication of democracy, it is now of central strategic importance that at the same time ideological support be given to all decentralizing or even secessionist social forces."[12]

A question that might be raised is whether the generality of humankind would endorse the tendencies that Hans is promoting. Would democratic populations (who have ceased to be *citoyens* (citizens) or *Staatsbürger* in any meaningful sense) really want to live in the decentralized, elitist society that Hans recommends, one in which a "natural elite" possess "natural authority," and, because of "selective mating" and the "laws of civil and genetic inheritance," these "positions of natural authority are more likely than not passed on within a few noble families."[13] Why would the majority want to acknowledge these "authority persons," who presumably would arbitrate conflicts on the basis of the social deference that others extend to them? It is hard to see why most people would accept such arrangements, as opposed to a democracy, in which the promise is made and often fulfilled of redistributing goods to the voters. The question is not whether the democratic state robs from Peter to pay Paul (it obviously does that!) but whether Hans's "natural order" offers most people what they want. The answer is an emphatic "no" and therefore this order (which looks a bit like Friedrich Hayek's conception of "spontaneous order") depends for its realization on the possibility of "decentralization and secession." Absent such a possibility, this order is in no way feasible.

---

[11]Ibid., p. 71; and Hans-Hermann Hoppe, *Eigentum, Anarchie und Staat: Studien zur Theorie des Kapitalismus* (Opladen: Westdeutscher Verlag, 1987).

[12]Hoppe, *Democracy*, p. 74; and Hans-Hermann Hoppe, *The Economics and Ethics of Private Property: Studies in Political Economy and Philosophy* (Boston: Kluwer, 1993).

[13]Hoppe, *Democracy*, p. 71.

Two other observations may be appropriate for understanding more fully the libertarianism of the Right that Hans exemplifies. One, this libertarianism is a recognizable subspecies of what the Italian Marxist Domenico Losurdo calls "aristocratic radicalism," which he explores in voluminous works on Friedrich Nietzsche (1844–1901). According to Losurdo, Nietzsche's "critique of modernity" is based on his opposition to the leveling tendencies that he perceives in democracy and socialism.[14] It was therefore perfectly consistent for Nietzsche to praise aristocratic societies, including the Indian caste system, and to advocate liberty in the Western world of his time. That is because the state, as Nietzsche understood it, was becoming an instrument of equalization; and its attack on property relations would belong to a larger effort to remove all social and gender distinctions. Nietzsche, as Losurdo points out, also disliked Christianity, because he thought the "slave morality" that pervaded this religion and the culture it nurtured rendered them ineffective against the Left. He therefore broke with classical conservatives, who had viewed established religions as bulwarks against revolution. From Nietzsche's perspective, Christianity and the Left were related worldviews, and only a new aristocratic order, one that had shed its Christian past, could save civilization from the unfolding of the egalitarian ideal, going from democracy into socialism and feminism.

In addition to the aristocratic radicalism that animates Hans's libertarianism (albeit without Nietzsche's passionate dislike for Christianity), there is another influence on his work that deserves to be stressed. His German background has made him allergic to the "American democratic" ideal, as Hans states candidly in the opening lines of the Preface to the German edition of his *magnum opus*:

> "Politically incorrect" is what the rulers and in particular the victors among the rulers proclaim. The great victor of the 20th century, in particular as far as Germany is concerned, is the USA. Hence, the USA has determined the "correct" interpretation especially of recent history. Defeated Germany was not only occupied, but also

---

[14]Domenico Losurdo, *Nietzsche il Ribelle Aristocratico: Biografia Intelettualle e Bilancio Critico* (Turin: Bollati Boringhieri, 2002).

reeducated. Germany's schools and universities, under almost complete government control, and the governmentally licensed mass media, have proclaimed to this day the official American view of history and in particular of the 20th century as a triumph of good over evil.[15]

It is hard to ignore the likely connection between Hans's detestation of the "State" in all of its modern manifestations and the use of postwar public administration in West Germany, perhaps even more than in the Communist East, to humiliate his nation. His sense of what was done to "reeducate" defeated Germans after the War, which is documented in detail in Caspar von Schrenk-Notzing's *Charakterwäsche: Die Politik der amerikanischen Umerziehung in Deutschland*, has left Hans understandably skeptical about the modern democratic project.[16] His relation as a student to Jürgen Habermas, the German thinker and publicist who more than anyone else in his country has called for a rejection of a German national identity and for the creation of a new "constitutional patriotism," based on supposedly universal democratic values, may explain even more about Hans's intellectual odyssey.

Hans has seen the ugliest side of modern, guided democracy, which is the side that keeps getting shoved into the faces of its critics. The fact that the advocates of an American global democratic mission, a group now insanely referred to as "conservatives," have elevated German reeducation to a global model is further proof of the imperialistic side of the ideology that Hans goes after. This new democratic undertaking may have added to his discomfort with "the god that failed." If this is the case, then his discomfort is fully justified. ❧

---

[15]Hans-Hermann Hoppe, *Der Gott, der keiner ist*, Robert Grözinger, trans. (Waltrop & Leipzig: Manuscriptum Verlagsbuchhandlung, 2003), pp. 7–8 (English translation from Hans-Hermann Hoppe, "Demokratie. Der Gott, Der Keiner Ist," LewRockwell.com (December 5, 2003)). See also similar comments in Hoppe, *Democracy*, pp. x–xi; and xxiii, noting that "both Mises and Rothbard had a soft spot for democracy and tended to view the transition from monarchy to democracy as progress."

[16]Caspar von Schrenck-Notzing, *Charakterwäsche: Die Politik der amerikanischen Umerziehung in Deutschland* (Graz: Ares Verlag, 2004); and Ernst von Salomon, *Der Fragebogen*, seventeenth ed. (Rowohlt Taschenbuch Verlag, 2007).

5

Marxism Without Polylogism

Jeffrey A. Tucker

L udwig von Mises believed that the topic of polylogism was important enough to put up front in the introduction of *Human Action.*

> Marxism asserts that a man's thinking is determined by his class affiliation. Every social class has a logic of its own. . . . This polylogism was later taught in various other forms also. Historicism asserts that the logical structure of human thought and action is liable to change in the course of historical evolution. Racial polylogism assigns to each race a logic of its own.[1]

He was writing in 1949 but he saw where trends were headed: polylogist thinking—the belief that a multiplicity of conflicting forms of logic exist within the human population, subdivided by some group-based characteristic—would become a prevailing feature of modern social science. So today a vast amount of modern politics is based on some form of this idea. We speak of the group-based interests not just about class but also in the areas of race, sex, religion, ability, looks, and more. Even environmentalist politics

---

Jeffrey A. Tucker (tucker@mises.org) is Editorial Vice President of the Ludwig von Mises Institute.

[1]Ludwig von Mises, *Human Action*, Scholar's Edition (Auburn, Ala.: Ludwig von Mises Institute, 1998 [1949]), p. 5.

might be understood in these terms: that nature itself operates according to a different logical matrix from the human population, so that we are exploiting nature all the time and might not know it.

An additional point about polylogism: it is believed that not only are there are a variety of forms of logical structure existing in the world but that these forms of logic create a conflict, rooted in exploitation, that forms the basis of society and cries out for correction by some external means. Thus do all these forms of polylogism generate a supposed need for some social (state) action to accommodate these varieties of thinking. The exploiters must be overthrown, even in the case of the environment. So pervasive is this perspective that it nearly defines the whole of the social sciences as practiced in academia today.[2]

Becoming aware of this through reading Mises, the reader is shocked at Hans-Hermann Hoppe's presentation of the core claims of Marxian class theory and his summary conclusion: "I claim that all of them are essentially correct."[3]

How can we account for Hoppe's apparent softness toward the Marxist idea, even as Mises is so thoroughly against it? There is an answer here: what Hoppe has done is purge Marxism of its epistemological assumptions and retained its analysis of the material world. This permits us to draw for Marxism many important insights while disregarding the polylogism that has led to so much insidious rhetoric of the past and present.

A classic example of the use of polylogism can be found in *Karl Marx and the Close of His System* by Eugen von Böhm-Bawerk in 1896.[4] Böhm-Bawerk offers a painstakingly detailed argument, stretching over 150 pages, that Marx never got around to fully explaining why it is that goods do not exchange in proportion to the value of labor in them but rather that the profit of capital is in proportion to the capital invested. Had Marx attempted to explain

---

[2]My friend B.K. Marcus sums up his entire college experience as a four-year case for polylogism.

[3]Hans-Hermann Hoppe, *The Economics and Ethics of Private Property* (Auburn, Ala.: Ludwig von Mises Institute, 2006), pp. 117–38.

[4]Eugen von Böhm-Bawerk, *Karl Marx and the Close of His System* (New York: Augustus M. Kelley, 1949).

this, as he kept promising he would, it would have been obvious that his entire theory of surplus value was inherently contradictory to the facts on the ground. This is a fatal flaw in Marx's work, because he doesn't allow the reader to logically or empirically test his claim concerning the surplus value extracted by the capitalist and not given to workers. Böhm-Bawerk further writes that Marxism seems to have built into the system a strategy that belies any attempt to refute it. Every disagreement is dismissed with *ad hominem* of sorts, that the writer is hopelessly mired in bourgeois thinking. "Is it too much to demand that if he introduces subjective interpolations into his system they should be correct, well founded, and non-contradictory? And this reasonable demand Marx has continually contravened." This was Böhm-Bawerk's protest against the use of polylogist assertions embedded in Marxist defense tactics.

Marxist theorist Rudolf Hilferding responded to Böhm-Bawerk in a way that underscored the problem with polylogism: he does precisely what Böhm-Bawerk would predict that a Marxist would do. He dismissed the source, and with long-winded criticism tossed aside all of Marx's critics in the same way that Marx did. Concerning the great professor's detailed attempt to grapple with the details of Marx's theory, Hilferding writes:

> As spokesman for the bourgeoisie, it enters the lists only where the bourgeoisie has practical interests to defend. In the economico-political struggles of the day it faithfully reflects the conflict of interests of the dominant cliques, but it shuns the attempt to consider the totality of social relationships, for it rightly feels that any such consideration would be incompatible with its continued existence as *bourgeois* economics.[5]

Hilferding further says that the professor's argument can be disregarded because he failed to deal with Marxism "it its entirety" as a complete system of thought, that, one supposes, must be accepted on faith. Whereas Böhm-Bawerk talks about subjective values, and individual prices and their relationship with capital invested, Marx, writes Hilferding, "looks upon the theory

---

[5]Ibid., p. 121.

of value, not as the means for ascertaining prices, but as the means for discovering the laws of motion of capitalist society."

Hilferding writes:

> Instead of taking economic or social relationships as the starting point of their system, they have chosen for that starting point the *individual* relationship between men and things. They regard this relationship from the psychological outlook as one which is subject to natural and unalterable laws. They ignore the relationships of production in their social determinateness, and the idea of a law-abiding evolution of economic happenings is alien to their minds.[6]

Hilferding's criticism can be summed as an application of this polylogist dismissal: as a member of the ruling class who is wedded to bourgeois ways of thinking, Böhm-Bawerk is just not capable of thinking the right away about these things. Marxist thought, which is all about the laws of history and the social determinates driving the material world, is alien to him simply because his mind is incapable of seeing the truth.

And so it is today with so many political arguments. The rhetoric is on a much lower level today, but this is the usual way in which political discussion takes place in the post-Marxist society in which the polylogist assumption drives discussion. Capitalists can't possibly understand the logic of environmentalist thinking because they are out of touch with nature and its need. Whites cannot even begin to comprehend the demands of blacks for preference and redistribution because the black experience and way of thinking are alien to the white experience and way of thinking. So too with issues of sex, sexuality, religion, and physical ability. It is usually assumed that one may not even speak about the controversies of our time unless one belongs to the "victim group" being discussed. Even then, if a woman or a block or a gay offers a point of view that runs contrary to the dominate political agenda of the mainstream lobby for these groups, that person is dismissed as somehow lacking higher consciousness or hopeless mired in a different mindset. She is not a *real* woman, he is not a *real* black, they

---

[6]Ibid., p. 196.

are not *really* disabled, he doesn't *genuinely* represent the views of Islam, etc.

What's at work here is an unraveling of the entire basis for any form of intellectual discussion. If we can't agree on universal rules of establishing the veracity of truth claims, all discussion is reduced to a series of demands followed by *ad hominem* attacks on anyone who resists those demands. Mises himself understood that if we are to avoid this fate, there had to be some understanding and agreement on the rules of logic. George Koether reports[7] that Mises told his seminar students that the first book on economics that they should read is a book on logic by Morris Cohen, a book which is in fact one of the last complete texts on logic to published for universal use in the college classroom.[8] Meanwhile, forums on academic discussion board filled with complaints that logic as a discipline is no longer part of high-school study or even under-graduate college study, which means that after 16 years of formal study, hardly any students are taught even the basic rules on how to think.

This is further evidence that this one aspect of Marxism — its radical attack on the core of clear thinking, a subject that (along with grammar and rhetoric) has been part of the "trivium" since the middle ages — has triumphed in mainstream thinking today, so much so that any professor suspected of holding to logical univer-sals and refusing to accept class-interest arguments as self-evi-dently true can be driven out of the university merely for holding "politically incorrect" opinions.

Hoppe's attachment to Marxism, however, eschews polylogism completely and instead embraces universal logical principles as the very method by which to reapply Marxian political theory in a completely different context. In his writings on class theory, he ticks through the familiar list: history is defined by class struggle; the ruling class has a common interest; class rule is defined by ownership relations involving exploitation; there is a tendency toward centralization of class interest; and centralization and

---

[7] *Austrian Economics Newsletter* 20, no. 3 (Fall 2000).

[8] Morris Cohen, *An Introduction to Logic and Scientific Method* (New York: Read Books, 2007); originally published in 1934.

expansion of exploitative rules leads to an unviable attempt at global domination. What he is speaking of here is not polylogism as such but a narrower aspect of Marxian politics and its claims concerning the social forces of history. And he says that they are all essentially correct. The basis for Hoppe's claim reflects his views of the Marxist theory of exploitation, which he regards as correct in its analytical features but not it its application.

Hoppe deals with the application error in Marxist theory swiftly and decisively. The Marxist view says it is exploitation for the worker to labor five days and receive only three days of product value back in wages. And yet it remains true that workers willingly accept wage contracts. It is a strange sort of exploitation that is mutually beneficial to all parties and engaged in willingly and happily by billions of people every day. The interests of the worker and the capitalist are harmonious: the worker accepts a smaller portion of goods in the present over a larger one in the future, while the capitalist has the opposite preference. Marx didn't see this because he failed to comprehend that it is impossible to exchange future goods against present goods except at a discount.

But what about the theory of the reality of exploitation itself? Hoppe argues that it is fulfilled in the Austrolibertarian framework of looking at the world, once we understand that the ruling class is distinguished by its access to state power. This follows from Hoppe's new definition of exploitation, which occurs when a person successfully claims partial or full control over scarce resources that he has not homesteaded, saved, or produced, nor acquired contractually from a previous producer-owner. The state can be seen as a firm devoted entirely to the task of exploitation in this sense. This exploitation creates victims, who can overthrow their exploiters once they develop a consciousness of the possibility of an exploitation-free society in which private property is universally respected and not systematically violated by a ruling class.

What's interesting about the Hoppean account of the Marxian theory, and his recasting of the theory in light of Austrolibertarian theory, is that it completely bypasses the core polylogist assumption of Marxist theory. There is no need to postulate that the exploiters and the exploited are somehow socially hardwired into thinking differently according to conflicting logical principles. On the contrary, Hoppe's approach assumes the universal applicability of one set of logical principles. Here is the main point of departure, one that clarifies the seeming difference between Mises and Hoppe, and highlights an important ideological agenda for the future.

In what ways might Hoppe's reconstruction of Marxism apply to Marxism's modern spinoffs? Once we strip away the polylogist assumption underlying modern politics, we can see that many group relations are indeed characterized by varieties of Hoppe-style exploitation. And it is precisely law and legislation that make this possible. Laws that privilege one race, one religion, one sex, one class of abilities, over another generate a group of victims and solidify a form of group solidarity that might have previously existed only in nascent form. Whereas group differences might resolve themselves through trade, the entry of the state into the association amplifies and institutionalizes group conflicts. This is true as regards, for example, religion. Once the state begins to subsidize one form of religious expression, it generates the impression on the part of other religions that they are being ripped off or put upon in some way, and the only means of defense is to organize and coalesce to take back what is rightly theirs. This trajectory can become particularly explosive when it involves issues of race and sex, but conflict also appears in other areas, such as environmental legislation and disability legislation.

In the same way that state-subsidized exploitation led Marx to observe but misdiagnose the nature of exploitation in his time, forms of state exploitation today can lead people to embrace anti-capitalistic creeds based on a misdiagnosis of the root of conflicts over race, sex, religion, ability, and the environment today. It is not the case that demographic groups are inherently in conflict; the illusion is created by the absence of what Hoppe calls "clean capitalism," in which all relationships in society are characterized by voluntary exchange and association. Part of that misdiagnosis drives people to embrace a polylogist understanding of the structure of the human mind. But once the Hoppean understanding of the exploitation and conflict—those kernels of truth in Marxism— becomes clear, there is no need to resort to far-flung explanations to account for them. The root problem is not somehow embedded in the structural diversity of operating logics in the world; the explanation of conflict in society is rooted in a much more direct and simple cause: the state itself.

In this way, then, the Hoppean theory of social conflict has the potential to not only do away with old-time Marxist politics and its destructive effects in the world but to hold within itself the potential for uprooting and overthrowing the entire polylogist basis of the social sciences as they have developed in the last hundred years—and the state apparatus of interventionism that results from them. As to whether this is possible, it comes down to the question of which is more fundamental to the Marxist worldview: its polylogism or its exploitation theory. A major job of the Hoppean project is to toss out the former while retaining a version of the latter in a way that can be used against the state and its interests. ❧

A Knight of
Anarcho-Capitalism

Yuri N. Maltsev

H ans-Hermann Hoppe is the most ardent advocate of liberty in our time. He has done more to advance our understanding of philosophical, legal, economic, and cultural aspects of liberty and private property than any other living intellectual. A favorite student and close personal friend of Murray and Joey Rothbard, Hoppe developed the anarcho-capitalist tradition of the Austrian school of economics after Murray's untimely death in January 1995. A prolific writer, great teacher, and very popular public speaker, he has attracted tens of thousands of people in all parts of the world to the ideas of liberty.

Hoppe is not a "secondhand dealer in ideas" (using Hayek's expression).[1] He is a generator of new knowledge, new ideas, and new interpretations of well established facts, and his understanding of history is second to none. In his books and public appearances, he provides a crystal clear vision of social phenomena and develops his own pioneering theory of history based on the methodology of the Austrian School.

Yuri N. Maltsev (maltsev.yuri@gmail.com) is Professor of Economics at Carthage College and Senior Fellow of the Ludwig Von Mises Institute.

[1]F.A. Hayek, "The Intellectuals and Socialism," *University of Chicago Law Review* (Spring 1949), reprinted in *Studies in Philosophy, Politics and Economics* (Chicago: University of Chicago Press, 1967), p. 178.

His seminal work, *A Theory of Socialism and Capitalism*,[2] provides a logical and ethical case for capitalism and against socialism, and shows that no system but capitalism is ethically justifiable. Hans has become the most well-known, living critic of socialism in our time. He stared the beast in the face and called it by its name, providing an unparalleled analysis of the evil nature of socialism; he made an airtight case that "socialism is economically and morally inferior to capitalism."[3]

Continuing his analysis of the ethical foundations of capitalism in his *The Economics and Ethics of Private Property*, he provided a logical and ethical case for a purely private economy based on the absolute right to self-ownership and to private property. The appendix to this book, "Four Critical Replies," again shows him at his best. Critically engaging Osterfeld, Lomasky, Steele, Rasmussen, Yeager, and Conway, Hoppe gives a brilliant outline of the theory of anarcho-capitalism based on crystal clear definitions of anarchism, natural rights, private property, self-ownership, and many other terms.

The same year as the *Economics and Ethics of Private Property* was published (1993), he contributed the chapter "Marxist and Austrian Class Analysis" to the volume on Marx of which I was the editor.[4] His twenty-two page contribution is the most devastating critique of the Marxist belief system ever written. He focuses his analysis on the heart of Marxism—the Marxian theory of capitalist exploitation—showing that Marx could "not understand the phenomenon of time preference as a universal category of human action"[5] and built his whole theory of history underlying his secular religion of "scientific communism" on the wrong premises. Hoppe writes: "If Marx's theory of capitalist exploitation and his

---

[2]Hans-Hermann Hoppe, *A Theory of Socialism and Capitalism: Economics, Politics, and Ethics* (Boston: Kluwer Academic Publishers, 1989).

[3]Ibid., p. 166.

[4]Hans-Hermann Hoppe, "Marxist and Austrian Class Analysis," in *Requiem for Marx*, Yuri N. Maltsev, ed. (Auburn, Ala.: Mises Institute, 1993); first published under the same title in the *Journal of Libertarian Studies* 9, no. 2 (Fall 1990), pp. 79–93.

[5]Hoppe, "Marxist and Austrian Class Analysis," p. 56.

ideas on how to end exploitation and establish universal prosperity are false to the point of being ridiculous, it is clear that any theory of history derived from it must be false, too."[6]

The goal of social ownership of the means of production is the most important prerequisite of the Marxist plan for socialism, communism, and the withering of the State. Hoppe shows that, if achieved, it will lead to human slavery, misery, and the omnipotent State. He writes:

> In fact, social ownership is not only economically inefficient . . . it is incompatible with the idea that the state is "withering away." For if means of production are owned collectively, and if it is realistically assumed that not everyone's ideas as to how to employ these means of production happen to coincide (as if by miracle), then it is precisely socially owned factors of production which require continued state actions, i.e., an institution coercively imposing one person's will on another disagreeing one's.[7]

He was also the first to systematically demonstrate that democracy inevitably leads to the growth of socialism and the omnipotence of big government. Enemies of freedom understood this nature of democracy and were using democracy for their own evil ends. In the Marxist textbook on revolution, *The State and Revolution*, published in 1917, Lenin wrote:

> Democracy means equality. The great significance of the proletariat's struggle for equality and of equality as a slogan will be clear if we correctly interpret it as meaning the abolition of classes. But democracy means only formal equality. And as soon as equality is achieved for all members of society in relation to ownership of the means of production, that is, equality of labor and wages, humanity will inevitably be confronted with the question of advancing further, from formal equality to

---

[6]Ibid., p. 58.
[7]Ibid., pp. 72–73; internal footnotes omitted.

actual equality, i.e., to the operation of the rule "from each according to his ability, to each according to his needs."[8]

Hoppe shows that socialism's centralized control over property would require a gargantuan state and oppressive state machinery, and that the history of world communism has been one of individual and collective executions, deaths in concentration camps, mass murder, genocide, government-organized mass starvation, and deportations. These crimes were the direct results of the Marxist theory of capitalist exploitation and its collateral theory of class struggle which justified the need for "elimination" of people who were not considered useful to the construction of a new society.

In terms of numbers of victims, communists outperformed any other mass murderers in human history. Professor R.J. Rummel, the leading authority on genocide and democide, estimated communist crimes have resulted in the loss of 171,035,000 innocent lives.[9] The victims of communism lived in the squalor of shabby public barracks and collective farms, received pittance wages, and were killed "for trying to leave the country."[10]

I remember a discussion of the fate of freedom in Eastern Europe when Hoppe told me that he detests nationalism as a form of collectivism, but nationalism of the small countries is preferable to that of the modern day empires, as is it is closer to individuals.

He has devoted his life to the search of truth and defense of liberty, to the fight against ideologies of slavery in all their forms and shapes, to "continuous ideological struggle, for if the power of government rests on the widespread acceptance of false indeed absurd and foolish ideas, then the only genuine protection is the

---

[8]V.I. Lenin, *Gosudarstvo I Revolucija* (Moskva: Politizdat, 1968), str. 27 (translation by the author).

[9]Calculated by author from data available at <www.hawaii.edu/powerkills /20TH.HTM>.

[10]Hans-Hermann Hoppe, "The Case for Free Trade and Restricted Immigration," *Journal of Libertarian Studies* 13, no. 2 (Summer 1998), pp. 221–33, at p. 230.

systematic attack of these ideas and the propagation and proliferation of true ones."[11]

Following the rationalist tradition of the Austrian School, further developed by his mentor and friend Murray N. Rothbard,
Hans-Hermann Hoppe is an outspoken rationalist and critic of
social relativism in all its forms: empiricism, deconstructionism,
historicism, positivism, post-structuralism, post-modernism, anar-
cho-syndicalism, skepticism, and post-anarchism. Hans developed
the theory and practice of epistemological and methodological
individualism to its present heights.

> Only individuals act; consequently, all social phenom-
> ena must be explained — logically reconstructed — as the
> result of purposeful, individual actions. Every "holistic"
> or "organicist" explanation must be categorically
> rejected as an unscientific pseudo-explanation. Like-
> wise, every mechanistic explanation of social phenom-
> ena must be discarded as unscientific.[12]

Hans celebrates individualism and opposes all forms of collectivism which makes people

> easily deluded and sunk into habitual submission. Thus
> today, inundated from early childhood with govern-
> ment propaganda in public schools and educational
> institutions by legions of publicly certified intellectuals,
> most people mindlessly accept and repeat nonsense
> such as that democracy is self-rule and government is of,
> by, and for the people.[13]

Hoppe's seminal treatise on democracy[14] provides readers with
deep insights into the reasons for decivilization that we all witness

---

[11]Hans-Hermann Hoppe, *Democracy — The God that Failed: The Economics
and Politics of Monarchy, Democracy, and Natural Order* (New Brunswick, N.J.:
Transaction Publishers, 2001), p. 93.

[12]Hans-Hermann Hoppe, "Murray N. Rothbard: Economics, Science, and
Liberty," in *15 Great Austrian Economists*, Randall G. Holcombe, ed. (Auburn,
Ala.: Mises Institute, 1999), p. 224.

[13]Hoppe, *Democracy*, p. 92.

[14]Ibid.

and experience. Following Mises's question "Are We Historians of Decline?," Hans investigated the logical reasons for the deep-rooted sickness of the West, swamped by welfare dependency, family break-up, random violence and crime, drug culture, graffiti, and deteriorating public health. His answer is a revelation for many and it is as true as it is discomforting for the apologists of the State:

> As a result of subsidizing the malingerers, the neurotics, the careless, the alcoholics, the drug addicts, the Aids-infected, and the physically and mentally "challenged" through insurance regulation and compulsory health insurance, there will be more illness, malingering, neu-roticism, carelessness, alcoholism, drug addiction, Aids infection, and physical and mental retardation.[15]

Hoppe provides a clear and humanistic alternative: society based on pure private property, private law, and voluntary exchange. "Instead, the withering away of the state, and with this the end of exploitation and the beginning of liberty and unheard of economic prosperity, means the establishment of a pure, private-property society regulated by nothing but private law."[16]

Born in Peine, a small town between Braunschweig and Hanover in Central Germany, into a loving and intellectually nourishing family, he received his education at the Johann Wolf-gang Goethe University in Frankfurt am Main (also known as Frankfurt University). When Hoppe was celebrating his first birth-day in 1950, Max Horkheimer, Theodor W. Adorno, and Friedrich Pollock re-opened the *Institut für Sozialforschung* (Institute for Social Research) which was shut down by the Nazis. The Institute was a home of the Frankfurt School of neo-Marxist critical theory, social research, and philosophy which attempted to adapt Marxism to the realities of the Twentieth century. Leading German intellectuals—Jürgen Habermas, Herbert Marcuse, Erich Fromm, Walter Benjamin, Karl Mannheim, and Hans-Georg Gadamer—worked in the Institute, and one of the most interesting and popular ones, Habermas, became Hans's mentor and Ph.D. advisor.

---

[15]Ibid., p. 99.

[16]Hoppe, "Marxist and Austrian Class Analysis," p. 73.

How easy it would be for Hoppe to accept his mentor's ideas and become another brilliant Frankfurt School disciple! Instead he chose another path—the path of truth and liberty.

His study at the Johann Wolfgang Goethe University with Habermas and Karl-Otto Apel was time well spent, however, as it shaped Hoppe as a first class social scientist and helped him to put forth an "argumentation ethics" defense of individual rights, based in part on the discourse ethics theories of the Frankfurt School. His intellectual independence prevented him from accepting his mentors' apology for socialism and their anti-capitalist mentality. As one reviewer noted, "Hoppe believes his former teacher Habermas's discourse-ethics theories, while correct at core, are applied incorrectly by Habermas to yield a socialistic ethic; Hoppe feels that Habermas's theories, if correctly applied (as Hoppe himself does), yield the libertarian non-aggression norm."[17]

It is not a coincidence that popularity of Hoppe's scientific findings, and his books and lectures, is extremely high in the post-communist world—among people who were used as guinea pigs by their own governments to be experimented on for the sake of a bloody, Marxist utopia. Latvians and Lithuanians, Estonians and Bulgarians, Russians and Armenians, Poles, Germans, Czechs and other victims of communist murder and slavery are a most attentive audience for Dr. Hoppe. Hoppe's worldwide outreach with lectures and seminars in the United States, Europe, and Asia, his contribution to the intellectual demise of socialism in the post-communist world from Estonia to Georgia, Lithuania to the Czech Republic and Poland, have made him even more famous in Eastern and Central Europe and Asia than he is in the United States and Germany.

At all of the dozens of events that I have heard Hans speak— conferences, seminars, and other intellectual events of the Ludwig von Mises Institute in the United States; conferences overseas, in

---

[17]Stephan Kinsella, "The Undeniable Morality of Capitalism [review essay of Hoppe's *The Economics and Ethics of Private Property* (1993)]," *St. Mary's Law Journal* 25 (1994), p. 1434.

Vilnius, Lithuania, and Copenhagen, annual meetings of the Property and Freedom Society in Bodrum, Turkey—he was the most thought-provoking, intellectually stimulating, and admired speaker.

His intellectual rigor and austerity peacefully co-exist with his warm and humorous character. I remember well the Southwestern Economics Association Meeting in San Antonio, Texas. After the conference we decided to explore the "Venice of the Southwest" with its well-known River Walk and took a water taxi which brought us to a Brazilian restaurant with the richest choice of tastiest meats that I have ever experienced before (not surprisingly, as I was raised in an almost meatless USSR). Hoppe jumped on the occasion to poke fun at vegetarians and tree huggers, and to stress that our brain needs to be honed and pampered not only by food for thought, but by the nicest delicacies and drinks providing excellent nourishment for great ideas. How true! Moscow bureaucrats with whom I've spent most of my life did not have clear thinking with brains on a meager diet of vodka, borscht, and potatoes.

I first met Hoppe in April 1990 at the conference on Economics of Desocialization in Washington D.C. One of my few friends in Washington was Gottfried von Haberler (1901–1995), an eminent economist, active participant in the famous "Mises-Kreis"— Mises's Viennese seminars—and later professor at Harvard and fellow of the American Enterprise Institute. A well-known Austrian economist most of his life, Gottfried followed the widespread fashion for cheap money and abandoned his previous support of the international gold standard. Haberler also abandoned his early Austrian School views on business cycles and became a critic of Misesian theory. Thus, Hoppe was very critical of Haberler's ideas. Yet, during the conference, he was most cordial and helpful to the frail 89 years old man. He told me that the conference in Washington was a good opportunity for a reconciliation of Dr. Haberler with the modern Austrian school and to inform him of the progress in Austrian economics and the activities of the Ludwig von Mises Institute. The conference turned out to be a great success, and Haberler paid a moving tribute to Ludwig von Mises and praised the role of the Institute in the development of the Austrian School of economics.

In 2006, Hans-Hermann Hoppe founded the Property and Freedom Society, the true intellectual alternative to the Mont Pèlerin Society which had become monopolized by neo-conservatives, and organized its first international meeting at the beautiful, Mediterranean resort of Bodrum, Turkey. Together with his wife Guelcin, the most charming economist that I have ever met, they have graciously hosted annual meetings of the Society at the Guelcin's Mediterranean resort, the Hotel Karia Princess. Each of these meetings has been a true celebration of free thinking and intellectual fellowship, and provided me with enough intellectual oxygen for the whole year.

Calm, logical and focused, Hoppe is a Sherlock Holmes of economics, in constant search for truth, rejecting any compromises and "sweet little lies" of "publicly certified intellectuals," beltway libertarians, and neo-conservatives. A most learned scholar, he has called upon all advocates of liberty to be "intellectual anti-intellectuals," as opposed to most "intellectuals" in the West, who have sold out to the state:

The first and foremost task of the intellectual anti-intellectuals, then, is to counter this dogmatic slumber of the masses by offering a precise definition of the state, as I have done at the outset, and then to ask if there is not something truly remarkable, odd, strange, awkward, ridiculous, indeed ludicrous about an institution such as this. I am confident that such simple, definitional work will produce some serious doubt regarding an institution that one previously had been taken for granted.[18]

I feel very lucky to have known Hans personally for almost twenty years. I am still amazed by his encyclopedic erudition in history, culture, economics, law, and philosophy, and fascinated by the amount of intellectual energy he generates and radiates to others! ❧

---

[18]Hans-Hermann Hoppe, "Reflections on the Origin and the Stability of the State," LewRockwell.com (June 23, 2008).

7

Helping Future Generations of Scholars

Edward Stringham

From criticizing democracy to advocating a stateless society Prof. Hans-Hermann Hoppe is well known for not backing away from controversy.[1] Hoppe has well earned reputation for not compromising his beliefs and not sugarcoating how he presents ideas. But I would like to highlight how in addition to being an uncompromising scholar, Professor Hoppe has been very supportive of others as well. My story has to do with Hoppe as the Editor of the *Journal of Libertarian Studies*, and myself at the beginning of what has become an academic career. In 1997, I finished my college honors thesis under the direction of my professor Walter Block. My topic was on privatizing law enforcement, for which I

Edward Stringham (edward.stringham@trincoll.edu) is Shelby Cullom Davis Visiting Associate Professor at Trinity College.

[1]See, e.g., Hans-Hermann Hoppe, *Democracy – The God that Failed: The Economics and Politics of Monarchy, Democracy, and Natural Order* (New Brunswick, N.J.: Transaction Publishers, 2001); idem, "Government and the Private Production of Defense," in idem, ed., *The Myth of National Defense: Essays on the Theory and History of Security Production* (Auburn, Ala.: Mises Institute, 2003).

[2]Idem, *A Theory of Socialism and Capitalism: Economics, Politics, and Ethics* (Boston: Kluwer Academic Publishers, 1989); idem, *The Economics and Ethics of Private Property: Studies in Political Economy and Philosophy*, 2nd ed. (Auburn, Ala.: Mises Institute, 2006 [1993]).

read a bunch of material including two of Professor Hoppe's books, *A Theory of Socialism and Capitalism* and *The Economics and Ethics of Private Property*.[2] I think the thesis was fine for my age, but it was not nearly as structured or polished as something one would write with years of experience. I hoped to be able to publish something from it, but I did not know where to begin. Walter Block said I should send the complete manuscript to Professor Hoppe to ask for advice.

One can only imagine how many other things Prof. Hoppe had on is plate, but not only did he look at my manuscript—he read all 120 pages. Professor Hoppe also took the time to highlight what was useful and what was potentially publishable. And I really appreciated what Prof. Hoppe had to say. My favorite part of the manuscript had been the final quarter, but Walter Block said he liked the first three quarters and not the last part. One can only imagine my dismay when I showed the manuscript to my mother and she said the same thing. Yet Professor Hoppe said that my important contribution was in the final part! I ended up following Hoppe's recommendations, and rewrote the final quarter as a stand-alone piece, which ended up as my first publication.[3] This pleasant experience paved the way for dozens of other publications, and so I am glad Prof. Hoppe was the way he was. The fact that such an established scholar took the time to help the young me is something for which I will always be grateful. ❧

---

[3]Edward Stringham, "Market Chosen Law," *Journal of Libertarian Studies* 14 no. 1 (Winter 1998–99): 53–77.

8

A "Lovable Son of a Gun"

Roland Baader

Hans Hoppe's first visit to my hometown and current domicile, Waghaeusel, (in Baden-Wuerttemberg, Germany) took place in June of 1995. My dear wife, Uta, was still alive at the time. With great pride she showed Hans the tidy garden she was so devoted to. She asked him: Do you like it? Hans answered dryly, "yes." A little later Uta assumed a dancer's pose and asked Hans if he liked what he saw. "Yes," he said. In the evening Uta prepared a delicious meal. She looked at the guest with anticipation and at last asked, "do you like it?" Hans: "Yes." Uta's reply: "Hans, you are a son of a gun, but the most lovable son of a gun I know. I love you anyway."

At the time we had a border in our house, a poodle named *Olga* who belonged to Professor Gerard Radnitsky. I put Olga on a porch chair next to Hans and said: "This is a very learned poodle. He insists on professorial company." Hans Hoppe commented: It is *a priori* true and needs no falsification, that a poodle is not a human being and therefore cannot be a scientific theorist. But he can remain seated if he likes.

Roland Baader (M.Econ.; Roland-Baader@t-online.de) is a private scholar and major representative of the Austrian School in Germany, author of 15 books and hundreds of articles in newspapers, magazines, and scholarly journals. This chapter was translated by Arlene Oost-Zinner.

Many years passed before Hans renewed the tiresome journey (with the intercity train from Frankfurt to Mannheim, and from there with the regional train) in July of 2004.

Because we hadn't seen each other in such a long time, our conversational cups were overflowing. And because Hans wanted to fly back to the USA on the very next day, we had but one evening to tackle a quota of intellectual exchange that would normally require an entire week. At the ready were four bottles of Sardinian red wine to serve as "Babbelwasser" (local dialect for alcoholic beverage that aids in the acceleration of linguistic and semantic gymnastics). When the first light of morning appeared the bottles were empty – and we were still lucid, but tired. A short sleep followed.

Now because Hans, who usually exercises caution with respect to false Gods (Bacchus among them), survived the Sardinian flood seemingly unscathed, I sent him a certificate a few days later. It read:

The Brotherhood of the Red Nose,
the Society of Sardinian Competitive Drinkers,
for having demonstrated uncommon bravery at the
Battle of Waghaeusel,[1]
on the night of the 27th to the 28th of July, 2004,
is pleased to honor

Professor Dr. Hans-Hermann Hoppe

As a lifelong member

Roland Baader
Signature of the President

---

[1] There really was a Battle of Waghaeusel in 1849 between the Baden rebels and the Prussian troops.

The fun and games came full circle with Hans's reply:

Dear Roland:

being recognized as a Sardinian competitive drinker and being named a life long member of your exclusive society moves me deeply.

Yours, Hans

Hans, on this the occasion of your 60th Birthday, I am deeply moved at how you've scattered the lies and the errors of mainstream economic battalions the world over, how you've so eloquently borne the torch of every flame started by Mises and Rothbard and have gone on to fan the same fire of freedom in millions of minds and hearts. ❧

9

Appreciation and Gratitude

John V. Denson

T hank you for the opportunity to convey my very high regard and great appreciation for the outstanding body of work of my friend Hans-Hermann Hoppe. Hans is an original thinker and tireless fighter for the ideas of individual freedom and a free market economy. We desperately need scholars like him now more than ever.

Congratulations, Hans. ✀

John V. Denson (donna.moreman@alacourt.gov) is a Circuit Judge in Lee County, Alabama and has been closely connected with the Ludwig von Mises Institute since it was founded. He is the editor of two books, *The Costs of War* and *Reassessing the Presidency* and is the author of a third book *A Century of War*.

10

A Student's Appreciation of Professor Hoppe

Jeffrey Barr

L ike German engineering, Professor Hans Hermann-Hoppe's worldview is orderly, robust, and ultimately compelling.

Yet, I came to discover (and then embrace) this worldview by accident. Though I was generally a good student, I miserably failed the first microeconomics class I ever took. The class was a morass of neoclassic incantations and mathematic models of human behavior that had no grounding in reality. Indeed, at the time, economics looked like Carlyle's "dismal science," and the experience was so bad that I vowed never again to set foot in another economics class. But because I had failed, I had to make up the class. Fortuitously, Professor Hoppe's microeconomics class happened to fit within my schedule in the following semester. My advisor counseled against taking Professor Hoppe, stating, "Many students find him to be . . . unorthodox."

Having had my fill of economic orthodoxy, I ignored my advisor and happily signed up for Professor Hoppe's class. Professor Hoppe did not disappoint. In contrast to the dismal science, Professor Hoppe refreshingly professed praxeology: the science of

Jeffrey Barr (BarrJ@cityofnorthlasvegas.com) practices law in Las Vegas, Nevada. He studied under Murray Rothbard and Hans-Herman Hoppe in the late 1980s and early 1990s.

human action. The subject matter made intuitive sense, and Professor Hoppe delivered crisp and articulate lectures, always punctuated with his dry wit and German accent. He eschewed standard economics textbooks; instead, his students read Henry Hazlitt's *Economics in One Lesson*[1] and Lew Rockwell's *The Free Market Reader*.[2] Even Professor Hoppe's exams poked subversive fun at mainstream economics.

Though I attended many of Professor Hoppe's lectures in several different classes, I was particularly fortunate to enroll in an unforgettable seminar entitled, "Marxism and Its Critics." Professor Hoppe devoted the first half of the seminar to indoctrinating the class in traditional, unadulterated Marxism. He insisted that his students be able to recite tenets of socialism better than any Soviet university student. The Good Professor then devoted the second half of the semester to systematically refuting each fundamental socialist contention. In session after session, Herr Hoppe methodically demolished the logical underpinnings of the communist system, attacking the rotten philosophy at its core. It was also this time that I devoured Professor Hoppe's first English-language book, *A Theory of Socialism and Capitalism*.[3] This treatise and the Marxism-and-Its-Critics course solidified Hoppe's brilliance in my mind. I also realized that I might be in the presence, ironically enough, of Marx's most formidable critic.

Despite all of the formal coursework with Professor Hoppe, I cherish his informal classes most. At the beginning of each semester, Professor Hoppe would announce that he would meet with students who were interested in joining the Political Economy Club at a local pub. He invited everyone in his classes, though few had the fortitude to attend. Those who did enjoyed long hours of debates on the many issues of the day—and what issues there were to discuss! The late-1980s/early 1990s were exciting times.

---

[1]Henry Hazlitt, *Economics in One Lesson*, rev. ed. (New York: Manor Books, [1962, 1974]; reprint New Rochelle, N.Y.: Arlington House, 1979).

[2]Llewellyn H. Rockwell, Jr., Ed. *The Free Market Reader: Essays in the Economics of Liberty* (Auburn, Ala.: Ludwig von Mises Institute, 1988).

[3]Hans-Hermann Hoppe, *A Theory of Socialism and Capitalism* (Boston-Dordrecht-London: Kluwer, 1989).

Murray Rothbard was at the zenith of his prestige. Communism's fall had vindicated Mises, and the so-called "grassroots Republican revolution" of the early 90s exuberantly confirmed the theories I was learning in university. These events provided much fodder for late-night, smoky meetings of the Political Economy Club. The sessions were less like meetings, and more like Professor Hoppe holding court. A bit detached, Professor Hoppe would often listen to the deliberations, sip his drink, put his hand to his chin, look into the air in deep contemplation, and finally, after gathering his thoughts, he would respond with a, "Ja, Ja, but, you see . . ." Much of the time, I would simply listen to these discussions, daring not to ask an unintelligent question because Hoppe's genius intimidated me. After knowing Professor Hoppe for nearly twenty years, I confess that I remain in awe of his brilliance so much so that I still feel a bit awkward addressing him as anything but "Professor Hoppe."

I am proud to be a part of this "festive-writing," honoring the remarkable career of Hans-Hermann Hoppe. Few individuals have had a more profound influence on my life. In an odd way, I will be forever grateful to that awful neoclassical economics professor whose microeconomics class I flunked. Without that failing grade, I might never have had the privilege to call Hans Hermann-Hoppe friend, mentor, and, most of all, professor. Congratulations, Professor Hoppe! ❧

11

The Vegas Circle

Lee C. Iglody

I was introduced to Professor Dr. Hans-Hermann Hoppe through Murray N. Rothbard, whom I had followed from New York's Brooklyn Polytech to the University of Nevada, Las Vegas, in order to study Austrian Economics. Having recently finished his Mises Institute booklet on the Austrian Method, I almost trembled when reaching out to shake his hand. Almost twenty years later, I still remember fondly that brief moment in the hallway. It was, to exaggerate only slightly, more exciting than meeting Mick Jagger and David Bowie. Right off the bat, anyone who knew Professors Rothbard and Hoppe back in the late 80s and early 90s will confirm that this dynamic duo had a chemistry that at once made them very accessible and yet strangely distant. Accessibility came from the fact that Rothbard was always willing to entertain even the most foolish questions with his characteristic cackle and an explanation of the way things are. Professor Hoppe, on the other hand, had a much more methodological, Teutonic way of dealing with stupid inquiries, a form of Socratic

Lee Iglody (leeiglody@yahoo.com), an attorney in Las Vegas, completed his Bachelor of Arts in Economics with honors under the guidance of Professors Murray N. Rothbard and Hans-Hermann Hoppe at the University of Nevada, Las Vegas.

dialogue with a lot of "ja, so" thrown in to punctuate the conversation. ("Government provides goods that the market cannot produce? Ja, so what do you mean by 'goods'?")

At the time, I traveled the "libertarian" seminar circuit quite a bit. At each of these programs, I always found individuals who were amazed by the depth and breadth of the works of Rothbard and Hoppe, and could not stop asking questions about them and their work. And each time this happened, I took a moment to thank God again for the chance I had to learn at the feet of the actual masters, Rothbard and Hoppe. And this is where part of the distance came in. Rothbard and Hoppe were operating on a different level altogether. There are those of us who are lucky enough to go through life with some vague understanding of what things are and how they became so. A few, select, blessed individuals transcend everything, see almost everything and are adept at imparting the gift to see to others. In this regard, Hoppe simply soared.

In the classroom, Professor Hoppe was not some lecturer regurgitating the sanitized and sterile "knowledge" of textbooks (he didn't use them), but a great "professor" of truth, with a clear, concise style of delivery punctuated by his wonderful dry wit, and a reading list that included books such as Hazlitt's *Economics in One Lesson* and Rothbard's *Man, Economy, and State*. I personally witnessed him convert many students to libertarianism. "You know, he really makes sense," was uttered by countless students after class. He made even generally disinterested students think about and grapple with fundamental questions of economics and, thus, civilization.

Predictably, although Professor Hoppe regularly received outstanding student reviews, and his publication list put to shame most of the economics department, there came a time when the University attempted to deny him tenure. With perseverance and dignity, Professor Hoppe overcame his opponents and achieved tenure. Thereafter, twice more his enemies came after him, and twice more he repulsed them, at great personal cost. I personally witnessed the immense time and effort Professor Hoppe had to expend defending against these onslaughts, and it saddens me to think how many new ideas humanity has been deprived of because of this diversion of his time and thoughts.

One of our regular activities outside the classroom was the weekly Political Economy Club meeting that took place at a local tavern, with cheap beer and a suitably quiet corner for us to gather around Professor Hoppe. Usually, by the third or fourth round, Professor Hoppe became "Hans" and the discussions became animated. Various visiting students, and the occasional dignitary, would often stop by to inject new energy into the discussion of diverse topics. Aside from the educational and social benefits of talks that went into the wee hours, I was privileged to observe the evolution of Hoppe's thoughts on many issues.

True, Hans is genuinely Teutonic in his reserve and detachment, but like so many great Germanic Thinkers, beneath this Teutonic exterior is a passion for freedom and knowledge that propels him to seek answers and solutions precisely because the consequences for humanity are so great. Anyone who has read his theoretical or practical works can imagine him a sincere defender of Western Civilization, with all that implies; but to have sat across from him when he is "Hans" explaining why, for example, methodological individualism is indispensible to real knowledge or democracy is a false god, is to see and feel that here sits another brave soul who has taken *"Tu ne cede malis, sed contra audentior ito"* to heart. Ludwig von Mises is said to have regretted, not the times he stood fast, but the times he compromised. By this standard, Professor Hoppe will have but few regrets.

I salute you, Hans. ✍

Part Two

Crossroads of Thought

12

Uncompromising Radicalism as Promising Strategy

Philipp Bagus

he first time I came across Professor Hoppe's work was when, still in high school, I read his introduction to a reprint of the German edition of Mises's *Liberalism*. I was fascinated both by Mises's book and by Hoppe's compelling statements, and glad to discover in him a leading living scholar in the tradition of Austrian economics, which I was then in the process of discovering. As he was a fellow German I overcame my timidity, traced him on the Internet and sent him an e-mail asking for advice for a place to study Austrian economics in Germany.

To my surprise and pleasure he actually answered my e-mail quickly. I learned to my disappointment that it was impossible to study Austrian economics at a German University. But Professor Hoppe suggested that I attend the Mises University in Auburn, Alabama to get an introduction to this school of thought. He also generously offered his recommendation to get me a scholarship to this event. Later he would recommend me for a fellowship at the Mises Institute; outline an epistemological table for my methodology class; invite me to the Property and Freedom Society Meetings

Philipp Bagus (philipp.bagus@web.de) is assistant professor of economics at the Universidad Rey Juan Carlos in Madrid.

and Private Seminars, and in various other ways promoted and shaped my professional development.

As a mentor, Prof. Hoppe surely can serve as a role model. Supportive though he is as a professor, however, as a scholar he is known to be intransigent. The words he wrote about Mises in the above-mentioned text describe his own attitude very well: "After all Mises was a man of principles, who categorically opposed compromises that were contrary to his theoretical insights; in a time where at republican Universities flexibility and opportunism were demanded for more than ever."[1] In adopting such an uncompromising attitude, Prof. Hoppe has bewildered and antagonized many colleagues and readers. However, it is precisely this attitude that is also attracting the attention and admiration of individuals who value principles, consistency, rigor, and truth. In what follows I will analyze Prof. Hoppe's uncompromising radicalism *as a strategy to spread Austro-Libertarian theory*, and make the case that it is an excellent – and possibly the only suitable – strategy to attain this end.

Prof. Hoppe has never made any compromise in economic theory, even though this could have brought him more influence in the mainstream economic profession. He is well known for his strong methodological stand against the mainstream by defending an extreme rationalism and apriorism.[2] Moreover, he is an uncompromising scholar also in the political sphere. Here he goes one step beyond Mises, who remained in favor of a minimal state and did not come to the logical conclusion of his own statement:

> [t]he program of liberalism . . . if condensed into a single word, would have to read: property, that is, private ownership of the means of production (for in regard to commodities ready for consumption, private ownership is a matter of course and is not disputed even by the

---

[1]Ludwig von Mises, *Liberalismus* (Jena: Gustav Fischer, 1927; reprint Sankt Augustin: Academia Verlag, 1993) p. 16.

[2]Hans-Hermann Hoppe, "In Defense of Extreme Rationalism: Thoughts on Donald McCloskey's The Rhetoric of Economics," *Review of Austrian Economics* 3 (1989): 179–214; idem, *Economic Science and the Austrian Method* (Auburn, Ala.: Ludwig von Mises Institute, 1995).

socialists and communists). All the other demands of
liberalism result from this fundamental demand.[3]

While Mises remained throughout his life a staunch defender of
a minimal state defending the violation of property rights by the
government in order to secure them, Prof. Hoppe is more consistent in his political theory and does not hesitate to follow the
implication of liberalism to its logical end:

> For those members of the movement who still hold on to
> the classic notion of universal human rights and the idea
> that self-ownership and private property rights precede
> all government and legislation, the transition from liber-
> alism to private property anarchism is only a small intel-
> lectual step, especially in light of the obvious failure of
> democratic government to provide the only service that
> it was ever intended to provide (that of protection). Pri-
> vate property anarchism is simply consistent liberalism;
> liberalism thought through to its ultimate conclusion, or
> liberalism restored to its original intent.[4]

The intellectual radicalism of Prof. Hoppe and his strategy
towards a free society, i.e., private property anarchy, go hand in
hand. Following Etienne de la Boétie, David Hume, and Ludwig
von Mises, he emphasizes that government's power rests on public opinion rather than sheer force.[5] Without widespread support
and voluntary cooperation on part of a large portion of a population governments cannot enforce their will. Consequently, governments can be brought down if a large part of population just ceases
its support. In order to achieve this, a minority must convince a
majority to end its support of the rulers. Prof. Hoppe likes to call
such an energetic minority "anti-intellectual intellectuals" referring

---

[3]Ludwig von Mises, *Liberalism: In the Classical Tradition*, Ralph Raico,
trans. (Irvington-on-Hudson, N.Y.: Foundation for Economic Education,
[1927] 1985), p. 19.

[4]Hans-Hermann Hoppe, *Democracy — The God that Failed: The Economics
and Politics of Monarchy, Democracy, and Natural Order* (New Brunswick, N.J.:
Transaction Publishers, 2001), p. 236.

[5]Ibid., p. 289.

to the fact that the vast majority of intellectuals function as corrupted intellectual safeguards of the rulers. The anti-intellectual intellectuals, however, have a good chance of being successful only if they are idealistic and strongly committed, as well as inspired by the vision of a free society, because they will face difficulties in a state-ruled world. Thus, they must have the energy and patience to convince the masses to end their support to the rulers. Here is where Prof. Hoppe's intellectual radicalism comes in. He rightly assures that:

> In fact, there must never be even the slightest wavering in one's commitment to uncompromising ideological radicalism ("extremism"). Not only would anything less be counterproductive, but more importantly, only radical—indeed, radically simple—ideas can possibly stir the emotions of the dull and indolent masses. And nothing is more effective in persuading the masses to cease cooperating with government than the constant and relentless exposure, de-sanctification, and ridicule of government and its representatives as moral and economic frauds and impostors: as emperors without clothes subject to contempt and the butt of all jokes.[6]

Intellectual radicalism is not only adequate to convince the masses of government failure but also to recruit a dedicated minority, especially among the young. In fact, Rothbard regarded education as the key to success on the road to a free society.[7] In my opinion the educational efforts should be concentrated on the young. As I can tell from my own experience, young people that are still idealistic can be ignited by excitement and enthusiasm for a logical consistent theory or program. Moreover, young people might still be intellectually flexible, change their world view and have not invested a long time in cooperating with, being assisted by or approving publicly or privately of the state. They do not have to consider their past as a great error having cooperated with the

---

[6]Ibid., p. 94.

[7]Murray N. Rothbard, *For a New Liberty: The Libertarian Manifesto*, rev. ed (San Francisco: Fox & Wilkes, 1996), p. 297.

state. Without such a psychic mortgage they are easier convinced of the prospects of a free society. Specifically, they might see their role in the change of the state of affairs into a better direction, the direction of an inspiring ideal. An inspiring uncompromising ideal was already called for by F.A. Hayek:

> We must make the building of a free society once more an intellectual adventure, a deed of courage. What we lack is a liberal Utopia, a program which seems neither a mere defense of things as they are not a diluted kind of socialism, but a truly liberal radicalism which does not spare the susceptibility of the mighty (including the trade union), which is not too severely practical and which does not confine itself to what appears today as politically possible. We need intellectual leaders who are prepared to resist the blandishments of power and influence and who are willing to work for an ideal, however, small may be the prospect of its early realization. They must be men who are willing to stick to principles and fight for their full realization, however remote. . . . Free trade and freedom of opportunity are ideals which still may rouse the imaginations of large numbers, but a mere "reasonable freedom of trade" or a mere "relaxation of controls" is neither intellectually respectable nor likely to inspire any enthusiasm. The main lesson which the true liberal must learn from the success of the socialists is that it was their courage to be Utopian which gained them the support of intellectuals and thereby an influence on public opinion which is daily making possible what only recently seemed utterly remote. Those who have concerned themselves exclusively with what seemed practicable in the existing state of opinion have constantly found that even this has rapidly become politically impossible as the result of change in a public opinion which they have done nothing to guide. Unless we can make the philosophic foundations of a free society once more a living intellectual issue, and its implementation a task which challenges the ingenuity and imagination of our liveliest minds, the prospects of freedom are indeed dark. But if we can regain that belief in

the power of ideas which was the mark of liberalism at
its best, the battle is not lost.[8]

Prof. Hoppe is such a Utopian in the best Hayekian sense. He
has, in a sense, fulfilled Hayek's call, especially with his bestseller
Democracy — The God That Failed. With his theory of argumentation
ethics and building upon Rothbard's natural law theory, he has
shown that an objective and consistent ethical theory is possible.
His work combines two branches, a consistent economic theory
with a consistent political and ethical theory into a consistent theory of the social sciences — Austro-Libertarianism — that by its logical consistency, rigor, radicalism, clarity, and explanatory power
is capable of inspiring the excitement and enthusiasm necessary to
achieve its radical social ends.

I regard his uncompromising position as a good strategy to
gain influence in the long term. In the process of persuading others to accept a particular viewpoint, a coherent theory should prevail over an opportunistic strategy. Science always must tell the
truth. One should not overthrow principles, tell an untruth, or lie
just to persuade others about a particular point of view. Such a
strategy is not ethical, and it will destroy one's consistency and
undermine one's argumentative basis, so much so that in the long
run this strategy becomes self-defeating. Making compromises in
theory eventually thwarts the one's own aims as a theorist.

Perhaps making compromises will help to get one's articles
published in a top journal. Maybe dealing with applied topics that
are in vogue in the mainstream can help garner a position in a top
university. Opportunistic behavior might help assure tenure,
respect, and a better income. The temptation to get into ever
higher-ranked top journals, ever-better universities, and media
outlets can lead some to make ever more substantial compromises.
But once one starts with compromises he is on a slippery slope. Of
course, this strategy can help one achieve more impact and influence, especially in the short run and among certain intellectuals.
But it entails the great danger that one starts to gradually resemble
these intellectuals in order to convince them. In fact, the Chicago

---

[8]F.A. Hayek,"The Intellectuals and Socialism," in *Studies in Philosophy, Politics, and Economics* (Chicago: University of Chicago Press, 1967), p. 194.

School has had more influence in academics and politics than the Austrian school through making compromises and advocating various forms of state intervention.

However, what is important for an economist or an economic school is not to have influence but to tell the truth. *Fiat veritas, et pereat mundus*, to change a famous Latin phrase. There shall be truth even if the world perishes. The original phrase and motto of the Habsburg Emperor Ferdinand (1503–1564) is: *Fiat iustitia, et pereat mundus*. There shall be justice even if the world perishes. Fortunately, it lies in the nature of man that we do not have to choose between justice and the flourishing of civilization. Justice does not stand in contrast to wealth production but is actually necessary for it. As Rothbard states, "the proper groundwork for this goal [liberty] is a moral passion for justice."[9]

Sticking to the truth is the best strategy to achieve the flourishing of civilization and liberty. Ultimately it is public opinion that changes the course of the world. People must be convinced of the benefits of liberty and told about the evil of government. Therefore, the truth about liberty must be unequivocally stated again and again. Nothing is more attractive in theory than a coherent, consistent, and stringent position. Prof. Hoppe has demonstrated that consistent theory is beautiful and liable to attract a hard core of students strongly committed to the cause of truth. By sticking to the truth one will not need rhetoric that makes compromises to convey a position since the truth seekers will find the truth. Neither will one need to approve of others' inconsistent, compromising, and socialistic positions.

By contrast, intellectual compromise entails a strategic disadvantage. An inconsistent theory will lead to false conclusions and will attract those with shallow reasoning who will easily abandon the cause of truth. But compromise—deliberate inconsistency—does even greater harm. There is no logical end in continuing with compromises until the whole original theory is abandoned and falls apart. Eventually the compromising scholar loses respect for his own original position. He ends up in intellectual sloth, stagnating

---

[9]Murray N. Rothbard, *The Ethics of Liberty* (New York: New York University Press., 1998), p. 264.

debates, muddled positions, and boring superficialities — an unappealing potpourri.

Prof. Hoppe's economic and political theory avoids this pitfall. A consistent, rigorous, and radical theory is proposed by a man who does not make compromise in his goal of achieving a free society. In so doing, he inspires others to follow him on the path to that goal. I, for my part, will try to make my own contribution towards that end following Prof. Hoppe's model. I would like to express my deepest gratitude to him for directing my path from the moment at which I first started reading his introduction to Mises's *Liberalism,* and wish him all the best in the future. ✧

13

Abraham Lincoln and the Modern State

Luigi Marco Bassani

While still revered by a great majority of Americans as crucial for national freedom, the "Lincoln episode" is considered by some peripheral scholars to be the final nail in the coffin of the American experiment in self-government. At the very best, it drastically changed the Founders' Republic, and in a way that cannot sit well with conservative and libertarian political outlooks. According to Thomas Fleming, for instance, "Lincoln's presidency was . . . the second American founding . . . which turned a constitutional system established by Washington, Adams and Jefferson, as a regime of liberty, into a radical Jacobin State rooted in the principle of equality."[1]

In this brief treatment of Lincoln—upon which I will venture very much aware, but not afraid of what a scholar aptly defined "the stranglehold that Jaffa and Thurow have on Lincolnian political theory"[2]—there is no room or even need to treat the question of

Luigi Marco Bassani (marco.bassani@unimi.it) is professor of History of Political Theory at the Università di Milano, Italy.

[1]Thomas Fleming, "Three Faces of Democracy: Cleisthenes, Jefferson, and Robespierre," *Telos* 104 (Summer 1995), p. 51.

[2]William S. Corlett, Jr., "The Availability of Lincoln's Political Religion," *Political Theory* X, no. 4 (Nov. 1982) p. 521.

slavery. The well-known letter to Horace Greely is, in any case, the plainest refutation of the idea that Lincoln waged a war against the South to uproot slavery. As he most clearly acknowledged, his foremost preoccupation was always the preservation of the Union, and concern for the black slaves had no part in it. He plainly stated that he did not want "to leave any one in doubt" that

> My paramount object in this struggle is to save the Union, and is not either to save or to destroy slavery. If I could save the Union without freeing any slave I would do it.[3]

While for most people in those days antislavery *was* unionism, and vice versa, Lincoln took a simpler line of argument and stated very clearly that the Union was the one and only goal of the struggle. It is exactly the notion of the Union as an end in itself, as the only moral institutional arrangement for Americans, which is central to the understanding of Lincoln as the agent of the establishment of the modern State in America.

Much of the Lincoln debate in the past generations has centered on whether the Republic survived the Civil War drama unscathed or was fundamentally altered. Lincoln always insisted that he trod in the footsteps of Washington and Jefferson regarding all relevant questions of government. Later on, however, both Lincoln's devotees and a great number of historians (the two categories tend to merge in the "Lincoln cult") have contended that the American nation was in fact very much in need of another founding, thus refuting the claims of continuity with the republican past attributed to Lincoln's policies and actions. At any rate, nowadays the notion that Lincoln, for better or for worse, instigated a radical renovation and changed the American political landscape forever is common ground.

Here I shall very briefly contend that Lincoln indeed brought about a change of the first order, and probably much greater than most historians of ideas would concede, as it obliterated the original, American Republic. Put bluntly, Lincoln precipitated the final

---

[3]Abraham Lincoln to Horace Greely, August 22nd, 1862, *The Collected Works of Abraham Lincoln*, R.P. Basler, ed., 9 vols. (New Brunswick, N.J.: Rutgers University Press, 1953), vol. V, p. 388; hereinafter *Collected Works*.

migration to America of European categories of power and the State.

Prima facie, Lincoln appears simply to be the victorious successor to the progression of characters running from Alexander Hamilton to Daniel Webster and Henry Clay. But with the idea of the Union as an end in itself, Lincoln discovered the Trojan horse for bringing the European categories of the modern State into America. That is, in securing the Union and uprooting slavery, Lincoln was not merely upholding a moral stance; rather he was interpreting the *Zeitgeist*, whose real focus was on the consolidation of the modern State.

Lincoln's Constitution

Lincoln generally denied that his actions violated the Constitution or were otherwise outside its framework. In spite of his reassurances, Lincoln's Constitution became, in effect, a profoundly different document from the one ratified in 1788. Even the most superficial reading of the Constitution and the *Bill of Rights* (1791) will show that the revolutionary generation thought that nearly all serious threats to the freedom of the individual came from government. All the freedoms and rights that the Founders were talking about were understood as safeguards of the individual *against* government. That was the rationale, unsophisticated as it may be, behind the Founders' notion of minimal government. All the basic freedoms were deemed in need of protection from one and only one potential aggressor, namely government (more properly the federal government, rather than States' governments). While other individuals could always be a threat to property, government could obliterate both property and property rights.

With Lincoln the focus of threats to liberty changes from government to individuals. It is not government, but private individuals that can become potentially abusive. The government, therefore, ought to be charged with the task of taking the necessary steps to protect individuals from exploitation by other persons. This is a turning point of the first order and it betokens an entirely different way of thinking about government. Expanding upon these ideas, George Fletcher has written a thoughtful book called *Our Secret Constitution: How Lincoln Redefined American Democracy*.

In his opinion there are now two Constitutions in this country. Alongside the first, original Constitution, there now is a "secret" unwritten one crafted by Lincoln himself. The two documents entail two different sets of values, locked in an ongoing contradiction. "The first Constitution commits itself to freedom and the second builds both on a preference for equality and the recognition that freedom is often an illusion."[4]

While the first Constitution is built on a deeply-felt distrust of government, the second presupposes confidence in a forceful government, the protector of citizens from other citizens. In the profound change engendered by the presidency of Abraham Lincoln, a new understanding of the relation between the individual and the government was brought to America, a notion that prevailed – and still prevails – in Europe. The conclusion is such as to tear the very fabric of the old constitutional instrument: "The view that comes to the fore in the Secret Constitution recognizes that freedom as well as rights depend on the proper interaction with government."[5] Sympathizers and critics alike agree on one point: Lincoln changed the Constitution and the American system of government forever.

Lincoln bent the Constitution to his own purposes. The explanation of the logic behind all the abuses came in a very important letter to Albert Hodges. He wrote in April 1864:

> I did understand, that my oath to preserve the constitution to the best of my ability, imposed upon me the duty of preserving, by every indispensable means, that government – that nation – of which that constitution was the *organic law*. Was it possible to lose the *nation*, and yet preserve the *constitution*? By general law life and limb must be protected; yet often a limb must be amputated to save a life; but a life is never wisely given to save a limb. I felt that measures, otherwise unconstitutional, might become lawful, by becoming indispensable to the preservation of the constitution, through

---

[4]George P. Fletcher, *Our Secret Constitution: How Lincoln Redefined American Democracy* (New York: Oxford University Press, 2001), p. 223.

[5]Ibid.

the preservation of the nation. Right or wrong, I
assumed this ground.[6]

This is the most important single statement of the "Lincoln persuasion" for two reasons. It is the best illustration of his political
thought and the manifest death warrant for classical liberalism in
America.

Lincoln believes the Constitution to be an "organic law," a
European notion that was quite a novelty in American political
discourse. He goes on to draw an unambiguous parallel between a
human and a collective body. In a few sentences one can find all
the elements of the modern State theory of European origin, artic-
ulated by a man who may never have heard of Machiavelli, Bodin,
Hobbes, but was nonetheless singing to their tune. In Lincoln's
mind, the Constitution is in fact an organic law as it is meant to
protect and give form to an organic society by creating an organic
State. The crucial thing is that the society or the nation that it
should protect is much more important than the law itself, the
Constitution. In other words, the Nation comes first.

For Lincoln the Constitution had no particular meaning when
detached from its more significant "progenitor," the Union. While
the question in earlier American political discourse would have to
be summarized as "whether the Union had any meaning apart
from the Constitution,"[7] Lincoln was effectively reversing the
dyadic relation. In fact, the Union had become a mystical and self-
justifying end.

Herman Belz and a number of other scholars deny altogether
that the President ever violated the Constitution. According to him,
"Lincoln's example, is to insist on fidelity to the text, forms, and
principles of the framers' Constitution."[8] For Lincoln, "American

---

[6]Abraham Lincoln to Albert G. Hodges (April 4th, 1864), *Collected Works*,
vol. VII, p. 281.

[7]Richard Gamble, "Rethinking Lincoln," in *The Costs of War: America
Pyrrhic Victories*, John V. Densen, ed. (New Brunswick, N.J.: Transaction,
1999), p. 141.

[8]Herman Belz, *Abraham Lincoln, Constitutionalism, and Equal Rights in the
Civil War Era* (New York: Fordham University Press, 1998), p. 100.

nationality was defined by the Constitution . . . the nation was the Constitution."[9] In fact, Lincoln declared exactly the opposite: the nation was *not* the Constitution and Lincoln was ready to violate the latter to save the former.

The most revealing part of Lincoln's frank statement on the Nation and the Constitution is the use of the organic metaphor. This equation between a living body and a polity is of the utmost importance, since it is crucial to the emergence of the categories and the terminology of the modern State in political theory. The (modern) State, in fact, is not only a set of rules, a novel way of looking at the political community; it is also embodied in a terminology which subtly compels one to think of and about the State within the mental framework of the State itself. The emergence of the modern State in Europe went hand in hand with the change in the political lexicon that took place from the 1500s. The State had to be construed by jurists as an artificial person that transcended the person of the princely ruler and, ultimately, his very dynasty, guaranteeing its perpetuation. The new body politic had a life of its own, beyond subjects and even the sovereign; it did not represent anybody, it simply existed and it was nurtured by myths produced by historians, jurists, theologians, as well as politicians (first and foremost the myth of having always existed).

Vital to such a creation, almost as crucial as the notion of sovereignty itself, was the extensive use of the organic metaphor. This is the idea that the set of relationships between human beings forms a real entity, a living organism, which the State, this artificial person, has the duty to regulate. At best, it simply implies that political rule is natural to society, as society itself is a body politic. While it is true that such metaphors may be found in ancient Greek political thought, chiefly in Plato's *Republic*, they were not particularly popular prior to the rise of the modern State.

A civil war is utterly disruptive, as it conflicts directly with the State dogma: it duplicates, or multiplies the unity upon which the State is predicated. It presents a "house divided," or a sick organism, and "it cannot stand." In a modern State, the contenders, the disruptors of unity, must be treated as unredeemable foes,

---

[9]Ibid., p. 98.

absolute enemies, to be erased from the face of the Earth: for they have challenged the most sacred principle of them all, that of unity. If this perspective of the Civil War as the "modern State coming to America" is correct, then the war was not *unnecessary*, as Thomas DiLorenzo suggests,[10] because the minimalist and decentralized Republic of the Founders needed to be replaced by the "rationality" of the modern State, and the war was the means to that end.

America experienced in a few years, roughly between 1832 and 1865, a telescoped replica of what happened to Europe from 1525 to 1815. In Europe it was the sovereign — first the King and then the assembly — who promised to free all individuals from the tyrannical as well as outmoded loyalties that were the core of liberty in the Middle Ages: church, city, corporation, family and the like. The individual had to be liberated of all previous social ties in order to become a good and free citizen.

In this tragedy the federal government took the part of the sovereign power in European history, while the States were left with the role of relics. The war was indeed necessary because the Republic of the Founders was based on principles that were not only at odds with the modern State, but utterly inimical to it. A genuine federalism is, in fact, not an option for a modern State.

For Lincoln the Union was the organic metaphor of choice. As evidence of Lincoln's stance on the Union, the message to Congress of December 1st, 1862 is invaluable. The moving description of the United States as a physical living entity, as "our national homestead," is the premise on which the President builds his claim that such an organic entity

> in all its adaptations and aptitudes . . . demands union, and abhors separation. In fact, it would . . . force re-union, however much of blood and treasure the separation might have cost.[11]

---

[10]Thomas J. DiLorenzo, *The Real Lincoln: A New Look at Abraham Lincoln, His agenda, and An Unnecessary War* (New York: Three Rivers Press, 2003).

[11]Abraham Lincoln, "Annual Message to Congress" (December 1st, 1862), *Collected Works*, vol. V, p. 529.

In this important message to Congress Lincoln also stressed very clearly why there should be no separation, at any cost:

> That portion of the earth's surface which is owned and inhabited by the people of the United States, is well adapted to be the home of one national family; and it is not well adapted for two, or more. . . . [Everything in this country is] to be an advantageous combination, for one united people.[12]

To Lincoln, the Union was the great guardian of the principle of equality and he was ready to sacrifice everything to preserve it. He wanted America to take the place of Europe in world supremacy because he firmly believed that Europe was doomed by her history of oppression, brutality, and radical inequality, and that America was going to be a better, fairer leader: a leader that would eventually bring equality and democracy to all mankind.

THE CIVIL RELIGION OF ABRAHAM LINCOLN

A further element of interest in this appraisal of the irruption of the categories of the modern State in America is Lincoln's notion of "civil religion." In modern times, the idea of a civil religion was hinted by Machiavelli and later it was fully developed by Jean-Jacques Rousseau. The search of a civil religion that would replace Christianity goes hand in hand with the intellectual construction of the modern State. One of the secular dogmas of the modern State is that the "mystery of being" is to be located in this world and in the political community, not in heaven above us. Machiavelli, Rousseau, and many others, looked to a "civic (or civil) religion" as the most suitable tool for guaranteeing the obedience of the citizenry to political institutions.

Lincoln thought of himself as a pure Christian and is still regarded by many as an inspirational character in this field. Still, his only clear reference to the notion of an "American political religion" is characterized by distinctly un-Christian overtones. I am referring to his famous speech of 1838, in which he advocated the

---

[12]Ibid., p. 527.

"reverence for the laws" to become the supreme virtue of the country:

> Let it be taught in schools, in seminaries, and in colleges
> ... let it be preached from the pulpit, proclaimed in leg-
> islative halls, and enforced in courts of justice. And, in
> short, let it become the *political religion* of the nation; and
> let the old and the young, the rich and the poor, the
> grave and the gay, of all sexes and tongues, and colors
> and conditions, sacrifice unceasingly upon its altars.[13]

Once again, the reader and the scholar must wonder at the fact that somehow Lincoln had Rousseau engraved in his heart, without, probably, ever having heard of him.

FRANCIS LIEBER AND THE GERMAN *STAATSTHEORIE* SCHOOL

When confronted with all these threads – Union, Nation, organic metaphors, civil religion – all leading to one single goal, the renewal of the American political community in the shape of a modern State, the historian of ideas faces one big question: "Where was it coming from?" While Lincoln was the most brilliant American politician of his times (and possibly of American history), he was quite uneducated in political philosophy. In some ways, however, the works of Francis Lieber, who in 1827 was one of the first German academics to migrate to America, may well have made it through to Lincoln's own mindset. Lieber served as a conduit between the intellectual and political cultures of Germany, England, and America. Lieber's influence in bringing the modern State categories to the New World cannot be overstated. As remarked by two historians of the German cultural influences in the United States:

> [Lieber's] contributions to political theory marked the
> beginning of a new era in American ideas on the nature
> of the state. There had been anticipatory statements of
> the theory he advanced, but these had been fragmentary

---

[13]Abraham Lincoln, "Address Before the Young Men's Lyceum of Springfield, Illinois" (January 27th, 1838), *Collected Works*, vol. I, p. 112; emphasis added.

and unsystematic as compared with the organic system presented in his learned treatises. The publication between 1838 and 1853 of his three books on political ethics, on legal and political hermeneutics, and on civil liberty and self-government put him at the head of the new school of political thought, at the same time putting the then regnant theory of natural law to rout.[14]

Since its beginning with Francis Lieber, American "political science" was—and remained for decades—stamped in the mold of the Teutonic *Staatstheorie*, albeit without the philosophic subtleties of the Kant-Fichte-Hegel tradition. It was predicated on continental notions, first and foremost on the worshipping of "[t]he state whose origin is in history, whose nature is organic, whose essence is unity, whose function is the exercise of its sovereign will in law, and whose ultimate end is the moral perfection of mankind."[15]

Or, as Lieber himself declared in one of his most significant works:

> The State is aboriginal with man; it is no voluntary association . . . no company of shareholders; no machine, no work of contract by individuals who lived previously out of it; no necessary evil; . . . the State is a form and faculty of mankind to lead the species toward greater perfection—it is the glory of man.[16]

Lieber's doctrine is "a prophetic conception," according to Vernon Parrington, based on "the principle of an evolving state that draws all lesser sovereignties into its orbit by the law of attraction."[17]

---

[14]Henry A. Pochmann & Arthur R. Schultz, *German Culture in America, 1600–1900: Philosophical and Literary Influences* (Madison: University of Wisconsin Press, 1957), p. 125.

[15]Sylvia D. Fries, "Staatstheorie and the New American Science of Politics," *Journal of the History of Ideas* 34, no. 3 (July–September 1973), p. 11.

[16]Francis Lieber, *Manual of Political Ethics, Designed Chiefly for the Use of Colleges and Students at Law (1838–1839)*, 2nd rev. ed., Theodore D. Woolsey, ed. (Philadelphia: Lippincott, 1888), vol. II, p. 162.

[17]Vernon L. Parrington, *Main Currents in American Political Thought: An Interpretation of American Literature from the Beginnings to 1920, The Romantic Revolution in America (1800–1860)* (New York: Harcourt, Brace, 1927), vol. II, p. 89.

Parrington was well aware of the importance of Francis Lieber, who "provided a philosophical background" to the legal theory of Joseph Story. "Under the combined legal and philosophical attack the compact theory found its philosophical breastworks leveled, its natural rights theory undermined, and its commanding position effectively turned."[18] Alan Grimes places Lieber at the transition between "the constitutional and legal approach to an understanding of the nature of the American Union, and the rise of the organic concept of the nation."[19] The importance of the German professor in shaping the ideas which Lincoln exploited fully has been noticed by other historians. Lieber "had indeed argued before the war that the original Constitution was insufficient to the needs of the nation . . . in the 1830s and 1840s, he had gained prominence, North and South, by attacking the idea of a fixed Constitution." A staunch advocate of federal growth, he thought "that federal power should expand slowly and organically—and thus constitutionally—as the nation grew. . . . He believed that the war would solidify the Union and thus fulfill his dream, nurtured during his school years in Germany, of living in a modern nation-state." Later on, during the war Lieber became very popular, wrote dozens of articles and pamphlets in order "to popularize his distinctive brand of nationalism." In practice, "[h]is many public statements used the South's insurrection to justify an expansion of federal power beyond what the Constitution expressly sanctioned."[20]

Although probably the most important, Lieber was not alone in fostering these concepts all across the country. William T. Harris of St. Louis, one of the first American Hegelians, and the German educated John W. Burgess, Lieber's own successor at Columbia College, were joining forces in rendering familiar the new nationalist dogma to the citizenry. In this respect the war was clearly a turning point. As Merle Curti put it:

---

[18]Ibid.

[19]Alan Pendleton Grimes, *American Political Thought* (New York: Holt, 1960), p. 283.

[20]Michael Vorenberg, *Final Freedom: The Civil War, the Abolition of Slavery, and the Thirteenth Amendment* (Cambridge: Cambridge University Press, 2001), p. 64.

During and after the Civil War, Northern intellectuals developed the incipient organic theory, which at first did not reach the rank and file even in the North. In the Old World the organic theory was likewise serving the integral type of nationalism that had largely replaced the older, humanitarian variety of the early nineteenth century.[21]

CONCLUSION

In the words of Karl Marx, the Civil War was a "world-transforming . . . revolutionary movement."[22] Dating from the year 1862, this must be considered as one of his few correct prophecies, albeit an easy one.

The whole political landscape of America was changed by the war in an unparalleled way. The call for centralized power was the theme of the day and became the everlasting legacy of the war. As far as the States were concerned, it was not only the idea of a perpetual and not so voluntary union that had prevailed, but also the notion that the States were mere provinces of a vast empire.

The sectional crisis beginning in 1828 (with the publication of South Carolina's *Exposition and Protest*, penned by John Calhoun) up to the Southern bid for independence developed on two intertwined issues: constitutional interpretation and tariffs. The victory of the North on both fronts was absolute. The Constitution was transformed by the post-war amendments and could be freely interpreted by the Supreme Court, with the States — *qua* States — having no part in its reading. The Constitution became a typical matter for the federal power to deal with. Likewise, by the end the economic supremacy of the federal government was unchallenged. A system of national banks chartered by the national government rendered the decade long struggle against a national bank

---

[21]Merle Curti, *The Roots of American Loyalty* (New York: Columbia University Press, 1946), p. 175.

[22]Karl Marx to Friedrich Engels, October 29th–November 17th, 1862, in *Karl Marx on America and the Civil War*, Saul K. Padover, ed. (New York, McGraw-Hill, 1972), p. 263.

obsolete. If the fight of the Jeffersonians had been for "hard currency and hardly any government," by the end of the 1870s an all-powerful government was sponsoring fiat money.

> The Supreme Court, under Chase . . . upheld the constitutionality of the Legal Tender Act. Before the end of Reconstruction, Greenbackers were clamoring for more paper money. Few citizens before the war had contributed directly to the treasury. By the war's close everyone and everything was taxed.[23]

In the end, it was the presidency of Lincoln—the very statesman who said "the principles of Jefferson are the definitions and axioms of free society"[24]—that wrote *finis* to those very same principles and ended the American experiment in limited government and self-government. One of the major consequences of the meta-constitutional theory of the Union as an end in itself (and of equating its dissolution with a "moral catastrophe") embraced by Abraham Lincoln was that of making American political thought more receptive to European theories.[25] America proceeded towards a "normalization" of sorts, growing ever more similar to Europe. And this process of "convergence" was to reach its peak during the last century. Lincoln "normalized" America, thus opening the door for the Americanization of the world.

American constitutional liberalism of the origins, namely federalism, having lost its moorings in the theory of natural rights, became increasingly transformed into an instrument of ideological conflict between the two sections of the country, which were by now tantamount to veritable distinct nations.

---

[23]James A. Rawley, *The Politics of Union: Northern Politics during the Civil War* (Lincoln: University of Nebraska Press, 1980), p. 184.

[24]Abraham Lincoln to H.L. Pierce et al. (April 6th 1859), *Collected Works*, vol. II, p. 375.

[25]Just as an example, in the late Nineteenth century John W. Burgess offered a definition of sovereignty as an "original, absolute, unlimited, universal power over the individual subject and over all associations of subjects," and of "the State . . . [as] the source of all titles to land and of all powers over it," John W. Burgess, *Political Science and Comparative Constitutional Law* (Boston-London: Ginn, 1891), vol. I, pp. 47, 52.

The sea changes that I have tried here to summarize are better understood as the triumph of the modern State, but they might likewise be seen, in a more classical, American approach, as the final displacement of the Founding Fathers' design for self and limited government. This conclusion, of course, is liable to grate on the ears of those—scholars, popular historians, journalists and politicians—who subscribe to the standard, fashionable view that the gigantic upheaval occasioned by the Civil War was first and foremost a moral crusade for the eradication of slavery and the redemption of the white race in this country from its original sin.

In conclusion, we must turn again to the American *Staatstheorie* professors. It is true that their dominance in the profession faded after World War I, and their ultimate failure might be linked to the fact that they were "unable to apply the German idea of the state to the American Political tradition."[26] But this is true only from a purely theoretical perspective. Abraham Lincoln was not engaging in such a complex pursuit. He did not have to render the two traditions compatible, but rather to burn the bridges with the old American notion of "liberty vs. government." In addition, he did not have to win any sophisticated scholarly dispute, as he had better weapons than continental authorities on the subject of liberty and the State. It was his army that, in fact made every citizen, North and South of the Potomac, appreciate the notion that there was an identity of interest between the individual and the State (by now understood as the Nation).

The conventional wisdom concedes that Abraham Lincoln, in uprooting slavery, also uprooted the old notion of an opposition between the individual and the State. I would contend, however, that a more careful reading of history gives us a materially different picture. Lincoln's primary object was, in fact, to eradicate the eighteenth century opposition between the individual and the State, depriving of any meaning a Constitution that was constructed on such a dichotomy. The principal result was the end of the Founders' Republic and the emergence of the United States as a Modern State. The end of slavery was only a side effect, albeit a much welcomed one, of Lincoln's primary goal. ֍

---

[26]Fries, "Staatstheorie and the New American Science of Politics," p. 403.

14

The Sociology of the Development of Austrian Economics

Joseph T. Salerno

lthough this paper was presented as a lecture in 1996, I have chosen to publish it in this volume in nearly its original manuscript form.[1] It was never previously published or posted electronically, but the paper achieved a limited circulation in manuscript form via copy and fax machines during the primitive days of the Internet. Despite its relatively restricted exposure, however, it generated a remarkably heated discussion in Austrian economics circles — much of it based on an inaccurate hearsay version of the paper — that lasted for a number of years.[2] So the first reason for publishing the paper now without

Joseph T. Salerno (salerno@mises.com) is the Academic Vice-President of the Ludwig von Mises Institute, a Professor of Economics (Graduate Program Chair) at the Lubin School of Business at Pace University, and editor of the *Quarterly Journal of Austrian Economics*. This paper is an edited version of a speech presented at the Ludwig von Mises Institute's First Annual Austrian Scholars Conference, Auburn University, Alabama, January 26–27, 1996, on a panel entitled "The Future of the Austrian School."

[1]Footnotes have been added and the title has been changed, but save for the correction of grammatical errors and the insertion of a few clarifying words here and there, the text has remained substantially unaltered.

[2]See, for example, David L. Prychitko, "Thoughts on Austrian Economics, 'Austro-Punkism,' and Libertarianism," in idem, *Markets, Planning and Democracy:*

major revision is to set the record straight regarding the actual claims and supporting arguments contained in it. A second reason for proceeding with belated publication of the manuscript is to acquiesce in and thus put a halt to the numerous importunities to publish that I have been subjected to over the years by colleagues and friends who were broadly aware of the prolonged controversy that swirled around the paper but were neither in the audience at its original presentation nor had the opportunity to read it subsequently. The third, and perhaps the most important, of my reasons for complying with the editors' request to publish the paper is that, despite the fact that the situation in Austrian economics has greatly changed for the better since the paper was originally written and despite my dissatisfaction with its imperfections of style and tone, I think its substantive claims have stood up quite well and bear repeating. In particular, I believe the paper identifies counterproductive attitudes peculiar to proponents of a heterodox intellectual movement. Such attitudes are always liable to recur and must be vigilantly guarded against because they are likely to impede the movement's further progress, if not threaten its very survival.

AUSTRIAN ECONOMICS DEFINED

Before we venture to speculate on the future of the Austrian School, we must first define the distinct intellectual paradigm adherence to which characterizes a member of this school.

Specifying a vague methodological attitude or stance, for example "subjectivism" or "methodological individualism," is not sufficient. These labels arguably apply to a broad array of modern economists—from the late George Shackle to Milton Friedman the price theorist—as well as to the contemporary followers of Carl Menger and Ludwig von Mises. To capture the essence of the distinctively Austrian approach to economics, therefore, we must do much more. Namely, we must define the precise and realistic method utilized by the acknowledged masters of Austrian economics for discovering

---

Essays after the Collapse of Communism (Lyme, N.H.: Edward Elgar Publishing, 2002), p. 186, *et pass.*

and explicating what Menger called the "exact" laws of econom-ics.[3]

For my money, this method is praxeology, which was given its name and first comprehensive explication by Mises. Mises did not conceive praxeology as a metaeconomic discourse unrelated to the workaday concerns of the economic theorist; he himself used it as a tool of research in revolutionizing the theories of money, busi-ness cycles, and socialism. Even before Mises, however, this method was actually employed by the great founders of the Aus-trian school, Menger and Böhm-Bawerk, to discover new eco-nomic truths. What Mises calls "the modern theory of value and prices,"[4] first systematically expounded by Böhm-Bawerk, is a tan-gible creation of praxeology. Going back further still, this method was also adumbrated and used by some of the most creative eigh-teenth- and nineteenth-century economists, namely Cantillon, Say, Senior, and Cairnes.

The essence of Austrian economics may be defined, then, as the structure of economic theorems that is arrived at through the process of praxeological deduction, that is, through logical deduc-tion from the reality-based Action Axiom. In addition to providing a unique and practicable method for developing the science of eco-nomics, this definition is useful precisely because it clearly excludes Shackle and Friedman, as well as many other economists, past and present, from being considered as practitioners of Aus-trian economics. It is childish to seek to define an intellectual par-adigm, or even to use a definite term to designate it, while at the same time bemoaning a particular definition because it excludes or is "intolerant of" those whose views are essentially inconsistent with the paradigm so defined. It must not be forgotten that a defi-nition, by *definition*, is meant to be rigidly essentialist and, hence, exclusivist.

---

[3]See Carl Menger, *Problems of Economics and Sociology*, Louis Schneider, ed. (Urbana: University Illinois Press, 1963), pp. 61, 69; idem, *Investigations into the Method of the Social Sciences with Special Reference to Economics*, Francis J. Nock, trans. (New York: New York University Press, 1985 [1883]), chaps. 4–5.

[4]Ludwig von Mises, *Human Action: A Treatise on Economics* (Chicago: Con-temporary Books Inc., 1966), p. 201.

Having given a definition of Austrian economics, I now turn to a discussion of two problems which cloud its future. Both of these problems, I will argue, betray a peculiar reluctance on the part of some of its practitioners to define precisely what is meant by Austrian economics. Perhaps this reluctance is due to a fear that to define a science or the specific method of pursuing it is to peremptorily foreclose the possibility of any future progress in the discipline. The enormous advances that have occurred within the praxeological paradigm since Say and Senior first began to self-consciously articulate its method, I think, render this fear baseless. Indeed, I would argue that it is hardly accidental that Mises, the first economist to deliberately utilize praxeology as a comprehensive research method, was the economist who made the greatest substantive advances in the Austrian theoretical paradigm. However, due to a severe constraint of time, I will not pursue this point any further here.

Austro-Punkism

The first problem beclouding the future of the Austrian school I call "Austro-punkism." My use of this neologism here is not intended to evoke the older, indefinite sense of the term "punk" as anyone, "especially a youngster, regarded as inexperienced, insignificant, etc."[5] Rather, I use it in the more specific and now widely-accepted sense to indicate the harboring of an impious attitude toward the accomplishments of the past and, hence, toward all authority. This attitude is the driving force of the phenomenon of "punk" rock, which from its narrowly musical roots in the late 1970s has grown into a broad cultural movement today. The broad social acceptance of the punk phenomenon is exemplified by the fact that its music, now blandly but significantly entitled "alternative rock," permeates the airwaves of even mainstream, commercial radio stations. (I must confess I am bitter that the last remaining "classic" rock station in New York City has recently and abruptly converted to the "alternative" rock format.)

---

[5]*Webster's New Twentieth Century Dictionary of the English Language,* unabridged 2nd ed. (New York: Simon & Schuster, 1983), p. 1462.

Now, I am not trying to suggest here that the roots of Austro-punkism lie in popular culture. I will deal with the causes that underlie it shortly. My immediate purpose in the allusion to punk rock is to justify my use of the "Austro-punkism" label as a non-pejorative and meaningfully descriptive term, which contributes precision and clarity to our discussion of the prospects for Austrian economics.

Austro-punkism, as I employ the term, then, identifies a movement within Austrian economics that recognizes no masters of the discipline and that, therefore, calls all received doctrine into question. It views Austrian economics as a discipline in a state of constant and radical flux, devoid of any fundamental and constant principles but rife with a myriad of endlessly debated questions. Indeed, leading proponents of Austro-punkism proudly trumpet that an Austrian economist is one for whom there should eternally exist more questions than answers. To venture a more meaningful definition of Austrian economics than this represents for Austro-punks an attempt to intolerantly close off the perpetual and open-ended conversation that they uphold as the hallmark of scientific inquiry.[6]

With no acknowledged masters, any self-proclaimed Austrian (whether equipped with formal training in economics or not) is judged fit to try his hand at radically reconstructing the discipline. In other words, Austrian economics can and should be revolutionized on a daily basis, by anyone and everyone. This means that the works of Mises, Hayek, and Rothbard are not treated as authoritative texts to be learned from and built upon in the painstaking labor of systematically adding to the inherited structure of economic theory. Instead these texts provide Austro-punkism with a common vocabulary in which to carry on their incessant and carping metaeconomic discussion about the dire need for radical reconstruction of economic theory. But the plans for reconstruction

---

[6]See Murray N. Rothbard, "The Hermeneutical Invasion of Philosophy and Economics," *Review of Austrian Economics* 3, no. 1 (1989): 45–59; Hans-Herman Hoppe, "In Defense of Extreme Rationalism: Thoughts on Donald McCloskey's *The Rhetoric of Economics*," *Review of Austrian Economics* 3 no. 1 (1989): 179–214; idem, "Comment on Don Lavoie," Mont Pèlerin Society, General Meeting (1994), available at www.HansHoppe.com.

that issue forth from such metaeconomic griping never amount to more than casual and wildly implausible glosses on the texts of the masters. This explains the centrality of hermeneutics to Austro-punkism; it provides a justification for treating the meaning of the texts as infinitely elastic and capable of bearing almost any interpretation, however outlandish. Without recourse to the exercise of deconstructing the texts of the masters, the metaeconomic discourse of Austro-punkism would come to a screeching halt, because it has offered no practical alternative to praxeology as a method for systematically elaborating economic theory.

The treatment meted out by the Austro-punks to Mises and Rothbard sharply contrasts with the pious treatment accorded by these creative geniuses to their own masters. Mises confesses that he felt himself competent to criticize the value and price theory that he learned from Menger and Böhm-Bawerk only after he himself had reached a mature understanding of the issues.[7] This occurred only at the age of 52, after he already had published his major treatises on money and socialism and had achieved eminence as one of the leading economists on the Continent. And, despite their substantive and long-standing differences in political economy, the first time Murray Rothbard ever ventured to directly criticize Mises in public was in the classic paper he presented at South Royalton in 1974 on "Praxeology, Value Judgments and Public policy."[8] Murray was then already 48 years old and yet,

---

[7]Ludwig von Mises, *Notes and Recollections* (South Holland, Ill.: Libertarian Press, 1978), p 60. On the moral obligation entailed in pronouncing on a specialized subject, Rothbard stated: "It is no crime to be ignorant of economics, which is, after all, a specialized discipline and one that most people consider to be a 'dismal science.' But it is totally irresponsible to have a loud and vociferous opinion on economic subjects while remaining in this state of ignorance." Murray N. Rothbard, "Anarcho-Communism," in *Egalitarianism as a Revolt Against Nature and Other Essays*, 2nd ed. (Auburn, Ala.: Mises Institute, 2002 [1974]), p. 202; originally published as "Anarcho-Communism," The Libertarian Forum II, no. 1 (January 1, 1970).

[8]Murray N. Rothbard, "Praxeology, Value Judgments, and Public Policy," in Edwin G. Dolan, ed., *The Foundations of Modern Austrian Economics* (Kansas City: Sheed and Ward, 1976), pp. 89–111, also published in Murray N. Rothbard, *The Logic of Action One* (Cheltenham, U.K.: Edward Elgar, 1997), pp. 78–99.

after his talk had ended, I remember him confiding to a few of us that he was still a "little shaky" from the experience of publically disagreeing with his mentor for the first time. (This of course is precisely the attitude one should have when attempting to advance beyond the acknowledged master of a discipline, even in a minor area.)

Austro-punkism itself, indeed, raises more questions than there are answers for. Most significantly, why Austro-punkism? Why is the neo-Austrian school—of all schools of economics past and present—seemingly the only school ever to be afflicted with the scourge of punkism? Why not Ricardian-punkism or Chicago-punkism? The works of Milton Friedman, George Stigler, and Gary Becker, after all, are never casually derided or subjected to grossly distorted reinterpretations by those professing to be Chicago economists. This is not to deny, of course, that almost all schools spawn radical internal critics. But generally such dissidents, sooner or later, promote a schism among the like-minded in the discipline. One only has to think of Paul Davidson and the Post-Keynesians, Robert Mundell and the Supply-siders, Robert Lucas and the Rational Expectations school, Gregory Mankiw and the other New Keynesians to recognize the pervasiveness of this phenomenon in contemporary economics.

Yet, schismatics differ from punks in three important respects. First, the promoters of schism are generally individuals who have completely absorbed and may even have substantially contributed to the orthodoxy they are now seeking to escape. Second, they are eager to proclaim their apostasy to the world by relabeling themselves. And, third, at least some in the ranks of the schismatic movement are willing and able to embark upon the arduous task of substantively reconstructing the edifice of the orthodox economic theory they object to. Austro-punks, in contrast, tend to be innocent of a profound understanding of the orthodoxy they criticize. Moreover, their interest lies not mainly in theoretical or applied research in economics proper, but in promulgating meta-norms for economic theorizing and dawdling glosses on the texts of the masters. Most significantly, rather than seizing the first opportunity to break free of the oppressive orthodoxy they disdain, Austro-punks cling to their proclaimed position within Austrian economics like Leonidas and his Spartans at Thermopylae.

So, I ask again, why the peculiar phenomenon of Austro-punkism? I have pondered on this question for a few years and I think I have a few answers.

The causes of Austro-punkism are threefold. Briefly, they are the lack of formal graduate training in Austrian economics, the influence of 1970s-style left-libertarianism, and the work (not the person) of Ludwig Lachmann. I will say a few words about each of these causes in turn.

1. Lack of a Graduate School

Lack of formal graduate training in Austrian economics represents the objective or institutional deficiency that has bedeviled Austrian economics from the inception of its modern renascence. Despite several laudable programs in Austrian economics associated with universities in the U.S., there is still not available to the interested young scholar a conventional graduate program in which he or she may obtain comprehensive and rigorous training in Austrian economic theory. But rigorous theoretical training is essential not only to the development of the aspiring Austrian economist but also to the healthy flourishing of the overall discipline.

Graduate education is the means of fostering respect for the masters of the science by enforcing a disciplined interpretation of their texts. The chairman of my dissertation committee, an unreconstructed IS/LM Keynesian,[9] once told me that the first time he read Patinkin's *Money, Interest, and Prices*,[10] William Fellner led him through it by the nose; the second time, Fellner sent him through it on his ear; and by the third reading, humbled and scraped, he had begun to understand it. Needless to say, my advisor neither lacked respect for Patinkin, nor foisted upon me any bizarre reinterpretations of his work. A similar engagement with *Human Action* or *Man, Economy and State*[11] would work wonders for our metaeconomists.

---

[9]IS/LM stands for "Investment Saving/Liquidity preference Money supply."

[10]Don Patinkin, *Money, Interest, and Prices*, 2nd ed. (New York: Harper & Row, Publishers, 1965).

[11]Mises, *Human Action*; Murray N. Rothbard, *Man, Economy, and State: A Treatise on Economic Principles, with Power and Market: Government and the*

In fact, it is precisely the inadequacy of their grounding in technical Austrian economic theory that accounts for their absorption in metaeconomics. When pushed to analyze a real-world problem, Austro-punks generally resort to Chicago price theory, Public Choice theory, Game theory, or Transactions-costs economics depending upon the era and institution of their graduate training. Those who have not been relentlessly drilled in the technical aspects of price theory as taught by Böhm-Bawerk, Wicksteed, and Mises or compelled to master the intricacies of Austrian production and capital theory in their intellectually formative years will hardly be inclined to pursue meaningful research in theoretical or applied Austrian economics.

But graduate schools are essential to a flourishing discipline not only for how they teach but also for whom they exclude. There are no other means available for weeding out those who are unsuited by ability or temperament to pursue research in economics and who, therefore, are apt to develop into sterile and punkish malcontents. This all-important exclusionary function is generally performed by rigorous drilling in the fundamentals of the discipline. For example, beginning with what Paul Samuelson calls the "terror" employed by Viner in his theory course in the 1930s, the University of Chicago's Economics Department has not lacked for a mechanism for screening out unfit candidates for advanced degrees. Thus one rarely encounters individuals proclaiming to be "Chicago economists" who seek to overturn Chicago price theory or, for that matter, "MIT economists" who repeatedly express doubts about the efficacy of mathematical modeling. Would that we could say the same about so-called "Austrian economists" who regard Rothbard as merely a libertarian theorist and ridicule praxeology as a simplistic and intolerant methodology.

This singularly promiscuous use of the label "Austrian economist" cries out for the implementation of an institutionalized exclusionary process in Austrian economics. Of course, this is not a call for anointing a particular person or institution as final arbiter of who does and who does not qualify as an "Austrian economist."

Economy, Scholars edition (Auburn, Ala.: Mises Institute, 2004; *Man, Economy and State* originally published 1962).

This would be a ridiculous and less than ingenuous inference from my argument. Rather, the existence of a graduate program in Austrian economics would provide the critical objective test—a "market test," if you will—to facilitate the natural process of doctrinal *self-exclusion*, as is the case currently, for example, with Chicago economists. Those individuals who flunk out of the Chicago graduate economics program or whose interests or aptitudes divert them into a graduate philosophy program rarely, if ever, refer to themselves as "Chicago economists." Why should matters be any different with Austrian economists?

2. 1970s-Style Left-Libertarianism

Many of those interested in pursuing Austrian economics are naturally motivated by ideology. They are intensely interested in learning how to rationally defend a free society. This motivation, in and of itself, should present no difficulties for our science. But many of the ideologically-inclined individuals who found their way into Austrian economics since the beginning of its revival in the 1960s have been proponents of 1970s-style left-libertarianism. This variant of libertarianism fosters a punkish worldview, since its adherents tend to promote atomistic individualism, which neglects the distinction between State power and bureaucracy on the one hand and the necessarily hierarchical and authoritarian structures and institutions of culture, religion, scholarship and business on the other. They do not realize that society and all its institutions are pervasively and inescapably elitist and authoritarian.[12] They chafe against the operation of the iron law of oligarchy, which

---

[12]The word "authoritarian" is not used here in its usual sense as a description of a political system or an individual psychological trait; rather it is used, for lack of a better term, to refer to a social process in which authority in some area or subject is voluntarily and spontaneously invested in specific individuals, families, and organizations. On the nature and constitution of authority in this sense, see Robert Nisbet, *Twilight of Authority* (New York: Oxford University Press, 1975). For more on the topic of natural elites and related matters, see Hans-Hermann Hoppe, *Democracy – The God That Failed: The Economics and Politics of Monarchy, Democracy, and Natural Order* (New Brunswick, N.J.: Transaction Publishers, 2001), p. 71 *et pass.*

ensures that an elite will always tend to coalesce and predominate in any human endeavor.

Accordingly, as Mises has pointed out, "There never lived at the same time more than a score of men whose work contributed anything to economics."[13] Yet the Austro-punk is not humbled by this insight; from his perch in metaeconomics, he behaves as if literally anyone is competent to prescribe a method of proceeding for the wholesale reconstruction of Austrian economics. The Austro-punk is also not chastened by the fact that the great methodologists of our science were each one of the score of those then currently living who made genuine contributions to economic theory. Moreover, it was generally only later in their careers, after prolonged meditation on and practice of economic theory, that men such as Say, Senior, Cairnes, Menger, Hayek, and Mises took up methodological concerns.

3. Ludwig Lachmann

While left-libertarian ideology goes a long way toward explaining the predisposition that many Austro-punks harbor to dismiss the body of theory inherited from the past masters of the science as inconsistent with their prescribed meta-norms, it is the work of Ludwig Lachmann that supplies the content of these norms. Without embarking on a detailed evaluation of Lachmann's work, or of his position in Austrian economics, suffice it to say that Austro-punks have seized upon his well-known assertions that the "future is unknowable" and that "expectations, like human preferences, are autonomous."[14] These propositions are then wielded by Austro-punkism as a rhetorical bludgeon to bash any systematic elaboration of economic theory that employs, in however subsidiary a manner, the equilibrium construct. Thus, for example, the mighty edifice of praxeological economic theory laboriously constructed over the years by economists from Menger to Rothbard is

---

[13]Mises, *Human Action*, p. 873.

[14]On this topic see Hans-Hermann Hoppe, "On Certainty and Uncertainty, Or: How Rational Can Our Expectations Be?", *Review of Austrian Economics* 10, no. 1 (1997): 49–78; also idem, "In Defense of Extreme Rationalism" and "Comment on Don Lavoie."

summarily rejected as "too equilibrium" and "failing to meaning-fully incorporate expectations."

Of course, the Austro-punk project that seeks to formulate a system of economic theory completely dispensing with any refer-ence to the mental construct of equilibrium has not yet advanced beyond the meta-plane. Nor will it ever, because human action always and everywhere embodies an inherent tendency toward equilibrium. Furthermore, Austro-punkism will never succeed in its program of expanding economic theory to incorporate learning and expectations-formation processes. As Mises has demon-strated, the content of specific individuals' knowledge and expec-tations, which renders the economist's praxeological theorems rel-evant to real-world analysis, can only be derived from the histori-cal discipline of thymology.[15]

THE SOUTH ROYALTON SYNDROME

A second problem besetting the contemporary Austrian School of economics and threatening to stunt its future development is what might be called the "South Royalton Syndrome." It also is attributable to a failure to clearly define a uniquely Austrian para-digm. South Royalton, Vermont was the site in June 1974 of the first conference on Austrian economics held in North America. The main speakers at the conference were Murray Rothbard, Israel Kirzner, and Ludwig Lachmann, and its participants included a surprisingly large number of graduate students who have since gone on to academic careers, while continuing to pursue research in Austrian economics. Together with the wholly unexpected awarding of the Nobel Prize in economics to Hayek later in the same year, it was truly a defining moment in the Austrian revival whose galvanizing effect on the young acolytes is difficult to over-estimate.[16]

---

[15]Ludwig von Mises, *Theory and History: An Interpretation of Social and Eco-nomic Evolution* (New Rochelle, N.Y.: Arlington House, 1969 [1957]). See also Joseph T. Salerno, "Ludwig von Mises on Inflation and Expectations," *Advances in Austrian Economics*, vol. 2B (1995): 297–325.

[16] See Murray N. Rothbard, "The Present State of Austrian Economics," paper delivered at the Tenth Anniversary Scholars' Conference of the Ludwig

Given these circumstances, there is an understandable, although unfortunate, tendency among those who participated in the South Royalton conference to define Austrian economics as a closed network of South Royalton participants and their immediate students. The focus of the definition is thus not on a specific body of truth and the method of advancing it but on a specific group of people, whose work is viewed as the exclusive source of new contributions to the discipline. Those who are afflicted with the South Royalton syndrome, consequently, are inclined to ignore or dismiss the work of those outside the network and treat them as unwanted interlopers into Austrian economics. This is especially the case if the newcomer's approach is fresh and diverges from the familiar or, even worse, directly challenges the work of a revered insider.

A living science, however, requires the new blood of those who display the vision and drive to diverge from well-worn paths and to venture beyond the boundaries tentatively marked out by the current leaders of the discipline. These young visionaries should be enthusiastically welcomed into the Austrian fold and encouraged and supported in their exploration for new truth. This was always Murray Rothbard's view of how Austrian economics should progress. He was always urging others, especially the young, to "go beyond" his own work while adhering to the basic praxeological paradigm. He once wrote to me that "I welcome change and advances in Austrian theory provided they are true, i.e., that they work from within the basic Misesian paradigm. So just as I think that I have advanced beyond Mises in developing the Misesian paradigm, [other] people ... have advanced the paradigm still further, and great!"

---

von Mises Institute, October 9, 1992; published in *Journal des Economistes et des Etudes Humaines* 6, no. 1 (March 1995), pp. 43–89 and in *The Logic of Action One: Method, Money, and the Austrian School* (Cheltenham, U.K.: Edward Elgar Publishing, 1997); also Karen I. Vaughn, "The Rebirth of Austrian Economics: 1974–99," *Journal of the Institute of Economic Affairs* 20, Issue 1 (March 2000); Peter Lewin, "Biography of Ludwig Lachmann (1906–1990): Life and Work" <http://mises.org/about/3236> (accessed Jan. 12, 2009).

CONCLUSION

It is interesting to note that Austro-punkism and the South Royalton syndrome, although they appear to denote attitudes that are polar opposites, may actually be complementary. After all, given their self-conscious aversion to defining a common intellectual paradigm, the bonds linking the network of Austro-punks tend to be personal rather than purely scientific. And their much-ballyhooed devotion to tolerance as the *beau ideal* of the scientific method does not seem to be manifested in the treatment accorded those young scholars who are eagerly advancing the frontiers of the praxeological paradigm.

My purpose in making these remarks is not to accuse particular persons of error, and so I have studiously tried to avoid any references to particular persons. Rather my purpose is cautionary; we are all as fallible human beings in a shared intellectual movement confronted with similar temptations to err. I have been moved to speak out because the errors in this case are capable of destroying a recently reborn and still fragile science with a great and glorious tradition and much to offer the human race. ❧

15

Business Ethics: In the Crossfire Between a Code of Conduct and Black Sheep

Eugen-Maria Schulak

Lieber Hans,

Die vielen guten Gespräche, die ich bislang mit Dir führen konnte, haben mich, nebst der Lektüre Deiner Schriften, ganz außerordentlich bereichert und beflügelt, wofür ich Dir von Herzen danken will. In meiner Heimatstadt Wien, deren Blüte längst Geschichte ist, fand ich im Zuge meiner philosophischen Entwicklung wohl manchen guten Lehrer, doch letztlich niemanden, der imstande war, die Welt in Form einer grundlegenden Kritik philosophisch gegen den Strich zu bürsten. Nichts hob sich wohltuend vom Üblichen und Erlaubten ab,

Eugen-Maria Schulak (schulak@philosophische-praxis.at) is an entrepreneur serving as philosophical counselor in Vienna, Austria (www.philosophische-praxis.at). A university lecturer and author of six books, he is the director of the Department of Philosophy at the Siemens Academy of Life.

This paper is an English version (translation by Ciaràn Cassidy) of a lecture delivered on the occasion of the inaugural meeting of the Society for Austrian Economic Thought, July 7, 2008, Hotel Imperial, Vienna.

*nichts wies in eine neue Richtung. Die Klarheit und zwin-
gende Logik Deiner Gedanken haben mich, das kann ich heute
sagen, aus einer Art dogmatischem Schlummer geweckt. Es
wurde mir eine neue und wertvolle Gedankenwelt eröffnet,
deren Wurzeln – und das ist die Pointe – hier in Wien zu
suchen sind. Du hast mir in gewissem Sinne meine Heimatstadt, in der ich mich philosophisch verloren glaubte,
wiederum zurückgegeben. Auch in emotionaler Hinsicht ist
dies für mich von unschätzbarem Wert.*

*Alles Gute und noch viel Kraft für weiteres fruchtbares Schaf-
fen*

– Eugen[1]

Business ethics is a topic which is currently very much in fashion and which confronts us at every turn. This leads us to ask, why should be so this; what might be the reason for this; and who, or what, could lie behind this development? But before we can hope to answer these questions, we must

---

[1]Translation (by Guido Hülsmann):

Dear Hans:

*It is with all my heart that I thank you for the many good discus-
sions we have had so far, as well as for your writings. They have
greatly enriched and inspired me. In my hometown of Vienna,
which flourished long ago, I encountered in the course of my
philosophical development many a good teacher, but ultimately
none of them were able to shed new philosophical light on the
world with a fundamental critique. There was no genius apart
from conventional and licit wisdom, no new directions in
thought. Today I can say that the clarity and stringent logic of
your thoughts have awakened me from dogmatic slumber. They
have introduced me to a new and precious intellectual universe,
the roots of which – and that's the irony of the story – are to be
found here in Vienna. In a certain sense, you have given back to
me my hometown, in which I had felt lost as a philosopher. From
an emotional point of view, too, this was a priceless feat.*

Best wishes for many more productive years

– Eugen

be quite clear as to what we mean by the expression "business ethics" and what we hope to obtain from its use. We must go deeper and ask, who was it that brought up the expression and introduced it into the discussion; who has the most to benefit from its application; and who is it directed against, or has most to lose?

One of the most important insights of Ludwig Wittgenstein was that the meaning of a word depends on the context in which it was used. The meaning of a word can only be evaluated and understood when we know the purpose for which the word is used. It is especially important to understand the meaning of words that are fashionable. Such words are used primarily because other people also use them. Fashionable words are governed by a certain dynamic that is more emotional than rational; they depend on their emotional impact much more than on a careful consideration of what one actually wishes to say.

Allow me a brief *excursio* into the realm of applied psychology. When some people speak of business ethics, their expression assumes a solemn, almost priestly characteristic. Some are so overcome with moralistic wrath that they come across as Commissioners of the *Politburo*. Others, again, radiate hypocrisy; one gets the impression that they feel *obliged* to discuss business ethics – and they invariably end up grinning self-consciously. With others, it is quite obvious that they have no idea what they are talking about. These are the people who always slavishly follow whatever ideas are "in" and will regurgitate whatever is deemed politically correct. And, yet again, there are those who know very well why they use this term, but who cleverly mask their true intentions. Finally, there are those who make no attempt to conceal their intentions and use this opportunity to speak once more about "capitalist pigs" and so-called "social necessity."

For more than a decade, the topic of business ethics has been a matter of intensive discussion. This trend is still growing. The reasons for this discussion are in no sense new. We can trace similar episodes back to the 19th century when the German economist, Gustav Schmoller, who founded the Verein für Socialpolitik, compared the role of his profession to that of the chorus in a classical Greek tragedy. The role of the professional economist, like that of the chorus, was to evaluate and comment on political and economic events that took place on the world stage; it was not, however, to actively participate on this stage. The economist, just like the choir, performed the role of an expert authority. In the modern era, the ethics of the economist has thus come to be based on concepts such as "the people," "social justice," "development," "progress," "equality" or "social compensation," which were consequently adopted into the programs of national governments.

Such conceptual developments were precursors of state socialism as well as of National Socialism. That such concepts could be developed with relative ease, in dictatorships of the right as well as of the left, and continue to be so developed to this day, provides ample food for thought. Both Socialism and National Socialism had this much in common: they utilized every conceivable force to manipulate and regulate every business movement. Dictatorship and business regulation always go hand in hand.

Modern dictatorships invariably describe themselves as "peoples' democracies," or they have evolved from democracies that have gradually begun to manipulate the population by means of new moral precepts. In addition, they have begun to control economies. In this way, they manage to implement and finance their political goals without fear of hindrance.

In the final analysis, political freedom and economic freedom amount to one and the same thing. Politics is financed exclusively by means of compulsory payments; in other words, from taxation. The more ambitious are political intentions, and the more far-reaching the required policy measures, the larger the administration that is needed and the more everything costs.

The revenue that is needed can only be obtained from those who create wealth, i.e., from those who produce goods and services, or who are involved in the exchange of goods and services. These people either produce goods and services that others are prepared to pay for, or they trade in merchandise which others are prepared to purchase voluntarily. Such people, and these alone, create wealth. Politics cannot create wealth. For this reason, politics is continually seeking to acquire as much wealth as possible from others through the medium of their monopoly of force.

The fact is that it is hardly possible to levy any more taxes in Austria today than are currently being collected. Any increase in the real tax burden would cause companies to leave the country in droves and induce private persons to flee to the black market. In other words, we have reached the ceiling of what is possible, or acceptable. In contrast to this, our state bureaucracy requires ever more revenue. More and more people are living off the state. Our public health system is bankrupt. The public pension funds are bankrupt. The public debt is rising continuously. We still shy away from public expropriations. But more and more privately-held wealth will have to be expropriated if we are to continue to finance our so-called socialist state.

They who would gladly dispossess us are busy spreading the opinion that we live in an era of neo-liberalism. Apart from the fact that very few have any idea what this is supposed to mean, it is quite inappropriate to consider the present age worthy of the designation "liberal." For one, the government's share of GDP is currently about 40 percent. At the zenith of Austrian liberalism, the taxation of income had just been introduced, with a top marginal tax rate of 5 percent.

They who would dispossess us continuously, step by step, never tire of pointing out that we are, apparently, a rich country. This can only be regarded as a fallacy, considering that anyone, making a net monthly income of €2,000 or more belongs to the top 10 percent of income-earners in Austria. In truth, we live in a paternalistic, socialist regime which has succeeded in steering our views and our behavior, and which has thus managed to produce an extraordinary uniformity of thought and consensual behavior. Slowly but inexorably, we are heading towards a new form of communism. At the moment, we cannot say exactly where this is leading to.

Let us now turn to the numerous debates on business ethics that are conducted in Austria. With regard to those varied discussion groups, it is possible to make an extraordinary observation: Among those who are active in business, we observe a deeply-rooted conviction that the economy can only prosper in the long run if it is driven by ethical considerations. Those who belong to professions far removed from daily business, tend to regard the expressions "business success" and "ethical attitudes" as mutually exclusive.

If we analyze these two groups more closely, we see that both participate in the economy—if only as consumers. However, it is noticeable that these groups are completely different as regards how they earn their livelihoods; while one group is active in economic enterprises, the other is dependent on income from the public sector.

Looking at these two groups in terms of their relationship to the state, we can designate them, in the interest of simplicity, as "net recipients" or "net payers." In public finance, we describe "net recipients" as "transfer payments recipients," which makes it quite clear that each recipient is being subsidized by someone who is paying. Transfer-payment recipients would include all those who work in the public sector, such as civil servants, teachers, the police, politicians, professors, scientists, employees of various trade guilds, and government employees of both the federal and regional governments, including associated tradesmen and manual workers. Quite clearly, pensioners and retirees belong to this group also. What is significant about "recipients" is that their tax liabilities, as well as their net incomes, are a burden on public budgets, which means that they must be met by the "net payer."

Transfer payments are payments of state institutions to private persons. They have to be financed either from a redistribution of national income, or through public borrowing. Transfer payment recipients are private persons who receive more from the state than they contribute to the finances of the state and who depend on the state, either wholly or in part, for their livelihood.

Let us pursue further the question of how the number of transfer payment recipients in Austria compares to that of contributors.[2]

---

[2]Statistics by Herbert Unterköfler.

Register of electors for the parliamentary elections, 2002   5,912,592

Net transfer-payment recipients (2004)

Pensioners	1,842,538
Public administration and social insurance employees	450,300
Employment in education[3]	143,532
Employment in health, veterinary medicine, and social services[4]	171,667
Unemployed/recipients of unemployment assistance[5]	306,236
Leave of absence (with pay)	110,489
Total (2004)	3,024,770

In 2004, there were about three million net recipients of transfer payments in Austria. Persons for whom transfer payments constituted only a part of their income are not included. Thus, for example, we find groups such as recipients of children's allowances, agricultural subsidies, or supplementary (state) pensions are not included in the statistics. In consequence, we can easily imagine that the number of net recipients constitutes a clear majority of the electorate. It is not too difficult to imagine what implications this might have for democracy.

Pensioners make up about two thirds of transfer-payment recipients. For all of their working lives, they were obliged to make regular contributions to state pension funds. The normal practice of such pension funds was, and still is, to squander this money, rather than invest it carefully. These people were, to put it bluntly,

---

[3]A minute proportion of those engaged in education are remunerated by means of fees or contributions, or are privately employed (e.g., in private schools).

[4]The financing of the health system, services of veterinary medicine, and social services occurs mainly by means of transfer payments. The available statistics cover only part of those employed in this sector.

[5]The data on unemployed and on unemployment assistance includes 42,645 "unemployed" undergoing retraining, 27,033 recipients of advance payments on pensions, and 2,166 recipients of "temporary payments."

dispossessed. Their wealth was confiscated, bit by bit, over the years. Today they are dependents — dependents of the state and at the mercy of political developments — and are confronted by an uncertain fate.

This system, which we call an "inter-generational contract" in Austria, is nothing more than a pyramid scheme. Can you imagine an insurance agent coming into your house and presenting you with the following proposition: "I have a fantastic offer to make to you. Every month, you will pay me €1,000. This money I will transfer to Mr. X as he is now old and needs the money. And, when you are old, I will find a Ms. Y to whom I will sell a contract similar to that which I now offer you. The money I will receive from Ms. Y, I will then pay to you when you are old."

I think we can agree that whoever signs such a contract is a complete idiot. Thus, the Austrian state does not offer us such contracts for our voluntary signatures, but compels them with the threat of force. Basically, we are dealing with nothing less than a pyramid scheme of the sort that, incidentally, the state itself has banned. Pyramid schemes are illegal; compulsory state insurance, not so.

᪥   ᪥   ᪥

Let us return to the many discussions and debates that now take place on the subject of business ethics, and focus on certain observations one can make when one analyzes what is happening in these debates.

First of all, it is readily apparent that the vast majority of those persons we might generally describe as the business ethics "moralists" belong to the category of net recipients of social transfers. It is typical of this group that they do not see themselves as part of the economy. Nevertheless, they claim the right to make the relevant rules. The overriding tenor of this discussion is that one cannot simply accept that trade alone can organize the world, or dictate how the world is run. *Their views* must also be taken on board. In the absence of detailed guidelines and regulations, which they formulate and which may need to be enforced by law if necessary, the economic system would spiral out of control.

Capitalism alone, driven, as it supposedly is, by naked greed and its narrow focus on self interest, lacks the perspective to know what it is doing. Self-regulation is a complete non-starter. For this reason, it is necessary to guide the thought processes of the economically productive, and the best way to achieve this is through "voluntary restrictions," preferably backed by state regulation. Thus, the spirit of the times, as well as the public interest, demands that they who pursue the profit motive possess an official stamp of legitimization as, by definition, they are not guided by business ethics.

Basically, it is quite obvious what this group of "moralists" wishes to achieve. Their objective is to perform an usher's role in society, allocating positions and rights on the basis of official certificates and seals of approval.

The "moralists'" contribution to the debate often displays significant shortcomings, both in terms of their personalities as well as their professional credibility, and reminds one a little of the forceful pronouncements on sexuality from a clergy living a life of celibacy. In principle, one is seeking to make authoritative statements about something one has rejected, which, indeed, they may despise. Their opponents may justifiably ask what right they have to make such proposals, on what moral authority is their claim based, and what professional or specialist qualification can they produce to add credibility to their views? Perhaps their claim is based on the view that, in order to observe and comment on something objectively, one must, in some sense, be an "outsider." However, it is obvious that their claims are little more than a striving for monopolistic power.

Taking a charitable view of the matter, claiming a right of co-determination in a context where one has no experience and, in particular, no responsibility can only be regarded as being rather forward, and more than a little embarrassing. In truth, we are confronted with a rather blatant case of chutzpah, because those who are most likely to argue in favor of economic regulation are precisely the same people who obtain their income from the tax payments of the persons they regulate. Pretty much all scientific civil servants and intellectuals, all politicians and officials live off donations from the state. Those "business ethics moralists" are not at all overjoyed to be reminded that their remuneration is obtained from tax revenues, which are extracted from taxpayers by means of the coercive monopolistic power of the state.

The "ethics moralists" are often to be found in vehement opposition to any suggestion that the state should disengage, either wholly or in part, from various economic activities and sectors. And it doesn't really help to point to the proven inefficiencies in the administration and the large-scale destruction of resources during the 1970s and 80s in the so-called "welfare states." The "moralists" will defend the inflated size of the government with all their might—much as a hunter would watch its prey.

It will be very interesting when the "moralists" are asked about their own ethical standards. Then, it is very noticeable that they who drive the business ethics debate forward almost never consider discussing the ethics of civil servants, or of the public sector of the economy. This is all the more surprising when one considers that the state, through taxation, accounts for almost half of the total economic activity of the country. How, then, can the "moralists" so resolutely ignore that the high rates of VAT drive by no means insignificant groups of the population under the poverty limit? And why is it never questioned that almost all major scandals of recent decades have occurred in the state sector, or sectors closely associated with the state?

Basically, it is perfectly obvious that the "moralists" are guided primarily by their own self-interest, just like everyone else, and as net-recipients of social transfer payments are simply concerned with safeguarding their incomes. That this must be couched in terms of ethics is simply an indication that their productive performance on the open market would probably attract no more than a fraction of what they currently earn. Their instinctive reaction is to cloak in moralistic terms what is, in reality, begging for their salaries.

It is obvious that this questionable motivation is strong enough to ensure that the "moralists" dominate just about every debate concerned with business ethics. However, the result contains many contradictions. Thus, one rejects economic growth as being destructive and unethical, but insists upon automatic wage increases as a matter of course, however they may have to be financed. One demands security of supply in the fields of energy and food supply, but of course rejects the concomitant construction projects as being detrimental. And, one fulminates against globalization while looking forward with pleasure to the next long-distance journey. Perhaps it is just not possible to build a better world without being active in the construction project.

Let us be in no doubt about one thing—a business ethic is an integrative force. The basic ethical principles, or virtues of corporate behavior, are perseverance (i.e., a willingness to make greater effort), trust in yourself and in others, ambition, curiosity, responsibility for capital and employees, uprightness in financial matters, frugality, loyalty, being a man of your word, honoring contracts, the prudence of a correct businessman, punctuality, a strong presence and honorable behavior, clarity of speech, a strong sense of vision, and entrepreneurship.

The fact is that businessmen and businesswomen must possess many of these qualities if they are to persevere and succeed in the marketplace. They can be regarded as ethical, *per se*. They make profit or, in other words, they create value. They supply people with goods that they need or want. They alone create genuine jobs. And they, along with their employees, are the only ones who pay taxes.

There is one clear conclusion we can draw from all of this. It is not business, and business people, who must prove that they adhere to adequate ethical standards. Rather, this burden of proof rests with the net recipients of transfer payments, as it is they who live off the compulsory deductions that are paid by businesses and their employees. The net recipients of these payments, from whom we naturally deduct pensioners, are the ones who are obliged to justify their incomes and the money they receive.

Commercial enterprises, and their employees, have already proven their case in that they have produced goods and services for sale which customers have been willing to buy. That means that they have been beneficial, or provided benefit, for other people. The same cannot be said for transfer recipients, or at least their case is not quite so clear. For this reason they ought to be obliged to try much harder to justify their entitlement to what they acquire from the economy. Nor should they be allowed to use the business ethics of others as a smoke screen to distract attention from the need to justify their own rent-seeking activities.

It is disgraceful how the business-ethic moralists of today succeed in keeping the business community on the run. All those who would like to regulate business are themselves "on the make" and extracting economic rent from their activities. The means of imposing such regulation is political power, through the medium of public law. In the case of non-governmental organizations (NGOs), justification is based on a certain morality, which is frequently rather dubious. In this way, business enterprises are paraded in public and pilloried in a manner formerly employed for political enemies in Stalinist show-trials.

Many enterprises play along in this ethical charade. The motives for this are varied; some cooperate from a habitual sense of obedience; others do so out of fear; others from downright stupidity. Rarely does this arise from a sense of conviction. There are about 250,000 SMEs (small and medium enterprises) in Austria. It is high time that these enterprises begin to reflect on what they really are, and what they actually do. Without this first step of reflection, they will never succeed in creating a spirit of solidarity to cast off their yoke.

Ultimately it will depend on us, friends of the Vienna School, to perform the task of opening eyes and raising awareness. This pedagogic task lies before us. ❧

16

Against Standard Law & Economics: Austrians and Legal Philosophers on Board

Martin Froněk and Josef Šíma

Hans-Hermann Hoppe made a lasting impact on the first generations studying (not only) economics in the Czech Republic and Slovakia after the fall of the Iron Curtain. We have repeatedly invited him to be a lecturer for our free-market summer program, the "Liberalni Institute Summer University." He also gave talks for journalists, academicians, and university students in Prague and recently has been awarded the "Franz Cuhel Memorial Prize for Teaching Excellence" and delivered a lecture at the opening day of the 2009 Prague Conference on Political Economy. He has been making an impact on Czech and Slovak students through his writings and lectures, both in English and Czech, for more than a decade. Consequently, he made a defense of property—a central point of his academic focus—a keystone of

Martin Froněk (fronek@libinst.cz) is a resident researcher at the Liberalni Institute, Prague, focusing on legal doctrines. He translated Bruno Leoni's *Freedom and the Law* into Czech. Josef Šíma (sima@vse.cz) is a professor and chairman of the Department of Institutional Economics, University of Economics, Prague. The authors would like to thank David Lipka for valuable comments and suggestions.

scholarly investigation for many young researchers, including the current authors.

ം   ം   ം

The Law & Economics movement emerging from the University of Chicago in the 1960s revolutionized the American legal academy. "Economic analysis of law" became a standard part of the top universities' curricula. Brian Bix, a leading legal theorist, considers this particular approach to law the most influential line of thought in contemporary jurisprudence.[1] Notwithstanding the prominence it has gained so far, the initial reaction of many influential legal thinkers to some assumptions and insights of L&E was suspicious rather than laudatory. Likewise, on the part of the economics profession, it was Austrian economics and its proponents who raised eyebrows when they first explored the writings of what is here referred to as "a standard Law & Economics," i.e., mainly the thought of judge Richard Posner.[2]

While we appreciate the importance of alternative paradigm building and the Austrian method of deriving conclusions from first principles, this time our aim is different and rather modest. We seek to point out the similarities between the criticisms of standard L&E, particularly the principle of "wealth maximization," presented by various legal philosophers (such as Jules Coleman, Ronald Dworkin, Anthony Kronman, Benjamin Zipursky and others) on one hand, and by Austrians on the other, and hence "build bridges." We will indicate that both lines of critique are, in many respects, compatible, though they rarely even recognize each other's existence.[3]

---

[1]Brian Bix, *Jurisprudence: Theory and Context*, 4th ed. (London: Sweet & Maxwell, 2006), p. 189.

[2]We have argued elsewhere that Austrian praxeology provides a much better framework for the study of the mutual relationship between economics and law than the Posnerian "economic" approach. See Josef Šíma, "Praxeology as Law & Economics," *Journal of Libertarian Studies* 18, no. 2 (2004): 73–89.

[3]But to the contrary, see Edward Stringham and Mark White, "Economic Analysis of Tort Law: Austrian and Kantian Perspectives," in *Law and Economics: Alternative Economic Approaches to Legal and Regulatory Issues*, Margaret

Wealth Maximization Principle — Positive Analysis

Building on Coase's insight that any conflict is of reciprocal character,[4] the general idea of Posner's *Economic Analysis of Law* is that any human activity has an impact on many people "if only by changing the prices of other goods."[5] However, Coasian bargaining that would maximize the joint production of all parties is likely to be prevented in the real world of transaction costs (not to mention the existence of the income effect, which may spoil the "invariability of the outcome" conclusion).[6] Thus, there will be conflicts among people due to losses inflicted on some that must be solved in non-market ways to assure an efficient outcome. Posner claims that this role of efficient problem solvers must be performed by judges and the legal system. Judges must assign property rights (liability) similar to how the market would have done so if transaction cost had not existed.[7]

Posner considers economics to be a source of insight regarding cost-benefit properties of alternative legal structures, which then can be used to *mimic the market* — i.e., redesign the legal system (and decide legal cases) that would lead to higher production in a broad sense. In short, Posner's principal idea is that judges should manipulate the limits of property rights in order to get an optimal — efficient — level of economic output.

Oppenheimer and Nicholas Mercuro, eds. (New York: M.E. Sharpe, 2004), pp. 374–92.

[4]Ronald H. Coase, "The Problem of Social Cost," *Journal of Law and Economics* 3 (October 1960).

[5]Richard A. Posner, *Economic Analysis of Law*, 5th ed. (New York: Aspen Law & Business, 1998 [1973]), p. 14.

[6]Walter Block, "Coase and Demsetz on Private Property Rights," *Journal of Libertarian Studies* 1, no. 2 (1977); idem, "Ethics, Efficiency, Coasian Property Rights, and Psychic Income: A Reply to Harold Demsetz," *Review of Austrian Economics* 8, no. 2 (1995).

[7]This interventionism is in the Coasean-Posnerian world "obviously desirable" even " when it is possible to change the legal delimitation of rights through market transactions." See the founding article of the Chicago approach, Coase, "The Problem of Social Cost," p. 19.

> The issue is rarely property right or no property right, but rather . . . limited property rights or unlimited property rights, with the limitation designed to induce the correct (not an insufficient or excessive) level of investment in the exploitation of a valuable resource.[8]

The criterion that should help judges in their endeavors is the "wealth maximization principle," which states that goods (resources, rights) should be assigned to those who value them most, i.e., to those who are willing and able to pay for them. Posner acknowledged that "wealth maximization," in fact, is the same as the well-known Kaldor-Hicks Efficiency.[9] A rule, decision or action in general is efficient, according to this view, if and only if those who benefit from it could *potentially* fully compensate those who loose and still have a net gain. Whether the actual payment to those made worse-off eventually takes place is, in this regard, irrelevant. We shall return to this aspect later.

The Role of Prices

To say anything meaningful about two states of the world when using the Kaldor-Hicks criterion, there have to be monetary prices to enable us to compare the actual gains and losses on both sides. Without prices, we could merely observe whether any transactions take place at all. If they do, from that very fact we could, in Rothbardian fashion, infer that the transaction makes both parties better off, at least *ex ante*.[10] Nothing more, nothing less. We would not be in a position to know whether the transaction is wealth-maximizing (or Kaldor-Hicks efficient) since the very concept presupposes the existence of prices. As Jules Coleman, a Yale law philosopher, put it, "only exchanges that involve prices can be wealth maximizing."[11] Thus, in a barter economy, a Posnerian

---

[8]Posner, *Economic Analysis of Law*, p. 42.

[9]Richard A. Posner, "The Ethical and Political Basis of the Efficiency Norm in Common Law Adjudication," *Hofstra Law Review* 8, no. 3 (Spring 1980): 491.

[10]Murray N. Rothbard, "Toward a Reconstruction of Utility and Welfare Economics," in Mary Sennholz, ed., *On Freedom and Free Enterprise: Essays in Honor of Ludwig von Mises* (New Haven, Conn.: D. Van Nostrand 1956).

[11]Jules Coleman, "Efficiency, Utility, and Wealth Maximization," *Hofstra Law Review* 8, no. 3 (Spring 1980): 523.

judge would have to either "refuse to decide"[12] or resort to some other principle that would guide his decision.

Not only barter economies pose problems for a Posnerian judge. This is where Austrians have a lot to say. Even if we assume that there are relative monetary prices generated in the market, the judge's inference from what he can observe at the moment is of little value. Building on Mises's insight about the nature of market prices as the mere data of economic history, Stringham denies the usefulness of such observation for any meaningful *pro futuro* decision. The willingness to pay and the prices change constantly, "so it would make no sense to base decisions on prices that no longer have relevance."[13] A similar point was made by Coleman as well. When he wrote about the need of prices for the application of the Kaldor-Hicks test, he stressed the importance of fixed relative prices.[14] There are no *fixed* relative prices out there, however. One of the important insights of Austrian economists is that individual actions of people on the real market generate prices in a never-ending process, or as Mario Rizzo put it, a "continual flux."[15] As such, they never be assumed to be fixed.

The unrealistic assumption of the "price fixedness" is essential for wealth maximization to hold its own. It is thus incoherent. The change of legal rules in the real world in the passage of time may have an impact on the structure of relative prices. The change of relative prices, however, affects the judge's previous calculation. At the time of the decision, the judge might conclude that to maximize wealth it is necessary to assign a right to A. Consequently, a new price structure emerges. If the judge was forced to decide the case again under the new circumstances he would assign the right to B. The need for a shift between legal rules becomes constant and

---

[12]Which, in standard account, "is not morally acceptable, since people expect access to justice." See Aleksander Peczenik, *On Law and Reason*, 2nd ed (Dordrecht: Springer 2008), pp. 26–27.

[13]Edward Stringham, "Kaldor-Hicks Efficiency and the Problem of Central Planning," *Quarterly Journal of Austrian Economics* 4, no. 2 (Summer 2001): 43.

[14]Coleman, "Efficiency, Utility, and Wealth Maximization," p. 524.

[15]Mario J. Rizzo, "Law amid Flux: The Economics of Negligence and Strict Liability in Tort," *Journal of Legal Studies* 9, no. 2 (March 1980).

immense uncertainty floods the system.[16] In other words, if we take into consideration what Austrians have always stressed in opposition to neoclassical economics — the dynamic nature of the market process in which no stable equilibrium can be achieved[17] — we can claim, concurring with legal philosophers, the wealth maximization principle to be unworkable.

Playing the Market

The above described criticisms of wealth maximization by both Austrians and some legal thinkers are relevant, but things are even worse. We have so far dealt with the problem of applying the wealth maximization principle as if the Posnerian judge were to operate in a real world context.[18] However, if the celebrated principle is in fact the same as the Kaldor-Hicks criterion, we enter the domain of pure fantasy — the judge is expected to weigh and compare the willingness to pay in the *absence* of the transaction itself and to consider the *potential* compensations of the victims. As has been repeatedly shown by Austrians, such a task is plainly impossible.[19] Posner

---

[16]Coleman calls this inconvenience a "circularity-of-preferences problem." Coleman, "Efficiency, Utility, and Wealth Maximization," p. 525.

[17]Gregory Scott Crespi, "Exploring the Complicationist Gambit: An Austrian Approach to the Economic Analysis of Law," *Notre Dame Law Review* 73, no. 2 (January 1998): 325–26.

[18]Except for the fixed prices assumption.

[19]In more difficult cases the complications multiply. As Rizzo explains:

> The efficiency approach requires not only the testing of hypotheses about the defendant's negligence, but also investigation into the (contributory) negligence of the plaintiff. If, however, the doctrine of contributory negligence is to be interpreted as a lesser-cost avoider defense, our task is still not complete. If we find that both defendant and plaintiff have been negligent, we must still determine which party could have avoided the accident at less cost. Therefore, we are driven to compare two counterfactual hypotheses. . . . The issue is not to compare or evaluate what has happened but, rather to speculate about what might have happened in two alternate worlds and then to compare the outcomes.

Rizzo, "Law amid Flux," p. 292; citations omitted.

himself admits in the first edition of his textbook (p. 139) that to determine who has the greater long-run accident-avoidance potential is "an intractable question, in most cases."[20]

Ronald Dworkin, the most cited legal philosopher of our times, eloquently summarizes the position of Posner and others:

> They concede . . . or rather insist, that information about what parties would have done in market transaction can be obtained in the absence of the transaction, and that such information can be sufficiently reliable to act on.[21]

Dworkin, for the sake of his particular argument against wealth maximization, accepts this. Needless to say, such concession is not very fortunate in general. Despite Posner's mere claims to the contrary,[22] no one has ever shown how a third party, be it a judge or a central planner playing the market, can get into the minds of potential parties to the transaction, find out their preferences and then do what they themselves would have done had the circumstances been different.

The similarity and impossibility of tasks that stand before both Posnerian judges and socialist planners is striking. In both cases, someone aspires to engage in non-price (non-market) allocation of resources. It is believed in both situations that more peace and more prosperity can be attained by such a device; that someone saves some resources by knowing in advance what the result of complex social phenomena will be; that one can *conceive* of markets without people really *having* and *making* markets. This belief is completely fallacious. Under socialism, as most of the economy got closer to the "socialist ideal" of non-market allocation, the less socialist planners knew about the real needs of the economy (the people) and the more pervasive was the ensuing chaos. The same will be true for the emergence of chaos and the spread of pure arbitrariness in law,

---

[20]Here he has been quoted by Rizzo. He also reminds us that Posner omits this phrase in subsequent editions of his book. Ibid., p. 308.

[21]Ronald Dworkin, "Is Wealth a Value?," *Journal of Legal Studies* 9, no. 2 (March 1980): 198.

[22]Richard A. Posner, *The Economics of Justice* (Cambridge, Mass.: Harvard University Press, 1981), p. 62.

the closer we get to the Posnerian "ideal." To claim otherwise would amount to requiring the judge to transform himself into a "cognitive superman."[23]

IMPLICATIONS OF L&E FOR INDIVIDUAL (PROPERTY) RIGHTS

Deficiencies in the positive arm of the L&E approach leads us to look into effects the Posnerian judge would bring about in reality if he was strictly adhering to wealth maximization.

The Continency of Right and Wrong

In his *Economics of Justice*, Posner illustrated how a judicial system would proceed to maximize social wealth in cases where external effects play a role.[24] Hoppe offers a summary:

> A factory emits smoke and thereby lowers residential property values. If property values are lowered by $3 million and the plant relocation cost is $2 million, the plant should be held liable and forced to relocate. Yet if the numbers are reversed—property values fall by $2 million and relocation costs are $3 million—the factory may stay and continue to emit smoke.[25]

The task of a judge is to reshape the existing structure of property rights. In fact, these rights do not count at all. The *value* of the rights is at stake. As the value cannot (as prices cannot), be assumed as fixed, there is no stable criterion by which we could determine *ex ante* who is going to prevail in each case. Whether property rights are allocated in a wealth maximizing manner "can

---

[23]Dieter Schmidtchen, "Time, Uncertainty, and Subjectivism: Giving More Body to Law and Economics," *International Review of Law and Economics* 13, no. 1 (March 1993): 78, quoting Bruce Ackerman, "Law, Economics, and the Problem of Legal Culture," *Duke Law Journal* 1986, no. 6 (December 1986).

[24]Posner, *The Economics of Justice*, p. 62.

[25]Hans-Hermann Hoppe, "The Ethics and Economics of Private Property," LewRockwell.com (Oct. 11, 2004). It must be admitted that Posner uses this example to show a possible divergence of wealth maximization from "happiness maximization"; nevertheless, it illustrates the alleged role of judges and how it would look like.

only be determined *ex post*."[26] Moreover, seconds after the dispute is settled, the value of property rights changes—at that moment the judge's calculation might be completely different if he were to decide the case again. This is something we would not expect of what we call law. The results of adjudication should, at least to some extent, be predictable. The wealth maximization negates this postulate.

Austrians like Hoppe are not alone in this particular criticism of L&E. Benjamin Zipursky, a representative of so called "pragmatic conceptualism," challenges the theory of economic analysis of tort law. According to him, tort law is, in essence, "backward-looking."[27] If we turn to the factory example, the right way of looking at the situation is to investigate the past, determine the structure of rights that was in place *before* the pollution, describe the actions of both plaintiff and defendant and, on this basis, decide who is to be held liable. On the other hand, the economic (Posnerian) approach is "forward looking;" the initial distribution of rights is of no importance—"where liability should lie ultimately depends on an answer to a question about the future, not about the past."[28] This, unfortunately, leads us to the conclusion that, for L&E what is right and what is wrong are merely contingent. A just legal system can hardly be based on the contingent notions of right and wrong.

The Irrelevance of (Some) Autonomous Individuals

The reliance on the wealth maximization principle has some unwelcome implications. If the redistribution of rights is based on willingness and ability to pay, what about those who are at the bottom of the society, who are willing but not able to pay? They simply do not count. As Anthony T. Kronman, a former dean of the Yale Law School, put it:

> The principle of wealth maximization necessarily favors those who already have money, or the resources with which to earn it, and are therefore able to pay more than

---

[26]Ibid.

[27]Benjamin Zipursky, "Pragmatic Conceptualism," *Legal Theory* 6, no. 4 (December 2000): 462.

[28]Ibid., pp. 462-23.

others to have a new legal rule defined in the way that is favorable to them.[29]

The nature of the proposed theory was acknowledged by its founder too when he stated:

> A less welcome implication of the wealth-maximization approach is that people who are very poor . . . count only if they are part of the utility function of somebody who has wealth.[30]

It is no surprise that Posner's insights outrage legal philosophers. The theory that aspires to be universal cannot count only some people while making others irrelevant for the sole fact that they are not endowed with enough wealth. This brings us to the problem of the initial assignment of rights.

According to Posner, not only property rights to chattels are to be instrumentally distributed according to the wealth maximization principle. Posner seeks to present a universal, normative benchmark for allocation of all sorts of rights, including the self-ownership of one's own labor. In other words, the issue of *initial assignment* of property rights is considered, since it is "the starting point for a market system."[31] The fact that people own their own lives and labor is, according to Posner, explicable by the wealth maximization principle itself; assignment of these rights to "natural owners" is a result of calculus. States Posner:

---

[29]Anthony T. Kronman, "Wealth Maximization as a Normative Principle," *Journal of Legal Studies* 9, no. 2 (March 1980): 240. Despite the fact that conclusions of Kronman and Austrians in this particular normative question coincide, we shall, for the sake of fairness, not forget that his approach to criticism of Posner is heavily influenced by the neoclassical notion of economics. Kronman, for example, uses utils and without hesitation engages in an interpersonal comparison of utility. Walter Block once rightly raised this objection in his reply to Kronman. See Walter Block, "Alienability, Inalienability, Paternalism, and the Law: Reply to Kronman," *American Journal of Criminal Law* 28, no. 3 (Summer 2001): 351–71.

[30]Richard A. Posner, "Utilitarianism, Economics, and Legal Theory," *Journal of Legal Studies* 8, no. 1 (1979): 119.

[31]Posner, "Efficiency Norm," p. 500.

> This is the economic reason for giving a worker the right
> to sell his labor and a woman the right to determine her
> sexual partners. If assigned randomly to strangers these
> rights would generally (not invariably) be repurchased
> by the worker and the woman respectively.[32]

Dworkin challenges this assertion by pointing out that we cannot simply assume, as Posner does, the rights to be repurchased by
their natural owners. These people must be willing and able to pay
for them what the random possessors of the right would demand
on the market. But all this necessarily depends on the initial
assignment of rights itself. The reasoning is, again, circular.[33] As
Ian Shapiro notes, the example assumes "exactly what Posner has
to establish if his theory is to make any sense."[34]

The difficulty was recognized by Kronman who, building on
Coleman's earlier work,[35] restated the problem in terms of auction.
No one has anything at his disposal and attends the auction where
the rights are to be sold to the highest bidder. The result of auction
will satisfy the wealth maximization principle, but the bids will
have a form of mere stipulation—for the time being the bidders
have nothing to pay with. The auction may result in enslavement
of A by B if the auctioneer concludes that the work of A will be better managed and allocated in more valuable uses by B than if it
was assigned to its "natural owner," i.e., A.[36]

The objections of legal thinkers are very similar to those made by
Austrians. Hans-Hermann Hoppe, using Posner's own example,[37]
showed that adherence to wealth maximization may well lead to

---

[32]Posner, "Utilitarianism, Economics, and Legal Theory," p. 125.

[33]Dworkin, "Is Wealth a Value?," p. 208. Dworkin indeed asserts that
under present conditions, it would be for most people today "impossible to
repurchase the right to their labor, because the value of that labor represents
more than half of their present wealth." Ibid., p. 209.

[34]Ian Shapiro, *The Flight from Reality in the Human Sciences* (Princeton, N.J.:
Princeton University Press, 2005), p. 111.

[35]Jules L. Coleman, "Efficiency, Exchange and Auction: Philosophic
Aspects of the Economic Approach to Law," *California Law Review* 68, no. 2
(March 1980).

[36]Kronman, "Wealth Maximization as a Normative Principle," pp. 240–41.

[37]Posner, *The Economics of Justice*, p. 77 n. 57.

the denial of self-ownership and justification of slavery. Suppose an alternative universe in which Henry Ford decided not to become an automobile manufacturer but a Trappist monk. In this universe, people would be poorer compared to our actual world; the wealth would be lowered. The notion of wealth maximization leads us to the conclusion that we could

> enslave Ford and put him into the Ford factory and just tell him: "Hey, keep on being the Ford that you were supposed to be instead of just being a Trappist monk."[38]

ETHICS VS. "POSNERIAN ECONOMICS"

It should be clear now how crucially important it is to contrast an ethically-based approach to property (such as self-ownership and its extension) to the efficiency theory of rights. Whereas the former approach (built-upon by Hoppe as a leading exponent of the Austrian approach and other prominent philosophers) gives us clear guidance, a Posnerian judge cannot perform the task assigned to him.

Whereas the former approach defends property as a building block of every viable social order, Posner dilutes its importance entirely. Over time, he adopted an even less property-friendly approach. He refuses, as he himself states, to keep the "faith in the power of science to take religion's place as the deliverer of final truth."[39] Soundness of theoretical arguments is not to be any more decisive because, as Posner claims,

> in my view the ultimate criterion should be pragmatic; we should not worry whether cost-benefit analysis is well grounded in any theory of value. We should ask how well it serves whatever goals we have.[40]

---

[38]Hans-Hermann Hoppe, "Law and Economics," Lecture delivered at Mises University, Mises Institute, Auburn, Alabama, Friday, August 5, 2005. Available at http://mises.org/multimedia/mp3/MU2005/mu05-Hopp2.mp3.

[39]Richard A. Posner, *Overcoming Law* (Cambridge: Harvard University Press, 1996), p. 394.

[40]Richard A. Posner, "Cost-Benefit Analysis: Definition, Justification, and Comment on Conference Papers," *Journal of Legal Studies* 29 (June 2000): 1156.

The Kaldor-Hicks concept of efficiency, the concept that was the cornerstone of the Chicago approach to Law & Economics, has been abandoned and nothing has been put in its place. As Posner put it:

> I do not want to stake my all on a defense of the Kaldor-Hicks concept of efficiency. For me the ultimate test of cost-benefit analysis employing that concept is a pragmatic one: whether its use improves the performance of government in any sense of improvement that the observer thinks appropriate.[41]

It is crucial to realize that "any sense of improvement that the observer thinks appropriate" may mean virtually anything from increasing taxes to building labor camps—a sad end of a once ambitious research project.

CONCLUSION

Our aim in the present paper was to show that the standard Law & Economics approach has to be challenged due to its shortcomings, and that scholars in both economic and legal fields understand that. Unfortunately, while presenting their arguments, they often ignore scholarship which could make their case stronger. Consider this quote from Markovits, an eloquent critic of using efficiency criteria in law:

> In fact, several highly respected economists and law-and-economics scholars have written well-known articles that make arguments purporting to justify the claim that economically efficient decisions are always just and/or desirable—arguments that they have not explicitly disavowed and *that no other economist had refuted.*[42]

This is simply not true, and we sought to provide sufficient evidence to support this claim. Austrian authors have written over the years a growing number of publications doing just that. The

---

[41]Ibid., pp. 1155–56.

[42]Richard S. Markovits, "On the Relevance of Economic Efficiency Conclusions," *Florida State University Law Review* 29, no. 1 (Fall 2001): 5.

Austrian broad approach to the study of social reality is something which legal theorists could very much benefit from. Regrettably, most of them seem to be unaware of the Austrian tradition,[43] and hence — to their detriment — work within the framework of neo-classical economics.

On the other hand, Austrians, too, rarely quote legal philosophers for the support of their thoughts, even though both groups may, in many respects, be developing, in essence, the same arguments. This fact alone should encourage Austrians to study more of their works. ❧

---

[43]For an author praising the humanistic approach of the Austrian economics see e.g. Michael Novak, "Economics as Humanism," in Edward Younkins, ed., *Three in One* (Lanham, Md.: Rowman & Littlefield, 2001).

 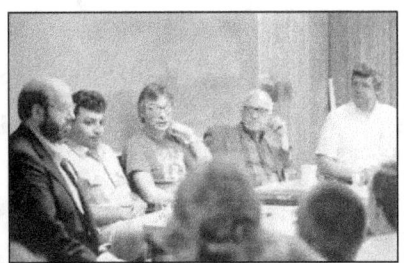

1991 Mises University. From left: Lew Rockwell, Yuri Maltsev, Hans Hoppe, Murray Rothbard, and Roger Garrison

1992 at Jekyll Island
From left: Hans Hoppe,
Murray Rothbard, and Lew Rockwell

Undated photo

From left:
Walter Block,
Hans Hoppe,
Roger Garrison,
and Richard
Ebeling

1996 Mises University Faculty. Front row, from left: Hans Hoppe, David Gordon, Robert Batemarco, Ralph Raico, Joseph Salerno, Andy Barnett, and Jeffrey Herbener. Back row: Mark Thornton, Thomas DiLorenzo, John Sophocleus, and Guido Hülsmann

Undated photo

Undated, with Norman Singleton and Paul Gottfried

With Guido Hülsmann at the 1999 Mises University

With Otto von Habsburg at the 1999 Mises Institute Supporters Summit and Schlarbaum Award presentation

Left:
With Joseph Salerno at the going-away party for Pat Barnett in 2001

Below: 2002

Above: With Eugen-Maria Schulak, September 2005

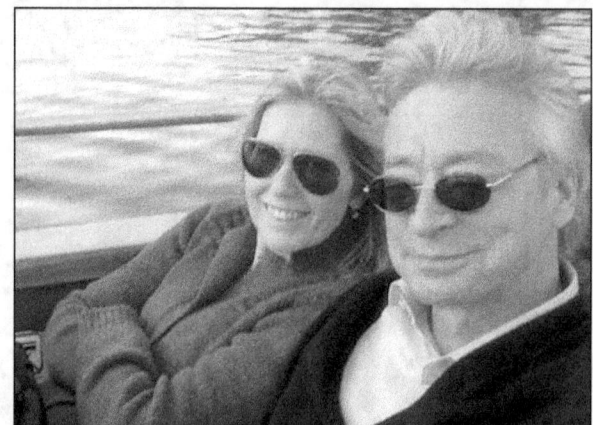

With his wife
Gülçin Imre in
Denmark, 2006

With Emily and
Nicholas
Hoppe, children
from his first
marriage,
in Auburn,
Alabama, 2006

With Gülçin in Bodrum, Turkey, 2007

At the 2007 meeting of the Property and Freedom Society, Bodrum, Turkey

2008 meeting of the Property and Freedom Society

Below: With David Gordon

Gülçin Imre (center), with members of the Property and Freedom Society writing for the German libertarian monthly magazine "eigentümlich frei." From left: Bruno Bandulet, Guido Hülsmann, Carlos Gebauer, Eugen-Maria Schulak, Rahim Taghizadegan, Andreas Tögel, Paul Gottfried, André Lichtschlag, Martin Stefunko, Sean Gabb, Robert Grözinger, Anthony Daniels, Christoph Schmidt-Krayer, and Hans-Hermann Hoppe, Bodrum, Turkey, 2009

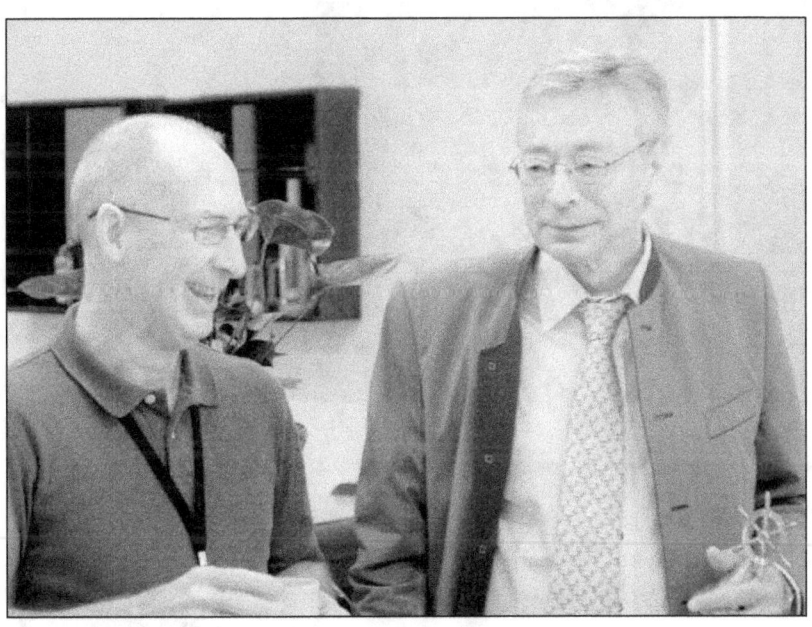

With Robert Higgs, Bodrum, Turkey, 2009

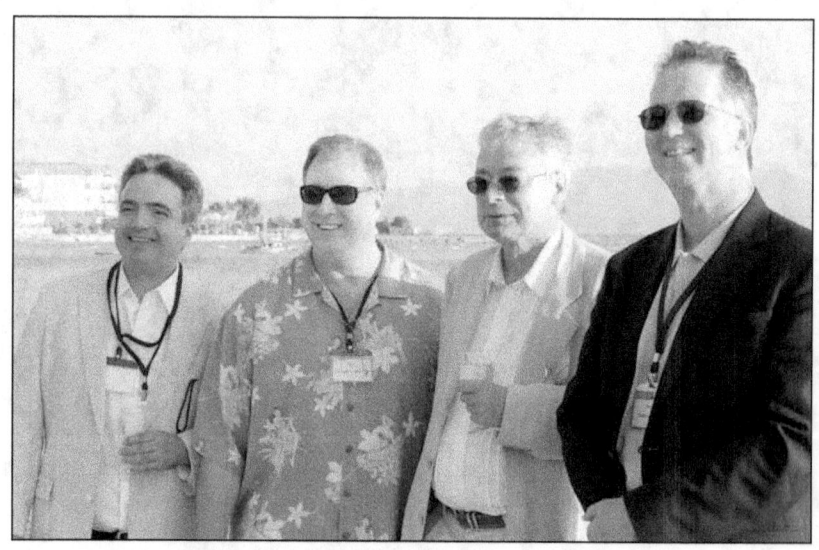

Lee Iglody, Doug French, Hans Hoppe, and Steve Sailer,
Bodrum, Turkey, 2009

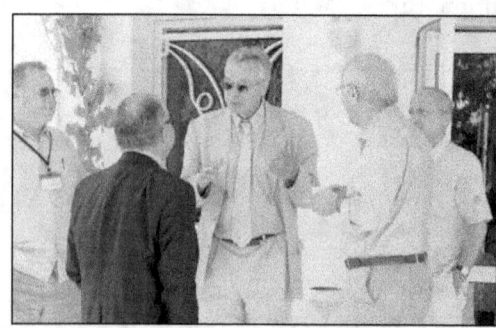

From left:
Andy Barnett,
Anthony Deden,
Hans-Hermann Hoppe,
Andreas Acavalos, and
Witold Falkowski,
Bodrum, Turkey, 2009

Hans, Gülçin, and
Peter Duesberg,
Bodrum, Turkey, 2009

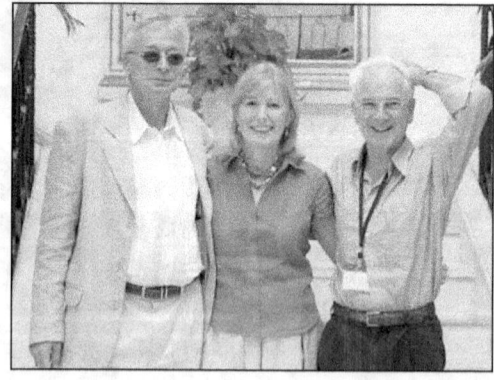

Part Three

Political Philosophy

17

Toward a Libertarian Theory of Guilt & Punishment for the Crime of Statism

Walter Block

T his paper is an attempt to combine the insights of Van Creveld concerning statism[1] with libertarian theory in order to forge a theory of justified punishment for the crime of engaging in statist, governmental, or other gangster activity.

GOVERNMENT VS. STATE

Van Creveld begins his analysis by distinguishing between governments and states. In his view:

> The state . . . is an *abstract* entity which can be neither seen, nor heard, nor touched. This entity is not identical with either the rulers or the ruled; neither President Clinton, nor citizen Smith, nor even an assembly of all the citizens acting in common can claim that they *are* the state.

Walter Block (WalterBlock.com; wblock@loyno.edu), a long time friend and admirer of Hans Hoppe, is Harold E. Wirth Endowed Chair and Professor of Economics, College of Business, Loyola University New Orleans and a Senior Fellow of the Ludwig von Mises Institute.

[1]Martin Van Creveld, *The Rise and Decline of the State* (Cambridge: Cambridge University Press, 1999).

On the other hand, it includes them both and claims to stand over them both.[2]

The hallmark of the state, for Van Creveld, is its impersonality. There is no one individual who can be clearly be described, distinctly, as a member of the state. On the other hand, it is possible to claim that *everyone* living within a certain location is a member of the state. He goes so far as to liken this institution to a

> corporation in the sense that it possesses a legal *persona* of its own, which means that it has rights and duties and may engage in various activities *as if* it were a real flesh and blood, living individual.[3]

But if the state is a corporation, it is distinguished from all other such, typically in two ways: it claims the right to initiate violence within a given geographical area (e.g., taxation), and demands a territorial monopoly in this regard (e.g., it will not tolerate the operation of any other state within "its" area). Van Creveld puts the matter in this way:

> the state differs from other corporations . . . first, [in] the fact that it authorizes them all but is itself authorized (recognized) solely by others of its kind; secondly, that certain functions (known collectively as the attributes of sovereignty) are reserved for it alone; and, thirdly, that it exercises those functions over a certain territory inside which its jurisdiction is both exclusive and all embracing.[4]

In sharp contrast, a government is an entity that, although it typically serves the same function as a state, consists of specific identifiable persons. Here, there is a clear line of demarcation, in any geographical area, between the rulers, who are part of the government, and the ruled, who are not.

---

[2]Ibid., p. 1.
[3]Ibid.
[4]Ibid.

According to Van Creveld:

> government and state are emphatically not the same.
> The former is a person or group which makes peace,
> wages war, enacts laws, exercises justice, raises revenue,
> determines the currency, and looks after internal secu-
> rity on behalf of society as a whole, all the while
> attempting to provide a focus for people's loyalty and,
> perhaps, a modicum of welfare as well. The latter is
> merely one of the forms which, historically speaking, the
> organization of government has assumed.[5]

Van Creveld further divides the government into various types, including tribes with rulers (chiefdoms), city-states, and empires.[6] To preview our findings, we shall maintain that while fomenting states and governments are equally criminal acts under the legal code of libertarianism, the distinction between them is still a highly useful one, in that the former presents far more analytic dif- ficulties than the latter.

WHAT IS LIBERTARIANISM?

Libertarianism is the philosophy that maintains it is illicit to threaten or initiate violence against a person or his legitimately owned property.[7] Defensive force may be used to ward off an attacker, but invasions of person or property are strictly prohibited by the non-aggression axiom.

---

[5]Ibid., p. 415.

[6]Ibid., p. 2. He actually includes a fourth category "tribes without rulers" but we ignore this possibility on the ground that it cannot be reconciled with our own view that all governments necessarily initiate (legally legitimate) vio- lence against their citizens, and demand a monopoly role in this regard.

[7]See on this Murray N. Rothbard, *The Ethics of Liberty* (Atlantic Highlands, N.J.: Humanities Press, 1982); Hans-Hermann Hoppe, *A Theory of Socialism and Capitalism* (Boston-Dordrecht-London: Kluwer, 1989); idem, *The Econom- ics and Ethics of Private Property: Studies in Political Economy and Philosophy* (Boston: Kluwer, 1993); John Locke, *An Essay Concerning the True Origin, Extent and End of Civil Government*, V, pp. 27–28, in *Two Treatises of Government*, P. Laslett, ed. (Cambridge: Cambridge University Press, 1960).

Given that both the state and government can be defined as a monopoly of legitimated violence within a given geographical area, it may then be fairly said that any such entity, which admits of rulers and ruled, whether private gang, government or state, necessarily violates the libertarian axiom of non-aggression.

Can it reasonably be objected that ruling entities, whether states or governments, are really embodiments of voluntary agreements between consenting adults, since they are based on constitutions?[8] Unfortunately for the supporters of dirigisme, such a contention cannot be maintained. Philosophers such as Spooner, Rothbard, and Hoppe have put paid to all such claims.[9]

If it is illicit to invade the person or property of another, what should be the appropriate response from the forces of law and order?[10] It is a combination of making the victim "whole" again,

---

[8]This is the position of the Public Choice School. See James M. Buchanan & Gordon Tullock, *The Calculus of Consent: Logical Foundations of Constitutional Democracy* (Ann Arbor: University of Michigan, 1962). For criticism, see Murray N. Rothbard, "Buchanan and Tullock's The Calculus of Consent," *The Logic of Action II* (Glos, U.K.: Edward Elgar Publishing, 1997), pp. 269–74; Walter Block & Thomas J. DiLorenzo, "Constitutional Economics and the Calculus of Consent," *Journal of Libertarian Studies* 15, no. 3 (Summer 2001): 37–56; idem, "Is Voluntary Government Possible? A Critique of Constitutional Economics," *Journal of Institutional and Theoretical Economics* 156, no. 4 (December 2000): 567–82; idem, "The Calculus of Consent Revisited," *Public Finance and Management* 1, no. 3 (2001).

[9]See Lysander Spooner, *No Treason: The Constitution of No Authority* (reprint Larkspur, Colo.: Pine Tree Press, [1870] 1966); Murray N. Rothbard, "The Anatomy of the State," *Rampart Journal* 1, no. 2 (Summer 1965); idem, *Power and Market: Government and the Economy* (Menlo Park, Calif.: Institute for Humane Studies, 1970); idem, *For a New Liberty* (New York: Macmillan, 1973); idem, *The Ethics of Liberty*; Hoppe, *A Theory of Socialism and Capitalism*; idem, *The Economics and Ethics of Private Property*. Spooner goes on to reject the claim that the government is really a voluntary organization, one agreed to on the part of its citizenry, on the ground that people do vote, pay taxes, serve in the army, and so on.

[10]These must of necessity be private, since public sector police violate the libertarian code of law in the first place, and can thus scarcely be relied upon to uphold it.

and punishing the aggressor.[11] What this amounts to, in effect, is "two teeth for a tooth" plus costs of capturing and scaring.[12] Consider the following scenario: A steals a car from B. A is now captured. What is the just punishment that will restore B, as much as possible, to his previous non-victimization state? First, the automobile must be returned from the carjacker to its rightful owner. That is the first "tooth." Then, what A did to B must be, instead, done to A, on B's behalf, by the forces of law and order. Since A relieved B of a car, and took it for himself, the same must now be done to A; that is, A's own car (*not* the one he just stole from B which has already been returned to B as the first tooth) must be given to B.[13] This is the "second tooth."[14] But more is needed if the

---

[11]On libertarian punishment theory, see Randy E. Barnett & John Hagel III, eds., *Assessing the Criminal: Restitution, Retribution and the Legal Process* (Cambridge, Mass.: Ballinger, 1977); Walter Block, "Radical Libertarianism: Punishment Theory for the State" (forthcoming); J. Charles King, "A Rationale for Punishment," *Journal of Libertarian Studies* 4, no. 2 (Spring 1980): 151–65; Stephan Kinsella, "Estoppel: A New Justification for Individual Rights," *Reason Papers* no. 17 (Fall 1992): 61–74; idem, "Punishment and Proportionality: The Estoppel Approach," *Journal of Libertarian Studies* 12, no. 1 (Spring 1996): 51–73; idem, "Inalienability and Punishment: A Reply to George Smith," *Journal of Libertarian Studies* 14, no. 1 (Winter 1998–99): 79–93; idem, "New Rationalist Directions in Libertarian Rights Theory," 12 no. 2 *Journal of Libertarian Studies* (Fall 1996): 313–26; idem, "A Libertarian Theory of Punishment and Rights," *Loyola of Los Angeles Law Review* 30 (1997): 607–45; Rothbard, *The Ethics of Liberty*.

[12]See on this Block, "Radical Libertarianism"; Rothbard, *The Ethics of Liberty*, pp. 85–96; idem, *For a New Liberty*, p. 97.

[13]If A does not have his own vehicle of equivalent value, then its value can be taken out of A's hide: that is, instead of putting A in a jail at B's (and all other taxpayers') expense, where he can spend his days in front of a color television, in cozy air conditioned circumstances, A will in effect be enslaved until he earns enough money to pay his debt to B. Our experience of this "curious institution" shows that private concerns are able to "sweat" more value out of their charges than the costs of feeding and guarding them. See Jeffrey Hummel, *Emancipating Slaves, Enslaving Free Men: A History of the American Civil War* (LaSalle, Ill.: Open Court, 1996); Mark Thornton, "Slavery, Profitability and the Market Process," *Review of Austrian Economics* 7, no. 2 (1994): 21–47; Robert W. Fogel & Stanley L. Engerman, *Time on the Cross: The Economics of American Negro Slavery* (Ann Arbor: University of Michigan Press, 1974). So would it be, nowadays, under fully private (slave) prisons.

scales of justice are to be once again righted. When A engaged in his act of car jacking, B was ordered, at the point of a gun, to exit from the automobile, and turn it over to A. B, reasonably enough, feared for his very life, not knowing whether or not compliance with A's orders would be sufficient to save himself. If all we do, now, is blithely turn two cars over to B from A, we will still be a long way from bringing matters to a just conclusion. Since A scared B, we must scare A, twice as much, if anything. Accordingly, to the "two teeth" penalty already imposed upon A, we additionally scare him. How can this be done? One reasonable option is to force him to play Russian roulette with himself, with the number of bullets and chambers to be determined by the severity of the crime perpetrated upon B by A. When we add to this a reasonable amount for the costs of capturing A,[15] our story in this regard is complete.

APPLYING LIBERTARIAN PUNISHMENT THEORY
TO POLITICAL RULERS

In those branches of athletics that have as their goal the movement of a spherical object such as golf, handball, racketball, baseball, softball, and soccer, the road to success is to "keep your eye on the ball." He who fails to do so, for even the slightest moment, cannot do as well as otherwise he might. A necessary condition for orchestral playing is to either memorize the notes — and their time value — or to keep your eyes *glued* to the musical score. Even a momentary lapse in this regard is almost a guarantee of less productivity than otherwise, if not outright failure. There are, to be sure, distractions; these account for failure to a great degree. But the high road to success is to strive to the utmost to focus on what you are doing.

---

[14]Note that we are not talking about 1.9 "teeth" or 2.1 "teeth" or any other amount of "teeth." Justice amounts to exactly twice what the bible recommended since we first return the stolen car, and then add on a second car as punishment.

[15]If A presents himself at the police station with a voluntary confession, this aspect of his punishment will be minimized.

It is the same with our present concerns. Only here, instead of a ball or musical notes, the aphorism of keeping your eye on the ball applies to the non-aggression axiom — and its applicability to those responsible for creating and running states and governments.The aim of the present paper is to apply the libertarian non-aggression axiom and punishment theory to the activities of the state. It is of the utmost importance that we act consistently with the basic building block of this philosophy, since the distractions will be numerous and powerful; allowing them to deter us from an accurate analysis will almost guarantee erroneous conclusions.

The "distractions" are so numerous and deeply embedded in our societal mores that even I, the author of this paper, feel a certain reluctance to overcome them. For one thing, politicians are the *leaders* of our present society. To contemplate incarcerating them, particularly *en masse*, is more than sufficient to make the most hardy intellect blanch.[16] But facts are facts, and we cannot take our eye off of the "ball" if we are to shed any sort of social scientific light on the problems to which we are addressing ourselves: given that governments are illicit invasive criminal institutions, and that people who aggress are justifiably punished, we must contemplate retribution, on a massive scale, against all those responsible.

JUST HOW MASSIVE?

But just how all-encompassing must be our vision? Suppose we were to contemplate a Nuremberg type trial for Cuba and North Korea. Would all inhabitants of these unhappy countries, without exception, be candidates for a jail sentence (or worse)? This, indeed, would be precisely the conclusion reached by what I would consider a rather unsympathetic interpretation of Van

---

[16]It is also undoubtedly illegal to contemplate any such activity. Accordingly, I hereby restrict the coverage of this discussion to the two political entities most people would agree are currently rogue states, or illegitimate governments, those of North Korea and Cuba, as of the time of the present writing (2008). Political entities operating in the past which fall into this category include the USSR, any of the countries of Eastern Europe until the fall of communism in that part of the world, Nazi Germany, Fascist Italy, Chile under Salvatore Allende, and Uganda under Idi Amin.

Creveld, along with the premises of libertarian punishment theory as we have adumbrated them. Specifically, this author has stated: "neither President Clinton, nor citizen Smith, nor even an assembly of all the citizens acting in common can claim that they are the state. On the other hand, it includes them both and claims to stand over them both."[17] The point is, if both Smith and Clinton are the state, and the latter is guilty of criminal behavior on this ground, then so must this apply to the former. But it would be a strange Nuremberg trial that found guilty the entire populace of Cuba; this would mean that there were no victims in that unhappy island country, only victimizers, a manifest impossibility, since the latter implies the existence of the former. From this we deduce that there must be at least *one* victim in Cuba. Further, it is only a particularly unsympathetic reading of Van Creveld to assume, on the basis of his analysis, that both Idi Amin and any one of his many victims would be not only guilty of political crimes, but equally guilty.

If it is not and cannot be the case that "we are all guilty" of statism, then it logically follows that some are culpable, and some are not. Let us consider a few candidates for the criterion separating the blameworthy from the innocent.

First, you are guilty of being part and parcel of government if you are employed by it, and not if not. This sounds like a good initial stab at making the distinction, but it is not. For one thing, virtually *everyone* in Cuba, North Korea, the USSR, East Germany either works or has worked for the state. Thus, this criterion would tend to collapse into the one which claims "we are all guilty," which has already been rejected. For another, surely there are people who are not formally employees of government, and yet who are guilty of statism to a great degree. Krupp and Messerschmit spring readily to mind in the Nazi era; Armand Hammer was an American businessman who cooperated with and effectively promoted Stalinism. Thus this criterion is both under- and over-inclusive.

---

[17]Van Creveld, *The Rise and Decline of the State*, p. 1. Again, let it be repeated, we are not in this paper contemplating punishing any such person as William Clinton for the crime of being the President of the United States. Rather, if we are to make use of this example, we are implicitly discussing the president or dictator of a country such as Cuba or North Korea.

Now consider a country where it is almost entirely a matter of choice, not physical necessity, to take a government job, for example, the U.S.[18] Use of the employment contract would condemn to criminality virtually every post office worker, teacher, professor,[19] social worker, street sweeper, garbage man, welfare recipient, toll booth collector, road repairman, and so on.[20] Again, we come perilously close to lapsing back into the "we are all guilty" scenario. Worse, no cognizance is taken of the distinction between a Marxist or leftist professor who supports totalitarianism, and those who oppose it.

Of course, it can be argued that even the libertarian professor or politician[21] who accepts a salary from government is still guilty of receiving what, by his lights, can only be considered stolen (e.g., taxed) property. And this cannot be denied. However, there are several replies open to the libertarian professor employed by a state school. First, there is the claim that he is only getting some of his own money back from the government, and not that of other people. Second, it is not exactly theft to take from a thief;[22] rather, such an act is best characterized as relieving a criminal of his ill-gotten gains. So, even if a post office worker takes a salary from the

---

[18]Let it be repeated once again that we are not considering the U.S., or any of the other western democracies as examples of countries that, if it is concluded that a person is part of the state apparatus, then he is guilty of violating the libertarian code of non-aggression, and is thus a subject fit for punishment.

[19]In the interests of full disclosure, I must note that I was previously employed by the University of Central Arkansas, a public institution of higher learning.

[20]This is somewhat of an exaggeration since some of these jobs have been privatized.

[21]Ron Paul is perhaps best known person in this latter category. Throughout his long career in the House of Representatives, he has served as a lone beacon for freedom.

[22]Actually, it is logically impossible to steal from a thief; one can only steal from the rightful owner, which, manifestly, the robber is not. An analogous situation occurs with regard to money. It is only possible to counterfeit legitimate money, not money which is already counterfeited, such as Cuban or North Korean money. On this see Walter Block, *Defending the Undefendable* (New York: Fox and Wilkes, [1976] 1991), pp. 109–20; Van Creveld, *The Rise and Decline of the State*, pp. 224–29.

government, this does not mean he is guilty of a libertarian legal code violation; far better that he, a non-thief, now has this money than that the government,[23] which stole it in the first place, gets to keep it. Ragnar Danneskjold, a fictional hero in Ayn Rand's *Atlas Shrugged*, made a career out of liberating (not stealing!) government property and returning it to its rightful owners.[24] This was a two stage act: first, taking money from the state, and second, giving it back to those from whom the state had stolen it from in the first place. If this complex act, consisting of two separate parts, was a righteous one, then each and every part of it, too, had to be licit; there cannot be a totally legitimate act one part of which is improper. But this means that not only returning stolen money to rightful owners should be lawful, but also taking it away from those with no valid title to it.[25]

Of course, the libertarian college professor who does not wish to open himself up to the charge of hypocrisy is subject to the "attack" on the part of taxpayers who may approach him and demand that he return to them those parts of their salary which cannot be accounted for on the grounds of him merely getting back his own (or his parents') tax revenues. What response does he have at his disposal? He has several. First, not all of these revenues (the difference, suitably capitalized, between what was stolen from him and what he has recovered) are up for grabs to the irate taxpayer who approaches him with charges of hypocrisy; it is only this amount subtracted from a reasonable "salvage" fee. According to the law of the sea merchant,[26] salvage fees amounted to one third of the value of a lost or abandoned boat. Applying this rule of thumb to our present situation, at most only two thirds of the

---

[23]Remember, we are still talking here about the North Korean or Cuban government.

[24]Ayn Rand, *Atlas Shrugged* (New York: Random House, 1957).

[25]E.g., the government of North Korea, or the fictional country of the U.S. in Rand's *Atlas Shrugged*.

[26]See "Marine Salvage Information For Recreational Boaters" (available at www.safesea.com/boating_info/salvage/salvage_main.html, accessed Nov. 19, 2008); "Salvage Law" (available at http://rms-republic.com/sal00.html, accessed Nov. 19, 2008).

libertarian professor's salary is vulnerable to this charge. Second, just as Ragnar chose his own victims of the state to whom to make restitution, so is this option open to our libertarian professor employed by a government institution. He need not satisfy any and all comers. Instead, he can direct these funds to worthy groups and organizations who have been victimized by taxation. Third, the would-be *claimant*'s hands must also be clean in this regard. *His* financial records must show that he is not a ruling class member or net tax consumer in the light of Calhoun's analysis.[27] Otherwise, he will be vulnerable to a counterclaim from the very person he is "attacking."

LIBERARTARIAN CLASS ANALYSIS

No, not all inhabitants of a geographical area are guilty of fomenting state institutions, nor are, even, all those who work for the government. The latter may constitute a presumption of political criminality, but this can be defeated, as we have seen. A better candidate for guilt and punishment emanates from libertarian class analysis.

This contention may be rejected out of hand by men of good will and good sense, because the Marxists have long polluted the concept with their own version of it. That is, in the more well-known Marxian class analysis, employers are guilty of exploitation, and employees are their victims.[28] But just because one version of class analysis is intellectually bankrupt does not mean that all others are. In the libertarian account, the distinction is, as might be imagined, between those who either directly or indirectly engage in violent attacks on innocent people, and those who do not.[29]

---

[27]John C. Calhoun, *A Disquisition on Government* (New York: Liberal Arts Press, 1953), pp. 16–18.

[28]For a refutation of this doctrine, see Eugen von Böhm-Bawerk, *Capital and Interest*, George D. Hunke & Hans F. Sennholz, trans. (South Holland, Ill.: Libertarian Press, [1884] 1959), particularly part I, chapter XII, "Exploitation Theory of Socialism-Communism."

[29]On libertarian ruling class theory see Rothbard, *The Ethics of Liberty*, pp. 176–77.

The state is of course the most well-organized group of exploiters of the innocent, but there are also non-governmental criminals, gangsters, etc., who must be included in the ruling class. Every car-jacker, every two bit thief, every perpetrator of fraud, every perpetrator of rape, assault and battery or murder, is, along with organizers and top managers of both government and state, a member of the ruling class from the libertarian perspective. As well, there are the aiders and abettors of the political system: members of the business, arts, and athletic communities who help politicians and bureaucrats in their mistreatment of the rest of society.

Perhaps the analogy that best illustrates this concept is that between officers and enlisted men in the army. The former are the rulers, the latter, the ruled. A colonel or a general typically receives far better treatment than a private or a corporal.[30] Who is a member of the ruling class: a welfare mother who accepts a check that would not be available to her in the free society, or the head of the Federal Reserve, an institution also incompatible with *laissez-faire* capitalism?[31] It is clearly not the former, but rather the latter. Yes, welfare is a clear theft of the rich taxpayer, in favor of the poor tax consumer[32] in this case, and is unjustified. But the single mom is more sinned against than a sinner. Put it this way: if somehow the "welfare queen" and all her ilk disappeared from the scene, the mixed economy, or socialism, would function pretty much as it has always done. On the other hand, were the politicians and top bureaucrats to decamp, and not be replicated, we would be well on our way toward the free society. ✷

---

[30]See Van Creveld, *The Rise and Decline of the State*, p. 161, on the different treatment accorded officers and enlisted men captured in war.

[31]It should not be forgotten that in this and other examples, we are discussing the Cuban or North Korean equivalents; e.g., the head of the central bank of those countries.

[32]Calhoun, *A Disquisition on Government*, pp. 16–18.

18

A Note on Intellectual Property and Externalities

Hardy Bouillon

I met Hans-Hermann Hoppe in 1991, I believe. Dissatisfied with inconsistencies in Hayek's concept of individual freedom, I was looking for an assessment that (at least) tried to avoid these inconsistencies. Hoppe's approach was and still is a representative of this rare species. Hoppe was refreshing. He did and does not take things for granted, for instance the classical liberal assumption that you cannot have individual freedom without government's monopoly to protect it. If we believe in free markets, why should we easily assume that they do not work when it comes to the private production of protection? On a more philosophical level: if we look for a consistent political philosophy that allows for a peaceful solution of man's most fundamental material problem, namely scarcity of resources under competing interests, why should not we look for a set of principles that do not contradict each other, no matter how difficult it appears to achieve these principles in practice?

Hardy Bouillon (hardy.bouillon@publicpartners.de) teaches philosophy at the University of Trier; is Hayek Institute Endowed Guest Professor at the Vienna University of Economics and Business; and is a Fellow of the International Centre for Economic Research (ICER) in Turin. His books include *Government: Servant or Master?* (1993), *Libertarians and Liberalism* (1997), and *Ordered Anarchy* (2007).

The anarcho-capitalism of Hans-Hermann Hoppe is a model developed along this guideline. Hoppe's principles of original appropriation of free goods and of production and trade of private goods are perfectly compatible. As long as goods are identifiable, all questions regarding their proper ownership can be solved – in principle. Of course, goods which are difficult to identify pose a problem – a problem that exists apparently for each approach that tries to solve the above-mentioned, most fundamental, material problem of man.

Material goods are identifiable, at least in principle. The place where you park your car cannot be taken by another car, at least not at the same time, because matter has extension. On a more general level: matter, whatever form it has or extension it takes, fills a spot in time and space. One and the same point in the time-space-coordinate-system cannot be taken more than once. This exclusive relationship between matter, time, and space helps to identify, i.e., locate, material goods: material goods can exist side by side, but they cannot collide, e.g., take simultaneously the same spot in the time-space-coordinate-system. Hence a society in which only material goods exist can solve its material conflicts without any collisions or conflict as long as we apply coherent principles of legitimate acquisition of property.

Things become more difficult if we include property in *imma-terial* goods. To say the least, the ontological status of immaterial goods is not the same as that of material goods. Whether immaterial goods fill spots in time and space, as material goods do, is much debated. It is also disputed whether or not it is possible to claim meaningfully that something exists if its alleged existence has no material form at all.

According to Popperian ontology, ideas have an immaterial status and began with language.[1] They are entities of World 3 and can be the subject of mental processes. These processes, in turn, belong to World 2. Of course, if we do not claim of ideas, problems, theories, arguments, etc. that they fill spots in time and

---

[1]Karl Popper, *The Open Universe: An Argument for Indeterminism* [The Post-script to *The Logic of Scientific Discovery*, vol. II] (Totowa, N.J., Rowman & Littlefield, 1982), p. 116.

space, what are they after all? Where do they go, when nobody thinks of them? Where have they been in the meantime, when someone "remembers" them? Do they disappear with mankind?

These questions address either deep philosophical problems or pseudo-problems. Whatever we think of the characteristics of these problems, it is clear that any meaningful concept of intellectual property presupposes that it is distinct from material property, hence *immaterial*. A further distinction between material goods and immaterial goods is that the former, in most cases, are tangible goods, whereas immaterial goods, for instance intellectual property, are intangible.[2] Ideas, melodies, and theories have no material extension *per se* as material goods do. Therefore, we cannot without further assumptions claim for them what we can claim for material goods, namely that they cannot collide with other material goods.

Intellectual property turns out to be a cumbersome element in an otherwise perfectly consistent political philosophy. Of course, Hoppe provides a solution to this problem. His solution rests on the introduction of a normative-functional explanation of private property into the debate and on the fact that immaterial goods are — unlike material goods — not scarce. As Hoppe has put it:

> [O]nly because scarcity exists is there even a problem of formulating moral laws; insofar as goods are superabundant ("free" goods), no conflict over the use of goods is possible and no action-coordination is needed. Hence, it follows that any ethic, correctly conceived, must be formulated as a theory of property, i.e., a theory of the assignment of rights of exclusive control over scarce means. Because only then does it become possible to avoid otherwise inescapable and irresolvable conflict.[3]

---

[2]Though some speak exclusively of tangible and non-tangible goods, I prefer to talk of material and immaterial goods. See, for instance, Stephan Kinsella, "Against Intellectual Property," *Journal of Libertarian Studies* 15, no. 2 (Spring 2001): 2. The point about material goods is not that they are tangible, for some are not. For instance, atoms and many other small material units are not tangible; they are identifiable only indirectly, though this does not prevent us from calling them material.

[3]Hans-Hermann Hoppe, *A Theory of Socialism and Capitalism* (Boston: Kluwer Academic Publishers, 1989), p. 235 n. 9.

In other words, assuming that scarcity is the reason for conflict over goods with competing interests[4] and that the very function of property rights is to solve these conflicts peacefully, there is no need to provide property rights for intellectual property, because intellectual goods are not scarce.

I shall return to this argument later. Until then we should keep in mind that intellectual property (if it exists at all) is, contrary to material property, difficult to identify and, hence, its philosophical treatment asks for special care. Before we address the analysis of intellectual property, let us look at some aspects of the role of definitions.

TYPES OF STATEMENTS: ANALYTICAL, EMPIRICAL, AND NORMATIVE

It goes without saying that statements in the sciences can have different forms. Three are of importance here: some statements are purely analytical (for instance definitions, tautologies), while others are mainly empirical (theories, hypotheses) or normative (imperatives, rules, laws). It also goes without further notice that it is sometimes quite complicated to tell whether a statement is meant to be (purely) analytical, empirical, or normative. Sometimes statements serve two or more masters. Take for instance your wife's message: "Darling, the garbage can is full." Not only do you suppose that she made an empirical statement (an assumption which is obvious because of the grammatical structure used in this sentence), you also clearly understand the implicit imperative: "Get the trash out of the kitchen and return with an empty bucket, please!"

---

[4] Ibid., p. 10:

> [B]ecause of the *scarcity of body and time*, even in the Garden of Eden property regulations would have to be established. Without them, and assuming now that *more than one person exists*, that their *range of action overlaps*, and that there is *no preestablished harmony and synchronization of interests among these persons*, conflicts over the use of one's own body would be unavoidable. (emphasis added)

Leaving the peculiarities of our language aside, it appears to be common sense among all scientists that language — despite all its imperfections — should be used as precisely as necessary for the theories in question and that analytical, descriptive, and prescriptive sentences should not be confused. It also appears to me that all three types of sentences have their distinct functions in all academic disciplines: definitions, being analytical statements, provide a field with abbreviations and meaning analyzes of the most central and frequently used concepts or terms,[5] while descriptive statements are mainly used for empirical assertions and prescriptive statements for normative recommendations.

Thus, when the existence or absence of some private property is either claimed or proposed, it is the definition of private property that tells us how private property, in either the empirical or normative context, is to be understood. Obviously, without knowing how private property is to be understood, we can neither definitely say what is empirically asserted, nor what the norm recommends.

In order to set the stage for the discussion of the role of functionalism in intellectual property rights, to which we turn later, we should mention here that some definitions look rather functional while others do not. The reason is quite simple. It rests on the fact that some concepts are mainly — if not exclusively — used to describe a functional relation while others do not. For instance, we usually define a wife by the relation to her husband (and *vice-versa*). The fact of bondage by marriage is constitutional for the definition of a wife — as it is for the definition of a husband. However, not for all terms are functional relations constitutional. Looking for a functional relation of the term that is to be defined might lead to the erroneous belief that this function, if found, is constitutional for the term.

For instance, it would be misleading to define private goods by their relation to public goods. Thus, it would be fallacious to conclude that unlike public goods, for which most authors claim

---

[5]On the role of definitions see Gerard Radnitzky, "Definition," in *Handlexikon zur Wissenschaftstheorie*, Helmut Seiffert & Gerard Radnitzky, eds. (Munich: Ehrenwirth, 1989), pp. 22–33.

non-exclusivity,[6] private goods are exclusive. Whether or not a good is exclusive is a coincidental character rather than a constitutional character of the good in question. Of course, this coincidental character comes along with most of the private goods. However, it all depends on the way the good is treated by its owner and others. If an owner shares his good with others, it loses its exclusivity.[7] Take for instance a boat that you share with your friends for a trip along the coast. Though, strictly speaking, it is not exclusive for the time of the trip, it is still your boat throughout the trip.[8]

Consequently, an appropriate definition of private property presupposes identifying the subject who privatized the good. This is because the reason for a good to become private is not in the good itself, but rather than in the relationship between the good in question and its "relator," i.e., someone who owns it privately, namely the owner. If the owner is sovereign over it, then the good in question is a private good, his private good. In other words: it

---

[6]We cannot deal here with the related question of how to define public goods appropriately. It seems, however, obvious that non-exclusion is an appropriate constitutional character of public goods. So while a likely concomitant of public goods, it is only coincidental. For instance: for the time a public library is used by just one person, it is, strictly speaking, not non-exclusive.

[7]Bringing in the owner's right to exclude others shifts the story onto another level for which different conditions hold. Foremost, talking of rights requires the inclusion of normative sentences in the debate, while the aforesaid operates with descriptive sentences exclusively.

[8]Analogously, it would be misleading to say that a private good is a good for which the owner has solved the exclusion problem, or paid the exclusion costs. Although this may hold for many private goods, it is accidental, but not constitutional. Some private goods do not have any exclusion costs, simply because there is nobody interested in being included. Think of bulky waste that nobody wishes to have. If placed on no-man's-land it becomes a common good (or a bad, for that matter); if placed on a public good (street) it becomes a public good (or bad, for that matter); if thrown in the neighbor's garden, it continues being private—and most likely becomes the subject of a fierce dispute among neighbors. However, it seems appropriate at least to indicate that an explication of the term "public good" would show that one of its main characteristics is non-sovereignty.

is sovereignty rather than exclusivity that defines private property.[9]

Having said this, it seems appropriate to add an observation on the exclusion and its costs. There are but two necessary preconditions for the existence of exclusion costs of a private good:

1. The owner is interested in excluding others from his property; and

2. Others covet his property.

Obviously, if the owner is uninterested in excluding others, then his property is likely to be taken away by someone who covets it. Nevertheless his exclusion costs are nil.[10] If the owner is interested in the exclusion of his property, whereas nobody covets it, he too faces no exclusion costs.

Though it may seem so at first, it is in fact not trivial to note that private property is appreciated by its owner mainly, if not exclusively, for the positive externalities that come with it. Also important is the insight that not all positive externalities that may come with a private good necessarily belong to the owner of that good. Think of a trumpet player in the street. His play might

---

[9]As Anthony de Jasay has put it: "Sovereignty may be delegated revocably, or transferred for good, but it cannot be shared, and that is why there is no true property that, after cancelling out agents, delegates and intermediaries, is not mine, yours, his or hers." Anthony de Jasay, *Choice, Contract, Consent: A Restatement of Liberalism* (London: Institute of Economic Affairs, 1991), p. 75.

[10]Talking of the exclusion costs for goods, from which the owner does not want to exclude others, is pointless. In any case, talking of costs is meaningful only if there exists at least one possible cost-bearer. It is equally pointless to speak of the costs or the price of a good for which there is no demand. The seller might have some clear ideas on the amount of money he wishes to get in return for the good, but he cannot determine the price alone. The price is determined by supply *and* demand, and this determination finds its expression in the market transaction.

To put it in Lockean terms, "costly" is a secondary quality of a good, but not a primary one. Plainly speaking, secondary qualities of any object presuppose a possible relation between the object and a subject. According to Locke, the primary qualities of an object exist with the object, for instance gravity, while secondary qualities, like color, come into existence through the relation of the object and an observer.

cause positive externalities (as long as it pleases the passers-by). However, we most likely do not view him as the owner of these externalities, not to mention having an associated right to ask for compensation for the positive externalities initiated.

We may list five reasons to be reluctant to maintain that the musician has a right in these externalities. First, implicitly we assume that the busker, though the unopposed owner of his instrument, is not the owner of the public space or the air in which he performs and that, hence, he has no privilege to use that sphere exclusively or ask for compensation if others use it. He uses the public space and the free good "air," and so do the passers-by.

Second, though the musician while playing initiates the sound waves, the listening of the passers-by is required in order to produce the full effect of listening to and enjoying music. In other words, though the musician is sufficient to produce the good "music," he is not sufficient to produce the positive externality that may accompany it. Third, the passers-by could also—*per impossibile*—claim a property right to remuneration of positive side effects, because their forming an audience attracts others to join the event and, hence, enlarge the group of possible donators.

Fourth, the internalization of positive externalities is a problem of its initiator. To the extent positive externalities are created without agreement (that would allow for compensation) and not internalized by its producer, these effects are nothing but free goods which can be internalized by anybody as he or she thinks fit. Fifth, since there is no agreement between the busker and the passers-by that would allow for compensation, the positive externalities generated by the guitar-player are at best an offer that one is free to accept or reject, and, if accepted, can be treated as a gift while the passers-by are free to respond to it by a return gift, i.e., throwing a few coins in the cap.

However one may view these considerations individually, they all seem to rest on the assumptions that property cannot generate new property for the owner if, in the process of this creation, property of others is included in one way or another; and that this holds true if the new "would-be property" is an externality. In other words, many positive externalities come into existence only by intermingling with property of others; and only if they don't, can the initiator claim a right in these without facing awkward queries.

These considerations are closely linked with the topic of intellectual property rights, although this might be not obvious at first sight. In order to become aware of this linkage, one might review the current debate on intellectual property rights.

LIBERTARIAN VIEWS OF INTELLECTUAL PROPERTY

Libertarians differ on the point whether intellectual property rights can be explained and legitimized in the same way as property rights in material goods and services.[11] Some, like Ayn Rand, argue that the origin of property rights lies in the creative process that leads to private goods and thus conclude that intellectual goods, as results of a creative process, are also private and endowed with property rights. In other words, the legitimacy of patent rights, copyrights, etc. rests on the creative act of the author or inventor.[12]

Others argue that the creative act as such would not initiate new property.[13] They rest their criticism on the fact that ideas can be reproduced without any loss of quality and can be shared by many without creating any scarcity problems. As mentioned before, assuming that scarcity is the potential reason of conflict and that the very idea of property rights is to solve these conflicts peacefully, they see no need to provide property rights for intellectual property.[14]

However we might judge these competing views, it is quite interesting that both camps bring in *functional explanations* of private property, not *functional definitions* or any other sort of definition, as defined in the "Types of Statements" section, above. From

---

[11] The best account on the different libertarian perspectives on this topic is given by Kinsella in "Against Intellectual Property."

[12] Ayn Rand, "Patents and Copyrights," *Capitalism: The Unknown Ideal* (New York: The New American Library, 1967), pp. 130–34. "Patents and copyrights are the legal implementation of the base of all property rights: a man's right to the product of his mind." Ibid., p. 130.

[13] For instance Boudewijn Bouckaert, Henri Lepage, Wendy McElroy, Benjamin Tucker and – partially – Murray Rothbard. See Kinsella, "Against Intellectual Property," p. 11.

[14] See note 2, above.

the proposed function of private property (be it "to give a man the right to the product of his mind" or "to assign rights of exclusive control over scarce means") they either defend or deny intellectual property rights. However successful these approaches may be, they do not provide definitions of intellectual property in terms of an exclusively analytical statement. In the above-mentioned cases, the definitions of private property serve at the same time descriptive and normative functions, i.e., they also say how private property is and *ought* be used in society.

Be this as it may, following the distinctions made herein, a definition of intellectual property has to take account of at least two implications. Assuming that talking of intellectual property is meaningful at all, the definition of intellectual property seems to imply that it shares with all other sorts of property the constitutional characteristic of property, namely being owned in a sovereign way by its owner. Another implication comes from the fact that intellectual goods are immaterial, hence not to be confused with material goods.

INTELLECTUAL PROPERTY, MATERIAL PROPERTY, AND EXTERNALITIES

Let us keep in mind that the most fundamental objection to intellectual property rights seems to be the following argument: as soon as we agree to the idea to establish intellectual property rights, we agree to the fact that they can collide *principally* with property rights in material goods. The reason for this collision is obvious: a patent forbids everybody, with the exception of the patentee and his licensees, from using their material property in ways that are forestalled by the patent. Thus a patent to bake a plum cake – given to a baker – would prohibit all (non-licensee) housewives from baking the cake in the patented way despite the fact that they would do it with their own ingredients. Hence, patents can collide *principally* with property rights in material goods (assuming that the patentee and the owner of the material goods in question are not identical).

Consequently, as soon as we include intellectual entities among the goods that can be private we end up with a political philosophy that has incoherent elements, while the very same political philosophy was coherent before this inclusion. In order to avoid this unpleasant problem, it seems to be necessary *either* to demonstrate that intellectual property and/or the right in it is non-existent or to show that the aforementioned collision does not exist at all. Hoppe's approach includes the former demonstration while the latter does not need to presuppose the non-existence of intellectual property and/or intellectual property rights.

In fact, against the background of some arguments mentioned earlier and some to come it appears to me that the alleged collision does not exist at all and that we can talk meaningfully of intellectual property and intellectual property rights. In order to show this, it is helpful to look at the widespread distinction of the three kinds of usage of goods, namely *usus, usus fructus*, and *abusus*. Following this categorization, we distinguish the use of a good, its fruits, and its sale or transformation. I may use my apple tree by sitting under it (*usus*), eating its apples (*usus fructus*), or by selling it to a neighbor (*abusus*). Material usus, usus fructus, and abusus of the apple tree are possible without any further material good added to it.

Obviously, when it comes to immaterial goods, things become different. The material *usus* of any immaterial good is not possible without material added to it. Take a melody. It takes a voice, a guitar, or any other instrument to use it materially.[15] Mixing the melody with an instrument makes for a *usus fructus*. Neither an idea nor its fruits are *per se* material. Even if transformed into another idea, an idea stays immaterial. The material "extension" of an idea, so to speak, comes into existence not prior to the mixture of the idea with matter.

That intellectual property alone cannot "breed" material property has far-reaching consequences. If it holds for intellectual property what holds for all private property,[16] namely that the sovereignty that comes with it does not go beyond the borders of that good, then no collision between intellectual property and material property is possible. Such a collision would require that the sovereignty that comes with an intellectual good would extend over material property.

---

[15]Of course, this change the fact that you may use it immaterially, namely mentally by thinking of it.

[16]In fact, this must hold for intellectual property if intellectual property is to be understood as a sort of private property.

Whatever intellectual property is (in ontological terms), the sovereignty over it does not extend to any material property. Thus an idea, whether patented or not, does not provide the owner of the idea with an extra sovereignty over any material property, be it his or the material property of somebody else.[17] That a patented idea (or any other intellectual good) cannot collide with material property means that the collision between the right of intellectual property and the homesteading principle simply does *not* exist. To put it differently, intellectual property rights and material property rights are in principle compatible.

Summary

The alleged collision between the two rights (material property rights and intellectual property rights) seems to rest on a misinterpretation of intellectual property. As some reflection on the different types of usage of goods shows, this misinterpretation rests on the confusion of intellectual property and its (material) externalities. These externalities are not, as shown, per se property of the owner of the idea. Only those externalities belong to him that derive from material goods he owned before or from free goods he appropriated. In particular he is not the owner of the material goods owned by others. Hence the owner of the plum cake recipe remains the owner of "his" idea but cannot claim sovereignty over the ingredients owned by housewives. There is no collision with his intellectual property and their "using his" recipe of baking a plum cake.

To put it differently, we can talk meaningfully of intellectual property and intellectual property rights. However, intellectual property as such — being free of any material "extension" — is of no immediate importance to business life. What counts in the market are the externalities that can be derived from intellectual property. How to deal with these externalities is, of course, a different matter. ❧

---

[17]The only sovereignty over his material property comes with that very material property, and with nothing else.

19

Classical Liberalism versus Anarcho-Capitalism

Jesús Huerta de Soto

I n this first decade of the twenty-first century, liberal thought, in both its theoretical and political aspects, has reached a historic crossroads. Although the fall of the Berlin Wall and of real socialism beginning in 1989 appeared to herald "the end of history" (to use Francis Fukuyama's unfortunate and overblown phrase), today, and in many respects more than ever, statism prevails throughout the world, accompanied by the demoralization of freedom lovers. Therefore, an "aggiornamento" of liberalism is

Jesús Huerta de Soto (huertadesoto@dimasoft.es) is Professor of Political Economy, Universidad Rey Juan Carlos, Madrid. This article was first published in Spanish as "Liberalismo *Versus* Anarcocapitalismo," *Procesos de Mercado: Revista Europea de Economía Política* 4, no. 2 (2007): 13–32, and is based on two separate lectures given under the same title, one at the summer university of the Universidad Rey Juan Carlos (Aranjuez, Friday, July 6, 2007) and the other at the summer university of the Universidad Complutense (San Lorenzo de El Escorial, Monday, July 16, 2007). In these lectures, I formalized my theoretical and political "break" with classical liberalism, itself a mere step in the natural evolution toward anarcho-capitalism. Back in September of 2000, at the general meeting of the Mont Pèlerin Society in Santiago, Chile, in a speech I gave as part of a joint presentation with James Buchanan and Bruno Frei, I clearly hinted at this break. Jesús Huerta de Soto, "El Desmantelamiento del Estado y la Democracia Directa," *Nuevos Estudios de Economía Política*, 2nd ed. (Madrid: Unión Editorial, 2007): chap. 10, pp. 239–45.

imperative. It is time to thoroughly revise liberal doctrine and bring it up to date in light of the latest advances in economic science and the experience the latest historical events have provided. This revision must begin with an acknowledgement that classical liberals have failed in their attempt to limit the power of the state and that today economic science is in a position to explain why this failure was inevitable. The next step is to focus on the dynamic theory of the entrepreneurship-driven processes of social cooperation which give rise to the spontaneous order of the market. This theory can be expanded and transformed into a full-fledged analysis of the anarcho-capitalist system of social cooperation, which reveals itself as the only system that is truly viable and compatible with human nature.

In this article, we will analyze these issues in detail, along with a series of additional, practical considerations regarding scientific and political strategy. Moreover, we will make use of this analysis to correct certain common misunderstandings and errors of interpretation.

The Fatal Error of Classical Liberalism

The fatal error of classical liberals lies in their failure to realize that their ideal is theoretically impossible, as it contains the seed of its own destruction, precisely to the extent that it includes the necessary existence of a state (even a minimal one), understood as the sole agent of institutional coercion.

Therefore, classical liberals commit their great error in their approach: they view liberalism as a plan of political action and a set of economic principles, the goal of which is to limit the power of the state while accepting its existence and even deeming it necessary. However, today (in the first decade of the twenty-first century) economic science has already shown: (a) that the state is unnecessary; (b) that statism (even if minimal) is theoretically impossible; and (c) that, given human nature, once the state exists, it is impossible to limit its power. We will comment on each of these matters separately.

The State as an Unnecessary Body

From a scientific perspective, only the mistaken paradigm of equilibrium could encourage belief in a category of "public goods" in which satisfaction of the criteria of joint supply and non-rivalry in consumption would justify, *prima facie*, the existence of a body with a monopoly on institutional coercion (the state) that would oblige everyone to finance those goods.

Nevertheless, the dynamic, Austrian conception of the spontaneous order entrepreneurship drives has demolished this entire theory put forward to justify the state: the emergence of any case (real or apparent) of a "public good," i.e., joint supply and non-rivalry in consumption, is accompanied by the incentives necessary for the impetus of entrepreneurial creativity to find a better solution via technological and legal innovations and entrepreneurial discoveries which make it possible to overcome any problem that may arise (as long as the resource is not declared "public" and the free exercise of entrepreneurship is permitted, along with the accompanying private appropriation of the fruits of each creative, entrepreneurial act). For instance, in the United Kingdom, the lighthouse system was for many years privately owned and financed, and private procedures (sailors' associations, port fees, spontaneous social monitoring, etc.) offered an effective solution to the "problem" of what "statist" economics textbooks depict as the most typical example of a "public good." Likewise, in the American Far West, the problem arose of defining and defending property rights concerning, for instance, head of cattle in vast expanses of land. Various entrepreneurial innovations which resolved the problems as they arose were gradually introduced (cattle branding, constant supervision by armed cowboys on horseback, and finally, the discovery and introduction of barbed wire, which, for the first time, permitted the effective separation of great stretches of land at a very affordable price). This creative flow of entrepreneurial innovation would have been completely blocked if the resources had been declared "public," excluded from private ownership, and bureaucratically managed by a state agency. (Today, for instance, most streets and highways are closed to the adoption of innumerable entrepreneurial innovations – the collection of a toll per vehicle and hour, the private management of security and noise pollution, etc. – despite the fact that most such innovations no longer pose any technological problem. Nevertheless, the goods in question have been declared "public," which precludes their privatization and creative entrepreneurial management.)

Furthermore, most people believe the state is necessary because they confuse its existence (unnecessary) with the essential nature of many of the services and resources it currently (and poorly) provides, and over the provision of which it exercises a monopoly (almost always under the pretext of their public nature). People observe that today highways, hospitals, schools, public order, etc. are largely supplied by the state, and since these are highly necessary, people conclude without further analysis that the state is as well. They fail to realize that the above-mentioned resources can be produced to a much higher standard of quality as well as more efficiently, economically, and in tune with the varied and changing needs of each individual, through the spontaneous market order, entrepreneurial creativity, and private property. Moreover, people make the mistake of believing the state is also necessary to protect the defenseless, poor, and destitute ("small" stockholders, ordinary consumers, workers, etc.), yet people do not understand that supposedly protective measures have the systematic result, as economic theory demonstrates, of harming in each case precisely those they are claimed to protect, and thus one of the clumsiest and stalest justifications for the existence of the state disappears.

Rothbard maintained that the set of goods and services the state currently supplies can be divided into two subsets: those goods and services which should be eliminated, and those which should be privatized. Clearly, the goods mentioned in the above paragraph belong to the second group, and the disappearance of the state, far from meaning the disappearance of highways, hospitals, schools, public order, etc., would mean their provision in greater abundance, at higher standards, and at a more reasonable price (always with respect to the actual cost citizens currently pay via taxes). In addition, we must point out that the historical episodes of institutional chaos and public disorder we could cite (for example, many instances during the years prior to and during the Spanish Civil War and Second Republic, or today in broad areas of Colombia or in Iraq) stem from a vacuum in the provision of these goods, a situation created by the states themselves, which *neither do* with a minimum of efficiency what in theory they should do, according to their own supporters, *nor let the private, entrepreneurial sector do,* since the state prefers disorder (which also appears to more strongly legitimize its coercive presence) to its dismantling and privatization at all levels.

It is particularly important to understand that the definition, acquisition, transmission, exchange, and defense of the property rights which coordinate and drive the social process do not require a body with a monopoly on violence (the state). On the contrary, the state invariably acts by trampling on numerous legitimate property titles, defending them very poorly, and corrupting the (moral and legal) behavior of individuals with respect to the private property rights of others.

The legal system is the evolutionary manifestation of the general legal principles (especially regarding ownership) compatible with human nature. Therefore, the state does not determine the law (democratically or otherwise). Instead, the law is contained in human nature, though it is discovered and consolidated in an evolutionary manner, in terms of precedent and, mainly, doctrine. (We view the Roman, continental legal tradition, with its more abstract and doctrinal nature, as far superior to the Anglo-Saxon system of common law, which originates from disproportionate state support for legal rulings or judgments. These judgments, through binding case law, introduce into the legal system all sorts of dysfunctions that spring from the specific and prevailing circumstances and interests in each case.) Law is evolutionary and rests on custom, and hence, it precedes and is independent of the state, and it does not require, for its definition and discovery, any agency with a monopoly on coercion.

Not only is the state unnecessary to define the law; it is also unnecessary to enforce and defend it. This should be especially obvious these days, when the use—even, paradoxically, by many government agencies—of private security companies has become quite common.

This is not the place to present a detailed account of how the private provision of what today are considered "public goods" would work (though the lack of *a priori* knowledge of how the market would solve countless specific problems is the naïve, facile objection of those who favor the current status quo under the pretext, "better the devil you know than the devil you don't"). In fact, we cannot know today what entrepreneurial solutions an army of enterprising individuals would find for particular problems—if they were allowed to do so. Nevertheless, even the most skeptical person must admit that "we now know" that the market, driven by creative entrepreneurship, works, and it works precisely to the extent that the state does not coercively intervene in this social process. It is also essential to recognize that difficulties and conflicts invariably arise precisely in areas where the free, spontaneous order of the market is hindered. Thus, regardless of the efforts made from the time of Gustav de Molinari to the present to imagine how an anarcho-capitalist network of private security and defense agencies, each in support of more or less marginally alternative legal systems, would work, freedom theorists must never forget that what prevents us from knowing what a stateless future would be like, the creative nature of entrepreneurship, is precisely what offers us the peace of knowing that any problem will tend to be overcome, as the people involved will devote all of their effort and creativity to solving it.[1] Economic science has taught us not only that the market works, but also that statism is theoretically impossible.

WHY STATISM IS THEORETICALLY IMPOSSIBLE

The Austrian economic theory of the impossibility of socialism can be expanded[2] and transformed into a complete theory on the impossibility of statism, understood as the attempt to organize any sphere of life in society via coercive commands which involve intervention, regulation, and control and emanate from the body with a monopoly on institutional aggression (the state). The state cannot possibly achieve its coordination goals in any part of the social-cooperation process in which it attempts to intervene, especially the spheres of money and banking,[3] the discovery of law, the

---

[1] Israel M. Kirzner, *Discovery and the Capitalist Process* (Chicago and London: University of Chicago Press, 1985), p. 168.

[2] Jesús Huerta de Soto, *Socialismo, Cálculo Económico, y Función Empresarial*, 3rd ed. (Madrid: Unión Editorial, 2005), pp. 151–53.

[3] Jesús Huerta de Soto, *Money, Bank Credit, and Economic Cycles*, Melinda A. Stroup, trans. (Auburn, Ala.: Mises Institute, 2006) (originally published in

dispensing of justice, and public order (understood as the prevention, suppression, and punishment of criminal acts), for the following four reasons:

(a) The state would need a huge volume of information, and this information is only found in a dispersed or diffuse form in the minds of the millions of people who participate each day in the social process.

(b) The information the intervening body would need for its commands to exert a coordinating effect is predominantly tacit and inarticulable in nature, and thus it cannot be transmitted with absolute clarity.

(c) The information society uses is not "given;" it changes constantly as a result of human creativity. Hence, there is obviously no possibility of transmitting today information which will only be created tomorrow and which is precisely the information the agent of state intervention needs to achieve its objectives tomorrow.

(d) Finally and above all, to the extent state commands are obeyed and exert the desired effect on society, their coercive nature blocks the entrepreneurial creation of the very information the intervening state body most desperately needs to make its own commands coordinating (rather than maladjusting).

Not only is statism theoretically impossible, but it also produces a whole series of distorting and highly damaging peripheral effects: the encouragement of irresponsibility (as the authorities do not know the true cost of their intervention, they act irresponsibly); the destruction of the environment when it is declared a public good and its privatization is prevented; the corruption of the traditional concepts of law and justice, which are replaced by commands and "social" justice;[4] and the imitative corruption of individuals'

Spanish in 1998 as *Dinero, Crédito Bancario, y Ciclos Económicos*, 3rd ed. (Madrid: Unión Editorial, 2006).

[4]F.A. Hayek, *Law, Legislation, and Liberty: A New Statement of the Liberal Principles of Justice and Political Economy*, 3 vols. (Chicago: University of Chicago Press, 1973–79).

behavior, which becomes more and more aggressive and less and less respectful of morality and law.

The above analysis also permits us to conclude that if certain societies thrive nowadays, they do so not because of the state, but *in spite of it*.[5] For many people are still accustomed to behavior patterns that are subject to substantive laws; areas of greater relative freedom remain; and the state tends to be very inefficient at imposing its invariably clumsy, blind commands. Furthermore, even the most marginal increases in freedom provide great boosts to prosperity, which illustrates how far civilization could advance without the hindrance of statism.

Finally, we have already commented on the false belief held by all those who identify the state with the provision of the ("public") goods it now provides (poorly and at great cost) and who wrongly conclude that the disappearance of the state would necessarily mean the disappearance of its valuable services. This conclusion is drawn in an environment of constant political indoctrination at all levels (especially in the educational system, which no state wishes to lose control of, for obvious reasons), an environment where standards of "political correctness" are dictatorially imposed, and the status quo is rationalized by a complacent majority which refuses to see the obvious: that the state is nothing but an illusion created by a minority to live at others' expense, others who are first exploited, then corrupted, and then paid with outside resources (taxes) for all sorts of political "favors."

The Impossibility of Limiting the Power of the State: Its "Lethal" Character in Combination with Human Nature

Once the state exists, it is impossible to limit the expansion of its power. Granted, as Hoppe indicates, certain forms of government (like absolute monarchies, in which the king-owner will, *ceteris paribus*, be more careful in the long term to avoid "killing the goose that lays the golden eggs") will tend to expand their power and intervene somewhat less than others (like democracies, in

---

[5]Carlos Rodríguez Braun, *A Pesar Del Gobierno: 100 Críticas al Intervencionismo con Nombres y Apellidos* (Madrid: Unión Editorial, 1999).

which there are no real incentives to worry about what will happen after the next elections). It is also true that in certain historical circumstances, the interventionist tide has appeared to have been dammed to a certain extent. Nevertheless, the historical analysis is irrefutable: the state has not ceased to grow.[6] And it has not ceased to grow because the mixture of human nature and the state, as an institution with a monopoly on violence, is "explosive." The state acts as an irresistibly powerful magnet which attracts and propels the basest passions, vices, and facets of human nature. People attempt to sidestep the state's commands yet take advantage of its monopolistic power as much as possible. Moreover, in democratic contexts particularly, the combined effect of the action of privileged interest groups, the phenomena of government shortsightedness and vote buying, the megalomaniacal nature of politicians, and the irresponsibility and blindness of bureaucracies amounts to a dangerously unstable and explosive cocktail. This mixture is continually shaken by social, economic, and political crises which, paradoxically, politicians and social "leaders" never fail to use as justification for subsequent doses of intervention, and these merely create new problems while exacerbating existing ones even further.

The state has become the "idol" everyone turns to and worships. Statolatry is without a doubt the most serious and dangerous social disease of our time. We are taught to believe all problems can and should be detected in time and solved by the state. Our destiny lies in the hands of the state, and the politicians who govern it must guarantee us everything our well-being demands. Human beings remain immature and rebel against their own creative nature (an essential quality which makes their future inescapably uncertain). They demand a crystal ball to ensure not only that they know what will happen in the future, but also that any problems which arise will be resolved. This "infantilization" of the masses is deliberately fostered by politicians and social leaders, since in this way they publicly justify their existence and guarantee their popularity, predominance, and governing capacity.

---

[6]Hans-Hermann Hoppe, *Democracy − The God that Failed: The Economics and Politics of Monarchy, Democracy, and Natural Order* (New Brunswick, N.J.: Transaction Publishers, 2001).

Furthermore, a legion of intellectuals, professors, and social engineers join in this arrogant binge of power.

Not even the most respectable churches and religious denominations have reached an accurate diagnosis of the problem: that today statolatry poses the main threat to free, moral, and responsible human beings; that the state is an enormously powerful false idol which is worshipped by all and which will not countenance anyone's freeing himself from its control nor having moral or religious loyalties outside its own sphere of dominance. In fact, the state has managed something which might appear impossible *a priori*: it has slyly and systematically distracted the citizenry from the fact that the true origin of social conflicts and evils lies with the government itself, by creating scapegoats everywhere ("capitalism," the desire for profit, private property). The state then places the blame for problems on these scapegoats and makes them the target of popular anger and of the severest and most emphatic condemnation from moral and religious leaders, almost none of whom has seen through the deception nor dared until now to denounce that in this century, statolatry represents the chief threat to religion, morality, and thus, human civilization.[7]

---

[7]Perhaps the most recent notable exception appears in Pope Benedict XVI's brilliant work on *Jesus of Nazareth*. That the state and political power are the institutional embodiment of the Antichrist must be obvious to anyone with the slightest knowledge of history who reads the Pope's reflections on the most dangerous temptation the devil can put in our way:

> The tempter is not so crude as to suggest to us directly that we should worship the devil. He merely suggests that we opt for the reasonable decision, that we choose to give priority to a planned and thoroughly organized world, where God may have his place as a private concern but must not interfere in our essential purposes. Soloviev attributes to the Antichrist a book entitled *The Open Way to World Peace and Welfare*. This book becomes something of a new Bible, whose real message is the worship of well-being and rational planning.

Joseph Ratzinger, *Jesus of Nazareth*, Adrian J. Walker, trans. (London: Bloomsbury, 2007), p. 41. Redford makes similar, though much more categorical, comments. James Redford, "Jesus Is an Anarchist," Anti-state.com (2001).

Just as the fall of the Berlin Wall in 1989 provided the best historical illustration of the theorem of the impossibility of socialism, the huge failure of classical-liberal theorists and politicians to limit the power of the state perfectly illustrates the theorem of the impossibility of statism, specifically the fact that the liberal state is self-contradictory (as it is coercive, even if "limited") and theoretically impossible (since once we accept the existence of the state, it is impossible to limit the expansion of its power). In short, the "law-based state" is an unattainable ideal and a contradiction in terms as flagrant as that of "hot snow, wanton virgin, fat skeleton, round square,"[8] or that evident in the ideas of "social engineers" and neoclassical economists when they refer to a "perfect market" or the so-called "perfect-competition model."[9]

ANARCHO-CAPITALISM AS THE ONLY POSSIBLE SYSTEM OF SOCIAL COOPERATION TRULY COMPATIBLE WITH HUMAN NATURE

Statism runs counter to human nature, since it consists of the systematic, monopolistic exercise of a coercion which, in all areas where it is felt (including those corresponding to the definition of law and the maintenance of public order), blocks the creativity and entrepreneurial coordination which are precisely the most typical and essential manifestations of human nature. Furthermore, as we have already seen, statism fosters and drives irresponsibility and moral corruption, as it diverts the focus of human behavior toward a privileged pulling on the reins of political power, within a context of ineradicable ignorance that makes it impossible to know the costs of each government action. The above effects of statism appear whenever a state exists, even if every attempt is made to limit its power, an unattainable goal which renders classical liberalism a scientifically unfeasible utopia.

---

[8]Anthony de Jasay, *Market Socialism: A Scrutiny: This Square Circle* (Occasional paper 84) (London: Institute of Economic Affairs, 1990), p. 35.

[9]Jesús Huerta de Soto, "The Essence of the Austrian School," lecture delivered at the Bundesministerium für Wissenschart und Forchung, March 26, 2007, in Vienna; published in *Procesos de Mercado: Revista Europea de Economía Política* 4, no. 1 (Spring 2007): 343–50, see esp. 347–48.

It is absolutely necessary to overcome the "utopian liberalism" of our predecessors, the classical liberals, who were both naïve in thinking the state could be limited, and incoherent in failing to carry their ideas to their logical conclusion and accept the implications. Hence, today, with the twenty-first century well under way, our top priority should be to allow the (utopian and naïve) classical liberalism of the nineteenth century to be superseded by its new, truly scientific, and modern formulation, which we could call libertarian capitalism, private property anarchism, or simply, anarcho-capitalism. For it makes no sense for liberals to continue saying the same things they said one hundred fifty years ago when, well into the twenty-first century, and despite the fall of the Berlin Wall nearly twenty years ago, states have not ceased to grow and encroach upon people's individual freedoms in all areas.

Anarcho-capitalism (or "libertarianism") is the purest representation of the spontaneous market order in which all services, including those of defining law, justice, and public order, are provided through an exclusively voluntary process of social cooperation which thus becomes the focal point of research in modern economic science. In this system, no area is closed to the drive of human creativity and entrepreneurial coordination, and hence efficiency and fairness increase in the solution of problems, and all of the conflicts, inefficiencies, and maladjustments which bodies with a monopoly on violence (states) invariably cause simply by virtue of existing, are eradicated. Moreover, the proposed system eliminates the corrupting incentives created by the state, and in contrast fosters the most moral and responsible human behaviors, while preventing the emergence of any monopolistic body (state) which legitimizes the systematic use of violence and the exploitation of certain social groups (those which have no choice but to obey) by others (those which at any time have the tightest hold on the reins of state power).

Anarcho-capitalism is the only system which fully recognizes the free, creative nature of human beings and their perpetual capacity to internalize increasingly moral behavior patterns in an environment in which, by definition, no one can arrogate to himself the right to exercise monopolistic, systematic coercion. In short, in an anarcho-capitalist system, any entrepreneurial project can be tried if it attracts enough voluntary support, and therefore many possible creative solutions can be devised in a dynamic and constantly changing environment of voluntary cooperation.

The progressive replacement of states by a dynamic network of private agencies which back different legal systems and also provide all sorts of security, crime prevention, and defense services constitutes the most important item on the political and scientific agenda, as well as the most momentous social change to take place in the twenty-first century.

CONCLUSION:
THE REVOLUTIONARY IMPLICATIONS OF THE NEW PARADIGM

The revolution spearheaded in the eighteenth and nineteenth centuries by the old classical liberals against the *ancien régime* finds its natural continuity today in the anarcho-capitalist revolution of the twenty-first century. Fortunately, we have discovered the reason behind the failure of utopian liberalism as well as the need to overcome it with scientific liberalism. Also, we know that the old revolutionaries were naïve and mistaken in pursuing an unattainable ideal which, throughout the twentieth century, opened the door to the worst statist tyrannies humanity has ever known.

The message of anarcho-capitalism is markedly revolutionary. It is revolutionary in its end: the dismantling of the state and its replacement by a competitive market process in which a network of private agencies, associations, and organizations take part. It is also revolutionary in its means, particularly in the scientific, economic-social, and political spheres.

(a) *Scientific Revolution.* On the one hand, economic science becomes the general theory of the spontaneous market order extended to all social realms. On the other hand, it incorporates the analysis of the social discoordination statism produces in any area it influences (including law, justice, and public order). In addition, the different methods for dismantling the state, the transition processes involved, and the ways and effects of wholly privatizing all services now considered "public" comprise an essential field of research for our discipline.

(b) *Economic and Social Revolution*. One cannot even imagine the spectacular human achievements, advances, and discoveries that will be possible in an entrepreneurial environment completely free from statism. Even today, despite continual government harassment, a hitherto unknown civilization has begun to develop in an increasingly globalized world. It is a civilization with a degree of complexity for which the power of statism is no match, and once it is totally rid of statism, it will expand without limit. For the force of creativity in human nature is such that it inevitably sprouts up through even the thinnest cracks in the government's armor. As soon as people gain a greater awareness of the fundamentally perverse nature of the state that restricts them, and once they perceive the tremendous opportunities removed daily from their reach when the state blocks the driving force of their entrepreneurial creativity, they will in large numbers join in the social clamor for reform, the dismantling of the state, and the advancement toward a future which remains entirely unknown to us but is bound to raise human civilization to heights unimaginable today.

(c) *Political Revolution*. The daily political struggle becomes secondary to that described in (a) and (b) above. It is true that we must always support the least interventionist alternatives, in clear keeping with the efforts of classical liberals to democratically limit the state. However, the anarcho-capitalist does not stop at that; he knows, and must also do, much more. He knows that the ultimate goal is the total dismantling of the state, and this fires his entire imagination and fuels all of his political action on a daily basis. Small advances in the right direction are certainly welcome, but we must never slip into a pragmatism that forsakes the ultimate goal of putting an end to the state. For purposes of teaching and influencing the general public, we must always pursue this objective in a systematic, transparent manner.[10]

---

[10]Jesús Huerta de Soto, "El Economista Liberal y la Política," in *Manuel Fraga: Homenaje Académico*, vol. 2 (Madrid: Fundación Cánovas del Castillo), pp. 763–88; reprinted at pp. 163–92 of *Nuevos Estudios de Economía Política*. For example, one indication of the growing importance of libertarian capitalism on

For instance, the anarcho-capitalist political agenda will include ever reducing the size and power of states. Through regional and local decentralization in all areas, libertarian nationalism, the reintroduction of city-states, and secession,[11] the aim will be to block the dictatorship of the majority over the minority and to permit people to increasingly "vote with their feet" rather than with ballots. In short, the goal is for people to be able to collaborate with each other on a worldwide scale and across borders, to achieve the most varied ends without regard to states (religious organizations, private clubs, Internet networks, etc.).[12]

Moreover, let us remember that political revolutions need not be bloody. This is especially true when they result from the necessary process of social education and development, as well as from popular clamor and the widespread desire to stop the deception, lies, and coercion that prevent people from fulfilling their aims. For example, the fall of the Berlin Wall and the Velvet Revolution, which brought an end to socialism in Eastern Europe, were both basically bloodless. Along the path to this important final result, we must use all of the peaceful[13] and legal[14] means that current political systems permit.

---

the current political agenda is the article "Libertarians Rising," which appeared in the Essay section of Time magazine in 2007. Michael Kinsley, "Libertarians Rising," *Time* (October 29, 2007), p. 112.

[11]Jesús Huerta de Soto, "Teoría del Nacionalismo Liberal," in *Estudios de Economía Política*, 2nd ed. (Madrid: Unión Editorial, 2004); idem, "El Desmantelamiento del Estado y la Democracia Directa."

[12]Bruno S. Frey, "A Utopia? Government Without Territorial Monopoly," *The Independent Review* 6, no. 1 (Summer 2001): 99–112.

[13]We must never forget the prescriptions of the Spanish scholastics of the Golden Age regarding the strict conditions an act of violence must satisfy to be "just": (1) all possible peaceful means and procedures must first have been exhausted; (2) the act must be defensive (a response to concrete acts of violence) and never aggressive; (3) the means used must be proportional (e.g. the ideal of independence is not worth the life or liberty of even one human being); (4) every attempt must be made to avoid claiming innocent victims; (5) there must be a reasonable chance of success (if not, it would be unjustifiable

An exciting future is opening up, in which we will continually discover new roads that will lead us, in keeping with fundamental principles, toward the anarcho-capitalist ideal. Though this future may seem distant today, at any moment we may witness giant steps forward which will surprise even the most optimistic. Who was able to predict five years in advance that in 1989 the Berlin Wall would collapse, and with it communism itself in Eastern Europe? History has entered into an accelerated process of change, and although it will never come to a halt, it will begin an entirely new chapter when humanity, for the first time in modern history, manages to rid itself of the state once and for all and reduce it to nothing more than a dark and tragic historical relic.

৭০   ৭০   ৭০

COMMENTS ON THE SPANISH ANARCHIST TRADITION

The chart shows the different political systems and how they evolve naturally into each other. They are grouped according to the degree to which they favor statism or antistatism, and support or oppose private property.

We see how the initial (mistaken and utopian) revolutionary movement of the classical liberals against the old regime slips into the pragmatism of accepting the state and opens the door to forms of socialist totalitarianism (communism and fascism-Nazism). The fall of real socialism ushers in social democracy, which today prevails far and wide (group-think).

The liberal revolution, which owes its failure to error and naïveté on the part of classical liberals, has a still-pending stage,

---

suicide). These are wise principles, to which I would add that participation and financing must be entirely voluntary. Any act of violence which goes against one of these principles is automatically delegitimized and becomes the worst enemy of the professed objective. Finally, Father Juan de Mariana's whole theory of tyrannicide is also relevant here. Juan de Mariana, *De Rege et Regis Institutione* (Toledo: Pedro Rodríguez, 1599).

[14]As Rothbard indicated, it is not advisable to violate current laws (basically administrative commands), because in the vast majority of cases, the costs outweigh the benefits.

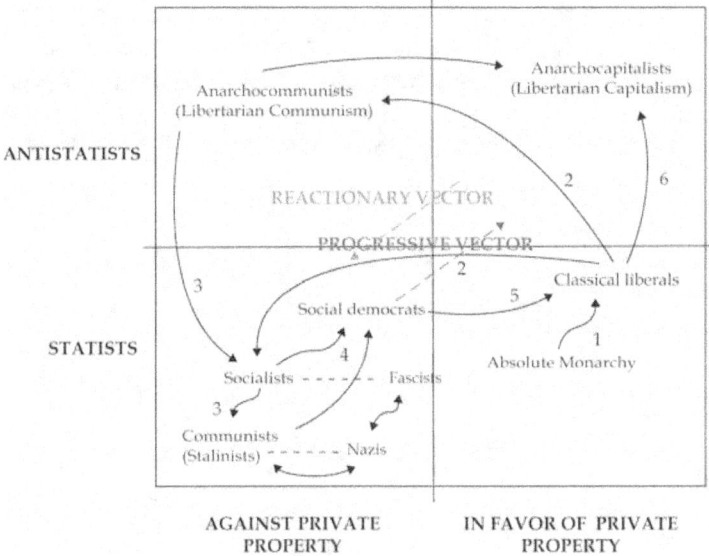

which will consist precisely of the evolution toward anarcho-capitalism.

One consequence which followed the failure of the liberal revolution was the appearance of libertarian communism, which was unanimously reviled and combated by supporters of the other political systems (particularly the most left-leaning ones), precisely due to its antistatist nature. Libertarian communism is also utopian, because its rejection of private property compels the use of systematic (i.e., "state") violence against it, thus revealing an insuperable logical contradiction and blocking the entrepreneurial social process which drives the only anarchist order scientifically conceivable: that of the capitalist libertarian market.

Spain has a long-established anarchist tradition. While we must not forget the great crimes committed by its supporters (in any case qualitatively and quantitatively less serious than those of communists and socialists), nor the contradictions in their thinking, it is true that, especially during the Spanish Civil War, anarchism was an experiment which enjoyed great popular support, though it was destined to fail. Just as with the old liberal revolution, today anarchists have before them their second great opportunity, which lies in overcoming their errors (the utopian quality of an anarchism which rejects private property) and accepting the market order as the sole, definitive path toward abolishing the state. If the Spanish anarchists of the twenty-first century can internalize these teachings from theory and history, Spain will very likely surprise the world again (this time for good, and on a large scale) by leading the theoretical and practical vanguard of the new anarcho-capitalist revolution. ❧

20

What Libertarianism Is

Stephan Kinsella

PROPERTY, RIGHTS, AND LIBERTY

Libertarians tend to agree on a wide array of policies and principles. Nonetheless it is not easy to find consensus on what libertarianism's defining characteristic is, or on what distinguishes it from other political theories and systems.

Various formulations abound. It is said that libertarianism is about: individual rights; property rights;[1] the free market; capitalism; justice; the non-aggression principle. Not all these will do,

Stephan Kinsella (stephan@stephankinsella.com) is Editor of *Libertarian Papers*. He thanks Juan Fernando Carpio, Paul Edwards, Gil Guillory, Manuel Lora, Johan Ridenfeldt, and Patrick Tinsley for helpful comments.

[1]The term "private property rights" is sometimes used by libertarians, which I have always found odd, since property rights are necessarily public, not private, in the sense that the borders or boundaries of property must be *publicly visible* so that non-owners can avoid trespass. For more on this aspect of property borders, see Hans-Hermann Hoppe, *A Theory of Socialism and Capitalism: Economics, Politics, and Ethics* (Boston: Kluwer Academic Publishers, 1989), pp. 140–41; Stephan Kinsella, "A Theory of Contracts: Binding Promises, Title Transfer, and Inalienability," *Journal of Libertarian Studies* 17, no. 2 (Spring 2003): n. 32 and accompanying text; idem, *Against Intellectual Property* (Auburn, Ala.: Ludwig von Mises Institute, 2008), pp. 30–31, 49; also Randy E. Barnett, "A Consent Theory of Contract," *Columbia Law Review* 86 (1986): 303.

however. Capitalism and the free market describe the catallactic conditions that arise or are permitted in a libertarian society, but do not encompass other aspects of libertarianism. And individual rights, justice, and aggression collapse into property rights. As Murray Rothbard explained, individual rights are property rights.[2] And justice is just giving someone his due, which depends on what his rights are.[3]

The non-aggression principle is also dependent on property rights, since what aggression is depends on what our (property) rights are. If you hit me, it is aggression *because* I have a property right in my body. If I take from you the apple you possess, this is trespass, aggression, only *because* you own the apple. One cannot identify an act of aggression without implicitly assigning a corresponding property right to the victim.

So capitalism and the free market are too narrow, and justice, individual rights, and aggression all boil down to, or are defined in terms of, property rights. What of property rights, then? Is this what differentiates libertarianism from other political philosophies—that we favor property rights, and all others do not? Surely such a claim is untenable. After all, a property right is simply the *exclusive right to control a scarce resource.*[4] Property rights specify

---

[2]Murray N. Rothbard, "'Human Rights' as Property Rights," in *The Ethics of Liberty* (New York and London: New York University Press, 1998); idem, *For A New Liberty: The Libertarian Manifesto* (rev. ed.; New York: Libertarian Review Foundation, 1985), pp. 42 *et pass.*

[3]"Justice is the constant and perpetual wish to render every one his due. . . . The maxims of law are these: to live honestly, to hurt no one, to give every one his due." *The Institutes of Justinian: Text, Translation, and Commentary*, trans. J.A.C. Thomas (Amsterdam: North-Holland, 1975).

[4]As Professor Yiannopoulos explains:

> *Property* may be defined as an *exclusive right to control an economic good . . .*; it is the name of a concept that refers to the rights and obligations, privileges and restrictions that govern the relations of man with respect to *things of value*. People everywhere and at all times desire the possession of things that are necessary for survival or valuable by cultural definition and which, as a result of the demand placed upon them, *become scarce*. Laws enforced by organized society

which persons own — have the right to control — various scarce resources in a given region or jurisdiction. Yet everyone and every political theory advances *some* theory of property. None of the various forms of socialism deny property rights; each socialism will specify an owner for every scarce resource.[5] If the state nationalizes an industry, it is asserting ownership of these means of production. If the state taxes you, it is implicitly asserting ownership of the funds taken. If my land is transferred to a private developer by eminent domain statutes, the developer is now the owner. If the law allows a recipient of racial discrimination to sue his employer for a sum of money — he is the owner of the money.[6]

Protection of and respect for property rights is thus not unique to libertarianism. What is distinctive about libertarianism is its *particular property assignment rules* — its view as to *who is the owner* of each contestable resource, and how to determine this.

> control the competition for, and guarantee the enjoyment of, these desired things. What is guaranteed to be one's own is property. . . . [Property rights] *confer a direct and immediate authority over a thing.*

A.N. Yiannopoulos, *Louisiana Civil Law Treatise, Property* (West Group, 4th ed. 2001), §§ 1, 2 (first emphasis in original; remaining emphasis added). See also *Louisiana Civil Code* (http://tinyurl.com/lacivcode), Art. 477 ("Ownership is the right that confers on a person direct, immediate, and exclusive authority over a thing. The owner of a thing may use, enjoy, and dispose of it within the limits and under the conditions established by law").

[5]For a systematic analysis of various forms of socialism, from Socialism Russian-Style, Socialism Social-Democratic Style, the Socialism of Conservatism, the Socialism of Social Engineering, see Hoppe, *A Theory of Socialism and Capitalism*, chaps. 3–6. Recognizing the common elements of various forms of socialism and their distinction from libertarianism (capitalism), Hoppe incisively defines socialism as "an institutionalized interference with or aggression against private property and private property claims." Ibid., p. 2. See also the quote from Hoppe in note 9, below.

[6]Even the private thief, by taking your watch, is implicitly acting on the maxim that *he* has the right to control it — that he is its owner. He does not deny property rights — he simply differs from the libertarian as to *who the owner is*. In fact, as Adam Smith observed: "If there is any society among robbers and murderers, they must at least, according to the trite observation, abstain from robbing and murdering one another." Adam Smith, *The Theory of Moral Sentiments* (Indianapolis: Liberty Fund, [1759] 1982), II.II.3.

PROPERTY IN BODIES

A system of property rights assigns a particular owner to every scarce resource. These resources obviously include natural resources such as land, fruits of trees, and so on. Objects found in nature are not the only scarce resources, however. Each human actor has, controls, and is identified and associated with a unique human body, which is also a scarce resource.[7] Both human bodies and non-human scarce resources are desired for use as means by actors in the pursuit of various goals.

Accordingly, any political theory or system must assign ownership rights in human bodies as well as in external things. Let us consider first the libertarian property assignment rules with respect to human bodies, and the corresponding notion of aggression as it pertains to bodies. Libertarians often vigorously assert the non-aggression principle. As Ayn Rand said, "So long as men desire to live together, no man may *initiate* — do you hear me? No man may *start* — the use of physical force against others."[8] Or, as Rothbard put it:

---

[7] As Hoppe observes, even in a paradise with a superabundance of goods,

> every person's physical body would still be a scarce resource and thus the need for the establishment of property rules, i.e., rules regarding people's bodies, would exist. One is not used to thinking of one's own body in terms of a scarce good, but in imagining the most ideal situation one could ever hope for, the Garden of Eden, it becomes possible to realize that one's body is indeed the prototype of a scarce good for the use of which property rights, i.e., rights of exclusive ownership, somehow have to be established, in order to avoid clashes.

Hoppe, *A Theory of Socialism and Capitalism*, pp. 8–9. See also Stephan Kinsella & Patrick Tinsley, "Causation and Aggression," *Quarterly Journal of Austrian Economics* 7, no. 4 (Winter 2004): 111–12 (discussing the use of other humans' bodies as means).

[8] Ayn Rand, "Galt's Speech," in *For the New Intellectual*, quoted in *The Ayn Rand Lexicon*, "Physical Force" entry (www. aynrandlexicon.com). Ironically, Objectivists often excoriate libertarians for having a "context-less" concept of aggression — that is, that "aggression" or "rights" is meaningless unless these concepts are embedded in the larger philosophical framework of Objectivism

The libertarian creed rests upon one central axiom: that no man or group of men may aggress against the person or property of anyone else. This may be called the "nonaggression axiom." "Aggression" is defined as the initiation of the use or threat of physical violence against the person or property of anyone else. Aggression is therefore synonymous with invasion.[9]

In other words, libertarians maintain that the only way to violate rights is by *initiating* force — that is, by committing aggression. (Libertarianism also holds that, while the initiation of force against another person's body is impermissible, force used *in response* to aggression — such as defensive, restitutive, or retaliatory/punitive force — is justified.[10]) Now in the case of the body, it is clear what

---

— despite Galt's straightforward definition of aggression as the initiation of physical force against others.

[9]Rothbard, *For A New Liberty*, p. 23. See also idem, *The Ethics of Liberty*: "The fundamental axiom of libertarian theory is that each person must be a self-owner, and that no one has the right to interfere with such self-ownership" (p. 60), and "What . . . aggressive violence means is that one man invades the property of another without the victim's consent. The invasion may be against a man's property in his person (as in the case of bodily assault), or against his property in tangible goods (as in robbery or trespass)" (p. 45). Hoppe writes:

> If . . . an action is performed that uninvitedly invades or changes the physical integrity of another person's body and puts this body to a use that is not to this very person's own liking, this action . . . is called *aggression*. . . . Next to the concept of action, *property* is the most basic category in the social sciences. As a matter of fact, all other concepts to be introduced in this chapter — aggression, contract, capitalism and socialism — are definable in terms of property: *aggression* being aggression against property, *contract* being a nonaggressive relationship between property owners, *socialism* being an institutionalized policy of aggression against property, and *capitalism* being an institutionalized policy of the recognition of property and contractualism.

Hoppe, *A Theory of Socialism and Capitalism*, pp. 12, 7.

[10]See Stephan Kinsella, "A Libertarian Theory of Punishment and Rights," *Loyola of Los Angeles Law Review* 30 (1997): 607–45; idem, "Punishment and Proportionality: The Estoppel Approach," *Journal of Libertarian Studies* 12, no. 1 (Spring 1996): 51–73.

aggression is: invading the borders of someone's body, commonly called battery, or, more generally, *using the body of another without his or her consent*.[11] The very notion of interpersonal aggression presupposes property rights in bodies—more particularly, that each person is, at least *prima facie*, the owner of his own body.[12]

Non-libertarian political philosophies have a different view. Each person has some limited rights in his own body, but not complete or exclusive rights. Society or the state, purporting to be society's agent, has certain rights in each citizen's body, too. This partial slavery is implicit in state actions and laws such as taxation, conscription, and drug prohibitions. The libertarian says that each person is the full owner of his body: he has the right to control his body, to decide whether or not he ingests narcotics, joins an army, and so on. Those various non-libertarians who endorse any such state prohibitions, however, necessarily maintain that the state, or society, is at least a partial owner of the body of those subject to such laws—or even a complete owner in the case of conscriptees or non-aggressor "criminals" incarcerated for life. Libertarians believe in *self*-ownership. Non-libertarians—statists—of all stripes advocate some form of slavery.

Self-ownership and Conflict Avoidance

Without property rights, there is always the possibility of conflict over contestable (scarce) resources. By assigning an owner to each resource, legal systems make possible conflict-free use of

---

[11]The following terms and formulations may be considered as roughly synonymous, depending on context: aggression; initiation of force; trespass; invasion; unconsented to (or uninvited) change in the physical integrity (or use, control or possession) of another person's body or property.

[12]"*Prima facie*," because some rights in one's body are arguably forfeited or lost in certain circumstances, e.g. when one commits a crime, thus authorizing the victim to at least use defensive force against the body of the aggressor (implying the aggressor is to that extent not the owner of his body). For more on this see Kinsella, "A Theory of Contracts," pp. 11–37; idem, "Inalienability and Punishment: A Reply to George Smith," 14, no. 1 *Journal of Libertarian Studies* (Winter 1998–99): 79–93; and idem, "Knowledge, Calculation, Conflict, and Law," *Quarterly Journal of Austrian Economics* 2, no. 4 (Winter 1999): n. 32.

resources, by establishing visible boundaries that non-owners can avoid. Libertarianism does not endorse just any property assignment rule, however.[13] It favors *self*-ownership over *other*-ownership (slavery).

The libertarian seeks property assignment rules *because* he values or accepts various *grundnorms* such as justice, peace, prosperity, cooperation, conflict-avoidance, civilization.[14] The libertarian

---

[13]On the importance of the concept of scarcity and the possibility of conflict for the emergence of property rules, see Hoppe, *A Theory of Socialism and Capitalism*, p. 134; and the discussion thereof in Stephan Kinsella, "Thoughts on the Latecomer and Homesteading Ideas; or, Why the Very Idea of 'Ownership' Implies that only Libertarian Principles are Justifiable," *Mises Economics Blog* (Aug. 15, 2007).

[14]"Grundnorm" was legal philosopher Hans Kelsen's term for the hypothetical basic norm or rule that serves as the basis or ultimate source for the legitimacy of a legal system. See Hans Kelsen, *General Theory of Law and State*, trans. Anders Wedberg (Cambridge, Mass.: Harvard University Press, 1949). I employ this term to refer to the fundamental norms presupposed by civilized people, e.g., in argumentative discourse, which in turn imply libertarian norms.

That the libertarian *grundnorms* are, in fact, necessarily presupposed by all civilized people to the extent they are civilized — during argumentative justification, that is — is shown by Hoppe in his "argumentation ethics" defense of libertarian rights. See on this Hoppe, *A Theory of Socialism and Capitalism*, chap. 7; Stephan Kinsella, "New Rationalist Directions in Libertarian Rights Theory," *Journal of Libertarian Studies* 12, no. 2 (Fall 1996): 313–26; idem, "Defending Argumentation Ethics," *Anti-state.com* (Sept. 19, 2002).

For discussion of *why* people (to one extent or the other) *do* value these underlying norms, see Stephan Kinsella, "The Division of Labor as the Source of Grundnorms and Rights," *Mises Economics Blog* (April 24, 2009), and idem, "Empathy and the Source of Rights," *Mises Economics Blog* (Sept. 6, 2006). See also idem, "Punishment and Proportionality," pp. 51 & 70:

> People who are civilized are . . . concerned about *justifying* punishment. They want to punish, but they also want to know that such punishment is justified — they want to legitimately be able to punish. . . . Theories of punishment are concerned with justifying punishment, with offering decent men who are reluctant to act immorally a reason why they may punish others. This is useful, of course, for offering moral men guidance and assurance that they may properly deal with those who seek to harm them.

view is that self-ownership is the only property assignment rule compatible with these *grundorms*; it is implied by them. As Professor Hoppe has shown, the assignment of ownership to a given resource must not be random, arbitrary, particularistic, or biased, if it is to actually be a property norm that can serve the function of conflict-avoidance.[15] Property title has to be assigned to one of competing claimants based on "the existence of an objective, intersubjectively ascertainable link between owner and the" resource claimed.[16] In the case of one's own body, it is the unique relationship between a person and his body—his *direct and immediate control* over his body, and the fact that, at least in some sense, a body is a given person and vice versa—that constitutes the objective link sufficient to give that person a claim to his body superior to typical third party claimants.

Moreover, any outsider who claims another's body cannot deny this objective link and its special status, since the outsider also necessarily presupposes this in his own case. This is so because in seeking dominion over the other, in asserting ownership over the other's body, he has to presuppose his own ownership of his body, which demonstrates he does place a certain significance on this link, at the same time that he disregards the significance of the other's link to his own body.[17]

Libertarianism realizes that only the self-ownership rule is universalizable and compatible with the goals of peace, cooperation, and conflict avoidance. We recognize that each person is *prima facie* the owner of his own body because, by virtue of his unique link to and connection with his own body—his direct and immediate control over it—he has a better claim to it than anyone else.

---

[15]See Hoppe, *A Theory of Socialism and Capitalism*, pp. 131–38. See also Kinsella, "A Libertarian Theory of Punishment and Rights," pp. 617–25; idem, "Defending Argumentation Ethics."

[16]Hoppe, *A Theory of Socialism and Capitalism*, p. 12.

[17]For elaboration on this point, see Stephan Kinsella, "How We Come To Own Ourselves," *Mises Daily* (Sept. 7, 2006); idem, "Defending Argumentation Ethics"; Hoppe, *A Theory of Socialism and Capitalism*, chaps. 1, 2, and 7.

PROPERTY IN EXTERNAL THINGS

Libertarians apply similar reasoning in the case of other scarce resources—namely external objects in the world that, unlike bodies, were at one point *unowned*. In the case of bodies, the idea of aggression being impermissible immediately implies self-ownership. In the case of external objects, however, we must identify who the owner is before we can determine what constitutes aggression.

As in the case with bodies, humans need to be able to use external objects as means to achieve various ends. Because these things are scarce, there is also the potential for conflict. And as in the case with bodies, libertarians favor assigning property rights so as to permit the peaceful, conflict-free, productive use of such resources. As in the case with bodies, then, property is assigned to the person with the best claim or link to a given scarce resource—with the "best claim" standard based on the goals of permitting peaceful, conflict-free human interaction and use of resources.

Unlike human bodies, however, external objects are not parts of one's identity, are not directly controlled by one's will—and, significantly, they are *initially unowned*.[18] Here, the libertarian realizes that the relevant objective link is *appropriation*—the transformation or embordering of a previously unowned resource, Lockean homesteading, the first use or possession of the thing.[19] Under this

---

[18]For further discussion of the difference between bodies and things homesteaded for purposes of rights, see Kinsella, "A Theory of Contracts," pp. 29 *et seq.*; and idem, "How We Come To Own Ourselves."

[19]On the nature of appropriation of unowned scarce resources, see Hoppe's and de Jasay's ideas quoted and discussed in Kinsella, "Thoughts on the Latecomer and Homesteading Ideas," and note 24, below. In particular, see Hoppe, *A Theory of Socialism and Capitalism*, pp. 13, 134–36, 142–44; and Anthony de Jasay, *Against Politics: On Government, Anarchy, and Order* (London & New York: Routledge, 1997), pp. 158 *et seq.*, 171 *et seq.*, *et pass.* De Jasay is also discussed extensively in my "Book Review of Anthony de Jasay, *Against Politics: On Government, Anarchy, and Order*," *Quarterly Journal of Austrian Economics* 1, no. 3 (Fall 1998): 85–93. De Jasay's argument presupposes the value of justice, efficiency, and order. Given these goals, he argues for three principles of politics: (1) if in doubt, abstain from political action (pp. 147 *et seq.*); (2) the feasible is presumed free (pp. 158 *et seq.*); and (3) let exclusion stand (pp. 171 *et*

approach, the first (prior) user of a previously unowned thing has a *prima facie* better claim than a second (later) claimant solely by virtue of his being earlier.

Why is appropriation the relevant link for determination of ownership? First, keep in mind that the question with respect to such scarce resources is: who is the resource's *owner*? Recall that ownership is the *right* to control, use, or possess,[20] while possession is *actual* control – "the *factual authority* that a person exercises over a corporeal thing."[21] The question is not who has physical possession; it is who has ownership. Thus, asking who is the owner of a resource presupposes a distinction between ownership and possession – between the right to control, and actual control. And the answer has to take into account the nature of previously-unowned things: to-wit, that they must at some point become owned by a first owner.

The answer must also take into account the presupposed goals of those seeking this answer: rules that permit conflict-free use of resources. For this reason, the answer cannot be *whoever has the resource or whoever is able to take it* is its owner. To hold such a view is to adopt a might makes right system where ownership collapses

---

seq.). In connection with principle (3), "let exclusion stand," de Jasay offers insightful comments about the nature of homesteading or appropriation of unowned goods. De Jasay equates property with its owner's "excluding" others from using it, for example by enclosing or fencing in immovable property (land) or finding or creating (and keeping) movable property (corporeal, tangible objects). He concludes that since an appropriated thing has no other owner, *prima facie* no one is entitled to object to the first possessor claiming ownership. Thus, the principle means "let ownership stand," i.e., that claims to ownership of property appropriated from the state of nature or acquired ultimately through a chain of title tracing back to such an appropriation should be respected. This is consistent with Hoppe's defense of the "natural" theory of property. Hoppe, *A Theory of Socialism and Capitalism*, pp. 10–14 & chap. 7. For further discussion of the nature of appropriation, see Jörg Guido Hülsmann, "The A Priori Foundations of Property Economics," *Quarterly Journal of Austrian Economics* 7, no. 4 (Winter 2004): 51–57.

[20]See note 4 and accompanying text, above.

[21]Yiannopoulos, *Property*, § 301 (emphasis added); see also *Louisiana Civil Code*, Art. 3421 ("Possession is the *detention* or *enjoyment* of a *corporeal thing*, movable or immovable, that one holds or exercises by himself or by another who keeps or exercises it in his name"; emphasis added).

into possession for want of a distinction.[22] Such a "system," far from avoiding conflict, makes conflict inevitable.[23]

---

[22]See, in this connection, the quote from Adam Smith in note 6, above.

[23]This is also, incidentally, the reason the mutualist "occupancy" position on land ownership is unlibertarian. As mutualist Kevin Carson writes:

> For mutualists, *occupancy and use* is the only legitimate standard for establishing ownership of land, regardless of how many times it has changed hands. An existing owner may transfer ownership by sale or gift; but the new owner may establish legitimate title to the land *only by his own occupancy and use.* A change in occupancy will amount to a change in ownership. . . . The *actual occupant is considered the owner of a tract of land,* and any attempt to collect rent by a self-styled ["absentee"] landlord is regarded as a *violent invasion of the possessor's absolute right of property.*

Kevin A. Carson, *Studies in Mutualist Political Economy* (Self-published: Fayetteville, Ark., 2004, http://mutualist.org/id47.html), chap. 5, sec. A (emphasis added). Thus, for mutualism, the "actual occupant" is the "owner"; the "possessor" has the right of property. If a homesteader of land stops personally using or occupying it, he loses his ownership. Carson contends this is compatible with libertarianism:

> [A]ll property rights theories, including Lockean, make provision for *adverse possession and constructive abandonment of property.* They differ only in degree, rather than kind: in the "stickiness" of property. . . . There is a large element of convention in any property rights system—Georgist, mutualist, and both proviso and nonproviso Lockeanism—in determining what constitutes transfer and abandonment.

Kevin A. Carson, "Carson's Rejoinders," *Journal of Libertarian Studies* 20, no. 1 (Winter 2006): 133 (emphasis added). In other words, Lockeanism, Georgism, mutualism are all types of libertarianism, differing only in degree. In Carson's view, the gray areas in issues like adverse possession and abandonment leave room for mutualism's "occupancy" requirement for maintaining land ownership.

But the concepts of adverse possession and abandonment cannot be stretched to cover the mutualist occupancy requirement. The mutualist occupancy view is essentially a *use* or *working* requirement, which is distinct from doctrines of adverse possession and abandonment. The doctrine of abandonment in positive law and in libertarian theory is based on the idea that ownership *acquired* by *intentionally* appropriating a previously unowned thing

Instead of a might-makes-right approach, from the insights noted above it is obvious that *ownership presupposes the prior-later*

may be lost when the owner's intent to own terminates. Ownership is acquired by a merger of possession and intent to own. Likewise, when the intent to own ceases, ownership does too—this is the case with both abandonment of ownership *and* transfer of title to another person, which is basically an abandonment of property "in favor" of a particular new owner. See Kinsella, "A Theory of Contracts," pp. 26–29; also *Louisiana Civil Code*, Art. 3418 ("A thing is abandoned when its owner relinquishes possession with the intent to give up ownership") and Art. 3424 ("To acquire possession, one must *intend to possess as owner* and must take *corporeal possession* of the thing"; emphasis added).

The legal system must therefore develop rules to determine when property has been abandoned, including default rules that apply *in the absence of clear evidence.* Acquisitive prescription is based on an implicit presumption that the owner has abandoned his property claims if he does not defend it within a reasonable time period against an adverse possessor. But such rules apply to *adverse* possessors—those who possess the property *with the intent to own* and in a sufficiently public fashion that the owner knows or should know of this. See Yiannopoulos, *Property,* § 316; see also Louisiana Civil Code, Art. 3424 ("To acquire possession, one must *intend to possess as owner* and must take corporeal possession of the thing"; emphasis added) and Art. 3476 (to acquire title by acquisitive prescription, "The possession must be continuous, uninterrupted, peaceable, *public,* and unequivocal"; emphasis added); see also Art. 3473. The "public" requirement means that the possessor possesses the proper openly as *owner,* adverse or hostile to the owner's ownership—which is not the case when, for example, a lessee or employee uses an apartment or manufacturing facility under color of title and permission from the owner. Rules of abandonment and adverse possession are default rules that apply when the owner has not made his intention sufficiently clear—by neglect, apathy, death, absence, or other reason.

(In fact, the very idea of abandonment rests on the distinction between ownership and possession. Property is more than possession; it is a right to possess, originating and sustained by the owner's *intention* to possess as owner. And abandonment occurs when the intent to own terminates. This happens even when the (immediately preceding) owner temporarily maintains possession but has lost ownership, as when he gives or sells the thing to another party (as I argue in Kinsella, "A Theory of Contracts," pp. 26–29).)

Clearly, default abandonment and adverse possession rules are categorically different from a working requirement, whereby ownership is lost in the *absence of use.* See, e.g., *Louisiana Mineral Code,* § 27 (http://law.justia.com/louisiana/codes/21/87935.html) ("A mineral servitude is extinguished by: . . . prescription resulting from nonuse for ten years"). Loss of ownership is *not* l ost by nonuse, however, and a working requirement is *not* implied by default rules

distinction: whoever any given system specifies as the owner of a resource, he *has a better claim than latecomers*.[24] If he does not, then he is *not an owner*, but merely the current user or possessor, in a might-makes-right world in which there is no such thing as ownership — which contradicts the presuppositions of the inquiry itself. If the first owner does not have a better claim than latecomers, then he is not an owner, but merely a possessor, and there is no such thing as ownership. More generally, latecomers' claims are inferior to those of prior possessors or claimants, who either

---

regarding abandonment and adverse possession. See, e.g., *Louisiana Civil Code*, Art. 481 ("The ownership and the possession of a thing are distinct. . . . Ownership exists independently of any exercise of it and *may not be lost by nonuse*. Ownership is lost when acquisitive prescription accrues in favor of an adverse possessor"; emphasis added). Carson is wrong to imply that abandonment and adverse possession rules can yield a working (or *use* or *occupancy*) requirement for maintaining ownership. In fact, these are distinct and independent legal doctrines. Thus, when a factory owner contractually allows workers to use it, or a landlord permits tenants to live in an apartment, there is no question that the owner *does not intend to abandon* the property, and there is no *adverse* possession (and if there were, the owner could institute the appropriate action to eject them and regain possession; see Yiannopoulos, *Property*, §§ 255, 261, 263–66, 332–33, 335 *et pass.*; *Louisiana Code of Civil Procedure* (http://tinyurl.com/lacodecivproc), Arts. 3651, 3653 & 3655; *Louisiana Civil Code*, Arts. 526 & 531). There is no need for "default" rules here to resolve an ambiguous situation. (For another critique of Carson, see Roderick T. Long, "Land-Locked: A Critique of Carson on Property Rights," *Journal of Libertarian Studies* 20, no. 1 (Winter 2006): 87–95.)

A final note here: I cite positive law here not as an argument from authority, but as an illustration that even the positive law carefully distinguishes between possession and ownership; and also between a *use* or *working* requirement to maintain ownership, and the potential to lose title by abandonment or adverse possession, to illustrate the flaws in Carson's view that an occupancy requirement is just one variant of adverse possession or default abandonment rules. Furthermore, the civilian legal rules cited derive from legal principles developed over the ages in largely decentralized fashion, and can thus be useful in our own libertarian efforts to develop concrete applications of abstract libertarian principles. See Stephan Kinsella, "Legislation and the Discovery of Law in a Free Society," *Journal of Libertarian Studies* 11, no. 2 (Summer 1995): 132–81; also idem, "Knowledge, Calculation, Conflict, and Law," pp. 60–63 (discussing Randy Barnett's views on the distinction between abstract legal rights and more concrete rules that serve as guides to action).

[24]See Kinsella, "Thoughts on the Latecomer and Homesteading Ideas."

homesteaded the resource or who can trace their title back to the homesteader or earlier owner.[25] The crucial importance of the prior-later distinction to libertarian theory is why Professor Hoppe repeatedly emphasizes it in his writing.[26]

---

[25]See *Louisiana Code of Civil Procedure*, Art. 3653, providing:

> To obtain a judgment recognizing his ownership of immovable property . . ., the plaintiff . . . shall:
>
> (1) Prove that he has acquired ownership from a previous owner or by acquisitive prescription, if the court finds that the defendant is in possession thereof; or
>
> (2) Prove a better title thereto than the defendant, if the court finds that the latter is not in possession thereof.
>
> When the titles of the parties are traced to a common author, he is presumed to be the previous owner.

See also *Louisiana Civil Code*, Arts. 526, 531–32; Yiannopoulos, *Property*, §§ 255–79 & 347 *et pass.*

[26]See, e.g., Hoppe, *A Theory of Socialism and Capitalism*, pp. 141–44; idem, *The Economics and Ethics of Private Property: Studies in Political Economy and Philosophy* (Boston: Kluwer, 1993), pp. 191–93; see also discussion of these and related matters in in Kinsella, "Thoughts on the Latecomer and Homesteading Ideas"; idem, "Defending Argumentation Ethics"; and idem, "How We Come To Own Ourselves." See also, in this connection, Anthony de Jasay, *Against Politics*, further discussed and quoted in Kinsella, "Thoughts on the Latecomer and Homesteading Ideas," as well as in Kinsella, "Book Review of Anthony de Jasay, *Against Politics*." See also de Jasay's argument (note 17, above) that since an appropriated thing has no other owner, *prima facie* no one is entitled to object to the first possessor claiming ownership. De Jasay's "let exclusion stand" idea, along with the Hoppean emphasis on the prior-later distinction, sheds light on the nature of homesteading itself. Often the question is asked as to what types of acts constitute or are sufficient for homesteading (or "embordering" as Hoppe sometimes refers to it); what type of "labor" must be "mixed with" a thing; and to what property does the homesteading extend? What "counts" as "sufficient" homesteading? We can see that the answer to these questions is related to the issue of what is the thing in dispute. In other words, if B claims ownership of a thing possessed (or formerly possessed) by A, then the very framing of the dispute helps to identify what the thing is in dispute, and what counts as possession of it. If B claims ownership of a given resource, he wants the right to control it, to a certain extent, and according to its nature. Then the question becomes, did someone

Thus, the libertarian position on property rights is that, in order to permit conflict-free, productive use of scarce resources, property titles to particular resources are assigned to particular owners. As noted above, however, the title assignment must not be random, arbitrary, or particularistic; instead, it has to be assigned based on "the existence of an objective, intersubjectively ascertainable link between owner and the" resource claimed.[27] As can be seen from the considerations presented above, the link is the physical transformation or embordering of the original homesteader, or a chain of title traceable by contract back to him.[28]

CONSISTENCY AND PRINCIPLE

Not only libertarians are civilized. Most people give some weight to some of the above considerations. In their eyes, a person is the owner of his own body — usually. A homesteader owns the resource he appropriates — unless the state takes it from him "by operation of law."[29] This is the principal distinction between libertarians and

---

else previously control "it" (whatever is in dispute), according to its nature; i.e., did someone else already homestead it, so that B is only a latecomer? This ties in with de Jasay's "let exclusion stand" principle, which rests on the idea that if someone is actually able to control a resource such that others are excluded, then this exclusion should "stand." Of course, the physical nature of a given scarce resource and the way in which humans use such resources will determine the nature of actions needed to "control" it and exclude others.

[27]Hoppe, *A Theory of Socialism and Capitalism*, p. 12.

[28]On the title transfer theory of contract, see Williamson M. Evers, "Toward a Reformulation of the Law of Contracts," *Journal of Libertarian Studies* 1, no. 1 (Winter 1977): 3–13; Rothbard, "Property Rights and the Theory of Contracts," chap. 19 in idem, *The Ethics of Liberty*; Kinsella, "A Theory of Contracts."

[29]State laws and constitutional provisions often pay lip service to the existence of various personal and property rights, but then take it back by recognizing the right of the state to regulate or infringe the right so long as it is "by law" or "not arbitrary." See, e.g., *Constitution of Russia*, Art. 25 ("The home shall be inviolable. No one shall have the right to get into a house against the will of those living there, except for the cases established by a federal law or by court decision") and Art. 34 ("Everyone shall have the right to freely use his or her abilities and property for entrepreneurial or any other economic activity not prohibited by the law"); *Constitution of Estonia*, Art. 31 ("Estonian

non-libertarians: libertarians are consistently opposed to aggression, defined in terms of invasion of property borders, where property rights are understood to be assigned on the basis of self-ownership, in the case of bodies; and on the basis of prior possession or homesteading and contractual transfer of title, in the case of other things.

This framework for rights is motivated by the libertarian's consistent and principled valuing of peaceful interaction and cooperation — in short, of civilized behavior. A parallel to the Misesian view of human action may be illuminating here. According to Mises, human action is aimed at alleviating some *felt uneasiness.*[30] Thus, means are employed, according to the actor's understanding of causal laws, to achieve various ends — ultimately, the removal of some felt uneasiness.

Civilized man feels uneasy at the prospect of violent struggles with others. On the one hand, he wants, for some practical reason, to control a given scarce resource and to use violence against another person, if necessary, to achieve this control. On the other hand, he also wants to avoid a wrongful use of force. Civilized man, for some reason, feels reluctance, uneasiness, at the prospect of violent interaction with his fellow man. Perhaps he has reluctance to violently clash with others over certain objects because he has empathy with them.[31] Perhaps the instinct to cooperate has is a result of social evolution. As Mises noted,

---

citizens shall have the right to engage in commercial activities and to form profit-making associations and leagues. The law may determine conditions and procedures for the exercise of this right"); *Universal Declaration of Human Rights*, Art. 17 ("Everyone has the right to own property alone as well as in association with others. . . . No one shall be arbitrarily deprived of his property"); Art. 29(2) ("In the exercise of his rights and freedoms, everyone shall be subject only to such limitations as are determined by law solely for the purpose of securing due recognition and respect for the rights and freedoms of others and of meeting the just requirements of morality, public order and the general welfare in a democratic society").

[30]Ludwig von Mises, *Human Action*, 4th ed. (Irvington-on-Hudson, N.Y.: Foundation for Economic Education, 1996), pp. 13–14, *et pass.*

[31]For further discussion of the role of empathy in the adoption of libertarian *grundnorms*, see note 14, above.

> There are people whose only aim is to improve the con-
> dition of their own ego. There are other people with
> whom awareness of the troubles of their fellow men
> causes as much uneasiness as or even more uneasiness
> than their own wants.[32]

Whatever the reason, because of this uneasiness, when there is the potential for violent conflict, the civilized man seeks justification for the forceful control of a scarce resource which he desires but which some other person opposes. Empathy—or whatever spurs man to adopt the libertarian *grundnorms*—gives rise to a certain form of uneasiness, which gives rise to *ethical action*. Civilized man may be defined as he who seeks justification for the use of interpersonal violence. When the inevitable need to engage in violence arises—for defense of life or property—civilized man seeks justification. Naturally, since this justification-seeking is done by people who are inclined to reason and peace (justification is after all a peaceful activity that necessarily takes place during discourse),[33] what they seek are rules that are fair, potentially acceptable to all, grounded in the nature of things, universalizable, and that permit conflict-free use of resources. Libertarian property rights principles emerge as the only candidate that satisfies these criteria. Thus, if civilized man is he who seeks justification for the use of violence, the libertarian is he who is *serious* about this endeavor. He has a deep, principled, innate opposition to violence, and an equally deep commitment to peace and cooperation.

For the foregoing reasons, libertarianism may be said to be the political philosophy that *consistently* favors social rules aimed at promoting peace, prosperity, and cooperation. It recognizes that the only rules that satisfy the civilized *grundnorms* are the self-ownership principle and the Lockean homesteading principle, applied as consistently as possible.

---

[32]Ibid, p. 14.

[33]As Hoppe explains, "Justification—proof, conjecture, refutation—is *argumentative* justification." Hoppe, *The Economics and Ethics of Private Property*, p. 384; also ibid, p. 413, and also Hoppe, *A Theory of Socialism and Capitalism*, p. 130 *et pass.*

And as I have argued elsewhere, because the state necessarily commits aggression, the consistent libertarian, in opposing aggression, is also an anarchist.[34] ❧

---

[34]See Stephan Kinsella, "What it Means to be an Anarcho-Capitalist," *LewRockwell.com* (Jan. 20, 2004); also Jan Narveson, "The Anarchist's Case," in *Respecting Persons in Theory and Practice* (Lanham, Md.: Rowman & Littlefield, 2002).

21

Classical Natural Law and Libertarian Theory

Carlo Lottieri

NATURAL RIGHTS AND LIVING LAW:
TOWARD AN INTEGRATION OF ROTHBARD AND LEONI

I f libertarianism wishes to give up modern political categories, it has to think about law in a different way.

Murray N. Rothbard, the most important exponent of the radical libertarian school, is right when he rejects the historicism and relativism of legal realism and when — for the same reasons — he criticizes Hayek and Leoni. But unfortunately, he does not really grasp the function of the evolution into classic natural law. Furthermore, his idea of building a libertarian code is completely inconsistent with his frequent references to the Greek and Christian legal heritage.[1]

Carlo Lottieri (lottieri@tiscalinet.it) is an Italian political philosopher with the University of Siena and Istituto Bruno Leoni whose main interests are in contemporary libertarian thought. Most recently he edited an anthology of writings by Bruno Leoni, *Law, Liberty and the Competitive* Market (New Brunswick, N.J.: Transaction, 2009).

[1]The notion of code — in despotic Prussia as well as in Napoleonic France — was connected to the needs of a sovereign power oriented to absorbing the legal order and changing any norm in a simple political decision.

In *For a New Liberty*, Rothbard points out that the history of a changing and evolving law can be useful in order to find just rules: "since we have a body of common law principles to draw on, however, the task of reason in correcting and amending the common law would be far easier than trying to construct a body of systematic legal principles *de novo* out of the thin air."[2] But the relationship between common law and natural law must be seen differently. Common law is not only an interesting tool for discovering natural law: it has its specific role. Positive law needs to interact with natural law principles, but even the latter cannot be considered as self-sufficient.

Moreover, in his defense of rationality, Rothbard does not realize that law cannot be entirely read into the praxeological framework, which is axiomatic and deductive. The division of theory and history puts some disciplines into opposition with others, but above all it makes a distinction within any single field of study. Economics, for instance, is a theoretical science if considered as political economics, but a historical and empiric activity if it analyzes what happened in the past.[3] This is also true for legal studies, because they have a theoretical part but, at the same time, include many other aspects which are, on the contrary, historical and cannot be examined using logical and *a priori* methods.

In his methodological writings, Rothbard distinguishes between *empiricism* and *experience*, and remarks that the refusal of the first does not imply a devaluation of the second. When he criticizes Mises for his Kantian approach, he finds in human experience exactly the main source of the axioms, the fundamental truths that are the starting point of a theory based on deductive logic.[4] But

---

[2]Murray N. Rothbard, *For a New Liberty: The Libertarian Manifesto* (Lanham, Maryland: University Press of America, 1973), p. 318.

[3]See Ludwig von Mises, *Theory and History* (Auburn, Ala.: Mises Institute, 1985).

[4]See Murray N. Rothbard "In Defense of 'Extreme Apriorism'," *The Logic of Action One* (London: Edward Elgar, 1997), pp. 100–08. Exactly in this sense Larry Sechrest outlines that a "careful examination of Austrian thought will reveal that the praxeological method itself is fundamentally empirical." See Larry J. Sechrest, "Praxeology, Economics, and Law: Issues and Implications,"

before the law, Rothbard seems to minimize the contextual and non-theoretical dimension of a large part of legal controversies and especially of positive law.

Using the Thomist framework, in this essay I will emphasize the importance of the *lex naturalis*, at the same time highlighting a *lex humana* deeply rooted in the complexity of different ages and societies, related to the subjectivity and specificity of opinions which cannot be fruitfully examined by a praxeological approach. Many problems, and even some inconsistencies of Rothbardian theory are a consequence of it.

Moreover, the way Rothbard deals with the arguments of causality and liability shows an inadequate understanding of the anthropology of the Austrian School, which moves from a study of human action (intentional and rational) and not by a simple behaviorist analysis.

In integrating Rothbardian libertarianism with positive law, an important contribution comes from Bruno Leoni, who in *Freedom and the Law* and other writings developed an original contribution to classical liberalism. The Italian scholar can help to improve some parts of Rothbard's libertarian theory of law. If the author of *The Ethics of Liberty* is much more grounded in natural law and even less naïve before *Wertfreiheit*,[5] Leoni can correct some limits of the Rothbardian approach and its incapacity to perceive the specificity of law: a practical and largely empirical science, historically situated and essentially oriented to finding reasonable solutions for very specific cases.

Quarterly Journal of Austrian Economics 7, no. 4 (Winter 2004): 22. In the Aristotelian-Thomist tradition, experience is a source of knowledge: we meet the world (which is common to all us) and we have experiences with a meaning. Rothbard shares this perspective when he distinguishes his position and that of Mises. For this reason, Sechrest opposes Hoppe (and Mises) because of their Kantianism and shares the Rothbardian perspective, embracing the project of "positing an empirical base for the Austrian School." Ibid., p. 23.

[5]See, in particular, Murray N. Rothbard, "The Symposium on Relativism: A Critique," 1960, memo conserved in the Ludwig von Mises Archives, now in Murray N. Rothbard, *Diritto, natura e ragione. Scritti inediti versus Hayek, Mises, Strauss e Polanyi*, Roberta Modugno, ed. (Soveria Mannelli: Rubbettino, 2005), pp. 125–45.

If philosophy of law has to investigate the eternal and immutable principles of justice, juridical scholarship must find the best translation of these for the specific problems of a society. For this reason, taking Leoni seriously means imagining a meeting point of natural law doctrine and the requirements of a positive law as a reality in evolution. And, it implies an effort to transfer into the legal context the Misesian methodology and its radical separation of theory and history: the sphere of axiomatic and deductive studies (*praxeology*) and the sphere of research based on experience (*history*).

We have to remember that specific attention to the historical and evolving features of legal orders has been a crucial element of the Austrian School since its origins. In his *Investigations into the Method of the Social Sciences*, Carl Menger praises the Historical School of Jurisprudence (Gustav Hugo, Friedrich Carl von Savigny, Barthold Georg Niebuhr), whose origins he dated back to Edmund Burke. Menger also highlights the individualistic content of evolutionary law with the goal of helping the classical liberal tradition to rediscover its lost roots: "law, like language, is (at least originally) not the product in general of an activity of public authorities aimed at producing it, nor in particular is it the product of positive legislation. It is, instead, the unintended result of a higher wisdom, of the historical development of the nations."[6]

It is exactly in this sense that we can understand Leoni's preference for evolutionary law (Anglo-Saxon law and Roman *jus civile*): a law not oriented to preserve tradition or spontaneous order *per se*. On the contrary, Leoni thinks that a polycentric and evolutionary order is in a better position to safeguard individual rights. Rules that emerge from the interpersonal exchange of claims are tools that can effectively protect society from the rulers.

As student of English legal history, Leoni shows a strong interest in the *common law of nature* that was at the heart of Edward Coke's perspective. In fact, in that theory law does not express an anti-rationalist attitude, but on the contrary, embodies natural reason emerging in an evolutionary way. This legal culture is

---

[6]Carl Menger, *Investigations into the Method of the Social Sciences*, Francis J. Nock, trans. (New York: New York University Press, 1985), pp. 174–75.

improved by various contributions (practical, pragmatic, professional) of many people. In this way, law is the consequence of a human activity oriented towards bettering reality using intelligence and experience.

Criticizing modern legal systems, Leoni remarks that

> there is far more legislation, there are far more group decisions, far more rigid choices, and far fewer "*laws written in living tables*," far fewer individual decisions, far fewer free choices in all contemporary political systems that would be necessary in order to preserve individual freedom of choice.[7]

Even if he never adhered to a consistent natural law theory, Leoni tried a sort of reconciliation of natural law and legal realism (positive law rightly understood), exploring the possibility of conjugating the flexibility of ancient common law and the just principles of a universal moral theory.

Leoni had a strong interest in the exploration of the libertarian potentialities of a similar perspective. In his writings, there are many elements of a radical libertarianism refusing any coercion. When some participants of the Claremont seminar about *Freedom and the Law* asked him who should choose the judges in a free society, he answered: "it is rather immaterial to establish in advance who will appoint the judges, for, in a sense, everybody could do so, as happens to a certain extent when people resort to private arbiters to settle their own quarrels."[8] In his opinion, the contemporary, statist system should disappear, leaving room for a competitive order of private courts. The convergence of Leoni and Rothbard is evident on many levels, because both imagine the end of the state monopoly on justice and security, with the purpose of opening the road to an institutional competition between people in charge to avoid criminal behaviors.[9]

---

[7]Bruno Leoni, *Freedom and the Law*, 3rd ed. (Indianapolis: Liberty Fund, 1991), p. 131; my italics.

[8]Ibid., p. 129.

[9]The notion of polycentric order—as it has been formulated by Michael Polanyi—can be useful to appreciate the complexity of a system based on

It is also for this reason that Rothbardian libertarian theory can find in Leoni and, above all, in his understanding of law, the way to overcome its theoretical and practical difficulties.

FROM PRAXEOLOGY TO THYMOLOGY:
THE ROLE OF POSITIVE LAW

In its daily development, law refers back to principles, but at the same time it concerns modest but not negligible disputes. Legal reasoning lives essentially in this pragmatic context and it leaves the specific topics of natural law in the background.

In Mises's thought, there is a notion that is extremely useful in helping us grasp the relationship between theory and practice in the law. In fact, in *Theory and History*, he opposes praxeology to thymology, which is in close relationship with history.[10] Thymology is a branch of history and "derives its knowledge from historical experience."[11] It stands for that set of empirical knowledge of psychological, sociological and even factual character that we use to find our way in relationships with other people. This "literary psychology" is the condition of a rational behavior: "for lack of any better tool, we must take recourse to thymology if we want to anticipate other people's future attitudes and actions."[12]

When Leoni returns to the legal realism tradition (to the law *in action* that Roscoe Pound opposes to the *law in books*) and remarks on a correspondence between positive law and what is foreseeable

---

checks and balances and operating without a written constitution imposed by an authority. Polanyi points out that the invisible hand pushing towards a free-market order is not so different from the forces defining *common law* and scientific research. The progress of knowledge is grounded on the principles that "every proposed addition to the body of science is subjected to a regular process of scrutiny." We find a similar logic in the legal order, because *common law* "constitutes a sequence of adjustments between succeeding judges, guided by a parallel interaction between the judges and the general public." Michael Polanyi, *The Logic of Liberty* (Chicago: University of Chicago Press, 1980), pp. 163, 162.

[10]Following Mises, "thymology is a historical discipline." Mises, *Theory and History*, p. 313.

[11]Ibid., p. 272.

[12]Ibid., p. 313.

(often using the formula *id quod plerumque accidit*),[13] he highlights that the positive law is always intelligible in a thymologic perspective. In his explicit purpose of applying Misesian methodology to law, Leoni discovers a praxeological dimension (the most theoretical part, coinciding with the analysis of the individual claims and their interaction), but also another thymological dimension (entirely depending on experience, common opinions and traditions).

His idea is that positive law has a strong relationship with customs. As practical activity, law must reduce uncertainty: it is for this reason that a creditor's claim is *legal*, because generally a debtor pays back what he has received, while the thief's claim is *illegal*, because generally people do not steal. The probabilistic analysis is purely empirical, but it is not unreasonable. Our behavior is led very often by the rationality of our past experiences and by our prejudices.

In this sense, Leonian theory of the individual claim is at the same time praxeological and thymological.

It is *praxeological* because it draws in a deductive way the theoretical conditions of the exchange and the meeting of different individual claims. When, in his writings, he opposes the point of view of the legal professionals (moving from the norms) and the perspective of the philosophers (interested in the origin of the rules), his aim is to reject the positivism prevalent in legal theory. He has the project of grasping the *a priori* categories—*à la* Reinach—subtending all legal orders. When he finds in the individual claim the starting point of a juridical relation, Leoni thinks he has understood a universal datum: his "demand and supply law." If prices emerge from the meeting of the actions of people supplying and demanding, the norms are the effect of the interaction of different claims. This is a universal regularity and, on this ground, he also develops his theoretical (praxeological) remarks about the relationship between legislation and living law, certainty and law, and so on.

But—as in Mises—this positive evaluation of praxeology does not imply a negative opinion of history or of the competence of

---

[13]Translation: "what usually happens."

lawyers. On the contrary, Leoni has the ambition of describing the distinct but connected roles of every sphere.

For this reason, his theory is largely thymological when he remarks that, if it is true – as Mises says – that "thymology tells no more than that man is driven by various innate instincts, various passions, and various ideas,"[14] then it is evident that norms are accepted when they satisfy the claims, the principles and the desires largely shared in a specific society; and the law profession-als are exactly well-informed about this peculiar and "local" envi-ronment. When Leoni emphasizes the qualities of the *ius civile* and the ancient common law, he aims to highlight the role of the lawyers and of all the people engaged in the solution to specific and concrete disputes.

Positive Law and History

This is a very important point in a large part of the philosophi-cal tradition. The main Greek and medieval thinkers were clear about the link between natural law (universal) and the contingent (historically defined and, *lato sensu*, subjective) dimension of situ-ations that we can understand only in specific contexts, as result of the cross of individual preferences.

In Aristotle, for instance, it is clear that there are some univer-sal principles judging every positive law. This passage is very out-spoken at this regard:

> Universal law is the law of nature. For there really is, as every one to some extent divines, a natural justice and injustice that is binding on all men, even on those who have no association or covenant with each other. It is this that Sophocles's Antigone clearly means when she says that the burial of Polyneices was a just act in spite of the prohibition: she says that it was just by nature.
>
> Not of to-day or yesterday it is,
> But lives eternal: none can date its birth.[15]

---

[14]Mises, *Theory and History*, p. 313.
[15]Aristotle, *Rhetoric*, 1373b.

At the same time, Aristotle holds the opinion that "there are two kinds of right and wrong conduct towards others, one provided for by written ordinances, the other by unwritten." In the second group, a class "springs from exceptional goodness or badness" and it is related to honor, gratitude, friendship, and so on. But the other "makes up for the defects of a community's written code of law. This is what we call equity." This Aristotelian notion of *equity* is very important. And, at the same time, we have to perceive the relationship between this idea of equity ("the sort of justice which goes beyond the written law")[16] and the idea of *phronesis*, as prudence and practical wisdom.

Equity and *phronesis* do not destroy the universal natural law, but they give us a way to understand how it can be possible to arrange some (difficult) situations. We can build a bridge from the natural law and the positive law of our — imperfect — relationship with the others. The perception of the human limits and the complexity of the world push us to appreciate the knowledge preserved by a complex system of legal notions, as developed through centuries of legal history.

For Aristotle, it was clear that a purely deductive method would not suffice to satisfy our exigencies.

Aquinas's lesson moves in the same direction, as is clear in his distinguishing between Natural Law (*Lex naturalis*) and Human Law (*Lex humana*). If the moral principles of natural law are unchangeable and can be rationally investigated by moving from some solid axioms, human law is the consequence of cultural and historic contingencies. As *Summa Theologiae* says, "the natural law contains certain universal precepts which are everlasting, whereas human law contains certain particular precepts according to various emergencies." At the same time, "nothing can be absolutely unchangeable in things that are subject to change. And, therefore, human law cannot be altogether unchangeable."[17]

---

[16]Ibid., 1374a.

[17]Saint Thomas Aquinas, *On Law, Morality, and Politics*, William P. Baumgarth and Richard J. Regan, eds. (Indianapolis-Cambridge: Hackett Publishing Company, 1988), p. 77.

Aquinas adds that "custom has the force of law, abolishes law, and is the interpreter of law."[18] He accepts customary law because it has the approval of individuals: "because, by the very fact that they tolerate it, they seem to approve of that which is introduced by custom."[19] This law that is dissolved in custom is not natural law, because Aquinas does not believe we can accept a legal order that has historically emerged if it is against justice; but historical evolution modifies positive law and even opens room for different interpretations.[20]

Law and Interpretation

In positive law, there is an essential function of interpretation, because there is always a distance between the norm and the cases in point. As Giorgio Agamben explains, "in the case of law, the application of a norm is no way contained within the norm and cannot be derived from it; otherwise, there would have been the need to create the grand edifice of trial law. Just as between language and world, so between the norm and its application there is no external nexus that allows one to be derived immediately from the other."[21]

What's the meaning of this? Using general rules in concrete and specific situations always implies a decision, and (at least hypothetically) an arbitrary power. The difference between the *law in the books* and the *law in action* is largely a consequence of this.

In many writings, Chaïm Perelmen remarks that legal logic is:

---

[18]Ibid., p. 80.

[19]Ibid., p. 81. As Anthony Lysska has pointed out, Aquinas "was aware of cultural diversity regarding mores." Anthony J. Lysska, *Aquinas's Theory of Natural Law: An Analytic Reconstruction* (Oxford: Clarendon Press, 1996), p. 112.

[20]In the latest development of his theory, Leoni introduced an interesting notion when he spoke about the *a-legal* claims (in Italian, *pretese agiuridiche*). Thus, we have not only *legal* and *illegal* claims, but also some claims not completely accepted today, that in the future might be considered lawful and legitimate. See Bruno Leoni, "Appunti di filosofia del diritto," in *Il diritto come pretesa* (Macerata: Liberilibri, 2004), p. 200.

[21]Giorgio Agamben, *State of Exception* (Chicago: The University of Chicago Press, 2005), p. 40.

> a very elaborated, individual case of practical reasoning, which is not a formal demonstration, but an argumentation aiming to persuade and convince those whom it addresses that such a choice, decision or attitude is preferable to concurrent choices, decisions and attitudes.

Perelman adds: "what characterizes an argumentation is its non-constraining character."[22] So, legal reasoning "is not presented as a formally valid deduction from non-temporal truths," because "reasons considered good at one period of time or in one milieu are not in another; they are socially and culturally conditioned as are the convictions and the aspirations of the audience they must convince."[23]

In spite of his disputable skepticism, Perelman is right when he points out that positive law is a "practical" activity, because it is a case-solving operation and often emerges from a transaction of different interests. To a large extent, law is not a science: it is a technique oriented to solving specific problems, because lawyers and judges do not search for the truth, but only the *legal* truth.

Law and Intentionality

If we analyze liability and causality in Rothbard, we have to recall the fundamental principles of the Austrian tradition.

In a recent article, Hans-Hermann Hoppe criticized his mentor and highlighted how it is contradictory to focus attention on the birth of property (with the homesteading of land) and then to exclude it, accepting a strict liability theory whose positivist and behaviorist origins are evident. Hoppe remarks that "homesteading implies intent," a subjective element; on the contrary, Rothbard's theory of causation and liability ignores this aspect.[24] Austrian School scholars emphasize the role of intentionality as a

---

[22]Chaïm Perelman, *Justice, Law and Argument. Essays on Moral and Legal Reasoning*, with an Introduction by Harold J. Berman (Dordrecht: Reidel, 1980), p. 129.

[23]Ibid., p. 131.

[24]For Hoppe, in Rothbard there is "a strict liability theory." Hans-Hermann Hoppe, "Property, Causality, and Liability," *Quarterly Journal of Austrian Economics* 7, no. 4 (Winter 2004): 88–89.

crucial element at the moment of the origin of private property and of its negation (theft, aggression, etc.).

Not all physical invasions imply liability and, to the contrary, some actions are liable even if there is no physical invasion. In economics, Rothbard was perfectly aware of this and was always very critical of economic schools with positivistic leanings. In 1985, in the Preface to *Theory and History* by Mises, he attacks mainstream positivism, remarking that "to become truly scientific like physics and the other natural sciences, then, economics must shun such concepts as purposes, goals and learning: it must abandon man's mind and write only of mere events."[25] But the main mistake of the American scholar is in analyzing *only simple events*, avoiding the problem of *intentionality* and *subjective liability*, and the consequent need to understand a specific action—made by a particular person, in that one moment and context.

Hoppe is right when he notes a contradiction in Rothbard between this theory of strict liability and the defense of homesteading, which implies another vision of ethics and a different anthropology. When Rothbard condemns as aggression the act of a man claiming and occupying a land previously "homesteaded" by other people, his arguments call for a well-defined idea of morality that it is not consistent with that oversimplified and behaviorist theory of causality and liability.

AN ARISTOTELIAN-THOMIST LIBERTARIANISM

For all these reasons, the Thomist distinction between natural law and human law is fundamental, especially if by *lex humana* we do not conceive of the state law, but our ever-imperfect translation, into norms, of our aspiration to live in a just society. As Paul Sigmund correctly remarked, "*human law* is the application to *specific circumstances* of the precepts of reason contained in the natural law."[26] This mediation is always unsatisfying, but at the same time necessary.

---

[25]Murray N. Rothbard, "Preface" to Mises, *Theory and History*, p. iii.

[26]Paul E. Sigmund, *Natural Law in Political Thought* (Cambridge Mass.: Winthrop, 1971), p. 39; the italics are mine.

Rothbard and Perelman make the symmetrically opposite mistake, because neither admits the autonomy of natural law and positive law. If Perelman reduces natural law to positive law (and reason to reasonableness), Rothbard reduces positive law to natural law (and reasonableness to reason). However, we have to admit the existence of a higher and objective dimension of law (where the rational method of Rothbard is justified) and of a much more prosaic and lower level, which can obtain many advantages from the dialogical and rhetorical approach used by Perelman.

The awareness of the need to mediate between the *a priori* principles of natural law and a largely inductive knowledge of the legal experience is not always present in Rothbard. But that's why the intellectual heritage of Leoni can be useful in the attempt to develop a libertarian legal theory aiming to protect the dignity and freedom of the individual. [27]

If, in Rothbard, there is the risk of ignoring the specificity of legal reasoning, Leoni remarks on the empirical features of the law and adopts a Misesian standpoint in putting into the right perspective human experience and the role it plays in the practical unfolding of our existence.

Leoni perceives the importance of the *positive law*, also in a libertarian and anti-statist perspective. The vision of what is *just by nature* has to be rooted in a particular time, embodied in specific institutions and recognizable in many different situations. But the Italian thinker was quite aware that this proposal was a return to the old tradition of natural law. In a very interesting passage, he criticizes Kelsen, saying that sociology of law is "the modern heir of the natural law."[28] And he specifies his idea in this way:

---

[27]In this sense, natural law has to be ever conceived in a strict relationship with the contingency of social reality. If all were governed by destiny, there would be no room for natural law (because its normative features imply human liberty). But at the same time it is true that the ever-changing character of social relationships forces natural law to have a specific link with history.

[28]Bruno Leoni, *Lezioni di filosofia del diritto* (Soveria Mannelli: Rubbettino, 2004), p. 160.

contemporary sociology of law schools can be considered, in a limited sense, and without the derogatory features used by Kelsen, the "modern heirs of natural law," exactly because they are inclined to re-evaluate in "law" the element of the "persuasions" leading the action of people, instead of the "legal order" conceived as dogmatics did.[29]

CONCLUSION

In spite of his positivism, Leoni can help us grasp the true nature of classical natural law, because he does not prospect for a "libertarian code" like the one envisioned by Rothbard, somewhat conceived on the model of the state legal systems. On the contrary, *Freedom and the Law* can be the starting-point for a more "classical" understanding of libertarian natural law actually rooted in the Aristotelian-Thomistic tradition.

In other words, in Leoni there is a wide scope for juridical research and for historical evolution, because of his belief in a *living law* in continuous and close interaction with reality. The legal order has some "essential" elements, but it changes through time, and for this reason it requires constant and challenging work to adjust rules and behavior.

If we return to the classics, we can better understand the main problems.

Thomist rationalism moves from the awareness of reason's limits. Sigmund highlights exactly this when he says that "Aquinas's system of natural law is and must be incomplete. He could not admit the Aristotelian possibility that nature could provide fully for man's fulfillment."[30] Rothbard himself is not far from this when he points out that a rational approach needs an understanding of the structural imperfection of our minds: "No man is omniscient or infallible—a law, by the way, of man's nature."[31] But this observation has to have significant consequences for legal theory. ᔋ

---

[29]Bruno Leoni, "Oscurità ed incongruenze nella dottrina kelseniana del diritto," in *Scritti di scienza politica e teoria del diritto* (Milan: Giuffrè, 1980) p. 202.

[30]Sigmund, *Natural Law in Political Thought*, p. 46.

[31]Murray Rothbard, *The Ethics of Liberty* (Atlantic Highlands, N.J.: Humanities Press, 1982), p. 11.

22

Why We Have Rights

Christian Michel

R ights are the means by which we can reasonably predict human behavior. Without predictability, the existence of higher life forms would be impossible. The water source should be found at the end of the same track beaten each morning; berries which have always been edible should not suddenly become poisonous; species which have never posed a threat should not suddenly become predatory. When humans or animals experience something that goes directly against fundamental expectations, stress and anxiety ensue, even when the consequences are not life threatening. The purpose of science and of gaining personal experience is to establish a chain of cause and effect with which we can then anticipate events. We can count on the bridge to bear our weight, the plane to defy gravity, and on drugs to cure us. Science boosts our sense of confidence in the world even if, through changing our environment, it itself, in turn, creates the unexpected.

The degree of confidence we have in our predictions diminishes when we are dealing with the behavior of higher life forms. Evolution programs in freedom; indeed freedom is fundamental to evolution. If in fleeing, antelope always veered to the right, their predators

Christian Michel (cmichel@cmichel.com) is a financial consultant in London and Geneva. He is president of Libertarian International and a director of ISIL and of the Libertarian Alliance.

would have already wiped out the species. We humans are programmed to find individual and original solutions to our problems; it is both the elevation and the tragedy of the human condition.

Natural Rights

Anticipating human behavior is therefore a risky business. We are one of many species whose members kill one another. Preying on our fellows is a fundamental feature of humanity that falls into direct conflict however with another feature — man as a social animal. How can we reconcile our violent impulses with the need to live together? Society demands that predation be checked. As a group member, we have reasonable expectations concerning other members: that they will not murder us in our sleep; that they will not assault us when we go out at night, for instance. These expectations do not only concern our person but our property as well. All human languages have a concept of a personal pronoun and a gerund. These indicate the bond that a human being establishes between herself and another, between himself and an object: not just any man, but *my* friend; not just any tool, but *mine*, one which I have made, which I have used and which I can reasonably expect to use again. That bond is established through birth (*my* child), between consenting adults (*my* spouse), through homesteading (*my* land, which I settled before anybody else did), through transfer by mutual consent (*my* book for which I have paid the price asked by the seller). Who could make a stronger claim? Those who are not the parents? Those who have not first tilled the soil? Those who have not paid for the book?

By publicly declaring this bond, we are counting on others to respect it. We are counting on reaping the harvest from the field we went to all the trouble of sowing. This expectation is reasonable and when it is dashed, especially through the deliberate actions of other members of our society (confiscating an owner's dwelling, taking a child away from her mother) we feel stress, anxiety and deep resentment.

A society that placed no bounds on rape, pillage, and murder would disintegrate. Its members would defect. Without these limitations, society would be impossible. It is intrinsic to the nature of every social group that each member can rely on others not to arbitrarily rob them of their lives or their assets. Each of us reasonably declares this as a *right*. Humans are fundamentally social animals (there is no such thing as a non-socialized human being), and it is in the nature of society for these rights to be at least partially respected. This is why these are termed *natural rights* – not that it is in the nature of human beings to have rights (I am not going to open this debate), but that it is in the nature of human societies.

These rights were not invented by governments, as the proponents of positive rights maintain, nor have they arisen on the back of nothing more than convention. They are the very stuff of social existence. A ragtag bunch of shipwreck survivors dragging themselves ashore on a desert island would have to respect these rights from the outset, simply in order to function as a social unit, even before establishing any institution. The purpose of politics is to create exceptions to rights, so that rights are no longer shared identically by all members of society.

There are two forms of exception:

- Everyone is exempted from respecting another person's rights in *certain* clearly defined circumstances (for instance, each of us has the right to kill our aggressor if we are acting in self-defense).

- Certain clearly defined persons are exempted from respecting other people's rights in *all* circumstances. They are the government. The government may rob and kill with impunity when they declare this transgression to be in the name of "taxation," "just war," or "reasons of state."

IMPLEMENTING RIGHTS

We not only demand of people that they refrain from attacking us, we base our own set of reasonable expectations on their behavior. Should their behavior fail to meet our expectations – we experience disappointment, stress, and anxiety; we feel wronged.

A custom is a good example of a behavior that it would be reasonable to assume will be perpetuated. In many societies, custom dictates the giving of gifts, for instance, at a wedding. A relative failing to respect this custom would offend, or at least annoy, the bride and groom. It would be appropriate to sanction this failure to comply with their reasonable expectations through a well-placed remark or by neglecting to invite the offending relative to the next family occasion. By the same token, if for years a villager has been taking a shortcut across a neighbor's field without any opposition on the neighbor's part, she would feel resentment and a sense of loss, should the neighbor suddenly bar her route.

These expectations would have been perfectly legitimate, just as the stress and anxiety at seeing them disappointed is understandable. They would have been even better founded, and would have become indisputable rights, had, for example, the villager signed an agreement according her the right of way across her neighbor's field.

The parties' intentions and their reasonable expectations concerning their respective behavior suffice to create a right. But as popular wisdom reminds us: "that which goes without saying is much better said, and even better written down!"

Rights born of such contracts and agreements are no longer natural, nor inherent, nor common to all societies (as is respect for life and property). They illustrate the wide breadth of human commitments according to their historical context and level of development (the sale of a radio frequency would have made scant sense in medieval times). Parties devise strategies, base investments, and enter into further agreements with other parties on the strengths of these promises. Were the contracting party to renege on their obligations, those relying on them would be disappointed and sometimes gravely injured.

THE TRANSFERENCE OF RIGHTS

Conflicting desires reign in every human heart. These desires compete fiercely for a human being's limited resources: his time, his body, his energy, the use of his material possessions. Our moral life centers on setting priorities for these irreconcilable desires (to work or laze around, to drink or drive, to have an affair or to stay faithful, to focus on career ambitions or to bring up a family). The majority of our choices indicate the value that we place on bonds, as each bond has a value, even if that value is "priceless" as when people say: "I wouldn't part with that for love or money." Value is that which one acts to gain and/or keep, as in the words of Ayn Rand.[1] We cannot make a distinction concerning the nature of the value we place on bonds—only concerning their intensity. The death of a child, the loss of an object, of a job, of a hope, causes us vastly different levels of anxiety and suffering, but that sense of loss is always felt. The best evidence for the common nature of these bonds is our ability to substitute one for another. Values are fungible. Some would refuse and others would jump at the chance of a juicy promotion at the expense of a colleague according to the respective value they place on loyalty and money.

Each of us has the right to attempt to create a bond—or to choose not to do so. Charlotte has the right to reject the bond that Werther would like to create between them, even if it drives the young Werther to commit suicide. He is expecting a form of happiness from this bond which is not what she has in mind. She is looking to achieve this happiness through creating a bond with someone else, Albert (whilst running the inevitable risk of being disappointed). In much the same way, the owners of the Cherry Orchard in Chekhov's play of the same name reject Lopakhin's crass offer to divide it into building lots. They badly need the money, but they place even a greater value on the orchard's magical beauty.

Therefore, the only limit to our creating new bonds with people (both in relation to themselves and to objects) is their right of refusal. We do not want to be forced into a marriage, friendship, employment, or to be forced to buy or sell, and we find it reasonable not to impose these demands on others. We intrinsically believe that each of us should have the possibility of evaluating his existing ties, to exchange these or not to do so, in accordance with what he believes will be the satisfaction that he and his counterpart will each derive from that exchange.

However, this is not always the case, as can be seen in the following discussion.

---

[1] *The Ayn Rand Lexicon: Objectivism from A to Z*, Harry Binswanger, ed. (New York: New American Library, 1986), "values" entry.

FALSE RIGHTS—POSSESSION

In the 1970s, I was a frequent visitor to New York. There, Cornell, a young man from the South Bronx, took me under his wing. His sense of property was highly selective: inviolable if it was a case of one of his acquaintances—he wouldn't have walked off with my ink pen; anyone else's was fair game. One day, when I made a passing remark about how nice it would be to cycle through Central Park, he immediately suggested he should get me a bike. "How many gears do you want? What color?" No doubt he would have got me the bike of my dreams within 48 hours.

My friend Cornell would have been bound by his promise. We would have entered into a contract, but concerning an article which did not belong to him, and consequently one which would not have belonged to me either. The chain of transfers by mutual consent would have been broken. Someone's deliberate act would have deprived a man, somewhere or other, of the bicycle he counted on. *His* bicycle. His travel plans thwarted, both the bike's usage value and its expected resale value gone.

What if Cornell had been a trickster trumped? Surely he would have felt the same anger and frustration as his victim if, looking forward to delivering to me what he had promised, one of his ilk had pinched that bike. But, in taking possession of that bicycle, Cornell had not been assigned the right to sever the bond between this object and its owner. Only through the parties' consent may a bond to an object be assigned, without disappointing their expectations and causing them suffering.

Only rights are transferable, not property itself. Those who take possession of a piece of property disregarding the owner's intention to transfer his right do not break the bond between that property and its owner.[2] What grounds would I have had to object, had

---

[2]Hoppe discusses the importance of objective ("intersubjectively ascertainable") links between owners and scarce resources in Hans-Hermann Hoppe, *A Theory of Socialism and Capitalism: Economics, Politics, and Ethics* (Boston: Kluwer Academic Publishers, 1989), pp. 12, 212 n.2, *et pass*; idem, *Eigentum, Anarchie und Staat: Studien zur Theorie des Kapitalismus* (Opladen: Westdeutscher Verlag, 1987), pp. 98–100); idem, "Four Critical Replies," in

the owner come and reclaimed what had never stopped being *his* bicycle?[3]

FALSE RIGHTS — THE LEGALIZATION OF THEFT

In others, we hope to find certain behaviors, although these behaviors neither stem from their personal commitment, nor are set in stone by custom: we would like them to be polite, helpful, and hospitable. If my car breaks down, I would like a driver to give me a lift to the next village, but it would be unreasonable to assume that the first one who comes along will be the one to do it; I do not have any right to assistance. I have a reasonable expectation that the employees of an establishment open to the public will treat me with courtesy, but is it my right? Precedents would imply so, but the right to demand deference towards customers belongs to the employer, if she has taken care to incorporate this specific written clause into her employment contracts.

On the other hand, if I pay pension contributions or health insurance premiums, I am "counting" on the service providers to deliver. As far as I am concerned, I am covered for these eventualities. I would feel seriously let down were these organizations to renege on their obligations through either dishonesty or bankruptcy. But can I reasonably require of people who do not know me, and who do not have any personal obligation to me, to care for me in my old age; to cover the cost of my hospitalization or to support me whilst unemployed?

Governments claim a quasi-monopoly on social support which lends them the legitimacy of their power. They create and fulfill expectations by forcing taxpayers to bail out social security and pension systems.

The Economics and Ethics of Private Property: Studies in Political Economy and Philosophy (Boston: Kluwer, 1993), p. 242. See also discussion of same in Stephan Kinsella, "How We Come to Own Ourselves," Mises.org Daily Article (September 7, 2006).

[3]On the importance of the prior-later distinction, see Hoppe, *A Theory of Socialism and Capitalism*, chaps. 1, 2, 7 et pass.; Kinsella, "How We Come to Own Ourselves," text at n. 4.

But, in fulfilling this expectation, doesn't this place them in the same position as Cornell, offering me something that doesn't belong to him? What's the difference? From him as well, I was certain of receiving the bike, but at the cost of the owner's frustration and resentment and by thwarting his travel plans, a cost that neither I nor Cornell were willing to bear, so how come we would impose it on someone else? Does not forced redistribution make each beneficiary a receiver of stolen goods?

Commands

This brings us to the other obvious ways of creating predictability in society: not through rights, but through commands. After all, as Benjamin Franklin famously remarked, there are only two certainties in this mortal coil: death and taxes. The government sends out tax demands to millions of households and can with reasonable certainty expect that at least 95% of people will comply. This predictability is even greater when members of another form of racket threaten to nail your kneecaps to the floor should you fail to stump up your protection money within three days.

Thus, there are two means of creating predictability in human societies: commands (to do something) and rights (that we may not be subjected to something). *The fundamental difference between liberalism and all other political philosophies is that, in all instances, liberals accord rights precedence over commands.*

The Moral Order

A command works better when it is internalized. Rather than waiting for the master to give an order, the individual carries that master within herself at all times. Information no longer needs to travel up and down the hierarchy. The individual is deemed to have already accepted the existence of commands to apply in each and every circumstance. This is the goal of morality.

But a moral code is intrinsically a personal commitment. It creates predictability for that individual. We can hope that a great number of individuals internalize certain core values, but just as we have seen with hospitality and mutual aid we cannot legitimately demand it. The confusion of morality with legislation forms the root of fundamentalism. Politics based on moral order is a contradiction in terms and are doomed to failure.

In a complex world where no situation ever presents itself in exactly the same fashion, rights foster negotiation to adjust individual actions. The market is the medium for these adjustments. But when the law has been internalized, the individual has no one with whom to negotiate adjustments (can one negotiate with oneself?). Faced with a new situation, an individual would be inflicting a useless privation on himself and/or his loved ones were he to apply a more rigorous moral criterion than his own morality would demand; on the other hand, he would end up experiencing guilt were he to act with laxity. Economists recognize that in this situation where dialogue is absent, contracts are impossible: it is called a command economy. Prices are set outside the market: too high—and production surplus results in wastage; too low—and demand will remain unsatisfied. In all cases, commands, either internal or external, in the moral realm or in the economy, coupled with the impossibility of negotiations weaken the social fabric.

There is no island left in our globalized world, no place to hide. History engages all. Those human groups where dialogue and negotiation are stifled are extremely vulnerable now that they are in contact with other groups that have reached a higher more liberal stage of development. Societies that are insufficiently complex adapt through violent transformation, as, say, many Muslim societies today, or are shattered out of existence, as are "first nations."

Of course, a fraught relationship exists between centers and margins, majorities and minorities, dominant and subordinate cultures, with the *realization that dissidence may not only be repressed by the dominant, but in a sense actually created by it.* In other words, herd morality, being intrinsically reactive, is defined by what it is not, by what it fears, and by what it excludes. It is the State police itself which produces the figure of the dissident; religion (of whatever persuasion) that of the heretic; the Moral Order, that of the pervert. Let us celebrate dissidents! Strength may preserve, but it is dissidence and transgression that advance man as a species.

THE "GOOD SOCIETY" AND ITS ENEMIES

The "Good Society" creates reasonable expectations through its institutions, its customs, and respect for contracts. It diminishes the stress and anxiety placed on its members. Through not subjugating them to any bond (no forced marriages, no castes, no legal monopoly of "public services" providers), people are allowed to form ones they choose: among themselves personally (friendships, partnerships); and among themselves concerning objects (property rights). In this way, the "Good Society" maximizes each person's chances of creating the most beneficial and strongest bonds.

The "Good Society" never offers the best possible circumstances for all its members from the outset. For how could its leaders possibly anticipate each person's wants? Particularly as human desires evolve. Each of us wants the ability to better our condition through substituting one bond with another that we believe to be of greater value (divorcing in order to marry a more considerate spouse, switching holdings in a securities portfolio, changing jobs, placing our children in a better school). Even if some people are mistaken in their expectations, others will not know this with complete certainty and, having prevented or forbidden the transaction, they could not compensate those who had wanted it in the first place and are now proven right in their assessment (time lost and opportunity costs cannot be compensated for). Therefore, any intervention that would ruin the parties' expectations pertaining to the exercise and formation of these bonds constitutes the most direct and the most harmful attack on the "Good Society." We have seen that two types of individuals commit this aggression.

In the first instance, we find those who cannot or will not obtain someone's consent to transfer a bond to an object to them. Murderers, rapists, robbers, swindlers, these all know they will never be granted this bond, but nevertheless choose to attack a person and to dispossess her of her rights to her body or possessions against her will.

The other group consists of a party with somewhat starker ambition, those who are aware that to simply seize an asset would make them nothing more than thieves. This gang instead forbids the creation of certain bonds between people and invalidates those which people have been able to create between themselves and objects.

Governments (they alone can harbor this outrageous pretension) impose restrictions on marriage contracts, employment and business contracts, on the free movement of people, on the construction of buildings, on what people can eat, drink, smoke, read, view, say, print and broadcast, what clothes we can wear, and what medicines we can use. They seize all or part of the assets of individuals and companies at will.

Yet, the desire to create new bonds underpins our initiatives, and as these bonds strengthen they bring us ever-greater satisfaction. So conversely, their violation causes us ever-greater distress.

This is why the common good of the "Good Society" is to protect these bonds without which it would not exist and to protect them especially against those who have the political power to infringe on them.

Will we ever achieve a "Good Society"? There is often cause for despair, I agree. It seems the battle is never won. But let me quote a wonderful Bulgarian poet, Blaga Dimitrova, with words that have inspired me for many years:

I'm not afraid
they'll stamp me flat.
Grass stamped flat
soon becomes a path.[4] ∽

---

[4]Blaga Dimitrova, "Grass," quoted in Harold B. Segel, *The Columbia Guide to the Literatures of Eastern Europe Since 1945* (New York: Columbia University Press, 2003 [1974]), p. 146.

23

Freedom and Property: Where They Conflict

Frank van Dun

FREEDOM AS PROPERTY AND THE NON-AGGRESSION PRINCIPLE

L ibertarian theorists like to trace social and economic problems to coercive, usually government-imposed or sanctioned interventions in the free market or restrictions on the exercise of the libertarian rights of self-ownership, private appropriation and use of material resources, and exchange by mutual consent. This sort of analysis of social and economic problems suggests, and is often meant to suggest, that in a situation where those rights are fully respected the problems would not arise or that they could and would be solved efficiently and peacefully by negotiation, mediation or arbitration. In other words, neither economic nor personal freedom is the cause of those problems; freedom is the condition for their solution.

Frank van Dun (Frank.vanDun@Ugent.be) teaches philosophy of law at the University of Ghent. He is the author of *Het Fundamenteel Rechtsbeginsel* (1983, 2008), a Dutch-language book that uses argumentation ethics as the basis for a non-positivist, libertarian theory of law.

This is fine as far as it goes – but how far does it go? As we shall see below, respect for the above-mentioned libertarian rights is not in itself sufficient to guarantee the freedom of every person. There may be cases where there is a conflict between claims on behalf of one person's freedom and claims on behalf of another person's private property. In such cases, the question arises, which claims should prevail. Unquestionably, the libertarian answer should be: freedom before property. Unfortunately, many libertarians are reluctant to give up the conception of "freedom as property" that (1) serves them so well in their critiques of interventionism and collectivism and (2) underpins their notion that the law of a libertarian order is merely the rigorous application of the so-called non-aggression principle.

The logical link between "freedom as property" and the non-aggression principle is the definition of aggression as an invasion of another person's property for any purpose other than getting restitution of one's property from, or securing compensation for damages resulting from a previous aggression committed by, that person. Thus, according to the non-aggression principle, only aggressive invasions of another's property are unlawful and every act of any other kind is lawful. In practical terms, libertarian judges have no right to authorize interference with non-aggressive acts, and libertarian enforcement agencies have no right to enforce any unilateral prohibition or restriction of such acts. However, if freedom is the supreme libertarian value, this will not do.

HOSTILE ENCIRCLEMENT ON LIBERTARIAN QUASI-EARTH

For the sake of the argument, let us suppose that, somewhere in the universe, there is a planet – let us call it Quasi-Earth – that is in all physical respects like our own planet Earth. In particular, Quasi-Earth is populated by beings that are in all respects like us, except that they are all law-abiding libertarians. Thus, unlike us Earthlings, the Quasi-Earthlings (1) unconditionally respect every person's rights of self-ownership, private appropriation of unowned resources, unrestricted non-invasive use his own property, and exchange by mutual consent, and (2) unconditionally abide by the non-aggression principle when it comes to dealing with interpersonal problems. In other words, there is no crime and every property owner is free to do with, to, and on his property whatever he likes provided his actions have no significant[1] physical effects on others or their properties. Consequently, there is no need for any political government and we may assume that states, if they ever existed over there, have long since withered away. In short, Quasi-Earth is the very model of a libertarian order according to the "freedom as property" paradigm. Nevertheless, it is easy to imagine how a person could lose his freedom because of non-invasive actions performed by others.

The most obvious case is encirclement. Suppose that every point on Quasi-Earth is privately owned by one or another individual person in such a way that every owner of a piece of the surface of Quasi-Earth finds that his property is surrounded by the properties of other persons, possibly by the property of a single other person. Because the inhabitants of that planet are very similar to us, we may expect that at least some people may find themselves surrounded by personal enemies or rivals or spiteful individuals who like to annoy or intimidate others. However, since they are all law-abiding people, they judiciously abstain from aggressive, invasive actions.

Clearly, a person's ability to move himself or his goods beyond the confines of his own property without trespassing on the property of others depends on their willingness to grant him a right of way. However, nothing in the Quasi-Earthlings' system of property rights obliges them either to grant him right of way or to permit third parties to cross their properties to reach his (if he has any). Consequently, because of a coincidence of decisions by his neighbors or because of an agreement among them, any person may find himself locked up on his own property or prevented from dealing with others outside the circle of his immediate neighbors.

Because, according to the libertarian conception of freedom as property, denying a person access to one's property does not count

---

[1] I shall not discuss the problem of drawing a line between significant and insignificant effects, although it is obviously a pervasive practical problem. A libertarian order cannot be viable unless it recognizes that a few particles of smoke crossing the boundary between two properties are different from a thick cloud of black smoke, a faint smell is different from an unbearable stench, and so on.

as a crime, his neighbors must be assumed to remain within their rights if they act in this manner. They do not infringe his property rights. Moreover, they must be assumed to remain within their rights if they then go on to grant him a right of way on condition that he complies with their demands, however onerous or demeaning these may be. Nevertheless, it would be absurd to regard their actions as respectful of his freedom, if by refusing him a right of way they turn encirclement into imposed isolation and his property into a prison (if he is on his property) or into an inaccessible resource (if he is not). In addition, we should remember that on Quasi-Earth encirclement is the normal condition of any person. Thus, given the assumed similarities between our planet and that supposed ideal planet, we should consider the possibility that entire groups may be made to suffer imposed isolation.

Some libertarians would argue that nothing in such a situation poses a threat to anybody's freedom. They would point out, for example, that the encircled person might tunnel under the adjacent properties or get a helicopter to fly over them.[2] However, such solutions are also available (if they are available at all) to people locked up in a regular prison—and it would be ridiculous to say that locking up a person in a prison does not deprive him of his freedom merely because he might have opportunities for making an escape. Moreover, the encirclement of a person could be three-dimensional, for example if some of the neighbors run mining operations under his property and others fill the airspace above it with antenna wires, power lines or weather balloons.

Other libertarians tend to belittle the problem with a general reference to the free market, noting, for example, that hostile encirclement is not without opportunity costs for those who practice it and that these costs will deter profit-maximizing individuals from engaging in the practice for any extended period. This argument is purely academic. First, we are not talking about people being excluded from one or a few bars or shopping malls but from the only means of access to their own property or to other places where they are welcome. Second, even if true, the argument only supports

---

[2]Thus, with respect to a related problem, see Walter Block, "Roads, Bridges, Sunlight and Private Property: Reply to Gordon Tullock," *Journal des Economistes et des Etudes Humaines* 8, no. 2/3 (June-September 1998): 315–26.

the proposition that, other things remaining the same, hostile encirclement *tends* to disappear over time. It does not support the proposition that it will ever actually disappear. Moreover, the reality is that profit-maximizing individuals often enough drift along with the prejudices of the majority of the population in their area, no matter what these prejudices are, no matter whether they themselves share them. All too often, the "sovereign consumer" is a herd or a mob. Accepting for the purpose of economic analysis that "all values are subjective," we should not expect market outcomes to be always and necessarily in support of objective, libertarian ethical values, such as freedom. Thus, we should not underestimate the lengths to which some people are willing to go to pester or boycott others, especially when they are emboldened by the cheers and nods of sympathizers. Neither should we make light of the ease with which a thing such as a privately owned road can be turned from a mere revenue-generating commercial asset into a means for exercising unilateral control over others and their properties.

Still other libertarians have been known to blame the victim: anybody can know that there is a risk of being surrounded by unfriendly neighbors; therefore, one should know that it is unwise not to take precautions against this eventuality. This may not be an unreasonable stance on a planet such as ours, which is not a model libertarian order. Here, few properties are surrounded on all sides by other private properties and even fewer are at a great distance from unowned open or public space. However, on Quasi-Earth, all of the accessible space can be converted into private property or pass into the hands of another owner at any moment. So, what sort of precautions against unfriendly encirclement could any individual take? Does being the owner of a road or canal imply that one should never be able to convert one's property to some other use, if the original owner of the road gave assurance of access to the first buyers or owners of the properties abutting it? Does having "guaranteed" access to a road imply that the road itself will remain connected to other roads, owned by the same or another road owner?

FREEDOM AND PROPERTY: CONFLICTING CLAIMS

Suppose a person complains about being isolated from the rest of the world by his neighbors' non-invasive actions and presents his case to a judge. Which judge is closer to the libertarian spirit and more likely to contribute to conditions of peaceful co-existence? One who dismisses the complaint because the neighbors do not trespass on the property of the complainant, or one who is willing to hear the complaint and, if it turns out to be justified, willing to decide that the neighbors are under an obligation to grant a right of way to the complainant? One who merely looks at observable movements across property boundaries, or one who considers that the protection of property, however vital to the preservation of freedom it may be, is nevertheless only a means to freedom and not its fulfillment? Which argument is more likely to be universalizable? That property rights are sacrosanct, or that freedom is sacrosanct?

We have assumed that on Quasi-Earth respect for private property is universal. Therefore, those who happen to become victims of imposed isolation must be assumed to bear their lot with equanimity, peacefully withering away in their ghettos and enduring being exploited by others. Surely, this assumption is not particularly plausible. However, should we weaken it then we must envisage the possibility that isolated groups resort to violence to break out of their confinement and regain their freedom. Should we condemn their revolt as criminal? Would we? Is isolation by hostile encirclement a just cause for resorting to violence or war against those who impose and refuse to lift it?

Freedom is not served by war, and neither is property. Just as aggressive violence threatens these values, acts that are prone to provoke violent reactions as well as wide-spread sympathy for those reactions among more or less distant observers similarly threaten the prospects for securing freedom and property, even if they are not in themselves 'aggressions,' i.e. invasions of property. Human nature being what it is, we should not overlook the irritability and irascibility of the "human animal." The principles of libertarian law should be entirely rational in the sense of being provably irrefutable "dictates of reason."[3] Both in formulating and

---

[3]This is the basic idea of Hans Hoppe's ethical justification of capitalism in his *A Theory of Socialism and Capitalism* (Boston-Dordrecht-London: Kluwer, 1989).

in applying them we should nevertheless be aware that in the rough-and-tumble of life the voice of reason has many competitors — and that some people know how to take advantage of that fact for the purpose of manipulating and provoking others to "fire the first shot." In other words, we should not adopt the stance of other-worldly sanctimonious saints ignoring the pervasive causal, physical and psychological aspects of the human condition.

If, as many libertarians believe, freedom is a natural right then we should be clear about whether it entitles one to destroy the freedom of others if only in ways that do not involve direct interference with their property. If it does then freedom can hardly count as a fundamental value in the sense of political philosophy; if it does not then the non-aggression principle can hardly count as the basic principle of libertarian law. Either way, there seems to be something wrong with equating libertarian law with the rigorous application of the non-aggression principle.

That should not come as a surprise. The principle does not refer to freedom, only to property; it would be adequate as the axiomatic law of freedom only if "freedom" and "property" were synonymous — but they are not. To paraphrase Anthony de Jasay,[4] we do not need a theory of "freedom as private property" anymore than we need any other theory of "freedom as something else."

RESTRICTING PROPERTY RIGHTS ON BEHALF OF FREEDOM

There is a straightforward solution to the problems of hostile encirclement or imposed isolation. The usual statement of the rights of a property owner already indicates that these rights are not "absolute" in the literal sense of the word. There is an "external effects" proviso that libertarians have come to take for granted. Even from the perspective of the non-aggression principle, one does not have the right to do what one wants with, to or on one's property. Such proprietary actions are within the law of a libertarian

---

[4]See the Antony de Jasay, "Justice as Something Else," in *Justice and Its Surroundings* (Indianapolis, Ind.: Liberty Fund, 2002), originally published in *Cato Journal* 16, no. 2 (Fall 1996): 161–73.

order only if they do not have significant physical effects on other persons or their properties.[5] The external effects proviso is necessary to link the concepts of property and freedom together into a plausible conception of an interpersonal order involving a multitude of diverse people inhabiting a world of scarce resources. However, it is still firmly within the "freedom as property" conception because it merely restricts the property rights of one person by invoking those of others.

As we have seen, the external effects proviso is not sufficient if it is intended to serve a libertarian purpose, i.e., to safeguard everybody's freedom, rather than a proprietorial one. At the very least, it needs to be supplemented to guarantee every person[6] not only access to his own property but also a way to go from there to any other place where he is welcome. In short, in addition to the external effects proviso, there is need to have a "free movement" proviso regarding ownership of material resources, to the effect that the rights of a property owner do not include the right to deprive others of the possibility of moving between their own property and any place where they are welcome. Of course, 'deprive' is too absolute for practical purposes: freedom of movement implies that there are no significant or unreasonable manmade obstacles to moving about.

Two logical points should be stressed here. The first is that if throwing an innocent person in a cell deprives him of his freedom then so does building a cell around him even on those occasions when one succeeds in doing so without touching him or his property. Thus, the free movement proviso appears implied in the very idea of freedom itself. The other point is that the new proviso no

---

[5]Unilaterally performing an action with significant physical effects on others or their properties is unlawful. I have argued elsewhere that certain non-invasive actions, such as misrepresenting [oneself as] another person and unilaterally changing the conventional meaning of the terms of a contract, should also be considered unlawful, if libertarian law is to serve its purpose of generating a viable order of human affairs rather than being a source of resentment, distrust and conflict. See my "Against Libertarian Legalism," *Journal of Libertarian Studies* 17, no. 3 (2003).

[6]Exceptions may no doubt be made, say, for criminals and the dangerously insane.

longer fits within the "freedom as property" paradigm. It is therefore likely to be controversial among libertarians – but at the very least, it has the merit of focussing their attention on the concept of freedom, forcing them to be much clearer and more explicit about their understanding of it.[7]

THINKING ABOUT PUBLIC SPACE IN A LIBERTARIAN ORDER

Assuming that the free movement proviso could be enforced, it would have the effect of steering the development and geographical arrangement of properties into the familiar pattern of a network of routes, trails and paths across open unowned space (for example, the seas, uninhabited, uncultivated land) and streets, roads, canals, and so on, connecting everyone's property with everybody else's. Let us use "route" as a catch-all term to designate any of the elements of this right-of-way network. It would appear that such a network is the most, perhaps even the only, efficient way for reconciling the rights of way demanded by the free movement proviso and the condition of exclusive control associated with private ownership.

Without the free movement proviso, under the "freedom as property" doctrine, routes would eventually be supplied as privately held property. This is what we should expect to see on Quasi-Earth, because we cannot very well imagine how a human civilization would function without such things as streets, roads and navigable waterways. However, the route owners would then have exactly the same rights as owners of the land, private houses or factories alongside the routes. They would have rights to exclude anybody for any reason or for no reason at all from using

---

[7]For other libertarian discussion of similar issues, see Stephan Kinsella, "The Blockean Proviso," Mises Economics Blog <http://blog.mises.org/archives/007127.asp> (Sept. 11, 2007); and Roderick T. Long, "Easy Rider," Austro-Athenian Empire <http://praxeology.net/blog/2007/09/11/easy-rider> (Sept. 11, 2007), both discussing Walter Block's view that someone who homesteads land that "encircles" unowned land must grant an easement to permit potential homesteaders access the unowned property. See, e.g, Walter Block, "Libertarianism, Positive Obligations and Property Abandonment: Children's Rights," *International Journal of Social Economics* 31, no. 3 (2004): 275–86.

their property, to demand any price or service in return for a permission to use it even in the most innocuous ways and for the most harmless purposes, and to form cartels with the owners of nearby routes to strengthen their bargaining positions.

In short, without the free movement proviso, private ownership of routes would exacerbate the problem of hostile encirclement and the risk of exploitation of some by others. It would jeopardize the freedom of every other person and provide the route owners with a basis in libertarian law for imposing all sorts of requirements on anybody who wishes to make use of their property. It would set them up as prospective "lords" or rulers with an effective lawful power to control the movements and trades of other property owners located in the area served by their routes. Indeed, in the past, the king's "sovereign right" was based, among other things, on his self-proclaimed or perceived role as the provider of "peace" in public space: unowned land, rivers, roads, and the like, that were available for use by all of his subjects.[8] The free movement proviso thus undercuts one of the most frequently offered justifications for the existence of state-power, as it derives the status in law of public spaces entirely from every person's right of freedom rather than from the kings' taking possession of those spaces.

With the free movement proviso in place, the ownership of routes would amount to no more than quasi-ownership, a right to manage an asset to guarantee the inviolable right of way for every law-abiding person. Such quasi-ownership would presumably include the right to claim the residual or profit from the management of routes. It would certainly not include the right to restrict access to the routes for lawful purposes, unless the restrictions are for sound technical or safety reasons (e.g., limitations of weight, length and width of vehicles; transportation of explosive or poisonous materials; etc.), or unless the routes have become redundant and are no longer in use.

Note that the proviso does not exclude the construction of fully privately owned routes, the owners of which would have the full

---

[8]This was a major element in Jean Bodin's natural history of the genesis of "absolute sovereignty" (in his *Six Livres de la République* [*Six Books of the Commonwealth*], 1576).

range of rights of exclusion and pricing that the owners of other types of property have. Such routes may be useful (and profitable) additions to the right-of-way network available under the free movement proviso. However, the proviso applies also to them. In other words, while permitted in a libertarian order, fully privately owned routes would not be allowed to break up the right-of-way network into disconnected segments, as this would constitute a violation of the free movement proviso and therefore the freedom of others.

The most important implication of the free movement proviso is the introduction or re-introduction into libertarian theory of the concept of public space as distinct from privately owned exclusive space. This is a neglected area in libertarian theorizing, in part because the conventional theory simply assumes away the existence of public spaces, except as sources of problems that would disappear without ill side-effects as soon as such spaces are "privatized." Indeed, under the influence of the "freedom as property" conception, which does not recognize the free movement proviso, libertarian theorists are prone to endorse the position that in public spaces people should be allowed to do as they wish, as long as they do not assault or physically harm others. Inclusion of the free movement proviso, in contrast, would invite libertarians to consider the proper use of the right-of-way network ("public space"), which is freedom of peaceful movement, and the dangers of other uses, such as disseminating propaganda, provoking confrontations, and the like. Since travelers and users of the right-of-way network are not its owners, it is appropriate to ask just which liberties they can legitimately claim and which obligations they incur while "on the road." Similar questions can be raised with respect to the quasi-owners or managers of the right-of-way network. The theoretical basis from which one should address these questions is, of course, the obligation to respect the freedom of movement of every person (more exactly, of every person who is not lawfully confined on account of his own criminal actions or his dangerous insanity).

There are, of course, other implications of the free movement proviso, e.g., concerning libertarian discussions of issues such as migration, but my aim here is not to explore all of its ramifications;

it is merely to draw attention to it and to suggest that it be seen as an integral part of the libertarian concept of ownership rights.

Obviously, the free movement proviso is a far-reaching restriction of the property right of route owners as it would be defined according to the "freedom as property" conception, but it is not an arbitrary restriction—in fact, it is rooted the idea of freedom, which is, or should be, the supreme libertarian value. Besides, the whole point of libertarian theorizing is to come up with a conception of an order of conviviality and cooperation in which people can enjoy their freedom and face the slings and arrows of life without having to worry that virtually every step they take requires them to agree to do another's bidding. ❧

Part Four

Democracy Reconsidered

24

The Trouble with Democracy:
Maslow Meets Hoppe

Doug French

H L. Mencken described politicians as "men who, at some time or other, have compromised with their honour, either by swallowing their convictions or by whooping for what they believe to be untrue."[1] "Vanity remains to him," Mencken wrote, "but not pride."[2]

The Sage of Baltimore had it correct, that to be elected and stay elected in American politics to any full-time position requires the suspension of any ethics or good sense a person may possess. Even those who begin political careers with the best intentions and have measurable abilities that would make them successful in any field soon realize that the skills required to succeed in politics are not those required outside politics.

Doug French (douglasinvegas@gmail.com) received his Masters degree in economics from the University of Nevada Las Vegas under Murray Rothbard with Professor Hoppe serving on his thesis committee. He, along with Deanna Forbush, was a benefactor for the publication of the second edition of Hoppe's *The Economics and Ethics of Private Property*. French is the President of the Ludwig von Mises Institute in Auburn, Alabama.

[1]H.L. Mencken, *Notes on Democracy* (New York: Alfred A. Knopf, 1926), pp. 114–15.

[2]Ibid., p. 115.

Lew Rockwell explains that, while competition in the market-place improves quality, competition in politics does just the opposite:

> The only improvements take place in the process of doing bad things: lying, cheating, manipulating, stealing, and killing. The price of political services is constantly increasing, whether in tax dollars paid or in the bribes owed for protection (also known as campaign contributions). There is no obsolescence, planned or otherwise. And as Hayek famously argued, in politics, the worst get on top. And there is no accountability: the higher the office, the more criminal wrongdoing a person can get away with.[3]

Thus it becomes "a psychic impossibility for a gentleman to hold office under the Federal Union,"[4] wrote Mencken. Democracy makes it possible for the demagogue to inflame the childish imagination of the masses, "by virtue of his talent for nonsense."[5] The king can do the same thing in a monarchy but only by virtue of his birth.

In stark contrast, in the natural order, as Hans-Hermann Hoppe explains in his monumental work, *Democracy – The God that Failed*, it is "private property, production, and voluntary exchange that are the ultimate sources of human civilization."[6] This natural order, Hoppe notes, must be maintained by a natural elite which would come by these positions of "natural authority," not by election as in the case of democracy, or birth as in the case of monarchy, but by their "superior achievements, of wealth, wisdom, bravery or a combination thereof."[7] This is just the opposite

---

[3]Llewellyn H. Rockwell, Jr., "Two Kinds of Competition," LewRockwell.com (August 12, 2004).

[4]Mencken, *Notes on Democracy*, p. 115.

[5]H.L. Mencken, *The Gist of Mencken: Quotations from America's Critic*, Mayo DuBasky, ed. (Metuchen, N.J.: Scarecrow Press, 1990), p. 352; originally from H.L. Mencken, "Off Again, On Again," *Smart Set* (March 1922), p. 50.

[6]Hans-Hermann Hoppe, *Democracy – The God that Failed: The Economics and Politics of Monarchy, Democracy, and Natural Order* (New Brunswick, N.J.: Transaction Publishers, 2001), p. 71.

[7]Ibid.

of what Mencken and Rockwell describe as a characteristic of democracy.

Instead, democracy affords the opportunity for anyone to pursue politics as a career. There is no need for the masses to recognize a person as "wise" or "successful," as Hoppe's natural order would require. Nor does one have to be born into the ruling family, as in the case of monarchy. As the great American comedian, Bob Hope, who was actually born in England, once quipped, "I left England at the age of four when I found out I couldn't be king." Maybe because he knows he can never have Prince Charles's job, Sir Richard Branson — knighted for "services to entrepreneurship" — sticks to business and reportedly owns 360 companies.

But, as Hoppe explains, democracies have expanded, and since World War I have been viewed as the only legitimate form of government. In turn, more people who have been successful at other pursuits are running for political office or becoming politically active. For instance, more and more wealthy billionaires are entering the political arena. While the wealthy tycoons of a previous generation were private and tended to covet seclusion, today's captains of industry such as Ross Perot, Michael Bloomberg, and Jon Corzine are running for office. And while Warren Buffett, Bill Gates, and George Soros haven't sought public office personally, they spend millions of dollars on political contributions and are visible in trying to sway the public debate on political issues, when their time would obviously be more productively spent (both for them and everyone else) on other, wealth-creating endeavors. Plus, a quarter of all House members and a third of all members of the Senate are millionaires.[8]

There may be politicians that pursue elected office for the money, but many elected officials are already wealthy by most people's standards. What makes the wealthy and otherwise successful want to hold office? Is it as Charles Derber describes in *The*

---

[8]See "Net Worth, 2007," OpenSecrets.org <www.opensecrets.org/pfds/overview.php> (accessed December 15, 2008); also "Millionaires Fill US Congress Halls," Agence France Presse <www.commondreams.org/headlines04/0630-05.htm> (June 30, 2004); Sean Loughlin and Robert Yoon, "Millionaires Populate U.S. Senate," CNN.com <www.cnn.com/2003/ ALLPOLITICS/06/13/senators.finances/ > (June 13, 2003).

Pursuit of Attention: Power and Ego in Everyday Life, that politicians since "Caesar and Napoleon have been driven by overweening egos and an insatiable hunger for public adulation"?[9]

The work of psychologist Abraham Maslow may provide an understanding as to why even successful entrepreneurs would seek public office. Maslow is famous for his "hierarchy of needs" theory that is taught in most management classes in American universities. The theory is generally presented visually as a pyramid, with the lowest or most basic human need—physiological need— shown as a layer along the base of the pyramid.

Maslow's view was that the basic human needs—thirst, hunger, breathing—must be satisfied before humans could accomplish or worry about anything else. The next tranche within the pyramid, shown on top of the physiological need, is the safety need. After satisfying thirst and hunger, humans are concerned about their continued survival. If a man is constantly worried about being eaten by a tiger, he doesn't concern himself with much else.

The next layer presented within Maslow's pyramid is the belonging need, which lies just above safety need. After the satisfaction of the two lower needs—physiological and safety—a person seeks love, friendships, companionship and community. Once this need is satisfied, according to Maslow, humans seek the esteem need. These first four needs were considered deficit needs. If a person is lacking, there is a motivation to fill that need. Once the particular need is filled, the motivation abates. This makes these needs different than the need at the top of Maslow's pyramid, the need for self-actualization. The need for self-actualization is never satisfied, and Maslow referred to it as a being need, or to be all you can be.

Thus, humans continually strive to satisfy their needs, and as the more basic needs are satisfied, humans move up the pyramid, if you will, to satisfy higher level needs. Of course, different humans achieve different levels, and it was Maslow's view that only two percent of humans become self-actualizing. Maslow

---

[9]Charles Derber, *The Pursuit of Attention: Power and Ego in Everyday Life*, 2nd ed. (New York: Oxford University Press, 2000), p. xxii.

studied some famous people along with a dozen not-so-famous folks and developed some personality traits that were consistent with people he judged to be self-actualizing. Besides being creative and inventive, self-actualizers have strong ethics, a self-deprecating sense of humor, humility and respect for others, resistance to enculturation, enjoyment of autonomy and solitude instead of shallow relationships with many people. They believe the ends don't necessarily justify the means and that the means can be ends in themselves.

One readily sees that Maslow's self-actualizers have nothing in common with politicians in a democracy, but closely fit the profile that Hoppe describes of the natural elite that would lead a natural order. But a step down from the top of the hierarchy of needs pyramid is the need for esteem. Maslow described two types of esteem needs according to Maslow expert Dr. C. George Boeree, a lower esteem need and a higher one. And while the higher form of esteem calls for healthy attributes such as freedom, independence, confidence and achievement, the lower form "is the need for the respect of others, the need for status, fame, glory, recognition, attention, reputation, appreciation, dignity, even dominance."

"The negative version of these needs is low self-esteem and inferiority complexes," Dr. Boeree writes. "Maslow felt [Alfred] Adler was really onto something when he proposed that these were at the roots of many, if not most, of our psychological problems."[10]

Now we see the qualities displayed by virtually all politicians in democracy: the constant need for status and recognition. The ends – compensating for an inferiority complex – justify whatever Machiavellian means.

Because democracy is open to any and all who can get themselves elected, either through connections, personality, or personal wealth, it is a social system where leadership positions become a hotbed for sociopaths. Maslow's self-actualizing man won't have an interest in politics. But those stuck on the need for esteem are drawn to it like flies to dung.

---

[10]C. George Boeree, "Abraham Maslow," www.ship.edu/~cgboeree/maslow.html (accessed December 15, 2008).

With leadership in such dysfunctional hands, it is no wonder. "In comparison to the nineteenth century, the cognitive prowess of the political and intellectual elites and the quality of public education have declined," Hoppe writes in *Democracy*.[11] "And the rates of crime, structural unemployment, welfare dependency, parasitism, negligence, recklessness, incivility, psychopathy, and hedonism have increased."[12]

So while the electorate recognizes that they are electing, at best incompetents, and at worst crooks, the constant, naïve, prodemocracy mantra is that "we just need to elect the right people." But, the "right people" aren't (and won't be) running for office. Instead, we will continue to have "the average American legislator [who] is not only an ass," as Mencken wrote, "but also an oblique, sinister, depraved and knavish fellow. . ."[13] ✎

---

[11]Hoppe, *Democracy*, p. 42.

[12]Ibid., p. 43.

[13]*The Gist of Mencken*, p. 423; originally from H.L. Mencken, "The Free Lance," *Baltimore Evening Sun* (January 10, 1913).

An Epistemic Justification of Democracy?

David Gordon

I n his great book *Democracy – The God that Failed*, Hans Hoppe argued that democracy leads to a growth in state power. In his view, the transition in European history from monarchy to democracy was a blow to liberty: "I [Hoppe] will explain the rapid growth in state power lamented by Mises and Rothbard as the systematic outcome of the democratic mindset, i.e., the (erroneous) belief in the efficiency and/or justice of public property and popular (majority) rule."[1]

This conclusion put Hoppe in polar opposition to the dominant opinion in contemporary Anglo-American political philosophy. In the mainstream, justifications for democracy abound. It is taken for granted that democracy, at least for modern Western political societies, is the only justifiable system of government. The question up for discussion is only how the justification is to be accomplished. I

David Gordon (dgordon@mises.com) is a Senior Fellow at the Ludwig von Mises Institute, the author of numerous books, including *Resurrecting Marx, The Philosophical Origins of Austrian Economics*, and *An Introduction to Economic Reasoning*, and editor of *The Mises Review*.

[1]Hans-Hermann Hoppe, *Democracy – The God that Failed* (New Brunswick, N.J.: Transaction Publishers, 2001), p. xxiii. See my review in *The Mises Review* 8, no. 2 (Spring 2002).

propose to examine a recent endeavor to justify democracy, one that has already won for its author considerable acclaim. David M. Estlund, in *Democratic Authority: A Philosophical Framework*[2] offers an "epistemic justification" for democracy. I shall endeavor to show that a crucial step in his argument fails.

Estlund wishes to show that democratic decision making has both authority and legitimacy:

> By *authority* I [Estlund] will mean the moral power of one agent (emphasizing especially the state) to morally require or forbid actions by others through commands.
> . . . By *legitimacy* I will mean the moral permissibility of the state's issuing and enforcing its commands owing to the process by which they were produced. (p. 2)

One way to show that the state has authority and legitimacy would be to claim that the rulers possess expert knowledge that others lack. The rulers know, e.g., how to run a complex economy and the proper foreign policy to adopt, while those not in authority lack such knowledge. (Such a claim would of course be risible in the actual world; but we are here concerned only with the structure of this particular argument, not the factual basis of its premise.)

As Estlund rightly recognizes, this argument cannot be accepted. Even if rulers did have superior knowledge, this would not suffice to generate an obligation by others to obey them.

> It is important to see that authority does not simply follow from expertise. Even if we grant that there are better and worse political decisions (which I think we must), and that some people know better what should be done that others), it simply does not follow from their expertise that they have authority over us, or that they ought to. . . . You might be correct, but what makes you boss? (p. 3)

---

[2]Princeton University Press, 2008. All subsequent references to this book will be by page numbers in parentheses in the text.

If expert knowledge does not ground authority and legitimacy, what does? One natural alternative would be to say that someone has authority over another only by consent. Unless people voluntarily have accepted the authority of the state, they stand under no obligation to obey its dictates. Libertarian anarchists would readily embrace this thesis, but Estlund is decidedly not of this persuasion. What then is he to do? If he rejects the necessity of consent, has he not committed himself to authoritarian rule? The question becomes more pressing because, as we have seen, he rejects the most natural basis for a claim to rule without consent, i.e., the superior knowledge of the rulers.

Estlund extricates himself from this difficulty by denying that he wishes to dispense with consent altogether.

> A traditional view says that there is no authority without consent. The state is not in a position to lay obligations on me unless I voluntarily and knowingly agree to their having this moral power. The main weakness of this approach is that it does not seem to account for the state's authority over very many people, since most people never consent to the authority of the state.[3] . . . [But] If there were some conditions that nullified non-consent, the result would be morally equivalent to consent . . . perhaps if the non-consent is morally wrong it should be without moral effect. (p. 9)

Estlund's conclusion does not follow. Suppose that you need to consult some documents that I own in order to complete your dissertation. Let us stipulate that I bear you no ill will and that it would cost me nothing to allow you to consult the documents. We might even suppose that you offer me a generous fee if I allow you to examine them. Unfortunately for your work, I refuse you access to them on no better grounds than a whim. Clearly, I have acted badly: I ought not to have impeded your project without cause. It does not follow, though, that because I acted badly, you now may

---

[3]Libertarians will not fail to note that for Estlund, it must turn out that the state is justified. Because strict consent fails to justify the state, it cannot be accepted as a criterion.

consult the documents, my wishes to the contrary notwithstanding. In like fashion, I suggest, it does not follow that if you failed to consent to a political decision when you ought to have, that your mistaken failure may be taken as equivalent to consent.

Let us put this point to one side and, *arguendo*, assume that Estlund's project of rule without actual consent remains in the field. Under what conditions ought people to consent to political decisions? Estlund, one will not be surprised to learn, finds the answer in democracy. In a political community, choices on certain matters of concern to all must be made. Everyone in the community has a chance to have his say on these matters, and the deliberations of a democratic community are likely to arrive at good decisions more than randomly. In these circumstances, people ought to consent to the results, even if they find themselves in the minority.

One might at first sight think that Estlund has retreated to a position he has already rejected. He appeals to the likelihood of correct decisions; but has he not rightly acknowledged that correctness does not generate authority? "You might be correct, but what makes you boss?" (p. 3) Further, has he not set his standard very low? All that he asks of democracy is that it leads to good decisions more than randomly. If one appeals to the authority of knowledge, should one not demand more?

But Estlund has not in fact embraced what he previously dismissed. It is not the epistemic merits of democracy by themselves that result in the claim to authority; it is these merits combined with mass participation in decision making.

> Democratically produced laws are legitimate and authoritative because they are produced by a procedure with a tendency to make correct decisions. It is not an infallible procedure, and there might even be more accurate procedures. But democracy is better than random and epistemically the best among those that are generally acceptable in the way that political legitimacy requires. (p. 8)

Estlund argues for his claim about democratic decision making in two stages. First, he contends that in an ideal system of democratic deliberation, decisions are likely to be right more than randomly. Second, even though actually existing democracy falls short of the ideal situation, it is still likely that it retains the required epistemic authority.

The principal failing of the argument lies in the first step. Estlund rightly calls attention to the advantages of deliberation and multiple points of view when one is trying to reach a decision. Has not Hayek taught us the advantages of dispersed knowledge, albeit his argument was for the free market rather than for democracy?

> If we ask why it is that two heads are better than one, or why thinking together in a communicative way is epistemically better than thinking alone, one element that deserves more discussion is the dispersal of knowledge. The idea of dispersed knowledge is central to Hayek's work on economic markets, and it is worth looking to his work for clues to how to use this idea to support the epistemic value of democracy. (p. 177)

Estlund has fallen into a glaring *non sequitur*. It seems entirely reasonable to say that deliberation that takes advantage of dispersed knowledge is better than decision that lacks this feature: in many cases, two heads are indeed better than one. But how does this in any way establish the conclusion that Estlund wants, i.e., that democratic decisions have a more than random chance of being right? From the fact that one method is better than another, nothing follows about whether either method is superior to chance.

There is a further problem with Estlund's assertion. In order to know how "good" democratic decision-making is, one would need to compare particular democratic decisions with the correct decisions. But Estlund nowhere presents any independent criteria for the correctness of political decisions. Even if he were right, we would have no way of knowing this.

Estlund's epistemic argument does not succeed. Given the sorry record of democracy that Hans Hoppe has abundantly documented, this failure was to be expected.[4]

---

[4]Estlund never refers to Hoppe.

26

Democracy and *Faits Accomplis*

Robert Higgs

N o institution of modern life commands as much vener-
ation as democracy. It comes closer than anything else
to being the supreme object of adoration in a global religion. Anyone who denies its righteousness and desir-
ability soon finds himself a pariah. One may get away with
denouncing motherhood and apple pie, but not with speaking ill of
democracy, which is now the principal icon of political and social
life throughout the world. Many people are atheists, but few are
anti-democrats.

Worship of this particular political arrangement has emerged
relatively recently, however, and in earlier ages political philosophers were more apt to condemn democracy than to praise it. Aristotle, whose views received great weight for millennia, did not recommend democracy highly. Along with many other criticisms of
this type of government, he wrote in his *Politics*:

> 1313b: 32-41: The final form of democracy has character-
> istics of tyranny: women dominate in the household so
> that they can denounce their husbands, slaves lack disci-
> pline, and flatterers—demagogues—are held in honor.
> The people wish to be a monarch.

Robert Higgs (RHiggs2377@aol.com) is a Senior Fellow in Political Economy
for the Independent Institute and editor of *The Independent Review: A Journal of
Political Economy*.

1295b: 39-1296a5: It is best for citizens in a city-state to possess a moderate amount of wealth because where some have a lot and some have none the result is the ultimate democracy or unmixed oligarchy. Tyranny can result from both these extremes. It is much less likely to spring from moderate systems of government.

1276a: 12-14: Some democracies, like tyrannies, rest on force and are not directed toward the common advantage.

1312b: 35-38: Ultimate democracy, like unmixed and final oligarchy, is really a tyranny divided [among a multitude of persons].[1]

The founders of the United States of America had mixed views about democracy. Nearly all of them seem to have feared it more than they respected it. They recognized that concessions to fairly wide participation in politics might have to be made to placate the masses—who, after all, had served as cannon fodder in the recently concluded war of secession from the British Empire—but they designed a system in which voting would be hobbled and circumscribed, so that the common people would be kept from giving direct vent to their passions by seizing control of the government and using it to plunder the rich. The founders conspicuously feared "mob rule" and associated it with untrammeled democracy. All of the newly independent states required property-holding and other qualifications for voting, and, in practice, the franchise was limited in most places to a small minority of the population—a subset of the adult, white males. The Constitution of the United States does not contain the word *democracy*, although it stipulates certain protocols for the election of officials, and it relies instead on federalism and the separation of powers to preserve liberty.

Although democracy made giant ideological strides in the nineteenth century, a few writers had the courage to condemn it even well into the twentieth century. Among the most astute of them

---

[1]Thomas R. Martin, with Neel Smith and Jennifer F. Stuart, "Democracy in the Politics of Aristotle," in *Demos · Classical Athenian Democracy · a Stoa Publication* (July 26, 2003). Available at: http://www.stoa.org/projects/demos/article_aristotle_democracy?page=2&greekEncoding=.

was Joseph A. Schumpeter. In *Capitalism, Socialism and Democracy*, he posits as a point of departure for analysis the classical conception of democracy: "the democratic method is that institutional arrangement for arriving at political decisions which realizes the common good by making the people itself decide issues through the election of individuals who are to assemble in order to carry out its will."[2] He then proceeds to demolish the pretension that this conception makes sense. "If we are to argue that the will of the citizens *per se* is a political factor entitled to respect," Schumpeter argues, "it must first exist. That is to say, it must be something more than an indeterminate bundle of vague impulses loosely playing about given slogans and mistaken impressions."[3] Schumpeter calls attention to "the ordinary citizen's ignorance and lack of judgment in matters of domestic and foreign policy" and adds, anticipating the *rational ignorance* concept of public choice theory, that "without the initiative that comes from immediate responsibility, ignorance will persist in the face of masses of information however complete and correct."[4]

Moreover, "even if there were no political groups trying to influence him, the typical citizen would in political matters tend to yield to extrarational or irrational prejudice and impulse." Matters are even worse once we recognize the "opportunities for groups with an ax to grind," who "are able to fashion and, within very wide limits, even to create the will of the people," leaving political analysts to ponder "not a genuine but a manufactured will" that is "the product and not the motive power of the political process."[5]

Schumpeter conceded that, in the long run, the general public may come to hold a more perceptive view of the world and to

---

[2]Joseph A. Schumpeter, *Capitalism, Socialism and Democracy*, 3rd ed. (New York: Harper and Brothers, 1950), p. 250.

[3]Ibid., p. 253.

[4]Ibid., pp. 261, 262.

[5]Ibid., p. 263. For a recent study that grapples with this problem, see Robert Higgs and Anthony Kilduff, "Public Opinion: A Powerful Predictor of U.S. Defense Spending," in Robert Higgs, *Depression, War, and Cold War: Studies in Political Economy* (New York: Oxford University Press, 2006), pp. 195–207.

reward or punish officeholders in its light when they cast their ballots, but this eventual adjustment itself has a fatal flaw, because history "consists of a succession of short-run situations that *may alter the course of events for good:*"[6]

> If all the people can in the short run be "fooled" step by step into something they do not really want, and if this is not an exceptional case which we could afford to neglect, then no amount of retrospective common sense will alter the fact that in reality they neither raise nor decide issues but that the issues that shape their fate are normally raised and decided for them.[7]

Because "electorates normally do not control their political leaders in any way except by refusing to reelect them or the parliamentary majorities that support them,"[8] the distinct possibility – nay, the great likelihood – exists that the voters will find themselves time after time concerned about a horse that has already fled the barn, never to be retrieved.

This bleak view of the political process under representative democracy becomes even bleaker once we recognize that office-seekers typically either speak in vague, emotion-laden generalities or simply lie about their intentions. After taking office, they may act in complete disregard of their campaign promises, trusting that when they run for reelection, they will be able to concoct a plausible excuse for their infidelity and betrayal of trust. Thus, the voters remain permanently immersed in a fog of disinformation, emotional manipulation, and bald-faced mendacity. No matter what a candidate promises, the voters have no means of holding him to those promises or of punishing his misbehavior until it may be too late to matter. In many cases, unfortunately, the officeholders' decisions give rise to irreversible consequences – outcomes that cannot possibly be undone *ex post*.

Garet Garrett had a similar vision of the uselessness of democracy as a means of making government accountable to the "will of the people" (or to anything else except the rulers' own desires).

---

[6]Ibid., p. 264; emphasis added.
[7]Ibid.
[8]Ibid., p. 272.

Writing at mid-century, shortly after Schumpeter's death, in an essay titled "Ex America," Garrett posed the following hypothetical scenario:

> Suppose a true image of the present world had been presented to them in 1900, the future as in a crystal ball, together with the question, "Do you want it?" No one can imagine that they would have said yes—that they could have been tempted by the comforts, the gadgets, the automobiles and all the fabulous satisfactions of midcentury existence, to accept the coils of octopean government, the dim-out of the individual, the atomic bomb, a life of sickening fear, the nightmare of extinction. Their answer would have been no, terrifically.[9]

Having set the scene, he asked: "Then how do you account for the fact that everything that has happened to change their world from what it was to what it is has taken place with their consent?" To which he added: "More accurately, first it happened and then they consented."[10]

Garrett proceeded to list and to discuss briefly a series of cataclysmic, course-altering political events in the United States, including getting into World War I, launching the New Deal, getting into World War II, and joining the United Nations, noting that in each instance the people did not vote for the government's action, yet "to all of this the people have consented, not beforehand but afterward."[11]

One might object at this point by asking, "What difference does it make whether the people consent beforehand or afterward, so long as they consent?" Indeed, Bruce Ackerman has written an entire book to argue precisely that the most profound constitutional changes in U.S. history occurred not when the people formally amended the Constitution, but when the government acted outside its constitutional authority in a crisis *and later received electoral and judicial validation of its actions*, and that these *de facto* constitutional

---

[9]Garet Garrett, *Ex America: The 50th Anniversary of The People's Pottage*, Introduction by Bruce Ramsey (Caldwell, Idaho: Caxton Press, 2004), p. 70.

[10] Ibid.

[11]Ibid., p. 72.

revolutions deserve our approbation; indeed, they ought to serve as models for future constitutional revolutions.[12]

Ackerman's view may be challenged by noting the frequency with which constitutional revolutionaries engineer the alleged *ex post* validation of their actions. People in power have the greatest ability to gerrymander the voting districts, bias the electoral rules, buy votes with taxpayers' money, stuff the ballot boxes, and otherwise ensure that those in power—regardless of how they got there—remain in power. Similarly, people in power have the greatest ability to appoint new judges, alter judicial jurisdictions, and change the size or number of courts of appeal to ensure that those in power—regardless of how they got there—gain judicial vindication of their (heretofore unconstitutional) actions.[13]

Despite the force of the preceding objections, Ackerman might refuse to consider them a knockout blow to his thesis. Sooner or later, he might insist, the people will be able to vote against policies they find offensive, and judges will be able to overturn the constitutionality of laws that transcend the government's true constitutional authority. The political winners can't rig the game forever, so if the people and the judges never avail themselves of opportunities to express their aversion to the constitutional revolutionaries and their policies, we may presume that they actually approve of what has been done—in Garrett's words, "first it happened and then they consented."

In a sense, this interpretation may be correct, but I doubt that the sense I have in mind is one that Ackerman would welcome. If the people never avail themselves of the opportunity to overturn what was done initially without their consent, they may thereby reveal only that people who have been fed thin gruel for a long time get used to eating it and even come to consider it nutritious.[14]

---

[12]Bruce Ackerman, *We the People 2: Transformations* (Cambridge, Mass.: Belknap Press of Harvard University Press, 1998).

[13]Robert Higgs, "On Ackerman's Justification of Irregular Constitutional Change: Is Any Vice You Get Away With a Virtue?" *Constitutional Political Economy* 10 (November 1999): 375–83.

[14]For visual representation of this phenomenon, nothing can surpass the Spartan regimen depicted in early scenes of the splendid film *Babbette's Feast* (1987).

In less metaphorical terms, my claim is that ideological change is often path-dependent: where a dominant ideology stands and where it is most likely to go in the future depend significantly on where it has been in the past.[15]

Bearing in mind this aspect of political, social, and economic dynamics, we may come to understand better how, for example, in each decisive episode in the great transformation of America's political economy between 1900 and 1950, "first it happened and then they consented," and afterward the people looked back on these episodes not so much with regret as with pride and a sense that the nation had overcome great challenges. Moreover, the people subsequently elevated to the pantheon of "greatness" the presidents who had taken it upon themselves to plunge the nation into these cauldrons and endowed them with sainthood in the Church of Democracy — thus, Woodrow Wilson and Franklin D. Roosevelt, and earlier, in the same mold, Abraham Lincoln.[16]

ço ço ço

After World War I erupted in Europe in August 1914, the overwhelming majority of Americans preferred that their government remain neutral and not become engaged in the fighting. "Aversion to joining in the carnage," writes Walter Karp, "was virtually unanimous."[17] President Wilson represented himself as striving above all to end the fighting and to resist the temptation to enter the war in reaction to various provocations by both warring sides. We may well doubt the sincerity of his avowals of neutrality, however. Thomas Fleming writes that "in an unguarded moment, Wilson confessed to a friend that he hoped for an Allied victory in the

---

[15]Robert Higgs, "The Complex Course of Ideological Change," *American Journal of Economics and Sociology* 67 (October 2008): 547–65.

[16]Robert Higgs, "Great Presidents?" in *Against Leviathan: Government Power and a Free Society* (Oakland, Calif.: The Independent Institute, 2004), pp. 53–56.

[17]Walter Karp, *The Politics of War: The Story of Two Wars Which Altered Forever the Political Life of the American Republic (1890–1920)* (New York: Harper and Row, 1979), p. 169.

war but was not permitted by his public neutrality to say so."[18] There is no doubt, however, that the president and his election managers perceived that the best way for him to gain reelection in 1916 was by continuing to represent himself as a man of peace; hence, the campaign slogan "He kept us out of war."

Yet, less than a month after beginning his second term, Wilson asked Congress for a declaration of war, resting his request on the astonishing ground that Americans had an absolute right to travel unmolested on the high seas on ships carrying munitions to a warring power. "Even after Wilson broke off relations with Germany in February 1917," Karp writes, "an overwhelming majority of Americans still opposed entering the war. Even when the United States had already been at war for some months, a majority of Americans remained a sullen, silenced opposition, more profoundly alienated from their own government than any American majority has ever been before or since."[19] Karp concludes: "Representative government had failed them at every turn."[20] Democracy in action?

Probably no single event of the past century has been such a prodigious source of evils as the U.S. entry into World War I and the Versailles Treaty that U.S. entry made possible. The conquests of Bolshevism, Nazism, and Fascism and the manifold catastrophes known collectively as World War II, not to mention endless troubles in the Middle East, arguably, may be traced directly to this source.[21] In the United States, World War I prompted the government to embrace what contemporaries called "war socialism" (though it was, in more precise language, "war fascism" for the most part), which provided blueprints for an immense variety of government interventions in the economy and society, many of

---

[18]Thomas Fleming, *The Illusion of Victory: America in World War I* (New York: Basic Books, 2003), p. 75.

[19]Karp, *The Politics of War*, p. 169.

[20]Ibid., p. 324.

[21]Among recent sources, see, for example, Jim Powell, *Wilson's War: How Woodrow Wilson's Great Blunder Led to Hitler, Lenin, Stalin & World War II* (New York: Crown Forum, 2005); and Patrick J. Buchanan, *Churchill, Hitler, and the Unnecessary War: How Britain Lost Its Empire and the West Lost the World* (New York: Crown, 2008).

which continue to impoverish Americans and to crush their liberties ninety years later.[22] The war could have such extreme and enduring consequences because it had also brought about abrupt ideological changes: many Americans became convinced by their perception of the wartime controls that the government was capable of successfully engaging in socio-economic engineering on a wide front. Thus, the war put the final nail into the coffin of nineteenth-century liberalism, at least in the eyes of the major political players. As Bernard Baruch, the wartime head of the War Industries Board, declared, "We helped inter the extreme dogmas of *laissez-faire*, which had for so long molded American economic and political thought."[23]

Democracy's next colossal failure in the United States occurred in 1932. By the time of the presidential election in November, the country had experienced more than three years of worsening economic performance: falling output, rising unemployment, increasing numbers of business failures, and growing numbers of homes and businesses lost to foreclosure or to seizure for failure to pay taxes. Not without plausible reasons, people blamed President Herbert Hoover for these dreadful developments and gave Franklin D. Roosevelt, the Democratic challenger, the benefit of the doubt.

Roosevelt campaigned on a platform that the old Grover Cleveland-style Democrats of the nineteenth century might have endorsed comfortably. As Jesse Walker summarizes it:

> The very first plank calls for "an immediate and drastic reduction of governmental expenditures by abolishing useless commissions and offices, consolidating departments and bureaus, and eliminating extravagance to accomplish a saving of not less than twenty-five per cent in the cost of the Federal Government." (It also asks "the states to make a zealous effort to achieve a proportionate result.") Subsequent planks demand a balanced

---

[22]Robert Higgs, *Crisis and Leviathan: Critical Episodes in the Growth of American Government* (New York: Oxford University Press, 1987).

[23]Bernard M. Baruch, *Baruch: The Public Years* (New York: Holt, Rinehart and Winston, 1960), p. 74.

> budget, a low tariff, the repeal of Prohibition, "a sound
> currency to be preserved at all hazards," "no interfer-
> ence in the internal affairs of other nations," and "the
> removal of government from all fields of private enter-
> prise except where necessary to develop public works
> and natural resources in the common interest." The doc-
> ument concludes with a quote from Andrew Jackson:
> "equal rights to all; special privilege to none."[24]

Having made these promises, Roosevelt swept to a lopsided victory at the polls.

Yet, the merest child knows that his New Deal, a huge hodge-
podge of domestic interventions, controls, subsidies, taxes, threats,
seizures, and other troublemaking amounted to nearly the exact
opposite of what he had promised the voters during the campaign.

So what, we may hear Professor Ackerman asking offstage;
didn't the people endorse these actions by reelecting Roosevelt
with an even greater margin of victory in 1936? Yes, of course, they
did. But, by that time, the president and his party had turned the
federal government into a vast vote-buying apparatus that covered the entire country and penetrated every county, town, and
village. As John T. Flynn described the situation:

> Roosevelt's billions, adroitly used, had broken down
> every political machine in America. The patronage they
> once lived on and the local money they once had to dis-
> burse to help the poor was trivial compared to the vast
> floods of money Roosevelt controlled. And no political
> boss could compete with him in any county in America
> in the distribution of money and jobs.[25]

Nor was this garden-variety political corruption the worst of it.
Far more significant in the long run was the loss of faith in the free
market among the masses and the boost given to ideological support for economic fascism. Owing to the Great Depression and the

---

[24]Jesse Walker, "The New Franklin Roosevelts: Don't Count on a Candidate's Campaign Stances to Tell You How He'll Behave in Office," Reason
Online, April 10, 2008, at http://www.reason.com/news/show/125921.html.

[25]John T. Flynn, *The Roosevelt Myth* (Garden City, N.Y.: Garden City
Books, 1949), p. 65.

New Deal, later generations would live in chronic fear of economic privation and rest their hopes for security in a fervent belief that if the economy turned down, the government could and would rescue them. The Employment Act of 1946 codified this public dependency. Rugged individualism, to the extent that it had ever really existed, died a cruel death at the hands of the New Deal — precisely the *opposite* of what Roosevelt had promised when he first campaigned for the presidency. Democracy in action?

Roosevelt was still in office when the next great travesty of democracy occurred, in 1940. War between the great powers had resumed in Europe, as everyone had expected it eventually would after the Versailles Treaty was signed in 1919. Just as the great majority of Americans had wished to keep away from the fighting in 1914, so a great majority again wanted nothing to do with the European bloodletting. Roosevelt, as the leader of the small minority that favored going to war — to save the British and (dare we conjecture?) to permit him to achieve the "greatness" that only wartime leadership brings — had to play his cards carefully. For two years, mendacity would be his major political device, as he sought to maneuver Germany and Japan into an "incident" so inflammatory that it would shock the public into supporting U.S. entry into the war.[26]

Roosevelt's vaulting ambition fed his quest for reelection to an unprecedented third term. Given the massive public opposition to war — opposition, that is, to the very objective whose attainment he sought above all others — the president, who had already begun to involve the country in the war in discreet ways, lifted his dishonesty to a higher level as the election approached. In a campaign speech at Boston on October 30, 1940, he declared bluntly: "I have said this before, but I shall say it again and again: Your boys are not going to be sent into any foreign wars." As David M. Kennedy notes, "Conspicuously, Roosevelt omitted the qualifying phrase

---

[26]Among the many sources relevant to this maneuvering, see the recent works by Robert B. Stinnett, *Day of Deceit: The Truth about FDR and Pearl Harbor* (New York: Free Press, 2000); Thomas Fleming, *The New Dealers' War: F.D.R. and the War within World War II* (New York: Basic Books, 2001); and George Victor, *The Pearl Harbor Myth: Rethinking the Unthinkable* (Dulles, Va.: Potomac Books, 2007).

that he had used on previous occasions: 'except in case of attack.'"[27] Relying on this seemingly frank promise, the electorate returned Roosevelt to office for another term.

In return, of course, they found themselves being pushed farther and farther toward open U.S. belligerency, until finally the Japanese attack on Pearl Harbor gave the president what he, his chief subordinates, and his closest supporters had been seeking from the start: declared engagement in the greatest armed conflict of all time. Democracy in action?

By the time it ended, Americans had suffered more than a million casualties, including more than 400,000 servicemen's deaths, and four years of economic fascism on the home front, with extensive controls and government takeovers that dwarfed those of any comparable episode in the United States before or since. Moreover, the entire world had been altered, as the Soviet Union, America's wartime ally, now stood astride all of eastern Europe and much of central Europe, too, as far west as Czechoslovakia, so that when the violence ended in 1945, only a tense pseudo-peace took its place, and the world was condemned to live in fear of nuclear annihilation indefinitely.

For this dismal result, we may credit the democratic system that put Franklin D. Roosevelt and his party in power and allowed them to make the United States the decisive factor in the war's outcome. Without America's active involvement in the war, the British might have been forced to sue for peace, and the Germans and the Soviets might have bled one another to death—a grisly outcome, to be sure, but would it have been any worse than what actually happened? We cannot know, of course; history is not ours to rerun, like a controlled experiment with reset conditions. Yet, we can scarcely deny that the devastated world of 1945, with 50 million dead, tens of millions left sick, wounded, or homeless, and a murderous Communist dictator in control of half of Europe, was scarcely what most Americans sought to bring about when they cast their votes for Roosevelt in 1940.

---

[27]David M. Kennedy, *Freedom from Fear: The American People in Depression and War, 1929–1945* (New York: Oxford University Press, 1999), p. 463.

જ જ જ

Democracy has always had its critics. No one claims that it is a perfect system for choosing political leaders or for putting in place the policies and laws the public prefers. Obviously, when individual preferences differ, no one political outcome can please everybody, and the "tyranny of the majority" stands as a constant menace to the lives, liberties, and property of unpopular minorities. Yet, most people continue to insist that democracy, with all its faults, offers to best institutional arrangement for making rulers accountable to the people. So long as elections continue to be held, the possibility always remains of "throwing the rascals out."

What has not been widely recognized, however, is the problem of *faits accomplis*. Once elected rulers have taken office, the democratic system provides little or no effective means for the people to bring them to heel short of the next election. The great problem is that, by that time, it may be impossible to reverse the outcomes the rulers have brought about. Wilson was not elected in 1916 to plunge the nation into the Great War. Roosevelt was not elected in 1932 to impose the New Deal on the country. Nor was he elected in 1940 to maneuver the United States into the greatest war of all time. Yet, in each case, the president did the opposite of what he had promised to do, and the people were left with no recourse. The world of 1919, the United States of 1936, and the world of 1945 — each was so massively, so irrevocably altered from the preceding status quo that any genuine restoration of the previous conditions was unimaginable. Like it or not, people were to a great extent simply stuck with what the deceitful politicians had done.

Worse, owing to "ideological learning," many people who initially had not desired these changes *did* approve of them in the circumstances in which they later found themselves — circumstances that they had in no way chosen, not even indirectly, but into which they had been forcibly shoved by the ruling decision-makers. Contemplating this situation, one readily recalls Goethe's dictum that "none are more hopelessly enslaved than those who falsely believe they are free."

Still worse, an altered ideological context then sets the stage from which a society may be propelled even further from the course it initially preferred during the next round of democratic choice, unconstrained decisions by elected officials, and the result-ing *faits accomplis*. If people believe that democracy is a means by which ordinary people may ensure that they exercise some control over their own societal fate, they are fooling themselves. If the per-sons elected to office have a free hand to act as they please, then the sense that they are truly accountable to the electorate is an illu-sion. It comes closer to the truth to say that the people are com-pletely at the mercy of the officials they have elected.

"Democracy," wrote H.L. Mencken, "may be a self-limiting dis-ease, as civilization itself seems to be. There are thumping para-doxes in its philosophy, and some of them have a suicidal smack."[28] Whether it will prove suicidal for its adherents, only time will tell, but we might note that, so far, only the United States of America, whose leaders and people tout their country as the greatest of all democracies, has employed nuclear weapons in war. It is not inconceivable that Woodrow Wilson's war to make the world safe for democracy, owing to the train of consequences it set in motion, may ultimately make the world safe for democracy, to be sure, but not safe for mankind. ❧

---

[28]H.L. Mencken, *A Mencken Chrestomathy* (New York: Knopf, 1949), p. 157.

27

Against the Primacy of Politics –
Against the Overestimation of
Majority Principle

Robert Nef

M uch as one may admire the clear-sightedness of Greco-Roman political philosophy and especially Aristotle, one should not shy away from fundamental criticism. It has had a pervasive and toxic influence on the history of political thought.

ATHENS – ON THE BACK OF AN ARMY OF SLAVES

For Aristotle, democracy was a *decayed form* of that "rule by the many" that he called a polity. So the career of the term "democracy," which is generally regarded nowadays as positive, began with radical criticism. Aristotle accurately identified and described the potential of the principle of majority rule to degenerate. His *Politics* is a plea for a mixed constitution. He differentiates between rule by *one, few* or *many*. All three forms of government can be *basically positive* if they "rule with a view to the common profit" and

Robert Nef (robertnef@bluewin.ch) is Chairman of the Liberales Institut in Zurich, a classical liberal think tank. This chapter is extracted from an address he gave on 28 June 2008 in Freiburg (Breisgau, Germany) on the occasion of receiving the Hayek Medal from the Friedrich A. von Hayek Gesellschaft.

fail if they serve only to benefit the one or the few or the many. Aristotle regards it as possible for the many to rule virtuously, but he considers it unlikely. His reasoning is entirely empirical:

> For while it is possible for one or a few to be outstandingly virtuous, it is difficult for a larger number to be accomplished in every virtue, but it can be so in military virtue in particular. That is precisely why the class of defensive soldiers, the ones who possess the weapons, has the most authority in this constitution.
>
> Deviations from these are tyranny from kingship, oligarchy from aristocracy, and democracy from polity. For tyranny is rule by one person for the benefit of the monarch, oligarchy is for the benefit of the rich, and democracy is for the benefit of the poor. But none is for their common profit.[1]

Although Aristotle showed himself to be a shrewd observer of his contemporaries when he defined man as a political animal (*zoon politikon*), in my opinion he prepared the way for a devastating overestimation of political, and a momentous underestimation of private, economic and civil society. For aristocrats like himself and Plato before him, and for many leisured aesthetes who came after him, *homo oeconomicus* – the farmer, the tradesman, the service provider and the merchant – was nothing but a philistine. These people – on the back of an army of slaves and other disenfranchised persons – concerned themselves with such banal activities as making a living. In continental Europe, this kind of division of labor between economics and politics has led to a widespread contempt for *homo oeconomicus* and for the economy as such, in both the broad and narrow sense of the word.

The intellectual preference for *homo politicus* over *homo oeconomicus* is alive and well. The "primacy of politics," as a fundamental principle of a grey-haired generation of believers in co-determination and grassroots democracy, still haunts the literature of social sciences.

---

[1] Aristotle, *Politics*, C.D.C. Reeve, trans. (Indianapolis: Hackett Publishing Company, 1998), Book III, chap. 7, 1279a39–1279b8.

APPENZELL AS THE COUNTERPART OF ANCIENT ATHENS

Direct democracy as embodied in the Appenzell "Landsge-meinde" differs markedly from the democracy of the Athenians.[2] In Athens, the popular assemblies were convened three or four times a month and those who attended received a *per diem* payment. The assembly of the people controlled the civil service, supervised the state-regulated distribution of grain, decided whether to go to war or make peace, passed verdicts in cases of treason, ostracized citizens considered a danger to the state, listened to petitions, and selected the key functionaries for military matters, for whom war then became crucial to their survival. The Council of 500 met practically every day! The Convention, which was established during the French Revolution and became the model for many contemporary parliamentary systems, took many of its ideas from this system. In this way, politics itself becomes the disease that it is supposed to cure.

A marked contrast is provided by the political system of the two Appenzells, which have managed to compete peacefully for centuries with politically comparable but religiously and culturally differing ways of governing and living.

This political system, which was practiced consistently for more than five hundred years, was in fact direct democracy. This refutes all assertions, including those of Aristotle, that rule by the many must collapse eventually under the weight of its internal deficiencies because it would inevitably lead to exploitation of the minority of rich citizens by the majority of the non-rich.

At the "Landsgemeinde," a kind of open-air general assembly, elections were held and laws passed — or thrown out if there was no consensus. The chief magistrate, who was mandated by the people to act in a part-time capacity as head of the government, was entrusted for one year with the state seal with which contracts were officially sealed and was required to render public account to the effect that any action taken had been "for the good of the country."

---

[2]Karl Mittermaier and Meinhard Mair, *Demokratie, Geschichte Einer Politis-chen Idee von Platon bis Heute* [Democracy, the History of a Political Idea from Plato to Today] (Darmstadt: Wissenschaftliche Buchgesellschaft, Darmstadt, 1995).

All posts in government and the judiciary were—and in some cases still are—part-time, unsalaried, and restricted to one year. There is no such thing as a professional politician; politics is merely a part of the function of each citizen. Those in positions of responsibility were elected and dismissed directly by the people. Their powers were always severely restricted. These involved, in particular, foreign policy, the legal system, and cantonal road construction. There was almost nothing to distribute apart from burdens. The decision to embark on a military campaign was taken by those who then made up the army. This co-identity of those taking the decision with those who had to implement it is crucial, especially in the area of military service where the collective demands that the individual put his life in jeopardy. In this case, Aristotle got it right. Where it is a matter of choosing war or peace—a fundamental political question—the many, who bear the consequences of the decision, are in fact more competent to decide than the few who may benefit from it.

This is the essential difference between the slave-owners and politicking idlers of Athens and the hard-working small farmers of Appenzell, who not only labored on their own land but also formed the militia that protected it. The importance of public and private issues—*res publica* and *res privata*—was fundamentally different.

Generally the minimum consensus was found at the "Landsgemeinde" through the procedures of direct democracy, often with very substantial majorities. Sometimes the assemblies would end in dispute, but although all those present were armed, the disputes did not lead to bloodshed. For one day in the year, each man was a *zoon politikon*. The other 364 days belonged to the "Häämetli" (i.e., the home farm), its private economy, the community of one's family, and the locally anchored culture. In summary, therefore, the process of building consensus within a democracy on the basis of the principle of majority rule is possible if it is limited in terms of scope, timeframe, and finance to the smallest possible portion of the life of a civil society, and if co-determination remains the exception to the rule of self-determination.

The practice of direct democracy in the two Appenzells has been presented here in a simplified and—admittedly—idealized way. It is regrettable that the open assembly, which had been an institution in Canton Appenzell Ausserrhoden, an industrialized area since the 19th century, was discontinued about ten years ago. However, it proved possible to retain the militia principle and the relatively lean political apparatus.

Without the instinctual distrust of all kinds of power, the principle of majority rule is in danger of doing away with that creative dissidence on which majorities too have to rely over the longer term. In the final analysis, protection for minorities protects the majority from collective stupefaction, but a great deal of nonsense is also propagated on the back of protection for minorities. It is often used to introduce group privileges of all kinds. We must not lose sight of the fact that, as Ayn Rand observed, the most important minority is the individual.

Self-determination is Better than Co-determination

Co-determination in accordance with the principle of majority rule is not an end in itself. It enjoys a subsidiary position *vis-à-vis* acts of individual self-determination. I remind readers of the priority enjoyed by the "home farm" over the wider community in Appenzell, namely 364 to 1. The burden of proof, as regards long-term practicability and common benefit, is borne by those who want to replace personal autonomy based on the principle of self-determination with collective autonomy based on the principle of majority rule.

One should not make it too easy for them to provide this proof before the intellectual forum that assesses political power in theory at first and then also in practice. Despite Alcuin's and Lichtenberg's formulation (*vox populi vox Dei*), and consonant with Hans Hoppe, the principle of majority rule is "a god that is none."[3]

The compulsion to do good and, above all, the compulsion to do what the majority holds to be good, turns diversity into uniformity and has a destructive impact on the community overall.

---

[3]See Hans-Hermann Hoppe, *Democracy – The God that Failed: The Economics and Politics of Monarchy, Democracy, and Natural Order* (New Brunswick, N.J.: Transaction Publishers, 2001).

Every creative community is based on peaceful competition, and if the principle of majority rule is misused to get rid of unpopular alternative solutions, it degenerates into rule by those populists who happen to have the ear of the majority at the time. ❧

Part Five

Economics

28

Hoppean Political Economy versus Public Choice

Thomas J. DiLorenzo

James M. Buchanan's 1986 Nobel prize in economics signified recognition of the fact that Buchanan and his colleagues in the sub-discipline of "public choice" had resurrected the study of *political economy* in the profession. From at least the time of Adam Smith until the early twentieth century, it was generally understood that one could not fully understand the economic world unless one included study of the impact of the state on the economy. In its zeal to mimic the physical sciences, the economics profession had abandoned the study of political economy, for the most part (with the exception of the Austrians), and embraced mathematical model building—usually of "models" that explained why markets always "failed."

Buchanan's pioneering work in public choice did not directly challenge the voluminous "market failure" literature; instead, he and others developed theories of the political process under democracy, based on economic theory and methodology, that helped to explain why government failure is likely to be far worse

Thomas J. DiLorenzo (tdilo@aol.com) is professor of economics at Loyola University-Maryland, and a senior fellow at the Ludwig von Mises Institute.

than any shortcomings of the free market, by any standard (certainly by the standard of Pareto optimality).[1] Thus, public choice is said to be a study of "comparative failures," of markets and governments.

Hans Hoppe's seminal work, *Democracy – The God that Failed*,[2] is in many ways far superior to the analysis of democracy that is provided by public choice analysis because it is grounded, not in neoclassical economic theory, but in "Austrian social theory" and is especially influenced by the work of Ludwig von Mises and Murray Rothbard. The combination of Austrian economics and the historical and philosophical insights of Mises and Rothbard enabled Hoppe to develop insights that are at times devastatingly critical of the much-acclaimed public choice theory while providing far superior explanations of the workings of democracy. The purpose of this paper is to point out or highlight some of these major insights and to explain how they are different from, and superior to, public choice insights.

DEMOCRACY AND THE PROCESS OF DECIVILIZATION

One of the first differences between Hoppean political economy and public choice has to do with Buchanan's standard explanation for why government is supposedly needed in the first place. In short, Buchanan has endlessly repeated the slogan attributed to the philosopher Thomas Hobbes that in a voluntary society without government, life would be "nasty, brutish and short." The implication is that without government, theft and violence would run rampant, creating a chaotic, unpleasant, and dangerous society.

But Buchanan has never offered much more than a repetition of this catchy slogan to make this argument. Hoppe, on the other

---

[1]See, e.g., James M. Buchanan and Gordon Tullock, *The Calculus of Consent: Logical Foundations of Constitutional Democracy* (Ann Arbor: University of Michigan, 1962); James M. Buchanan, *Cost and Choice: An Inquiry in Economic Theory* (Chicago: Markham, 1969).

[2]Hans-Hermann Hoppe, *Democracy – The God that Failed: The Economics and Politics of Monarchy, Democracy, and Natural Order* (New Brunswick, N.J.: Transaction Publishers, 2001).

hand, thinks the issue through very systematically. Yes, criminal activity can be destructive of civilization, but so can government itself, and much more than mere criminal activity. That is, "democracy" may not only fail to be "perfect" and in need of reform; it can be the *cause* of that "nasty" and "brutish" life that Hobbes and Buchanan so feared.

For one thing, victims (or potential victims) of crime can always legitimately defend themselves. This is not true whenever governments seek to confiscate one's property through taxation, "takings," or regulation. "In these cases a victim may *not* legitimately defend himself," writes Hoppe.[3] And "[t]he imposition of a government tax on property or income violates a property or income producer's rights as much as theft does."[4] Governmental money creation is also an act of theft, since it reduces the value of privately-held wealth. Regulation also constitutes theft, since ordering someone as to how he may use his property (beyond prohibiting him from harming someone else with it) amounts to "extortion, robbery, or destruction." And since property rights destruction by government becomes institutionalized (since citizens cannot legitimately defend against it), the entire society becomes more present-oriented and develops a higher rate of time preference due to the fact that people's expected rate of return on productive, future-oriented activity is reduced.

In a worst-case scenario many "formerly provident providers will be turned into drunks or daydreamers, adults into children, civilized men into barbarians, and producers into criminals."[5] Who could deny that this is a characteristic of modern democracies like the U.S.? As such, democratic government "presents a constant threat to the process of civilization," precisely the opposite of Buchanan's view of the "necessity" of government in defense of civilization.[6]

---

[3]Hoppe, *Democracy*, p. 12.
[4]Ibid., p. 13.
[5]Ibid., p. 15.
[6]Ibid.

In the first chapter of *Democracy — The God that Failed* Hoppe clearly states that he is not a monarchist and does not support monarchy. He merely applies logic and economic reasoning to a comparison of monarchy in order to highlight features of democracy that are typically ignored by public choice scholars (and most everyone else). Basing his analysis on a property rights perspective, something that public choice scholars rarely do, Hoppe makes the point that, since they own the entire country, monarchs will have incentives to minimize the destructiveness of crime, and will also moderate the extent to which they expropriate the wealth of their citizens lest they destroy their incentives to be productive.

Democratic politicians, by contrast, behave in exactly the opposite way: they will seek to maximize current income in a process of "continual capital consumption."[7] For what is not used up now by current officeholders will be gone forever (for *their* taking) in a few years.

Hoppe's analysis of government debt also differs from the standard public choice analysis. The latter contends that all politicians, regardless of party affiliation, have an inclination to vote to spend now and pay later — to engage in deficit spending as a means of creating a "fiscal illusion," i.e., making government seem less expensive than it actually is to current voters.

Hoppe focuses on the effects of property rights instead. Since politicians in a democracy are not held *personally* responsible for the debts that they incur while in office, the public debt will naturally increase. Taxes will have to be raised to service the increasing debt, which in turn will cause even higher rates of time preference as taxpayers anticipate higher future tax burdens. Society becomes progressively "infantilized."

As democracy grows, writes Hoppe, it tends to wage a constant war against individual responsibility by "increasingly relieving individuals of the responsibility of having to provide for their own health, safety, and old age."[8] The combination of high time preference, coupled with the lack of irresponsibility inevitably leads to *more crime* in society, not less, as society sinks into moral

---

[7]Ibid., p. 24.
[8]Ibid., p. 66.

relativism. Thus, democracy is not necessary to deter crime and maintain civilization; it causes crime.

FAILURES OF PUBLIC CHOICE

Although most members of the Public Choice Society, the professional academic organization of public choice scholars, would consider themselves to be political conservatives or libertarians, their research agenda has been tainted to some degree by fear of political incorrectness, a fear that no one would ever accusing Hoppe of having. Perhaps the most glaring example of this is the almost complete absence of any discussion of the topic of secession in a field that is supposed to be devoted to research of political institutions. Failure to consider the implications of political secession (unlike Mises, Rothbard, and Hoppe) has led public choice scholars to essentially waste thousands of pages of print, and years of research effort, in their writings on the topic of federalism and the political economy of state and local government.

What I am referring to is a large literature in public choice that models "competition" between local governments in a metropolitan area as being similar to competition in an industry. Voters are said to be able to "vote with their feet" if a particular governmental jurisdiction has say, excessively high taxes and/or low-quality "public services." Such mobility is said to "discipline" state and local politicians in the same way that marketplace competition disciplines corporate managers and gives them incentives to cut costs and prices and improve the quality of the goods and services they are selling.

But this entire literature, most of which is based on research on the U.S. political system, completely ignores the historical reality and effects of the U.S. government's violent destruction of the right of secession. After the U.S. government proved to the world that participation in its union was in no way voluntary, all of the states (not just Southern states) soon became mere appendages or franchisees of the central government. Government at all levels became more and more centralized and, as a result, there was very little difference in terms of tax burden between jurisdictions. Decades of research in public finance bears this out by showing that differences in interstate tax burdens do not provide much of an incentive at all for the migration of population or businesses. This is all simply ignored by public choice scholars who proceed with their analyses as though the American War Between the States never happened. Not Hoppe, though. He cites Ludwig von Mises who "had a soft spot for democracy," but believed that an essential feature of any democracy must be the right of secession.[9] He quotes Mises from his book *Liberalism* as saying that classical liberalism

> forces no one against his will into the structure of the state. . . . When a part of a people of a state wants to drop out of the union, liberalism does not hinder it from doing so. . . . [W]henever the inhabitants of a particular territory . . . make it known, by a freely conducted plebiscite, that they no longer wish to remain united to the state to which they belong at the time, their wishes are to be respected and complied with.[10]

This is how Mises believed a democratic government could be induced to respect property rights.

The right of secession was eliminated, of course, in 1865. As Hoppe writes:

> Mises's definition of democratic government was applicable to the U.S. until 1861. . . . However, after the crushing defeat and devastation of the secessionist Confederacy by Lincoln and the Union, it was clear that the right to secede no longer existed and that democracy meant absolute and unlimited majority rule.[11]

Hoppe does not make the mistake that public choice scholars make in assuming that state and local politicians are analogous to business managers who compete for "customers" by offering better services or lower (tax) prices. They do compete, says Hoppe,

---

[9]Ibid., p. xxiii.

[10]Hoppe, *Democracy*, p. 79, quoting Ludwig von Mises, *Liberalism: In the Classical Tradition*, Ralph Raico, trans. (Irvington-on-Hudson, N.Y.: Foundation for Economic Education, [1927] 1985), p. 109.

[11]Ibid., p. 80.

but they are competing for the "right" to plunder the taxpaying population. After all, Americans have a wide choice of post offices to do business with, but they are all a part of the same centralized U.S. Postal Service monopoly. Their choice among local governments is no more of a genuine choice than the "choice" among monopoly post offices is.

Many of the more prominent public choice scholars ignore the role of ideas in shaping public policy, most likely because of their positivist method. The influence of ideas on society is not something that can be easily "measured" and subjected to econometric testing, so it is simply ignored.

In contrast, following Mises and Rothbard, Hoppe shows how "the power of every government rests only on opinion and consensual cooperation," ultimately.[12] Moreover, "if the power of government rests on the widespread acceptance of false and indeed absurd and foolish ideas, then the only genuine protection is the systematic attack of these ideas and the propagation and proliferation of true ones."[13] Furthermore, if government becomes tyrannical and therefore illegitimate, then it is one's duty to consider "all federal law, legislation and regulation null and void and ignore it whenever possible."[14] Peaceful secession and non-cooperation with the illegitimate state is the only way to avoid being a slave to the state, says Hoppe.

This is dramatically different from the life work of James M. Buchanan, whose "constitutional economics," a branch of public choice, was established to pursue the project of constructing "a voluntary theory of the state," in the words of onetime Buchanan protégé, Viktor Vanberg.[15] Buchanan and others have spun many tales of a *theoretically* voluntary state, but of course there is nothing voluntary about the real-world state. Thinking of the American

---

[12]Ibid., p. 90.

[13]Ibid., p. 93.

[14]Ibid., p. 91.

[15]Viktor Vanberg, "The Impossibility of Rational Regulation? Regulation, Free-Market Liberalism, and Constitutional Liberalism," paper presented at the Annual Meeting of the Mont Pèlerin Society, Washington, D.C. (August 31, 1988).

state in the post-1861 era as somehow voluntary is simply ludi-crous.

Another major difference between Hoppean political economy and public choice is in the area of "class analysis." In their seminal work, *The Calculus of Consent*, Buchanan and Gordon Tullock adamantly denied that their analysis of political decision making and interest-group politics had anything to do with any kind of class analysis, especially Marxian class struggle analysis. This was a serious departure from classical liberalism, for there is a very long history of "libertarian class analysis" that is not based on any conflict between workers and capitalists, but on governmental exploiters versus the exploited taxpayers.

By definition, writes Hoppe, democracy means that everyone's income and property is immediately "up for grabs" by any politi-cal coalition that is powerful enough to grab it. "Majorities of 'have-nots' will relentlessly try to enrich themselves at the expense of 'haves'."[16] Following Rothbard, Hoppe is not fearful of quoting the great John C. Calhoun's *Disquisition on Government* that makes this point very eloquently.[17] (But because Calhoun is considered by some to have been the philosopher of Southern secession in the nineteenth century, political correctness in today's academe (including public choice scholars) demands that he be ignored.)

Hoppean political economy is nowhere more diametrically opposed to public choice theory than in Hoppe's statements on the subject of what to do about all of the decivilizing effects of democ-racy. The standard public choice approach is to try to recommend small changes at the margins of political decision making that will supposedly "improve" democracy, e.g., balanced-budget amend-ments to the Constitution, qualified majority-rule voting, term lim-its, etc. And of course thousands of pages of books and journal articles have been devoted to bolstering this approach by arguing, essentially, that democratic government really is voluntary, despite all outward appearances. Just read any issue of Buchanan's

---

[16]Hoppe, *Democracy*, p. 96.

[17]John C. Calhoun, *A Disquisition on Government* (New York: Liberal Arts Press, 1953).

Journal of Constitutional Economics for a look at this viewpoint. All of the attempts by such scholars to redesign modern constitutions, says Hoppe, are "hopelessly naïve."[18]

In sharp contrast, Hoppe writes that "The central task of those wanting to turn the tide and prevent an outright breakdown [of civilization] is the 'delegitimation' of the idea of democracy as the root cause of the present state of progressive decivilization."[19] Even the founding fathers, Hoppe points out, were "strictly opposed to" democracy and considered it to be "nothing but mob-rule."[20] The idea of democracy, in Hoppe's opinion, is immoral as well as uneconomical.[21] Practitioners of "constitutional economics" will be offended by such language, but in the tradition of Mises and Rothbard, Hoppe's first and foremost objective is the pursuit of truth, even if it comes at the expense of having a less-than-cozy relationship with other segments of the economics profession.

Hoppe attacks the hopelessly naïve views of "constitutional economics" head on, by recognizing that the long history of theorizing about "tacit" (but not actual) consent for government is patently absurd. In *The Calculus of Consent*, for example, Buchanan and Tullock argue that political decision making is *in theory* similar to marketplace decision making, especially if one can theorize about unanimous political consent. They recognize that there is never unanimous consent in politics, and that if there was, there would of course be no need for government. Truly voluntary behavior would emerge.

So they first make the case for "qualified" majority voting, still recognizing that 60 percent or 70 percent is not the same as 100 percent agreement. They then resort to the notion of "tacit" or "conceptual" consent. If one can conceive of unanimous consent, then one can declare government to be voluntary after all, say Buchanan and Tullock. This is pure nonsense, says Hoppe, and he is certainly

---

[18]Hoppe, *Democracy*, p. 110.
[19]Ibid., p. 103.
[20]Ibid.
[21]Ibid., p. 104.

correct. How this apology for statism ever became considered to be a part of classical liberalism is a mystery. (But perhaps this explains why the Swedish socialists who sit on the Nobel prize committee gave Buchanan the award in 1986.)

One further thing that characterizes the work of many public choice scholars, especially Buchanan and his followers, is an overblown degree of importance that is given to the "free-rider problem" in economics. Your author has personally heard Buchanan invoke the free-rider problem, the prisoner's dilemma, and Thomas Hobbes on dozens of occasions to justify the existence of the state, i.e., democracy. Having established the point that the "minimal state" is absolutely necessary, public choice scholars then go about their business of proposing minor tinkering at the margins with regard to the "rules of the game" of political decision making under the wishful belief that democracy can somehow be tamed.

Hoppe addresses this point head on as well by pointing out how one man's free-rider problem is often another man's profit opportunity (for solving the "problem"). Perhaps the most famous example of the alleged need for government to "solve" free-rider problems is national defense, which is always defined as a prototypical public good. As such, we are told that government must tax us to provide it and, furthermore, defense must be supplied by a government-run monopoly.

But isn't monopoly another form of "market failure?", Hoppe asks. Exactly how does one make the case for allocative efficiency by "solving" one "market failure" problem and replacing it with another one?

Austrian social theory, unlike all branches of "mainstream economics," including public choice theory, does not make the mistake of placing too much credence in the notion that truth about a subject as complicated as democracy can be arrived at in a theoretical vacuum that ignores history and philosophy. By largely ignoring history, or selectively using only the parts of it that support their research paradigm, public choice theorists have constructed a naïve and misleading view of constitutions and constitutionalism.

From the beginning of the American republic there were two distinct views of constitutional interpretation: the Jeffersonian view and the Hamiltonian view. Jefferson and his followers believed that the U.S Constitution could and should be seen as a set of limitations on the powers of the central government. Hamilton and his followers saw it exactly the opposite way: as a potential rubber stamp of approval (if "properly interpreted" by clever lawyers like Alexander Hamilton) for anything the central state ever wanted to do. It took several generations, but by the twentieth century the Hamiltonian view prevailed. Not a single federal law was ruled unconstitutional by the rubber stamp U.S. Supreme Court between 1937 and 1995.[22]

This did not happen overnight. It was the result of a long struggle in the war of ideas, combined with the brutal mass killing of the only group in American society to ever challenge the notion of unlimited powers wielded by the central government — the Southern secessionists. By 1865 the principle had been established that the federal government would be the sole authority with regard to issues of constitutionality. As the Jeffersonians had long warned, when the day ever came that the federal government assumed such authority, it would inevitably assert that there are, in fact, no limits at all to its powers. This is where America stands today, and has been standing for several generations.

Hoppe was never deluded by all the happy talk about constitutionalism. What can be done about the current state of affairs? "First," he writes,

> the American Constitution must be recognized for what it is — an error. . . . [G]overnment is supposed to protect life, property, and the pursuit of happiness. Yet in granting government the power to tax and legislate without consent, the Constitution cannot possibly assure this goal but is instead the very instrument for invading and destroying the rights to life, liberty, and the pursuit of happiness.[23]

---

[22]For further discussion of these issues, see Thomas J. DiLorenzo, *Hamilton's Curse: How Jefferson's Arch Enemy Betrayed the American Revolution — and What It Means for Americans Today* (New York: Crown Forum, 2008).

[23]Hoppe, *Democracy*, p. 279.

Austrian social theory is a far superior tool for understanding economic and political reality than is public choice theory. *Democracy – The God that Failed* is a true classic in the literature of liberalism, whereas it is a mystery as to why anyone would consider *The Calculus of Consent*, which is basically a social contract theory/apology for statism, to even be included in that literature. ❧

29

Securitization and Fractional Reserve Banking

Nikolay Gertchev

For good economists, the link between the operation of a fractional reserve banking system and the recurrence of boom-bust cycles is of little doubt. One of the paramount figures who has contributed to the intellectual elaboration of this relationship and to its transmission to young economists, among which the present writer has had the pleasure to count himself, is Professor Hans-Hermann Hoppe. Professor Hoppe has embedded the economic analysis of banking within a fairly general and carefully constructed theory of property rights.[1] In this way, he has further substantiated the relationship between an inflating banking system and the growing, illegitimate government invasion of property rights that Ludwig von Mises and Murray Rothbard

---

Nikolay Gertchev (ngertchev@gmail.com) is an economist with the European Commission, Brussels, Belgium. The views expressed in this article are strictly personal and do not engage the responsibility of the European Commission.

[1]Hans-Hermann Hoppe, "Banking, Nation States and International Politics: A Sociological Reconstruction of the Present Economic Order," *Review of Austrian Economics* 4 (1990): 55–87; idem, "How is Fiat Money Possible? — or, The Devolution of Money and Credit," *Review of Austrian Economics* 7, no. 2 (1994): 49–74; Hans-Hermann Hoppe, Jörg Guido Hülsmann, and Walter Block, "Against Fiduciary Media," *Quarterly Journal of Austrian Economics* 1, no. 1 (1990): 19–50.

have exposed.[2] Furthermore, he has demonstrated the consequences of state monopolies of money production (fiat paper monies) on international politics.[3]

While central banks, which provide fractional reserve banks (FRBs) and financial markets with liquidities created *ex nihilo*, have been systematically shown as the driver of inflation and of business cycles, other financial institutions have received significantly less attention in this respect. The purpose of this article is to investigate the extent to which securitization has played a role similar to that of central banks. Securitization has been growing for the last few decades and, like the use of derivatives, it has become a salient feature of present-day financial systems.[4] Despite lawyers', economists', and practitioners' analyses, and the renewed interest it has sparked since the 2007 subprime debt crisis, securitization's broad macroeconomic effects have not been fully expounded yet.[5]

---

[2]Ludwig von Mises, *Theory of Money and Credit* (Indianapolis, Ind.: Liberty Fund, 1981 [1912]); idem, *Human Action: A Treatise on Economics*, Scholars ed. (Auburn, Ala.: Mises Institute, 1998 [1949]); Murray N. Rothbard, *What Has Government Done to Our Money?* (Auburn, Ala.: Mises Institute, 1990 [1963]). Even though Mises and Rothbard are not the first to have demonstrated how the monopoly of money production can be used as a means of expropriation, they are the closest, by intellectual affinity and scholarly heritage, to the essentialist and ethical flavor of Hoppe's particular analysis.

[3]Hans-Hermann Hoppe, "Government, Money, and International Politics," *Etica & Politica/Ethics and Politics* 5, no. 2 (2003).

[4]Two technical specialists of the field even advance that securitization is as crucial as capital markets: "Securitization is as necessary to any economy as organized financial markets." Frank Fabozzi and Vinod Kothari, "Securitization: The Tool of Financial Transformation," Yale International Center for Finance, Working Paper No. 07-07 (2007), p. 11.

[5]Since 1996, the area is the central topic of a journal of its own – *The Journal of Structured Finance*. References to the large variety of legal studies, as well as basic treatment of the fundamental legal issues raised by securitization, can be found in Claire Hill, "Securitization: A Low-cost Sweetener for Lemons," *Washington University Law Quarterly* (Winter 1996): 1061–1120 and Steven Schwarcz, "The Alchemy of Asset Securitization," *Stanford Journal of Law, Business and Finance* 1 (1994): 133–54. The following technical presentations were all published by the research departments of central banks: Randall Pozdena, "Securitization and Banking," *Weekly Letter*, Federal Reserve Bank of San Francisco (July 4, 1986); Charles Carlstrom and Katherine

The goal of this contribution to Professor Hoppe's *Festschrift* is to suggest an economic interpretation of securitization. The first section defines this financial technique, presents a short history thereof and broadly quantifies its significance. Section two details its operational aspects when used by FRBs. Section three systematizes the main economic features of securitization by banks and offers a broad assessment of the technique.

DEFINITION, RATIONALE, AND SCOPE OF SECURITIZATION

In the course of production for exchange, economic actors obtain rights to future payments of money. For instance, a car dealer that sells his cars on credit for five years gets a claim on future receivables in exchange of his cars. Such credits are relatively illiquid because their characteristics tend to be sector- and client-specific. In some cases, non-financial companies may want not to get involved in the business of making credit. For these, and other possible reasons, economic actors who own claims on future payments may prefer to exchange them for an amount of money that is available now.[6] Each of these claims can be individually

---

Samolyk, "Securitization: More than Just a Regulatory Artifact," *Economic Commentary*, Federal Reserve Bank of Cleveland (May 1, 1992); Christine Cumming, "The Economics of Securitization," *Federal Reserve Bank of New York Quarterly Review* (Autumn 1987): 11–22; Ronel Elul, "The Economics of Asset Securitization," *Business Review*, Federal Reserve Bank of Philadelphia (Q3 2005), pp. 16–25; Emre Ergungor, "Securitization," *Economic Commentary*, Federal Reserve Bank of Cleveland (August 15, 2003). Practical issues, such as the impact of securitization on interest rates and on monetary policy, have been developed by James Kolari, Donald Fraser and Ali Anari, "The Effects of Securitization on Mortgage Market Yields: A Cointegration Analysis," *Real Estate Economics* 26, no. 4 (1998): 677–93; Arturo Estrella, "Securitization and The Efficacy of Monetary Policy," *FRBNY Economic Policy Review* 8, no. 1 (2002): 242–56; Yener Altunbas, Leonardo Gambacorta & David Marquès, "Securitisation and the Bank Lending Channel," *European Central Bank Working Paper Series* no. 838 (2007); and ECB, "Securitisation in the Euro Area," *Monthly Bulletin* (February 2008): 81–94. A complete multidisciplinary study, meant also to be a practitioners' guide, is Vinod Kothardi, *Securitisation — The Financial Instrument of the Future* (Wiley Finance, 2006).

[6]The underlying ultimate cause of these exchanges is rooted in individuals' time preference rates that are higher than the current interest rate. On the

passed to an economic actor that has just the opposite preferences. Or, relatively similar claims, possibly coming from different owners, could be grouped together within a single holding entity that could then create standardized claims on them to be sold to interested investors on the financial markets. This process of putting together relatively illiquid assets, of using them as collateral for backing new securities, and of using the proceeds from the sale of the securities to fund the owners of the illiquid assets is called securitization: "Securitization is the process of pooling and repacking loans into securities that are then sold to investors."[7] The general features of securitization can be presented by means of ordinary T-accounts (Table 1).[8]

Table 1
Synthetic Balance Sheets of Companies

Firm A		Firm B		Firm C	
Assets	Liabilities	Assets	Liabilities	Assets	Liabilities
Investments 120	Equity 100	Investments 80	Equity 50	Investments 350	Equity 200
Credits A 80	Debt 100	Credits B 20	Debt 50	Credits C 50	Debt 200

In aggregate, firms A, B and C have total liabilities of 700 (350 in owned capital and 350 in debts), out of which 550 are invested in production and 150 are lent to clients. In case all three firms securitize their credits to clients, economic relations can be summarized in the following way (after consolidation of A's, B's and C's books):

---

importance of time preference for the process of civilization in general and for economic analysis in particular, see Hans-Hermann Hoppe, *Democracy – The Gold that Failed: The Economics and Politics of Monarchy, Democracy, and Natural Order* (New Brunswick, N.J.: Transaction Publishers, 2001), especially chap. 1.

[7]Ergungor, "Securitization," p. 1.

[8]All numbers, in tables and in the text, refer to a quantity of well-defined monetary units (dollars, euros, ounces of gold, etc.), which we will avoid to mention systematically in order to avoid redundancy.

Table 2
Entities Involved in the Process of Securitization

Firms		SPV		Investors	
Assets	Liabilities	Assets	Liabilities	Assets	Liabilities
Investments 550	Equity 350	Credits A 80	Securities 1 100	Securities 1 100	Net Wealth
Reserves 150	Debt 350	Credits B 20	Securities 2 30	Securities 2 30	(savings 150)
		Credits C 50	Securities 3 20	Securities 3 20	

Firms sell their credits to a Special Purpose Vehicle (SPV) which makes the purchase with proceeds obtained through the issuance of securities bought by investors. The firms can use the reserves of 150 for consumption, investment or repayment of existing debts. The SPV is a separate legal structure, also referred to as a conduit, that issues asset-backed securities (ABSs). These securities can be structured in a variety of ways.[9] Some of them may be actual ownership titles in the SPV that give a *pro rata* property title on the credits held (pass-through ABSs). Others can be debentures that promise a rate of return that is only collateralized by the credits held (pay-through ABSs). Any of these types of ABSs can be issued in different tranches (three in our example), in which case the payment of income on a more junior tranche, i.e., with lower rating, is conditioned on the prior payment of income on the most senior tranches.[10] For investors, ABSs represent an additional opportunity for their savings.

On a technical level, other actors are involved also. The collection of the future receivables (repayment of the credits A, B and C) may be fulfilled by a specialized servicer.[11] The servicer's activities

---

[9]This explains why securitization is often considered as part of the broader area of *structured finance*, i.e., the engineering of structured financial products.

[10]Tranching is considered to be a form of insurance for the owners of the senior securities. Indeed, the junior securities act as cushions for losses on the credit portfolio of the SPV to the extent that these losses do not exceed the income payments on the junior securities.

may be monitored by a trust that defends investors' interests. More importantly, the very issuance of ABSs, especially when they are structured, requires the involvement of banks and rating agencies. Banks provide various degrees of liquidity facilities and credit-enhancement schemes that are crucial, together with tranching, for the evaluation of ABSs by rating agencies. In turn, this evaluation assesses the expected risk of investment in the ABSs, and determines the interest rate at which they could be issued. Analysts observe that securitization depends crucially on the rating process: "Rating agencies may be the single most important players in the securitization process."[12] However, to obtain a good rating seems to be a rather weak constraint for the success of an ABS issuance: "A securitization sponsor can theoretically structure the securitization to get any rating(s) it wants."[13]

From an economic point of view, securitization merely intermediates savings. One intuitive rationale for this rather roundabout technique is that competition between firms pushes them to accommodate clients with the financing of their purchases. Securitization then is the way to provide the funds, whose ultimate beneficiaries are the firms' clients. Clients, i.e., the ultimate debtors, may well appreciate and therefore remunerate that additional service enough for the ABSs to offer attractive yields to the investors. Firms may find this arrangement the best way to expand their turnover, rather than financing a more aggressive sales policy through additional fund raising that would become ever more expansive as it deteriorates their equity-to-debt ratio. There may be even a direct financial advantage for them, to the extent that

---

[11]It is most common for the firms who made the credits, often referred to as originators of the credits, to play this role. Securitization then allows a new business model with regard to credits — "originate and distribute" as opposed to "originate and hold."

[12]Joel Telpner, "A Securitisation Primer for First Time Issuers," *Global Securitisation and Structured Finance 2003* (Greenberg Traurig, 2003), p. 5. This is not an isolated opinion: "Rating agencies dictate a significant amount of the structure of securitization transactions. When the transactions were initially being structured, the rating agencies were heavily involved." Hill, "Securitization," p. 1071.

[13]Telpner, "A Securitisation Primer," p. 5.

market participants judge their activities riskier than the default risk of their clients. Under all circumstances, firms pass the credit risk of their assets to other market participants that are more willing to bear it.[14]

It is commonly admitted that securitization was created in 1970, when the Government National Mortgage Association (Ginnie Mae) issued a mortgage-backed security (MBS) in the form of a pass-through.[15] If the contemporary rise of this technique is indeed rooted in mortgage loans, securitization first occurred in the eighteenth century as a means for financing the West Indies plantations. Deon Deutz, a Dutch businessman, issued bonds with the proceeds of which he financed mortgage loans to plantation owners in Suriname. The bonds' yield was dependent on the return of the plantation loans, themselves guaranteed by the plantations and crops. These plantation loans "can be viewed as the forerunners of modern mortgage-backed securities."[16] Present-day MBSs developed in the US under the patronage of government-sponsored enterprises (GSEs) such as Fannie Mae and Freddie Mac that aim at creating a secondary market for home mortgage loans.[17] MBSs went through some innovations, such as the creation of collateralized mortgage obligations (CMOs) in 1983 and of Real

---

[14]As noted by an analyst: "The securitization process allows the company to separate financial assets from credit, performance and other risks associated with the company itself." Telpner, "A Securitisation Primer," p. 1. For a detailed and still clear-cut explanation of the possible benefits of securitization for all parties involved, see Philip R. Wood, *Title Finance, Derivatives, Securitisations, Set-off and Netting* (London: Sweet & Maxwell, 1995), pp. 41–68.

[15]Carlstrom and Samolyk, "Securitization," p. 2.

[16]K. Geert Rouwenhorst, "The Origins of Mutual Funds," Yale International Center for Finance, Working Paper no. 04-48 (2004), p. 5.

[17]A general account of the activities of Fannie Mae and Freddie Mac can be found in Scott Frame and Lawrence White, "Fussing and Fuming over Fannie and Freddie: How Much Smoke, How Much Fire?," *Journal of Economic Perspective* 19, no. 2 (2005): 159–84 and Richard Green and Susan Wachter, "The American Mortgage in Historical and International Context," *Journal of Economic Perspectives* 19, no. 4 (2005): 93–114, while Gordin Sellon and Deana VanNahmen, "The Securitization of Housing Finance," *Economic Review*, Federal Reserve Bank of Kansas City (July/August 1988): 3–20 present an early synthesis on their more specific role in the spread of securitization.

Estate Mortgage Investment Conduits (REMICs) that facilitate the issuance of CMOs. CMOs are specifically designed to address the prepayment risk in the event of falling interest rate, through the cushion system of the tranches.[18] Based on the model of MBSs, banks started issuing ABSs in the 1980s. Besides mortgage loans, ABSs use automobile, credit card and student loans as underlying assets. They are offered on the market either as long-term corporate bonds or as short-term commercial paper, better known as asset-backed commercial paper (ABCP).

Securitization has had an exponential growth (Chart 1). Securities issued by GSEs reached $7.5 trillion in the beginning of 2008, ABSs rose to $3.6 trillion, while the amount of ABCP stood at $0.8 trillion. If securitization represented only 2.5 percent of credit-market debt owed by all sectors in 1970, that ratio reached 24.0 percent in 2008. Home mortgages, which are almost the exclusive asset held by GSEs, have been in the portfolio of ABS-issuers varying from 35 percent of total assets in 2000 to 64 percent in 2006 (Chart 2).[19]

Evidence shows that securitization concerns mainly loans granted by banks, and not credits made by producers or distributors of commodities. The next question that needs to be addressed,

---

[18]With falling interest rates, fixed-rate borrowers are inclined to refinance their mortgages, thereby letting the lender bear the interest rate risk. Early repayment also changes the duration of a lender's portfolio, which may compromise other aspects of his investment strategy. Let us note that long-term home loans with fixed interest rates and low loan-to-value ratio are the outgrowth of government intervention during the Great Depression that aimed at rescuing bankrupt banks. Prior to the creation of the Federal Housing Administration in 1936 and of Fannie Mae in 1938, a typical mortgage had flexible rates, a maturity of up to five years, and a loan-to-value ratio of 50 percent. Green and Wachter, "The American Mortgage in Historical and International Context," pp. 94–96.

[19]The securitization growth trend has been less pronounced in Europe, where, for instance, ABCP represents only 30 percent of the commercial paper market, to compare with 50 percent in the US. FitchRatings, "The Importance of Liquidity Support in ABCP Conduits," *ABCP/Global Special Report* (October 25, 2007), p.1. The total outstanding volume of ABSs in the European market was estimated at €1.3 trillion in September 2007, 60 percent of which was eligible as collateral for liquidity at the European Central Bank. ECB, "Securitisation in the Euro Area," p. 92.

Chart 1
Growth of Securitization (1970–2008)[20]

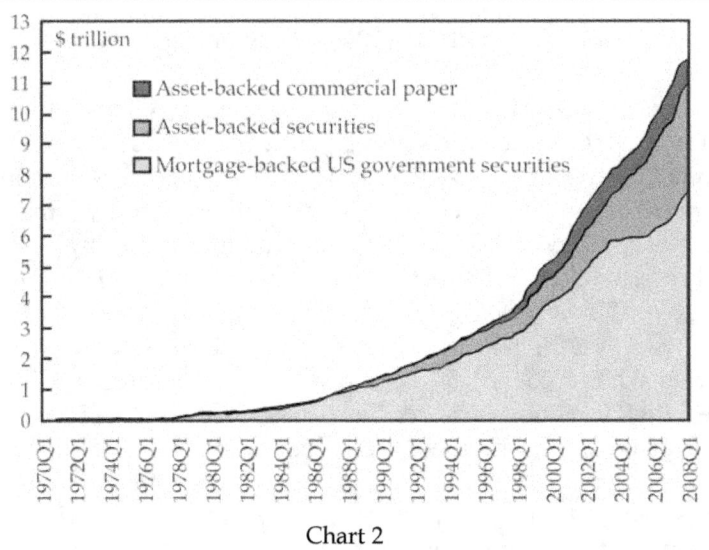

Chart 2
Structure of assets underlying ABSs (1984–2008)[21]

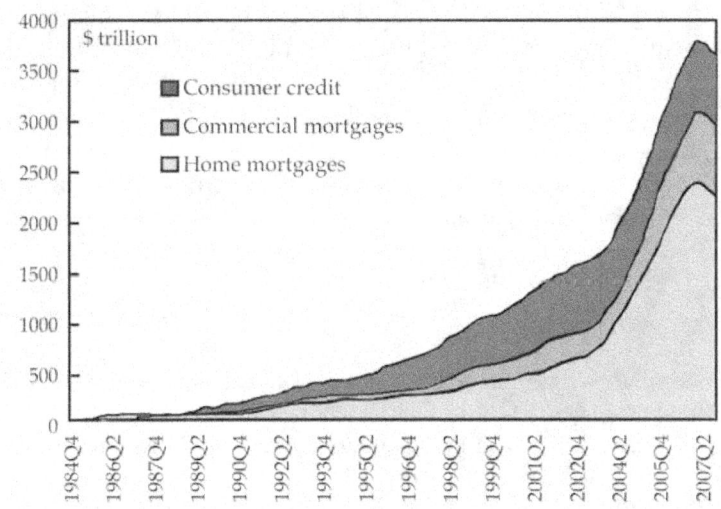

[20]Source: Flow of Funds Accounts of the United States. Data for ABCP since 2006 has been extracted from the Ecowin Reuters database. Government securities, i.e., privately issued securities that are eligible for open-market operations, are not to be confused with Treasury securities.

therefore, is how the general principles of securitization change when this financial technique is carried out by modern banks.

FRACTIONAL RESERVE BANKS AND SECURITIZATION

Contemporary commercial banks combine two essentially different functions. First, they serve as intermediaries between saver-capitalists and investor-entrepreneurs. Banks issue a debt instrument (bonds or commercial paper) only in order to lend the funds thereby collected to economic agents that need financing. As financial intermediaries, banks transform the maturity, risk and currency profile of existing savings.[22] This activity itself implies specific risks (credit, interest, currency, etc.) that banks may be willing to bear wholly, to manage partially or to hedge completely. Whatever their position toward these transformation-induced risks, their activity *qua* intermediaries consists in *pooling and channeling existing savings*. Because the loans that banks make come from actual wealth that is only transferred from one individual to another, one can speak of *real credit*. Real credit is the very foundation of capital accumulation and economic growth.

Second, banks act as fractional reserve depository institutions. This means that they are legally obliged to keep in reserves only a (very small) fraction of any amount of money that is deposited with them. The part of the money in excess of that fraction can be used for granting credits, i.e., for creating an additional deposit that is made available to the receiver of the credit. It follows that contemporary banks, in addition to channeling existing savings,

---

[21]Source: Flow of Funds Accounts of the United States. Mortgage-backed securities pooled and issued by GSEs are not included.

[22]The relations involved by this intermediation could be represented by the last two balance sheets of Table 2, where the SPV is to be replaced by the financial intermediary. Thinking of the SPV as of a standard financial intermediary strengthens our view that the most plausible rationale for securitization on the free market is to provide convenience to customers. As a matter of fact, they do not have to deal with the financial intermediary, but only with the seller (firms A, B and C in our example) who is in charge of the financial arrangement, precisely through securitization.

Table 3
Synthetic Balance Sheet of a Fractional Reserve Banking System

Bank A				Central Bank			
Assets			Liabilities	Assets			Liabilities
Reserves	200	Capital	1,000	Gold & Forex	100	Deposits	350
Credits	12, 500	Debt	600	Lending	550	Banknotes	400
Investments	900	Deposits	12,000	Investments	200	Capital	100

are also *creating deposits* that they lend out. Since such deposits are not brought about by existing savings, one can speak of *bank* (as opposed to *real*) *credit*.[23] It is precisely their ability to create bank credit through new deposits that makes banks specific and different from other companies, financial or not. The capacity to create deposits implies the capacity to increase the supply of media of exchange, for deposits are used as media of exchange. Since this is the particular feature of contemporary banks, we have to analyze securitization by banks especially in relation to its possible monetary impact. In order to do this, let us first briefly outline the operation of a fractional reserve banking system (Table 3).

Bank A has to comply with two basic regulations. It must keep reserves equal to 2 percent of its overall deposits and its capital (equity) should represent at least 8 percent of its credits.[24] Bank A's total assets include its liquidity reserves in the form of a deposit at the Central Bank (200), its credits to economic agents (12,500) and

---

[23]For a full-fledged theory of this important distinction, and a complete analysis of the legal and economic consequences of bank credit as opposed to real credit, see Jesus Huerta de Soto, *Money, Bank Credit, and Economic Cycles* (Auburn, Ala.: Mises Institute, 2006). Huerta de Soto convincingly shows, in line with findings by Chester Arthur Phillips and Milton Friedman, that from the standpoint of the entire banking sector, the limit on granting bank credit is a multiple of any initial monetary deposit, irrespective of which bank is the first to receive that money. The lower the required reserve ratio and individuals' demand for banknotes, the higher that multiple is.

[24]We borrow these numbers, for the sake of an example, from current practices in the euro area, according to which banks have to keep average reserves of 2 percent of their deposits, and from the Basle II capital requirements.

its investments in real estate and securities (900). Bank A has obligations towards its creditors (600) and towards depositors (12,000). The net difference between assets and liabilities is equilibrated by A's capital (1,000). The typical Central Bank's balance sheet also reports some of these asset and liability elements. Deposits held at the Central Bank (350) contain A's reserves among deposits from other institutions (other banks and government). The Central Bank's lending (550) is partly reflected in A's debt (as well as in the debt of government and of other financial institutions). The Central Bank's investments (200) represent holdings of securities, some of which may have been issued by A, as part of its debt. The other figures have been adjusted in order to equilibrate the balance sheet.[25]

It appears that A does not respect the liquidity reserve requirement. Assuming that it does not want to lose its shares on the deposit market, it needs to increase its reserves by 40, i.e., to replenish its account at the Central Bank. One means to achieve this consists in obtaining a credit by the Central Bank through open-market operations. A cedes a total of 40 worth of assets to the Central Bank, which creates a corresponding liquidity that is credited to A's account.[26] The Central Bank's total liabilities increase by that same amount, while A's total assets remain constant, due to the substitution of reserves and other assets. An alternative means for A would be to obtain liquidity from economic agents that have

---

[25]Other figures are not commented upon insofar as they do not concern the issue of securitization. The discussion of issues such as international monetary arrangements, demand for banknotes and central banks' histories would, of course, require elaborating on these other elements.

[26]We speak of cession rather than of selling, because open-market operations may take a variety of legal forms: outright purchases of Treasury securities (as conducted by the FED), extendable repurchase agreements (also typical of the Fed), or simply renewable short-term collateralized loans (as carried out by the European Central Bank). The economically relevant fact is the creation of liquidity for Bank A, not the concrete legal form it takes. For details on open-market operations, see FED, *The Federal Reserve System: Purposes and Functions* <www.federalreserve.gov/pf/pdf/pf_complete.pdf> (June 2005 [1939]); ECB, *The Implementation of Monetary Policy in the Euro Area: General Documentation on Eurosystem Monetary Policy Instruments and Procedures* <http://www.ecb.int/pub/pdf/other/gendoc2008en.pdf> (November 2008).

excess liquidity. Securitizing 40 of its credits is the proper way to capture that liquidity. This would also improve the capital-adequacy ratio. There is a substitution between different assets on A's balance sheet, while the Central Bank's total liabilities remain unaffected. From the standpoint of an individual bank, securitization appears, therefore, tantamount to refinancing at the Central Bank, the difference being that it does not imply an increase of total liquidities in the economic system, but only redistribution thereof among banks. The question then arises as to how securitization functions from the standpoint of the entire banking system.

From a systemic viewpoint, we must reject the assumption of liquidity shortage or excess. Let us consider A's balance sheet from Table 3, after refinancing at the Central Bank for 40 in exchange for part of its investments, as the consolidated banking system balance sheet. The question now is to identify how securitization economically affects the banking system, and how this is translated in accounting terms. One bank's mortgages are used to pay house builders, who in turn pay workers, producers of building material, etc. The latter spend the new monetary units on consumption and investment goods. Among the variety of goods that the receivers of the new deposits purchase are securities, some of which are ABSs.[27] When ABSs are purchased, bank checks are written or money order payments are made that de facto transfer ownership of bank deposits to the issuing SPVs. The SPVs then pass the ownership of the deposits on to the banks, from which they acquire mortgage or other type loans. The credit-selling banks thereby obtain claims on customers' deposits held by themselves or by other banks. After compensation, the system's deposits decrease exactly by the amount of credits sold to the SPVs, i.e., purchased by banks' customers. From the standpoint of the entire banking system, securitization implies, therefore, a simultaneous reduction in credits and deposits. If we turn back to our numerical example now, if 10 percent of all credits are securitized, credits that remain on the banks' books amount now to 11,250, while their obligations

---

[27]Our sequence of distributing new liquidity in the economic system starts with the construction sector, but it could start with any other economic sector, including the financial sector itself.

to depositors decrease concomitantly to 10,750. At this stage, total deposits of 10,750 are backed by reserves of 240, while total equity of 1,000 guarantees credits of 11,250. The liquidity reserve ratio increases from 2 percent to 2.23 percent, while the capital adequacy ratio rises to 8.89 percent. Securitization leads to excess liquidity and to improved compliance with capital provision regulations despite the fact that the Central Bank has not increased its total liabilities and additional savings have not been channeled into the banking industry.

What will then be the next step of the banking system, given the excess liquidity? Banks will grant new credits until the existing excess reserves (25, i.e., the existing 240 minus 2 percent of 10,750 of deposits) are just enough to cover the new deposits created through bank credit. Ignoring liquidity outflows driven by a higher demand for banknotes and by purchases abroad, it is straightforward that banks can grant as much new loans as credits have been securitized. Then the process can be repeated again and again, as long as there is demand for asset-backed securities, without ever returning to the Central Bank for refinancing. Securitization allows fractional reserve banks to grant more loans, while keeping total deposits, i.e., the money supply in the broad sense, constant in the economy. This is explained by the fact that the securitized credits are purchased by the SPVs by means of those same deposits that were created by banks in the very process of granting the credits. As a matter of fact, banks create both the object to be sold (credits) and the means by which it can be purchased (deposits). It is this aspect of FRBs that makes their use of securitization special.[28]

The operational aspects of securitization having been outlined, let us now address its economic characteristics.

---

[28]Banks that keep total reserves can make only real credit, i.e., they can lend out only funds collected through the issuance of securities (shares and bonds). Consecutive waves of securitization would imply consecutive reductions in investors' money holdings, whether cash or deposits, that could not be countered by the banking system.

The Illusion of Savings-Driven Growth
and the Spread of Securitization

Securitization allows FRBs to withdraw from the market the liquidities they have created and lent out. It reduces the money supply by the amount of liquid assets used to purchase the asset-backed securities. Therefore, it hides the reverse side of bank credit—the increase in the money supply, i.e., inflation. It makes the economic environment appear less inflationary than it should be, given individuals' growing indebtedness to banks. Securitization portrays a bank-credit driven boom as non-inflationary, savings driven growth. It contributes to the widespread illusion that more factors of production are available than in reality, and becomes thereby a factor in the generation of the error-induced boom-bust cycle.[29]

To a certain extent, economists have already recognized that securitization restrains the money-supply growth during a credit boom. From a different approach, central bank economists have come to the conclusion that securitization decreases the power of monetary policy: "securitization has likely weakened the impact of any policy move."[30] This, of course, means that securitization insulates banks' lending activity from the central bank's liquidity policy, which confirms our main conclusion and is even overtly stated by other economists: "Using a large sample of European banks, we find that the use of securitization appears to shelter banks' loan supply from the effects of monetary policy."[31] The central bankers' perspective is that of growing concern about loosening their grasp of the money supply. Such a concern implicitly admits that securitization disconnects the money-supply growth from bank-credit growth.[32]

---

[29]Jörg Guido Hülsmann, "Toward a General Theory of Error Cycles," *Quarterly Journal of Austrian Economics* 1, no. 4 (1998): 1–23.

[30]Estrella, "Securitization and The Efficacy of Monetary Policy," p. 1.

[31]Altunbas et al., "Securitisation and the Bank Lending Channel," p. 4.

[32]Further evidence of the acceptance of this result by other economists is easy to find: "securitization provides an ever-growing funding source to banks and may well be the most important engine of growth in bank lending." Ergungor, "Securitization," p. 4.

To a certain extent, our analysis is in conformity with the increasingly common view among economists, at least as far as the outer description of the phenomenon is concerned. However, when it comes to understand what contributes to the spread of securitization, we must part with the traditional approach, which mentions three main factors. First, securitization is presented as a way to circumvent capital adequacy regulations, because it transfers the credit risk of the loans from bank's books to the investors in the asset-backed securities. Second, the "originate and distribute model," according to which credits are only originated by banks and then distributed to investors who fund them, appears more attractive than the "originate and hold model" because of higher frequency of banking fees. Third, asset-backed securities add to the choice of investment opportunities and contribute to the efficiency of financial markets.[33] While these assertions may be true in themselves, it is not true that they systematically render securitization the best solution for FRBs.

Indeed, securitization improves banks' capital-adequacy ratio, as shown in our numerical example. However, given that banks have to raise capital only up to 8 percent of their new credits, it is never too expensive for them to pay dividends to new capital in order to grant 12.5 times more loans. In addition, the interest on the securitized loans is lost for the banks. Securitization, therefore, is not really saving the cost of capital raising, for expenses on capital are not an obstacle to the expansion of banks' activity.[34] The "originate and distribute" model does have the advantage of increasing banks' fees, but it has also the inconvenience of depriving the originator of the credit of the interest yield, which is transferred to the

---

[33]That third reason is presented sometimes as an overt syllogism: "For the issuer, the bottom line is to create a set of new securities that are worth more in aggregate than the value of the underlying assets." Lakshman Alles, "Asset Securitization and Structured Financing: Future Prospects and Challenges for Emerging Market Countries," *IMF Working Paper* WP/01/147 (2001), p. 5.

[34]If all outstanding asset-backed securities ($11.9 trillion at the beginning of 2008) were kept on US banks' balance sheets, this would have required, over the last 30 years, an additional capital injection of up to $ 952 billion. For comparison, at the beginning of 2008, the market value of all US corporate equities was $19.4 trillion, out of which $4.1 trillion were financial corporations' equities (Flow of Funds Accounts of the United States, Table L.213).

buyers of the asset-backed securities. There is no guarantee that the accumulation of servicing fees from securitized loans would be higher than the interest rates received on even a smaller amount of credits kept on the balance sheets. Finally, the assets-backed securities allow investors to obtain the same risk-revenue exposure as the one they would have obtained if investing in the banks and if banks have kept the loans on their books. It is therefore not clear in what sense there are new investment opportunities offered on the market.

All three traditional explanations of securitization assume that origination and funding of the securitized loans are two unrelated processes.[35] Our analysis shows that, to the contrary, they are two analytically inseparable aspects of FRBs' operation. As a matter of fact, securitization is of interest for economists only insofar as it is used by FRBs to dissimulate the inflationary impact of credit expansion. From this perspective, a full assessment of securitization needs, indeed, to explain how it became a widely used technique. The crucial point, from bankers' points of view, is to create a demand for part of their loans, repackaged as structured securities. It follows that securitization relies critically on the ABSs' quality as perceived by investors. Securitization by FRBs can work only if securitized loans are presented to the public as actually different from what they are. Hence, factors that change investors' preferences favorably toward these financial assets are the real determinants of the success of this technique. In a sense, securitization is based on institutions that create and maintain an illusion.[36]

Three illusion-creating institutions can be identified: government, rating agencies, and credit default insurers. All three contribute, in different ways, to change investors' perceptions of the ABSs' risk-return profile. Government, which was historically related to the modern inception of securitization in the USA, was providing an implicit guarantee of refinancing Fannie Mae and

---

[35]Alles, "Asset Securitization and Structured Financing," p. 15.

[36]To a certain extent, the illusionary nature of securitization by banks has been well captured by a legal analyst: "Securitization, in short, brings to financial technology what the sought-after philosopher's stone promised to bring to base metals—the ability to turn them into gold!" Schwarcz, "The Alchemy of Asset Securitization," p. 154.

Freddie Mac.[37] Rating agencies grant quality labels to privately issued ABSs. Credit insurers help enhance these labels through promises, namely to pay for defaulted creditors, that objectively cannot be carried out in the event of a systemic crisis.[38] All three contribute to an over-valuation of ABSs relatively to other financial assets.

Conclusion

Securitization is a financial technique that permits the exchange of relatively non-marketable credit claims for liquidities. As such, it exploits an exchange opportunity between individuals with opposite liquidity valuations in their preference scales. Its modern usage by fractional reserve banks has dissociated the growth of credit expansion from the growth of the money supply. Securitization has provided banks with an alternative source of liquidity, different from central banks' open-market operations, thereby weakening the latter's control of the total amount of credit in the economy. It has contributed to de-monetizing bank credits, thereby containing inflation under conditions of growing indebtedness. Securitization has therefore become a tool for spreading the illusion of savings-driven economic growth and for creating the economic cycle. ❧

---

[37]That guarantee became explicit in September 2008, when both companies were nationalized.

[38]The very important question of whether "credit insurance" is an instance of insurance rests out of the scope of the present paper. Let us, however, note here that, following Mises and Hoppe, we may conclude that credits cannot be insured, as the events "going bankrupt" are not independent, uncorrelated elements with an identifiable class probability. See Mises, *Human Action*, pp. 105–19; Hans-Hermann Hoppe, "On Certainty and Uncertainty, Or: How Rational Can Our Expectations Be?," *Review of Austrian Economics* 10, no. 1 (1997): 49–78; idem., "The Limits of Numerical Probability: Frank H. Knight and Ludwig von Mises and The Frequency Interpretations," *Quarterly Journal of Austrian Economics* 10, no. 1 (2007): 3–21. This implies that the very notion of credit insurance contributes to the creation of an illusion.

30

Hoppe in One Lesson, Illustrated in Welfare Economics

Jeffrey M. Herbener

E very schoolboy learns that, to reach a true conclusion, one must start with true premises and use valid logic. The lesson, unfortunately, is largely forgotten later in life. Most lack the intelligence, interest, or courage to apply the lesson rigorously. Many break or bend the rules to further their own agendas or careers. Others can only muster the will to follow the . rules in some part or in some cases. Rare is the person who masters the lesson.

Hans-Hermann Hoppe has demonstrated the intellectual heights that can be reached by employing the lesson with a brilliant mind, fervent devotion to the truth, and unflagging moral courage. What follows is a brief account of how he set right the entire field of Welfare economics.[1]

Jeffrey M. Herbener (jmherbener@gcc.edu) is professor of economics and chairman of the economics department at Grove City College. He is a Senior Fellow of the Ludwig von Mises Institute and associate editor of *The Quarterly Journal of Austrian Economics.*

[1]On the development of Welfare economics, see Mark Blaug, "The Fundamental Theorems of Welfare Economics, Historically Considered," *History of Political Economy* 39, no. 2 (2007): 185–207 and Jeffrey M. Herbener, "The Pareto Rule and Welfare Economics," *Review of Austrian Economics* 10 (1997): 79–106.

Old Welfare economics attempted to overturn the *laissez-faire* conclusions of the Classical school on the basis of the theory of marginal utility ushered in by the Marginalist Revolution. If utility can be compared interpersonally, by various assumptions such as cardinal utility or identical utility schedules or utility of money among people, the Old Welfare economists argued that diminishing marginal utility implied a social welfare gain from, among other interventions of the state, redistributing wealth from the rich to the poor. This line of argument was brought up short by the demonstration that the subjectivity of value precludes interpersonal utility comparisons. Therefore, social welfare can only be said to unambiguously improve from a change if it makes at least one person better off and no one else worse off. This Pareto Rule forbade economists from claiming social welfare improvements from state interventions since they do make some better off and others worse off.

New Welfare economics tried to weave a case for state intervention within the constraints of the Pareto Rule. The conclusions of New Welfare economics can be drawn from its main theorems. The First Welfare Theorem states that a perfectly-competitive general equilibrium is Pareto Optimal. From this theorem, the New Welfare economists conclude that a divergence of the real economy from this hypothetical condition justifies state intervention to improve social welfare. Economics journals are replete with cases demonstrating how the market economy fails to achieve a perfectly-competitive general equilibrium and what interventions the state should make to remove the market's inefficiency. The Second Welfare Theorem states that any Pareto Optimal solution can be brought about by a perfectly-competitive general equilibrium. For each pattern of initial endowments of income among persons, the perfectly-functioning market economy would reach a different Pareto Optimal outcome of production and exchange. From this theorem, New Welfare economists conclude that the state can distribute income, in whatever pattern it wants, e.g., to achieve a particular conception of equity, without impairing the social welfare maximizing property of the perfectly-functioning market economy.

In his article on utility and welfare economics in 1956, Murray Rothbard demonstrated that New Welfare economists were wrong to think that a case against *laissez-faire* could be constructed on the ground of the subjectivity of value.[2] He argued that New Welfare economists were correct to infer the impossibility of interpersonal utility comparisons from the subjectivity of value. Value is a state of mind without an extensive property that could be objectively analyzed. As such, no common unit of value exists among persons in which their mental states could be measured and thus, compared. Having accepted the subjectivity of value as the reason for the impossibility of interpersonal utility comparisons, which they made a pillar of their Welfare economics, New Welfare economists commit themselves to other corollaries of subjective value. In particular, Rothbard contended, they must embrace the concept of demonstrated preference. Because preferences exist solely in a person's mind, another person can acquire objective knowledge about them only by inferring it from his actions. Since no other objective knowledge of a person's preferences exists, only demonstrated preference can be used in the analysis of Welfare economics. Both the impossibility of interpersonal utility comparisons and demonstrated preference are deduced directly from the subjectivity of value, and therefore, New Welfare economists cannot, validly, accept one and reject the other. The impossibility of interpersonal utility comparisons constrains Welfare economics by the Pareto Rule, making it harder to justify state intervention than otherwise, but demonstrated preference raises the bar for justifying state intervention that much higher. According to New Welfare economists, the level set by the Pareto Rule is determined by the market's deviation from the optimal result of a perfectly-competitive general-equilibrium model, but demonstrated preference eliminates any use of hypothetical values, including the utility functions of economic agents that underlie such models. To be scientific, Welfare economics must confine itself to statements about preferences that actual persons demonstrate in their actions. Rothbard wrote:

> Demonstrated preference, as we remember, eliminates hypothetical imaginings about individual value scales. Welfare economics has until now always considered

---

[2]Murray N. Rothbard, "Toward a Reconstruction of Utility and Welfare Economics," *The Logic of Action, One* (Cheltenham, U.K.: Edward Elgar, 1997), pp. 211–54.

values as hypothetical valuations of hypothetical "social states." But demonstrated preference only treats values as revealed through chosen action.[3]

The First Welfare Theorem, reconstituted along Rothbardian lines, does not refer to the general equilibrium state of models invented by economists. It refers to the actual economy, for which it is more difficult to demonstrate social welfare improvements from state intervention. If market outcomes are compared to other realizable conditions reached in actual economic systems, instead of unrealizable outcomes of perfectly-functioning, fictitious models, then market failure seems unlikely. And, as Rothbard showed, the market does surpass the levels of social welfare reached in other, actual economic systems.

The Second Welfare Theorem, however, seemed unscathed by Rothbard's critique. New Welfare economists could still advocate one intervention of the state. Without impairing the efficiency of the market in bringing about a Pareto Optimal point, the state could still distribute income to achieve its conception of equity. Rothbard responded that private property was the proper initial distribution of wealth from which market activity renders a Pareto Optimal outcome. And, because the initial distribution of private property is not arbitrary, but follows the lines of self-ownership of labor, homesteader ownership of land, and producer ownership of goods, state intervention in property ownership could not produce an outcome commensurate in social welfare with the Pareto Optimal outcome of *laissez-faire*. New Welfare economists, however, not being adherents to Rothbard's natural rights theory of property, denied that state distribution of property ownership would lead to a market outcome inferior in social welfare to that of the unhampered market. Even some economists who favored *laissez-faire* agreed that the pattern of property ownership in society is arbitrary with respect to the market achieving a Pareto Optimal outcome and hence, the state can rearrange it without detrimental consequences on social welfare.

It was left to Hoppe to work out the logic of Rothbard's argument and reach a definitive conclusion about the effect on social

---

[3]Ibid., p. 240.

welfare of state distribution of property ownership.[4] In so doing, he reoriented Welfare economics to its true course. Although latent in Rothbard's analysis, Hoppe was the one who demonstrated that the Pareto Rule approach to social welfare economics leads, not to an optimization end point, but to a step-by-step Pareto Superior process with an objective starting point. As Rothbard had done before him, Hoppe confronted New Welfare economists with a logical inconsistency in their argument. They had accepted a basic principle, this time self-ownership, from which they inferred social welfare consequences of voluntary exchange, i.e., they pronounced on the social welfare consequences of voluntary exchange from the viewpoint of the traders themselves. But, in embracing self-ownership, they must also accept its logical corollary, namely Lockean property acquisition. Hoppe pointed out that self-ownership is a necessary precondition to all acquisition and use of property and not just voluntary exchange. Therefore, it is the starting point for each succeeding step of social interaction.

In critiquing Kirzner's view of Welfare economics, Hoppe writes:

> If, however, the Pareto criterion is firmly wedded to the notion of demonstrated preference, it in fact can be employed to yield such a starting point and serve, then, as a perfectly unobjectionable welfare criterion: a person's original appropriation of unowned resources, as demonstrated by this very action, increases his utility (at least *ex ante*). At the same time, it makes no one worse off, because in appropriating them he takes nothing away from others. For obviously, others could have homesteaded these resources, too, if only they had perceived them as scarce. But they did not actually do so, which demonstrates that they attached no value to them whatsoever, and hence they cannot be said to have lost any utility on account of this act. Proceeding from this Pareto-optimal basis, then, any further act of production, utilizing homesteaded resources, is equally Pareto-optimal on demonstrated preference grounds, provided only that it does not uninvitedly impair the physical

---

[4]Hans-Hermann Hoppe, "Review of *Man, Economy, and Liberty*," *Review of Austrian Economics* 4 (1990): 249–63.

integrity of the resources homesteaded, or produced with homesteaded means by others. And finally, every voluntary exchange starting from this basis must also be regarded as a Pareto-optimal change, because it can only take place if both parties expect to benefit from it. Thus, contrary to Kirzner, Pareto-optimality is not only compatible with methodological individualism; together with the notion of demonstrated preference, it also provides the key to (Austrian) welfare economics and its proof that the free market, operating according to the rules just described, always, and invariably so, increases social utility, while each deviation from it decreases it.[5]

Hoppe showed that the Pareto Rule needed to be applied to the social welfare consequences of the acquisition of property and not just its use. Self-ownership is the immutable starting point for the process of acquiring and then using property. State distribution of income to achieve an ostensibly more equitable "initial" endowment of income among persons fails to satisfy the Pareto Rule. In other words, the Second Welfare Theorem, reconstituted along Hoppean lines, is false. Only one initial endowment, the Lockean one, is capable of producing a Pareto Optimal outcome.

Moreover, Hoppe's argument dispatches entirely the notion of Pareto Optimality as a social-welfare maximizing end state. Welfare economics starts with the objective fact of self-ownership and then demonstrates that each step of voluntary acquisition and use of property satisfies the Pareto Rule and thereby, improves social welfare. Moreover, each instance of state intervention into the voluntary acquisition or use of property, benefits some and harms others and thereby, fails to improve social welfare. The actual market, then, is not compared to some end point it may eventually reach, but has not yet achieved. If that were the case, it might be claimed that some interventions of the state could facilitate the actual market in achieving the higher level of social welfare at its end point. Instead, Welfare economics is constrained to comparing the actual market to actual state intervention. No room is left for the claim that the market fails to attain some ideal which might be

---

[5]Ibid., pp. 257–58.

use to justify state intervention. Hoppe definitively established that the unhampered market is superior in improving social welfare.

Welfare economics is arguably the least of Hoppe's accomplishments in employing the lesson. In every field that has drawn his attention, he has, like Ludwig von Mises and Murray Rothbard before him, exemplified sound reasoning in social analysis. He improved the edifice they constructed by clarifying first principles and relentlessly and fearlessly tracing out the logical implications of these premises to their conclusions. He is an exemplar for all those who love the truth. ❧

31

The Demand for Money and the Time-Structure of Production

Jörg Guido Hülsmann

H ans-Hermann Hoppe is famous for his ground-break-
ing studies on the epistemology of the social sciences,
on the ethics of capitalism, and on democracy. But he
also made original and important contributions in various other fields, such as monetary economics.[1] Money and banking were actually our shared research interest may years ago, when
I first got in touch with him. It is therefore appropriate to offer an
essay on this topic to my dear friend Hans, a great mentor and a
magnificent source of inspiration.

Jörg Guido Hülsmann (jgh@guidohulsmann.com) is Professor of Economics at
the University of Angers, France; a Senior Fellow with the Ludwig von Mises
Institute; and the author of *Mises: The Last Knight of Liberalism* (2007) and *The
Ethics of Money Production* (2008). He would like to thank Nikolay Gertchev for
comments on a previous version of the present paper.

[1]See in particular Hoppe, "Banking, Nation States and International Politics. A Sociological Reconstruction of the Present Monetary Order," *The Economics and Ethics of Private Property* (Boston: Kluwer, 1993), chap. 3, pp. 61–92;
idem, "How is Fiat Money Possible? – or, The Devolution of Money and
Credit," *Review of Austrian Economics* 7, no. 2 (1994); idem with Jörg Guido
Hülsmann and Walter Block, "Against Fiduciary Media," *Quarterly Journal of
Austrian Economics* 1, no. 1 (1998): 1–50.

I. Introduction

The classical economists rejected the notion that the supply of and demand for money had any systematic impact on aggregate wealth. According to Adam Smith, the true factors determining economic growth were the division of labor and capital accumulation — real, not monetary factors. Austrian economists have always cherished and held onto these central insights, yet they have nuanced them in several respects. Most notably, Menger and Böhm-Bawerk have introduced the *time* dimension into the theory of capital, showing among other things the classical wage fund theory to be inaccurate in important respects.[2] Similarly, Mises stressed that *money is not neutral*. While the supply of money and the demand for money have no systematic impact on aggregate growth, these forces do affect the distribution and allocation of resources. They shape the type and relative quantities of goods being produced. In short, they determine the *structure*, though not the *level* of production.[3]

The purpose of present paper is to analyze the impact of the demand for money on the pure rate of interest, and thus on the *time* structure of production. Conventional Austrian monetary theory holds that while the supply of money does have a systematic impact on the rate of interest, the demand for money does not. The latter is so-to-say "time-neutral." We will criticize this contention and proceed as follows: after a reminder of some basic concepts (section II), we will briefly restate the traditional Austrian analysis of the time dimension of the money relation (section III), and then offer a critique, stressing that the demand for money is *not* time-neutral in the case of natural money, whereas it is in the case of fiat

---

[2]See Carl Menger, *Grundsätze der Volkswirtschaftslehre* (Vienna: Braumüller, 1871); Eugen von Böhm-Bawerk, *Positive Theory of Capital* (1959 [1921]); see also W.S. Jevons, *Theory of Political Economy* (1871).

[3]See Ludwig von Mises, *Theory of Money and Credit* (Indianapolis: Liberty Fund, 1980 [1924]), chap. 19; idem, *Human Action* (Auburn, Ala.: Ludwig von Mises Institute, 1998), chaps. 17–20. It goes without saying that the demand for and the supply of money concern cash balances; they do not concern short-term loans made on the so-called "money market" (see ibid., p. 400).

money (section IV). Finally we shall discuss some implications of our findings (section V).

II. THE DEMAND FOR MONEY

Definition

The demand for money can be defined either as the demand for monetary payments (flow), or as the demand for cash balances (stock). As far as the determination of the price level is concerned, both definitions lead to the same result. We will work with the second definition (money demand concerns cash balances) because it highlights the crucial fact that money renders its services not only at the moment when it is used in spending, but also during the entire period when it is being held or "hoarded." Money is the most marketable commodity. Thus cash balances, even while they are not being spent, provide liquidity services to their owners.

Cash balances are demanded for the liquidity services they provide. They are demanded for their purchasing power. The only exception is the merely nominal demand for money by collectors. The latter are not interested in the purchasing power of the bank notes and coins they collect. They are only interested in the notes and coins per se—that is why we call them collectors. But true money users do not demand mere *nominal* cash balances, but *real* cash balances. They demand a certain purchasing power.[5]

The Demand for Money and the Price Level

Standard demand and supply analysis shows that any increase of demand entails an increase of the price of the good in question.

---

[4]See Rothbard, *Man, Economy, and State* (3rd ed., Auburn, Ala.: Ludwig von Mises Institute, 1993), pp 662. Money itself is defined as a generally used medium of exchange; see ibid., p. 165; see also Menger, *Grundsätze der Volkswirtschaftslehre*, pp. 253f.; Mises, *Human Action*, p. 395.

[5]For a detailed discussion of the factors determining the demand for money, including a thorough critique of the Keynesian approach, see Rothbard, *Man, Economy, and State*, pp. 671–98. See also Philipp Bagus, "The Quality of Money" (Working paper, Universidad Rey Juan Carlos, 2008).

This price increase is not contingent (accidental), but systematic (necessary), which is what we mean when we assert that the increase of demand *causes* the price increase. Now in the case of money, its "price" can be defined as the total array of goods and services that can be exchanged for one unit of money.[6] In other words, the price of money is the purchasing power of a money unit. If the demand for money increases, therefore, the purchasing power of money tends to increase beyond the level it would otherwise have reached, which means that the general level of money prices will tend to decrease. Inversely, when the demand for money diminishes, the purchasing power of money will tend to fall below the level it would otherwise have reached, or, which is the same thing, the general level of money prices will tend to increase.

The Demand for Money and the Pure Rate of Interest

The question now is whether there is a systematic relationship between money demand, on the one hand, and the pure rate of interest (PRI) on the other hand. The latter can be defined as the pure return on investment as it would exist in general inter-temporal equilibrium or, equivalently, as the pure exchange rate between present goods (money and consumers' goods) and future goods (producers' goods and financial titles).[7] It follows that the demand for money could be said to affect the PRI only under one condition, namely, if it had a systematically *different* impact on present goods than on future goods. For example, if increases in the demand for money tended to reduce sales revenues more than cost expensiture, then there would be a *negative* relationship between the demand for money and interest rates (as held in standard Keynesian analysis).

III. The Time Dimension of the Money Relation in Conventional Theory

The time dimension of the "money relation" — of the demand for and supply of money — has been neglected in contemporary

---

[6]See Rothbard, *Man, Economy, and State*, pp. 204f.
[7]See ibid., p. 299.

economic analysis. Only the Austrian economists found it worthy of any systematic consideration. Conventional Austrian monetary theory holds that while the supply of money does have a systematic impact on the rate of interest, the demand for money does not.

The Time Dimension of the Money Supply

Mises and the Austrian literature after him focused on the supply side. Mises analysed in particular the impact of *increases* of the money supply on the time structure of production, distinguishing between systematic effects and non-systematic (accidental) effects.

On the one hand, increases of the money supply *systematically* provoke artificial reductions of the interest rate—"artificial" because they do not result from a lower time preference of the market participants, but from (unanticipated) increases of the money supply. Such artificial reductions of the interest rate entail inter-temporal misallocations of resources and, therefore, business cycles.[8]

On the other hand, increases of the money supply may also affect the interest rate *without* entailing misallocations, namely, to the extent that they modify the distribution of income and wealth. The increased money supply benefits the early users of the new money at the expense of the later users. Thus if the early users have a lower time preference than the later ones, then the average or social time preference will fall, thus entailing a reduction of the interest rate. Similarly, if the early users of the new money have a higher time preference than the later ones, then the average time preference will rise, thus provoking a higher rate of interest.

However, these distribution effects are *not systematic*. The early users of the new money do *not necessarily* have a lower or higher time preference than the later users. The increased money supply *might* therefore result in a lower interest rate; but it might just as well result in a higher interest rate, or not affect the interest rate at all.[9]

Analogous conceptions prevail in the case of changes of the *demand* for money.

---

[8]See Mises, *Human Action*, chap. 20.
[9]See ibid., pp. 545–47.

The Time Dimension of the Demand for Money

Mises dealt with the time dimension of the demand for money only incidentally. Still a clear case can be made that in his eyes changes of the demand for money does not have a systematic impact on the time structure of production. An increased demand for money (cash hoarding) merely entails a tendency for the prices of all goods to fall, but this event "does not require an adjustment of production activities" — it "merely alters the money items to be used in monetary calculation."[10] Changes in money demand can affect the interest rate only to the extent that they have an impact on the distribution of income and wealth. But, again, such distribution effects may work out one way or another — their impact "depends on the specific data of each case."[11]

Rothbard analyses this question in much more detail and comes to the same conclusion. He states that a "man may allocate his money to consumption, investment, or addition to his cash balance" and proceeds to show that, in the light of this distinction, the demand for money is time-neutral. Changes in the demand for money do not systematically affect time preference, and thus do not determine the PRI. Let us quote him here at length:

> His time preferences govern the *proportion* which an individual devotes to present and to future goods, i.e., to *consumption* and to *investment*. Now suppose a man's demand-for-money schedule increases, and he therefore decides to allocate a proportion of his money income to increasing his cash balance. *There is no reason to suppose that this increase affects the consumption/investment proportion at all.* It could, but if so, it would mean a change in his *time preference* schedule as well as in his demand for money.
>
> If the demand for money increases, *there is no reason why a change in the demand for money should affect the interest rate one iota.* There is no necessity at all for an increase in the demand for money to raise the interest rate, or a decline to lower it — no more than the opposite. In fact, there is no causal connection between the two; one is

---

[10]Ibid., p. 519.

[11]Ibid., p. 417.

determined by the valuations for money, and the other by valuations for time preference.

... An increased demand for money, then, tends to lower prices all around without changing time preference or the pure rate of interest Thus, suppose total social income is 100, with 70 allocated to investment and 30 to consumption. The demand for money increases, so that people decide to hoard a total of 20. Expenditure will now be 80 instead of 100, 20 being added to cash balances. Income in the next period will be only 80, since expenditures in one period result in the identical income to be allocated to the next period. If time preferences remain the same, then the proportion of investment to consumption in the society will remain roughly the same, i.e., 56 invested and 24 consumed. Prices and nominal money values and incomes fall all along the line, and we are left with the same capital structure, the same *real* income, the same interest rate, etc. The only things that have changed are nominal prices, which have fallen, and the proportion of total cash balances to money income, which has increased. . . .[12]

He concludes:

The only necessary result, then, of a change in the demand-for-money schedule is precisely a change in the same direction of the proportion of total cash balances to total money income and in the real value of cash balances. Given the stock of money, an increased scramble for cash will simply lower money incomes until the desired increase in real cash balances has been attained.[13]

---

[12]Rothbard, *Man, Economy, and State*, pp. 678f.

[13]Ibid., p. 679. Similarly, he states a few pages later:

A greater proportion of funds hoarded can be drawn from three alternative sources: (*a*) from funds that formerly went into consumption, (*b*) from funds that went into investment, and (*c*) from a mixture of both that leaves the old consumption-investment proportion unchanged. Condition (*a*) will bring about a *fall* in the rate of interest; condition (*b*) a rise in the rate of interest, and condition (*c*) will leave the rate of interest unchanged. Thus hoarding may reflect either a rise,

However, the conscientious Rothbard did not fail to remark that this conclusion stood on somewhat shaky grounds. In an endnote he wrote:

> Strictly, the *ceteris paribus* condition will tend to be violated. An increased demand for money tends to lower money prices and will therefore lower money costs for gold mining. This will stimulate gold mining production until the interest return on mining is again the same as in other industries. Thus the increased demand for money will also call forth new money to meet the demand.[14]

This observation will be the starting point for our following discussion.

<h3 align="center">IV. The Time Dimension of the Demand
for Money Reconsidered</h3>

The Demand for Commodity Money is Not Time-Neutral

Rothbard is correct in pointing out that changes in the demand for money do not have any systematic *direct* implications for the relative spending on consumers' goods and on the corresponding producers' goods. But as he admits, they do have implications for the return on investment (ROI) of money production, at any rate in the case of commodity monies such as silver or gold. An increased demand for silver will increase the ROI of silver production, because the factors of production needed to produce a given amount of silver now tend to become available at lower silver prices. This in turn will modify the spending on all other goods. In particular, capital will move from other industries into the silver industry, prompting the ROI of silver production to fall and the ROI of all other industries to rise, until the ROI of all lines of

---

a fall, or no change in the rate of interest, depending on whether *time preferences* have concomitantly risen, fallen, or remained the same. (Ibid., p. 690)

[14]Ibid., p. 916, endnote 10.

business is equal. Thus there will be a new PRI that is higher than the PRI that prevailed before the increase of the demand for money was priced into the market.

In other words, there is a positive causal relationship between the demand for commodity money and the PRI. The demand for commodity money is not time-neutral. Increases of the demand for commodity money tend to increase the PRI. Decreases of the demand for commodity money tend to decrease it.[15]

This relationship holds not only during a period of adjustment, during which more silver is being produced according to the higher demand. It also holds in *final equilibrium*, because the wear and tear increases along with the greater silver supply. The silver production will be increased permanently, and thus the PRI will also permanently be higher than it otherwise would have been.

The time structure of production will tend to be modified accordingly. A higher demand for money creates incentives to shorten the structure and to make it thicker than it otherwise would have been. And a lower demand for money will tend to lengthen the structure and make it thinner than otherwise. In short, the demand for money does affect the time structure of production.

The same effects hold in the case of *temporary* increases of the demand for money, as it is often the case at the onset and in the middle of the deflationary bust phase of the business cycle, when market participants seek to sell their non-monetary assets at a discount (thus the increase of the PRI), but a discount that is lower

---

[15]One could raise the question whether increases of the demand for money, because they entail a reduction of the price level and thus a corresponding wealth effect for money owners, did not actually *reduce* the PRI. Some Austrian economists such as Hoppe (*Democracy – The God that Failed*, p. 2) hold that increased wealth tends to lower time preference schedules. It seems to follow that an increased demand for money tends to diminish time preference schedules and thus implies a reduction of the PRI. However, the connection between wealth and time preference schedules does not hold *a priori*, but is a historically contingent relationship, as Barnett and Block have argued in "The Relationship between Wealth or Income and Time Preference is Empirical, Not Apodictic: A Critique of Rothbard and Hoppe," *Review of Austrian Economics* 19 (2006).

than the one they expect for the near future. In such cases the increase of the demand for money lasts only until the price structure has been adjusted to its new (lower) final equilibrium level.[16]

The Demand for Fiat Money Tends to Be Time-Neutral

Things are very different in the case of fiat money. The characteristic feature of fiat money is that the demand for it is at least partially determined by violations of property rights, in particular by monopoly or legal-tender laws. As a consequence, the producer of fiat money is able to choose for his product an inexpensive physical support, such as paper or electronic data.

Paper money and electronic money are fiat moneys *par excellence* because (1) their marginal cost of production is close to zero and (2) they need to be imposed on the market lest they would have no circulation *at all*, whereas other types of money such as the precious metals do not need fiat backing to be used at all. Typically, therefore, fiat money is being produced monopolistically and the producer enjoys complete discretion in maximizing his profits through time according to his inter-temporal value scales.[17]

Now here the causal mechanism that in the case of commodity monies links up the demand for money with the PRI vanishes. An increased demand for money will have next to no impact on the costs of fiat money and thus on the profitability of producing it. It will therefore not attract additional resources and thus increase the ROI in other industries. The long-run PRI is not modified–the demand for fiat money tends to be time-neutral.

Moreover, in the case of *temporary increases* of the demand for money, their tendency to increase the price level *can* be offset, without technical or commercial limitations, by a corresponding increase of the money supply, thus preventing the necessity to sell assets at a discount. As is well known, this is not a mere theoretical possibility. Present-day fiat money producers — the central banks — pursue a policy of price level stabilisation, and they vigorously

---

[16]This temporary impact of the demand for money on the PRI has been stressed by Rothbard, see *Man, Economy, and State*, pp. 692, 864f.

[17]See Hülsmann, *The Ethics of Money Production* (Auburn, Ala.: Ludwig von Mises Institute, 2008), chap. 1, sections 5 and 6; idem, *Logik der Währungskonkurrenz* (Essen: Management Akademie Verlag, 1996).

fight any form of price deflation. Thus we may say that, under the present-day fiat money regimes, any increases of the demand for money are actually *causing* corresponding increases of the money supply. It is true that such increases of the money supply will create a tendency for the price level to increase, thus entailing sooner or later a price premium within the *gross* rate of interest. But the crucial point is that the PRI need not increase. It follows that, even in the case of *temporary* increases of the demand for money, fiat money tends to have different consequences than commodity money.

Misleading Distinction between Money and Present Goods

Thus we see that the traditional Austrian position, according to which the demand for money is time-neutral, only applies to the case of fiat money. It does not apply to the case of commodity money. Why did the Austrians, and Mises and Rothbard in particular, overlook this fact? The main reason seems to be that they define money without reference to its physical characteristics. They see money as a particular "disembodied" class of goods that is therefore not subject to the laws ruling the time market. Changes in the demand for money do not affect time preference schedules because the latter concern only non-monetary goods ("real goods"), namely, consumer goods and producer goods. By contrast, money is a good in a class of its own.

Mises follows the German economist Carl Knies in classifying all economic goods into three mutually exclusive categories: consumers' goods, producers' goods, and media of exchange.[18] The

---

[18]See Mises, *Theory of Money and Credit*, pp. 96–102; Knies, *Geld und Credit* (2nd ed., Berlin: Weidmann, 1885), vol. 1, pp. 20ff. Mises argued (1) that money is not always "needed" in production processes. "There is no need for money either in the isolated household or in the socialized community. Nowhere can we discover a good of the first order of which we could say that the use of money was a necessary condition of its production" (p. 99). Furthermore, he contended (2) that money is not useful from an aggregate point of view. Whereas changes in the supply of consumers' goods or producers' goods make "mankind" poorer respectively richer, the "same cannot be said of the loss or gain of money" (p. 101).

Both arguments are weak. In *Socialism* (1922) and *Human Action* (1949), Mises stressed that only a monetary economy allowed for a complex and

pure interest rate is the inter-temporal exchange rate between present goods (consumer goods) and future goods (producer goods). The demand for money does not affect this exchange rate at all. As we have seen, this contention is correct in the case of fiat money. Here the marginal costs of producing paper money are virtually zero, and thus investment spending on money production does not depend at all on changes of demand. It follows that changes in the demand for paper money do not have any *a priori* impact on the proportion between consumption and investment, and thus on inter-temporal value-scales and the interest rate. But as we have seen as well, things are different in the case of commodity money.

Astonishingly, this fact has also been overlooked by Murray Rothbard. In chapter 11 of *Man, Economy, and State*, he modifies the analysis of present and future goods stated in earlier chapters, to take account of the impact of money hoarding.[19] Rothbard now abandons his previous classification of all goods into exactly two classes (present and future goods). Like Knies and Mises, he now champions the three-tier distinction between consumers' goods, producers' goods, and cash balances.

Clearly, a good case can be made that money is neither a consumers' good, nor a producers' good. However, for the determination of the PRI this is beside the point. Here the only relevant distinction is between present goods and future goods. Money could be said to be time neutral only if it fell into a third class of goods that would be neither present goods nor future goods. However, Rothbard does not deliver any demonstration to this

---

roundabout division of labour. Clearly, therefore, money is needed for most production projects. Similarly, the contention that the money supply has no positive or negative welfare implication for "mankind," even if true, has no scientific foundation whatever as long as we are unable to compare the subjective value judgments of different individuals.

[19]See Rothbard, *Man, Economy, and State*, p. 678. Previously he had identified hoarding as one of the *sources* of "the money that [capitalists] save and invest" — the other two sources being selling receipts from present production and money production (see ibid., p. 351). This classification begs the question whether money hoards are not in fact one of the *forms* in which one can save and invest one's capital.

effect, but simply *asserts* that money falls into a class of its own—an assertion that moreover contradicts his own previous emphasis that money is "the present good *par excellence.*"[20]

As soon as it is admitted that money is a present good, though not a consumers' good, the impact of the demand for money on relative spending between present goods and future goods is obvious. Let us recall Rothbard's argument, quoted above:

> A greater proportion of funds hoarded can be drawn from three alternative sources: (*a*) from funds that formerly went into consumption, (*b*) from funds that went into investment, and (*c*) from a mixture of both that leaves the old consumption-investment proportion unchanged.[21]

If money is a present good, then condition (a) does not imply any change inter-temporal value scales, but simply a different composition of present goods in one's portfolio. It follows that hoarding (a rise in the demand for money) in this case leaves the PRI unaffected, while in all other cases—conditions (b) and (c) it implies an *increased* PRI.

V. Some Implications of the Time-Dimension of the Demand for Money

The demand for commodity money is not time-neutral, but positively related to the pure rate of interest. By contrast, the demand for fiat money tends to be time-neutral. These results of our analysis seem to imply that fiat money, despite its manifold known shortcomings, conveys definite advantages over commodity

---

[20]Rothbard, *Man, Economy, and State*, p. 320. Rothbard's definition of present goods stresses the act of consumption (destruction). It would be more appropriate to define a present good as one that needs no further physical transformation to render the services for which it is ultimately desired. Money in one's cash balances no longer needs any physical transformation to be used, but is not destroyed through this use.

[21]Ibid., p. 690.

money, in particular, in facilitating economic growth.[22] Let us therefore briefly discuss some of these implications.

First of all we should point out that our foregoing analysis of the *comparative* impact of the demand for money on the PRI conveys no information about its *quantitative* impact. Considering that the long-run demand for money represents just a small fraction of aggregate wealth, and that it varies only marginally, it is very well possible that the long-run quantitative impact of changes in the demand for money on the PRI be negligible after all. On the other hand, there is scant empirical evidence about the behaviour of savers under a pure commodity-money standard. If and to the extent that saving occurs to a significant extent in the form of money hoarding, the quantitative impact on the PRI could increase accordingly.

It is obvious that such money-induced changes of the PRI can be highly useful, especially if we consider the reasons of a changing aggregate demand for money. Acting persons typically have an *increased* demand for money when they are concerned about looming deteriorations of the general economic and political environment. For example, they might expect troubles on the financial markets, or bad economic policy decisions such as tax hikes. Increased cash hoarding provides a partial protection against such events. Most importantly, the resulting increase of the PRI creates incentives to adjust the structure of production to the perceived riskier environment. More roundabout (and therefore riskier) investment projects will tend to be abandoned, while shorter investment projects will be encouraged. This helps preserving the all-important aggregate capital stock. Inversely, a *reduced* demand for money, which typically reflects a brighter outlook of the general economic and political environment, will induce a lengthening of the structure of production to the detriment of shorter (less physically productive) investment projects.

However, as we have seen, this mechanism for the protection of the capital stock only exists in the case of commodity money. In the case of fiat money, there are no similar incentives to adjust the

---

[22]For analysis of the economics, social and cultural consequences of paper money (respectively of electronic money), see Hülsmann, *The Ethics of Money Production*, chaps. 12 and 13.

structure of production, neither for switching it over to "safe mode" under the impact of an increased demand for money, nor in the opposite sense when the demand for money diminishes. It follows that fiat money regimes tend to waist more capital than commodity money regimes. Growth rates and living standards therefore would tend to be lower under fiat money than under commodity money.

Similarly, we should stress again the beneficial role of *short-run* variations of the PRI, resulting from increases of the demand for commodity money, in speeding up the adjustment of the structure of production after a boom phase, or in reaction to a looming crisis resulting from war, government interventionism, or natural disasters. These adjustments would not take place as quickly and automatically under a fiat money regime, as discussed above. It follows that, far from being advantageous from a macroeconomic point of view, the tendency to offset the impact of the demand for money on the PRI is actually another one of fiat money's major shortcomings.

Finally, as we have shown in a recent contribution, there is no systematic relationship between the aggregate volume of savings-investment and the PRI.[23] It follows that the demand for money, too, is not related to the aggregate level of savings-investment. Given individual inter-temporal value scales, it follows by logical necessity that both the demand and the supply of present goods are exclusively determined by those value scales, and that the latter are therefore the unique cause of the PRI. A higher demand for money not only implies an increased demand for present goods on the time market, but also a reduced supply. Therefore, the only necessary consequence of higher demand for money is for the PRI to increase. *But there is no systematic impact on the volume of the market (aggregate savings exchanged for aggregate future goods).* Depending on the (contingent) elasticity of supply and demand on the time market, the new final equilibrium might involve a somewhat larger volume of aggregate saving, but it might just as well, and with equal likelihood, involve a somewhat reduced volume of

---

[23]See Jörg Guido Hülsmann, "Time Preference and Investment Expenditure," *Procesos de Mercado* 5, no. 2 (2008): 13–33.

aggregate saving. Similarly, a lowering of the demand for money has only one necessary implication, namely, a reduction of the interest rate. Yet it has no systematic impact on aggregate saving, and thus on aggregate investment.

VI. Conclusion

In the present contribution we have shown that the demand for commodity money is *not* time-neutral. It affects the pure rate of interest and, therefore, the time-structure of production. By contrast, the demand for fiat money tends to be time-neutral — in other words, it tends not to affect the time structure of production. We have argued that this basic difference further bolsters the traditional Austrian case for commodity money and against fiat money. Indeed, the demand for commodity money is a very basic way for the unsophisticated citizen to bring the structure of production in line with his assessment of the macroeconomic environment. Fiat money takes this power out of his hands. The consequence is a greater tendency for capital to be wasted. ❧

32

Risk, Uncertainty, and Economic Organization

Peter G. Klein

I
n a recent paper, "The Limits of Numerical Probability: Frank H. Knight and Ludwig von Mises and the Frequency Interpretation," Hans-Hermann Hoppe explores Mises's approach to probability and its implications for economic forecasting.[1] Hoppe argues that Mises, like Frank Knight, subscribed to the "frequency interpretation" developed by Mises's brother, Richard von Mises,[2] along with others such as Ronald Fisher, Jerzy Neyman, and Egon Pearson. At first, this might seem surprising, as the frequency interpretation is usually contrasted with the "subjectivist" approach to probability advanced by de Finetti and, among economists, usually associated with Keynes.[3] A thoroughgoing commitment to

---

Peter G. Klein (pklein@missouri.edu) is Associate Professor in the Division of Applied Social Sciences at the University of Missouri, Adjunct Professor at the Norwegian School of Economics and Business Administration, and a Senior Fellow of the Ludwig von Mises Institute.

[1]Hans-Hermann Hoppe, "The Limits of Numerical Probability: Frank H. Knight and Ludwig von Mises and the Frequency Interpretation," *Quarterly Journal of Austrian Economics* 10, no. 1 (2007): 1–20.

[2]Richard von Mises, *Probability, Statistics and Truth* (New York: Dover Publications, 1957 [1939]).

[3]Bruno de Finetti, "Foresight: Its Logical Laws, Its Subjective Sources," in H.E. Kyburg and H.E. Smokler, eds., *Studies in Subjective Probability* (New

methodological subjectivism is, of course, a hallmark of the Austrian School. However, as Hoppe points out, Mises recognized two distinct kinds of probability, one applying to natural phenomena and another applying to human action. Just as Mises embraced "praxeology" in economics while endorsing the experimental method in the natural sciences, he thought a special kind of probability was relevant to economic decision-making, while accepting his brother's frequency interpretation for other kinds.

This paper extends the discussion by drawing out implications for economic organization of Mises's approach to probability, particularly regarding the entrepreneur's role in guiding the economic process by establishing and dissolving firms, directing their operations, and organizing them to create and capture value. After a brief review of Hoppe's interpretation of Knight and Mises, I summarize recent literature on the Knight-Mises approach to entrepreneurship and the firm, closing with some suggestions for future research.

KNIGHT, MISES, AND MISES ON PROBABILITY

Most economists are familiar with Knight's distinction between "risk" and "uncertainty." Risk refers to situations in which the outcome of an event is unknown, but the decision-maker knows the range of possible outcomes and the probabilities of each, such that anyone with the same information and beliefs would make the same prediction. Uncertainty, by contrast, characterizes situations in which the range of possible outcomes, let alone the relevant probabilities, is unknown. In this case the decision-maker cannot follow a formal decision rule but must rely on an intuitive understanding of the situation—what Knight calls "judgment"—to anticipate what may occur. Risk, in this sense, refers to "a quantity susceptible of measurement," and not a "true" uncertainty that cannot be quantified.[4] The essential function of the entrepreneur,

York: Wiley, 1964 [1937]); John Maynard Keynes, *A Treatise on Probability* (London: Macmillan, 1921).

[4]Frank H. Knight, *Risk, Uncertainty, and Profit* (New York: August M. Kelley, 1921), p. 26.

in Knight's system, is to exercise judgment, particularly in the context of purchasing factors of production.

Mises, in similar fashion, distinguished between "class probability" and "case probability." The former describes situations in which an event may be classified as a unique element of a homogeneous class, the properties of which are known. No one can predict whether a particular house in a particular neighborhood will burn down this year, but insurance companies know how many similar houses in similar locations have burned in the past, and from this the likelihood of a particular house burning within a particular period can be estimated. Case probability applies to cases in which each event is unique, such that no general class probabilities can be defined.[5] Here Mises, as argued by Hoppe, builds on his brother's defense of "frequentism," the idea that the probability of a particular event is the limit value of its relative frequency in a series of trials. In this understanding, probabilities can be defined only in cases in which repeated trials are feasible – i.e., in situations where each event can be meaningfully compared to other events in the same class. Moreover, and for this reason, probabilities can only be defined *ex post*, as learned through experience, and cannot exist *a priori*. Hence, Mises defines case probability, or uncertainty, as a case in which probabilities, in the frequentist sense, do not exist.[6]

---

[5]O'Driscoll and Rizzo adopt the terms "typical events" and "unique events" to get at this distinction. See Gerald P. O'Driscoll, Jr., and Mario J. Rizzo, *The Economics of Time and Ignorance* (Oxford: Basil Blackwell, 1985).

[6]Hence the use of the term "case probability" is misleading; what Mises really means is "case non-probability," or perhaps "case judgments without probabilities." Confusingly, Mises also argues elsewhere that "[o]nly preoccupation with the mathematical treatment could result in the prejudice that probability always means frequency" (Mises, *Human Action*, p. 107). Van den Hauwe argues, in contrast to Hoppe, that Mises's position is in some ways closer to Keynes's. See Ludwig Van den Hauwe, "John Maynard Keynes and Ludwig von Mises on Probability," *MPRA* Paper No. 6965 (2007); Hoppe, "Limits of Numerical Probability"; and Keynes, *A Treatise on Probability*.

Hoppe summarizes Knight's and Mises's views and argues persuasively that they are variants of Richard von Mises's position.[7] Hoppe also goes beyond Mises in explaining why human action, in Mises's sense of purposeful behavior, cannot be made part of a homogenous class. "Without a specified collective and a (assumedly) full count of its individual members and their various attributes no numerical probability statement is possible (or is, if made, arbitrary)."[8] Of course, as Hoppe notes, we can define such classes in a technical sense — me writing this chapter is an element of the class "economists writing book chapters" — but defining the class is not sufficient for applying class probability to an event. There must also be randomness, or what Richard von Mises calls "complete lawlessness," within the class.[9] And yet, this is not possible with human action:

> It is in connection with this randomness requirement where Ludwig von Mises (and presumably Knight) see insuperable difficulties in applying probability theory to human actions. True, formal-logically for every single action a corresponding collective can be defined. However, ontologically human actions (whether of individuals or groups) cannot be grouped in "true" collectives but must be conceived as unique events. Why? As Ludwig von Mises would presumably reply, the assumption that one knows nothing about any particular event except its membership in a known class is false in the case of human actions; or, as Richard von Mises would put it, in the case of human actions we know a "selection rule" the application of which leads to fundamental changes regarding the relative frequency (likelihood) of the attribute in question (thus ruling out the use of the probability calculus).[10]

---

[7]Hoppe, "Limits of Numerical Probability." One might also include Shackle's notion of "self-destructive, non-seriable" decisions. See G.L.S. Schackle, *Decision, Order, and Time in Human Affairs* (Cambridge: Cambridge University Press, 1961).

[8]Hoppe, "Limits of Numerical Probability," p. 10.

[9]Richard von Mises, *Probability, Statistics, and Truth*, p. 24.

[10]Hoppe, "Limits of Numerical Probability," p. 11.

Hoppe touches briefly upon, without treating in detail, the subjective approach to probability, in which *a priori* probabilities are treated simply as beliefs, rather than the outcome of some objective process of repeated trial and observation. Hoppe quotes Richard von Mises's remark that subjectivists such as John Maynard Keynes fail to recognize "that if we know nothing about a thing, we cannot say anything about its probability."[11] Adds Mises: "The peculiar approach of the subjectivists lies in the fact that they consider 'I presume that these cases are equally probable' to be equivalent to 'These cases are equally probable,' since, for them, probability is only a subjective notion."[12] Subjective probability has become central in contemporary microeconomic theory, however, particularly with the rise of Bayesian approaches to decision-making. Agents acting under conditions of uncertainty are assumed to have prior beliefs – correct or incorrect – about the probabilities of various events. These prior beliefs are exogenous, they may be common to a group of agents or unique to a particular agent, and they may or may not correspond to objective probabilities (in the frequentist sense). The Bayesian approach focuses on the procedure by which agents update these prior beliefs based on new information, and this updating is assumed to take place according to a formal rule (i.e., according to Bayes's law). Hence, the ex post probability, in such a problem, contains an "objective" element, even if it is a revision of a purely subjective prior belief.[13]

Langlois[14] argues for a tight connection between subjectivism in the Austrian sense of value theory and subjective probability theory, arguing that probabilities should be interpreted as beliefs about information structures, rather than objective events.

---

[11]Richard von Mises, *Probability, Statistics, and Truth*, p. 75.

[12]Ibid., p. 76.

[13]Bayesian updating can also be applied to objective prior probabilities, presumably to give guidance to the decision-maker in cases where repeated trials to determine the new *ex post* probability are not possible. The "Monty Hall paradox" is a classic example.

[14]Richard N. Langlois, "Subjective Probability and Subjective Economics," C.V. Starr Center for Applied Economics Research Report #82-09, Faculty of Arts and Science, New York University (1982).

> [I]t is not meaningful to talk about "knowing" a proba-
> bility or a probability distribution. A probability assess-
> ment reflects one's state of information about an event; it
> is not something ontologically separate whose value can
> be determined objectively.[15]

What distinguishes case from class probability, according to Langlois, is the character of the decision-maker's information about
the event. Objective probabilities (in the frequentist sense) are simply special cases of subjective probabilities in which the decision-
maker structures the problem in terms of classes of events. Entrepreneurship, in Langlois's interpretation, can be described as the
act of formalizing the decision problem. To use the language of
decision theory, a non-entrepreneur (call him, following Kirzner, a
Robbinsian maximizer) is presented with a decision tree, a set of
outcomes, and the probabilities for each outcome, and simply uses
backwards induction to solve the problem.[16] The entrepreneur, as
it were, re-draws the tree, by noticing a possible option or outcome
that other agents failed to see. The key distinction, according to
Langlois, is not whether the decision tree is populated with objective or subjective probabilities, but whether the tree itself is exogenous (Knightian risk) or endogenous (Knightian uncertainty).

Hoppe follows Richard von Mises in rejecting the subjectivist
position (and obviously sees no contradiction between the frequentist approach to probability and the subjective theory of
value). It is not clear exactly what is gained by redefining probabilities as "subjective with one information set" or "subjective with
another information set." As discussed in the next section, both
Knight and Mises saw probability theory in economics as playing
a particular role, namely allowing the theorist to distinguish situations in which prices are *predictable*, making profits and losses
ephemeral, and situations in which prices can only be anticipated,
using some form of *Verstehen*, by entrepreneurs. A subjectivist
parameterization of *Verstehen* may be possible, without being useful.

---

[15]Langlois, "Subjective Probability and Subjective Economics," p. 8.

[16]Israel M. Kirzner, *Competition and Entrepreneurship* (Chicago and London: University of Chicago Press, 1973).

UNCERTAINTY AND THE ENTREPRENEUR

Neither Knight nor Mises focused primarily on individual decision-making per se, but on the role of decision-making within the market system. "As economists," Hoppe observes, Knight and Mises "come upon the subject of probability indirectly, in conjunction with the question concerning the source of entrepreneurial profits and losses."[17] Indeed, while Knight devotes a chapter of *Risk, Uncertainty, and Profit* to a detailed discussion of knowledge, reasoning, and learning, his main purpose is not to analyze the ontology of judgment, but to explain the practical workings of the market. Specifically, his purpose in developing his account of probability was to decompose business income into two constituent elements, interest and profit. Interest is a reward for forgoing present consumption, is determined by the relative time preferences of borrowers and lenders, and would exist even in a world of certainty. Profit, by contrast, is a reward for anticipating the uncertain future more accurately than others (e.g., purchasing factors of production at market prices below the eventual selling price of the product), and exists only in a world of "true" uncertainty. In such a world, given that production takes time, entrepreneurs will earn either profits or losses based on the differences between factor prices paid and product prices received.

Mises, likewise, makes uncertainty central to his theory of profit and loss, a cornerstone of his well-known critique of economic planning under socialism. Mises begins with the marginal productivity theory of distribution developed by his Austrian predecessors. In the marginal productivity theory, laborers earn wages, capitalists earn interest, and owners of specific factors earn rents. Any excess (deficit) of a firm's realized receipts over these factor payments constitutes profit (loss). Profit and loss, therefore, are returns to entrepreneurship. In a hypothetical equilibrium without uncertainty (what Mises calls the "evenly rotating economy"), capitalists would still earn interest, as a reward for lending, but there would be no profit or loss.

---

[17]Hoppe, "Limits of Numerical Probability," p. 4. See also James Buchanan and Alberto Di Pierro, "Cognition, Choice, and Entrepreneurship," *Southern Economic Journal* 46, no. 3 (1980): 693–701.

Entrepreneurs, in Mises's understanding of the market, make their production plans based on the current prices of factors of production and the anticipated future prices of consumer goods. What Mises calls "economic calculation" is the comparison of these anticipated future receipts with present outlays, all expressed in common monetary units. Under socialism, the absence of factor markets and the consequent lack of factor prices, renders economic calculation — and hence rational economic planning — impossible. Mises's point is that a socialist economy may assign individuals to be workers, managers, technicians, inventors, and the like, but it cannot, by definition, have entrepreneurs, because there are no money profits and losses. Entrepreneurship, and not labor or management or technological expertise, is the crucial element of the market economy. As Mises puts it: directors of socialist enterprises may be allowed to "play market," to make capital investment decisions as if they were allocating scarce capital across activities in an economizing way, but entrepreneurs cannot be asked to "play speculation and investment."[18] Without entrepreneurship, a complex, dynamic economy cannot allocate resources to their highest valued use.

Why can't a central planning board mimic the operations of entrepreneurs? The key, for Mises, is that entrepreneurial appraisement is not a mechanical process of computing expected values using known probabilities, but a kind of *Verstehen* that cannot be formally modeled using decision theory. The entrepreneur, Mises writes, "is a speculator, a man eager to utilize his opinion about the future structure of the market for business operations promising profits."[19] The entrepreneur relies on his "specific anticipative understanding of the conditions of the uncertain future," an understanding that "defies any rules and systematization."

This concept of the entrepreneurial function is difficult to reconcile with the optimization framework of neoclassical economics. In this framework, either decision-making is "rational," meaning

---

[18]Ludwig von Mises, *Human Action: A Treatise on Economics*, Scholars Edition (Auburn, Ala.: Ludwig von Mises Institute, 2001 [1949]), p. 705.

[19]Ibid., p. 585.

that it can be represented by formal decision rules, or it is purely random. T. W. Schultz poses the problem this way:

> [I]t is not sufficient to treat entrepreneurs solely as economic agents who only collect windfalls and bear losses that are unanticipated. If this is all they do, the much vaunted free enterprise system merely distributes in some unspecified manner the windfalls and losses that come as surprises. If entrepreneurship has some economic value it must perform a useful function which is constrained by scarcity, which implies that there is a supply and a demand for their services.[20]

The key to understanding this passage is to recognize Schultz's rejection, following Friedman and Savage, of Knightian uncertainty.[21] If all uncertainty can be parameterized in terms of (possibly subjective) probabilities, then decision-making in the absence of such probabilities must be random. Any valuable kind of decision-making must be modelable, must have a marginal revenue product, and must be determined by supply and demand. For Knight, however, decision-making in the absence of a formal decision rule or model (i.e., judgment) is not random, it is simply not modelable. It does not have a supply curve, because it is a residual or controlling factor that is inextricably linked with resource ownership. As discussed above, it is a kind of understanding, or *Verstehen*, that defies formal explanation but is rare and valuable. In short, without the concept of Knightian uncertainty, Knight's idea of entrepreneurial judgment makes little sense.

Nor is judgment simply luck.[22] To be sure, one could imagine a model in which entrepreneurs are systematically biased, as in

---

[20]T. W. Schultz, "Investment in Entrepreneurial Ability," *Scandinavian Journal of Economics* 82, no. 4 (1980): 437–48, esp. pp. 437–38.

[21]Milton Friedman and Leonard Savage, "Utility Analysis of Choices Involving Risk," *Journal of Political Economy* 56, no. 4 (1948): 279–304.

[22]Kirznerian alertness is compared to luck in Harold Demsetz, "The Neglect of the Entrepreneur," in Joshua Ronen, ed. *Entrepreneurship* (Lexington: Lexington Press, 1983), pp. 271–80.

Busenitz and Barney[23] – individuals become owner-entrepreneurs because they overestimate their own ability to anticipate future prices – and the supply of entrepreneurs is sufficiently large that at least a few guess correctly, and earn profits. In such an economy there would be entrepreneurs, firms, profits, and losses, and profit (under uncertainty) would be distinct from interest. However, as Mises emphasizes, some individuals are more adept than others, over time, at anticipating future market conditions, and these individuals tend to acquire more resources while those whose forecasting skills are poor tend to exit the market.[24] Indeed, for Mises, the entrepreneurial selection mechanism in which unsuccessful entrepreneurs – those who systematically overbid for factors, relative to eventual consumer demands – are eliminated from the market is the critical "market process" of capitalism.[25]

Entrepreneurial Judgment and the Firm

In a series of papers, Nicolai Foss and I have used the Knight-Mises concept of the entrepreneur to explain important aspects of economic organization.[26] We start with Knight's view that entrepreneurship represents judgment that cannot be assessed in terms

---

[23]Lowell W. Busenitz and Jay B. Barney, "Differences between Entrepreneurs and Managers in Large Organizations: Biases and Heuristics in Strategic Decision-Making," *Journal of Business Venturing* 12, no. 1 (1997): 9–30.

[24]Ludwig von Mises, "Profit and Loss," in Mises, *Planning for Freedom* (South-Holland, Ill.: Libertarian Press, 1952), pp. 108–50.

[25]Peter G. Klein, "The Mundane Economics of the Austrian School," *Quarterly Journal of Austrian Economics* 11, nos. 3–4 (2008): 165–87.

[26]Nicolai J. Foss and Peter G. Klein, "Entrepreneurship and the Economic Theory of the Firm: Any Gains from Trade?" in Rashjree Agarwal, Sharon A. Alvarez and Olaf Sorenson, eds., *Handbook of Entrepreneurship Research: Disciplinary Perspectives* (Dordrecht: Springer, 2005); Kirsten Foss, Nicolai J. Foss and Peter G. Klein, "Original and Derived Judgment: An Entrepreneurial Theory of Economic Organization," *Organization Studies* 28, no. 12 (2007): 1893–1912; Kirsten Foss, Nicolai J. Foss, Peter G. Klein and Sandra K. Klein, "The Entrepreneurial Organization of Heterogeneous Capital," *Journal of Management Studies* 44, no. 7 (2007): 1165–86; Peter G. Klein, "Opportunity Discovery, Entrepreneurial Action, and Economic Organization," *Strategic Entrepreneurship Journal* 2, no. 3 (2008): 175–90.

of its marginal product and which, accordingly, cannot be paid a wage.[27] In other words, there is no market for the judgment that entrepreneurs rely on, and therefore exercising judgment requires the person with judgment to start a firm. Of course, judgmental decision makers can hire consultants, forecasters, technical experts, and so on. However, in doing so they are exercising their own entrepreneurial judgment.[28] Judgment thus implies asset ownership, for judgmental decision-making is ultimately decision-making about the employment of resources. The entrepreneur's role, then, is to arrange or organize the capital goods he owns. As Lachmann puts it: "We are living in a world of unexpected change; hence capital combinations . . . will be ever changing, will be dissolved and reformed. In this activity, we find the real function of the entrepreneur."[29]

This approach to the firm combines Knight's concept of judgment with the Austrian notion of capital heterogeneity. Foss, Foss, Klein, and Klein operationalize capital heterogeneity by incorporating Barzel's idea that capital goods are distinguished by their *attributes*.[30] Attributes are characteristics, functions, or possible uses of assets, as perceived by an entrepreneur. Assets are heterogeneous to the extent that they have different, and different levels of, valued attributes. Attributes may also vary over time, even for

---

[27]Knight, *Risk, Uncertainty and Profit*, p. 311.

[28]In the terminology of Foss et al., "Original and Derived Judgment," the entrepreneur-owner exercises "original" judgment, while hired employees, to whom the owner delegates particular decision rights, exercise "derived" judgment as agents of the owner. This implies that top corporate managers, whose day-to-day decisions drive the organization of corporate resources, are acting only as "proxy-entrepreneurs," except to the extent that they themselves are part owners through equity holdings.

[29]Ludwig M. Lachmann, *Capital and Its Structure* (Kansas City: Sheed, Andrews and McMeel, 1956), p. 16. Lachmann does not require the entrepreneur to own the assets he recombines; see Foss et al., "Entrepreneurial Organization of Heterogeneous Capital," for a more detailed argument that ownership, as residual rights of control, is a necessary part of this entrepreneurial function.

[30] Foss et al., "Entrepreneurial Organization of Heterogeneous Capital"; Yoram Barzel, *Economic Analysis of Property Rights* (Cambridge: Cambridge University Press, 1997).

a particular asset. Given Knightian uncertainty or Misesian case probability, attributes do not exist objectively, but subjectively, the minds of profit-seeking entrepreneurs who put these assets to use in various lines of production. Consequently, attributes are manifested in production decisions and realized only *ex post*, after profits and losses materialize.

Entrepreneurs who seek to create or discover new attributes of capital assets will want ownership titles to the relevant assets, both for speculative reasons and for reasons of economizing on transaction costs. These arguments provide room for entrepreneurship that goes beyond deploying a superior combination of capital assets with "given" attributes, acquiring the relevant assets, and deploying these to producing for a market: Entrepreneurship may also be a matter of experimenting with capital assets in an attempt to discover new valued attributes, either by trying out new combinations through the acquisition of or merger with another firm or by trying out new combinations of assets already under the control of the entrepreneur. The entrepreneur's success in experimenting with assets in this manner depends not only on his ability to anticipate future prices and market conditions, but also on internal and external transaction costs, the entrepreneur's control over the relevant assets, how much of the expected return from experimental activity he can hope to appropriate, and so on. Moreover, these latter factors are key determinants of economic organization in modern theories of the firm, which suggests that there may be fruitful complementarities between the theory of economic organization and Austrian theories of capital heterogeneity and entrepreneurship.

Foss, Foss, Klein, and Klein show how this approach provides new insights into the emergence, boundaries, and internal organization of the firm.[31] Firms exist not only to economize on transaction costs, but also as a means for the exercise of entrepreneurial judgment, and as a low-cost mechanism for entrepreneurs to experiment with various combinations of heterogeneous capital goods. Changes in firm boundaries can likewise be understood as the result of processes of entrepreneurial experimentation. And

---

[31]Ibid.

internal organization can be interpreted as the means by which the entrepreneur delegates particular decision rights to subordinates who exercise a form of "derived" judgment on his behalf.[32]

CONCLUSION

Uncertainty, in Knight's and Mises's sense, is thus fundamental to understanding not only the profit-and-loss system, and the market's process of allocating productive resources to their highest-valued users, but also the economic nature of the business firm itself. Unfortunately, contemporary neoclassical economics tends to reject both the distinction between case and class probability and the entrepreneur. If there is no "true" uncertainty, then profits are the result of monopoly power or random error. If any firm can do what any other firm does, if all firms are always on their production possibility frontiers, and if firms always make optimal choices of inputs, then there is little for the entrepreneur to do.

Fortunately, the modern entrepreneurship literature has begun to recognize the need for a more sophisticated treatment of uncertainty (along with other cognitive issues—see the discussion in Alvarez and Barney[33]), and concepts of resource heterogeneity are common in to the resource- and knowledge-based views of the firm, transaction-cost economics, and the real-options approach to the firm. Far from rehashing old controversies, the reexamination of Mises's and Knight's views on uncertainty in Hoppe's paper provides fresh insight into the entrepreneur, the firm, and the market process. ೪

---

[32]Ibid.

[33]Sharon Alvarez and Jay B. Barney, "Discovery and Creation: Alternative Theories of Entrepreneurial Action," *Strategic Entrepreneurship Journal* 1, nos. 1–2 (2007), pp. 11–26.

33

The Nature of Socialism

Mateusz Machaj

> *In hampering and of course even more so, in making it out-*
> *right illegal for private entrepreneurs to bid away means of*
> *production from caretakers, a system of socialized production*
> *prevents opportunities for improvement from being taken up*
> *to the full extent they are perceived.*

—Hans-Hermann Hoppe[1]

I first met Professor Hans-Hermann Hoppe in 2003, when he visited Poland for a libertarian conference. Most of the participants were interested in normative issues and political philosophy, whereas very few were interested in Austrian economics. Hence, I was coincidentally the only one to engage with Professor Hoppe in extensive discussions on theories of the Austrian School. I did not hesitate shamelessly to consume his time for the personal benefit of learning more about economics from one of Rothbard's most important followers. After this meeting, fortune continued to smile on me—it turned out that despite substantial geographical distance, I have enjoyed such productive conversations with my German mentor at least few times a year.

One of my favorite books, and among the most important for my intellectual development was Hoppe's *A Theory of Socialism and*

Mateusz Machaj (mateusz.machaj@mises.pl) is Instructor of economics at the University of Wrocław in Poland.

Capitalism, which could be labeled "property economics in one lesson," and, in the opinion of the present writer, is as important for introduction to Austrian economics as Hazlitt's classic. After reading Hoppe's book, one understands that political economy and comparative analysis of economic systems are about the external effects of different property regimes. As Hoppe proves, society and economy are themselves great positive external effects of private property,[2] whereas socialism and interventionism are associated with negative external effects that eventually lead to destruction of society and economy.[3] We would like to follow Hoppe's insights here: the article below attempts to reformulate Mises's calculation argument into a property argument. Private property provides enormous, positive, external effects that will disappear once it is abolished.

A Bad, Good Analogy

Imagine a dancing contest in which a group of judges is assessing the dancers. Three essential elements are required, without which any judging of that kind would not be possible. The first one is a cardinal numeration system. Every judge has certain qualitative evaluations about each performance; he could rank all the performances in order according to his view. However, there would

---

[1]Hans-Hermann Hoppe, *A Theory of Socialism and Capitalism: Economics, Politics, and Ethics* (London: Kluwer, 1989), p. 28

[2]A motto of Hoppe's Property and Freedom Society is Bastiat's aphorism, "Property does not exist because there are laws, but laws exist because there is property." Frédéric Bastiat, "Property and Law," in *Selected Essays on Political Economy*, Seymour Cain, trans., George B. De Huszar, ed. (Irvington-on-Hudson, New York: Foundation for Economic Education, 1995 [1848]); the website of the Property and Freedom Society is located at <www.PropertyAndFreedom.org>.

[3]Curiously, it is often argued that free market economists, as opposed to more interventionist ones, ignore "external effects." In fact, rather the opposite statement is true. Free market economists analyze these elements in detail, but perhaps do not use the term "external effects" very often. On the other hand, interventionist theorists use the term quite often, but usually completely ignore *external effects of institutionalized aggression* in their analysis. This defect is completely absent from Hoppe's works.

be no way to compare those individual assessments *vis-à-vis* each other without the existence of a common denominator. The use of cardinal numbers serves this function. Numbers offered by judges are simply added, and then the final result shows us a ranking of all performances.

The second element, necessarily connected to those numbers, is a quasi-"competition" between views of judges. Obviously, if all judges expressed the same opinion, there would be no point in having more than one. To certain extent, they do differ and do make different judgments (even though they might end up with the same conclusion). Having more than one judge justifies the use of numeric rankings, because these will serve as common quantitative denominator for all qualitative opinions. If there were only one judge, then we would not need cardinal numbers, as he could just rank the performances without assigning cardinal numbers to them.

The third essential element is a set of rules and constraints. Judges act within certain limits set by the rules. For example, they are constrained in their choice of numbers 1–10 and, therefore, cannot bid their scoring infinitely. Apart from this, no judge is allowed to overrule the decision of another judge, and there is no supreme judge who would assign possible numbers to other judges of a lower level. Otherwise, if there were one ultimate judge, for example, allowing judges to use only certain numbers, then he would of course decide about the final assessment, and not the judges themselves. Under this absurd condition, the decision process would boil down to a process in which neither the judges of the lower level nor the numbers they use would be needed. The situation in place would be the same as one in which one judge assesses the performances based on his preferences. In this case, qualitative valuation could substitute for a numerical one.

These three elements are integrated and cannot do without one another. Without numbers, there can be no common denominator for all qualitative assessments. If judges do not differ in their assessments, then there is no point in using numbers in the first place. (The use of a denominator would not be needed.) And if there are no rules concerning numerical assessment, then the whole process will not make sense.

However trivial this might seem, it actually provides us with a demonstration of the difference between socialism and capitalism.

I call this analogy a "bad, good analogy," because it is both good and bad. It is good, because it demonstrates some connections that are also present in the capitalist economy. The analogy is also very bad, because the market process is not otherwise like a dancing competition, hence the analogy could be easily misinterpreted.

CALCULATION IN CAPITALISM:
THE ANALOGY APPLIED

The purpose of this paper is to point out that "price ratios," as numerical ratios *per se*, are not the key element in the analysis of socialism, for it is a property structure that makes it differ from capitalism. Although the above, contest analogy does not exactly describe the market process, we can make sense of some observations concerning it. The market itself is necessarily linked to three interconnected elements, which cannot exist apart from each other: economic calculation, the intellectual division of labor, and private property constraints.[4]

Economic calculation allows for the comparison of many different ways of producing things. Imagine that one wants to produce a table – the range of possibilities is huge. One can use different tools, machines, resources, or laborers. These all are heterogeneous and cannot be added together in either physical terms or labor hours. Fortunately, there is economic calculation – all the factors have their monetary prices, hence one can add them together in terms of money and then decide which decision is the most economical. In this sense, money units are a way to "measure" the

---

[4]The term "intellectual division of labor" was used by Mises. Ludwig von Mises, *Economic Calculation in the Socialist Commonwealth* (Auburn, Ala.: Mises Institute, 1990), p. 18. See also the great work by Misesian Joseph Salerno, "Ludwig von Mises as Social Rationalist," *Review of Austrian Economics* 4 (1990). In Mises's *Socialism*, the term was translated as "mental division of labor." *Ludwig von Mises, Socialism: An Economic and Sociological Analysis* (New Haven, Conn.: Yale University Press, 1951), p. 118. Both terms might be misleading – it would be better to use the term "entrepreneurial division of labor," as I discuss in my "Market Socialism and the Property Problem: Different Perspective of the Socialist Calculation Debate," *Quarterly Journal of Austrian Economics* 10, no. 4 (December 2007): 257–80.

amount of used factors of production, which cannot be expressed together in one physical unit.

The term "intellectual division of labor" conveys the idea that different entrepreneurs have their own property and that they compete within property boundaries for factors of production. Each of them speculates and assesses conditions of the market. Competition between them allows for factors to be valued in terms of money. The calculus becomes the link that connects different opportunities and entrepreneurial expectations. Without competition transmitted through prices this way, there would be no point to economic calculation.[5]

The third group of elements, private property constraints, is a set of rules without which the process of competition could not be realized. Each entrepreneur controls money capital and factors that he owns — his economic decision-making about these scarce resources is the driving force for successful employment of the factors. He does not decide about all the other factors, and his current decisions will have an important effect upon his future income. This introduces a real boundary on his choices, for he personally will lose or gain in the process of competition (in terms of ownership). Only because of this influence can the intellectual division of labor have real effects on the economy. The owner of particular resources is making a decision only about a small element of the whole economy, since only he controls his ownership, and not the ownership of other people. In this sense, the intellectual division of labor is shaped by distribution of ownership. Without this division of ownership we could not speak of the entrepreneurial division of labor.

Socialist systems differ from the capitalist process by being establishing one compulsory owner, who becomes the ultimate decision maker in the economic system.[6] The consequences of that

---

[5]Different firms exist because of the competition within the uncertain world; this differs from the Coasian view that some monetary costs cause the existence of firms. See Ronald H. Coase, "The Nature of the Firm," *Economica* 4, no. 16 (1937).

[6]Writes Mises:

> The essential mark of socialism is that one will alone acts. It is immaterial whose will it is. The director may be an

step are unavoidable, since without private property there can be no intellectual division of labor. Instead of the market process, there is a physical and compulsory exclusion of competition, which substitutes for the market one ultimate decision making process, directing allocations of factors. The central owner does not determine the value of factors of production as the market process does, because he has no means to relate his assessment to other opportunities that might have been perceived by other entrepreneurs. There is no basis for quantitative discrimination between production projects, for there only can be a straight ordinal valuation of them (a valuation of completely vertically integrated processes). The so-called "social appraisement process" is abolished once private property is abolished.[7]

Possible Responses and Suggested Replies

Socialists have responded to Mises's challenge in many different ways. Unfortunately, in his critique he concentrates too much on only one aspect of the problem, namely economic calculation. In the previous section, Mises's argument has been reformulated mainly in terms of the following emphasis: we have now changed the focus from prices to the intellectual division of labor being a product of property distribution.

Socialism is a system organized by one owner, where there are no entrepreneurs competing for the most valuable use of resources. Even if one owner establishes some numerical system, this in no way differs from a straight ranking of all the possible ways of producing things. These centrally administered "prices" do not change anything since one owner establishes them, one

> anointed king or a dictator, ruling by virtue of his charisma, he may be a Fuhrer or a board of Fuhrers appointed by the vote of the people. The main thing is that the employment of all factors of production is directed by one agency only.

Ludwig von Mises, *Human Action: A Treatise on Economics* (Chicago: Contemporary Books, 1966), p. 695.

[7]This is the term used by Salerno, "Ludwig von Mises as Social Rationalist."

owner acts upon them, and one owner changes them *ex post*. From the very beginning he employs the managers (there is no market for corporate control) and decides what in the accounting books is registered as profits and losses. In contrast, market economy prices are the result of different actions of competing owners and this is their nature: as a *common denominator for different property assessments*.[8] If only one owner establishes prices, then they lose their basic feature as a denominator for the competition process and become only the expression of one owner's preferences (hence they cannot be used as an independent economic indicator).[9] Using prices in a socialist system is equivalent to a straight ordinal ranking of the processes by a central planner.

Let us now consider some responses to Mises.

1. *Abolish property and leave prices for the factors*

This certainly makes calculation possible, but does not get us far, since prices alone are not enough. Along with prices *allocation decisions* are needed, which will then reconstruct the price system. In a capitalist system, expectations and property decisions of competing owners constantly rearrange prices. In socialist systems, we have one owner and previous capitalist prices. But what's next? How is a planner supposed to act upon these prices or reshape them? Competition is not based on the existence of past prices, but on speculations upon the future state of the market.[10] Just because

---

[8]See also Jeffrey M. Herbener, "Calculation and the Question of Arithmetic," *Review of Austrian Economics* 9, no. 1 (1996): 151–62.

[9]On this point see G.D.H. Cole, *Economic Planning* (New York: Kennikat Press, 1971), pp. 183–85; Walter Eucken and Terence H. Hutchinson, "On the Theory of the Centrally Administrated Economy: An Analysis of the German Experiment. Part I," *Economica*, n.s. 15, no. 58 (1948); idem, "On the Theory of the Centrally Administrated Economy: An Analysis of the German Experiment. Part II," *Economica*, n.s. 15, no. 59 (1948); Morris Bornstein, "The Soviet Price System," *American Economic Review* 52, no. 1 (1962).

[10]See Mises, *Human Action*, p. 58:

> Understanding is not a privilege of the historians. It is everybody's business. In observing the conditions of his environment everybody is a historian. Everybody uses

some prices existed in the past does not solve the problem of economic calculation as posed by Mises.[11]

2. A mathematical solution[12]

We do not have enough room here to criticize the mathematical approach, but we take the opportunity here to reject the myth that Barone solved the problem on paper. A completely neglected quote *in extenso* from the source should suffice:

> Many of the writers who have criticized collectivism have hesitated to use as evidence the practical difficulties in establishing on paper the various equivalent; but it seems they have not perceived what really are the difficulties — or, more frankly, the impossibility — of solving such equations *a priori*. If, for a moment, we assume that economic variability of the technical coefficients may be neglected and we take account of their technical variability only, it is not impossible to solve on paper the equations of the equilibrium. . . . But it is frankly inconceivable that the *economic determination* of the technical coefficients can be made *a priori*, in such a way as to satisfy the condition of the minimum cost of production which is an essential condition for obtaining that maximum to which we have referred. *This economic variability*

understanding in dealing with the uncertainty of future events to which he must adjust his own actions. The distinctive reasoning of the speculator is an understanding of the relevance of the various factors determining future events. And — let us emphasize it even at this early point of our investigations — action necessarily always aims at future and therefore uncertain conditions and thus is always speculation. Acting man looks, as it were, with the eyes of a historian into the future.

[11]For Mises's response to initial criticism that was particularly weak, see Ludwig von Mises, "New Contributions to the Problem of Socialist Economic Calculation," in Richard Ebeling, ed., *Selected Writings of Ludwig von Mises: Between the Two World Wars: Monetary Disorder, Interventionism, Socialism, and the Great Depression* (Indianapolis, Liberty Fund, 2002).

[12]Sometimes improperly mixed with a dynamic market socialism model.

of the technical coefficients is certainly neglected by the collectivists. . . . The determination of the coefficients economically most advantageous can only be done in an experimental way: and not on a small scale, as could be done in a laboratory; but with experiments on a very large scale.

Some collectivist writers, bewailing the continual destruction of firms (those with higher costs) by free competition, think that the creation of enterprises to be destroyed later can be avoided, and hope that with organized production it is possible to avoid the dissipation and destruction of the wealth which such experiments involved, and which they believe to be peculiar property of "anarchist" production. Thereby these writers simply show that they have no clear idea of what production really is, and that they are not even disposed to prove a little deeper into the problem which will concern the Ministry which will be established for the purpose in the Collectivist State.[13]

3. *The collectivist decision*[14]

In this proposition, the planner is supposed to employ the specialists, perhaps past entrepreneurs and businessmen; while sitting around the table, they should figure out which range of production processes would be the best (or as in the case of democratic socialism this could be put to a vote). As we saw above, this would be only a paper game since the real competitive process requires that each market participant owns some resources and by his expectations and anticipations, within the property limits, competes with others for more ownership. As a planner and his employees determine the range of production processes in absence of bidding and exclusion based on property boundaries, their effort is completely different in nature than in capitalism. No competition exists in this scenario, for "competition" in it is as real as that between children

---

[13]Enrico Barone, "The Ministry of Production in the Collectivist State," in F.A. Hayek, ed. *Collectivist Economy Planning* (London: Routledge and Kegan Paul, 1935 [1908]), p. 287; emphasis added.

[14]See, for example, G.D.H. Cole, *Chaos and Order in Industry* (London: Metheun & Co. Ltd., 1920).

who, without funds, bid at the auction. Our "good, bad" analogy shows us that juries in the dancing contest must act within properly set numerical limits. Somewhat similarly, entrepreneurs are acting within real limits — possibility of control of resources. If they sit around the table without the limit set by property constraints, how can they compete and bid for the factors? How can one discriminate within plain proposition and suggestions? The fact that public service differs from business transactions in the marketplace does not stem from the incentive problem, or from the vanity of government employees. The problem lies exactly in the difference between acting on paper and actually bidding on prices with the use of property. Otherwise, the bidding process is in no way different from a game of Monopoly.[15]

4. *The central planner should introduce competition between managers of public enterprises*[16]

This solution mistakenly assumes that entrepreneurship is a result of management, not of control. It ignores the fact that entrepreneurship is a result of being an owner, supreme controller, i.e. final decision maker.[17] Naturally, in capitalism, owners might delegate to others the authority to act on their behalf, but this does not change the nature of entrepreneurship, i.e. ultimate control of a particular resource.[18] But, this feature changes under socialism, where only one owner delegates responsibility for decisions to subordinates in the economy. Following our dancing analogy, if there was one person deciding which judge should use which

---

[15]We can echo here Mises's phrase "play[ing] market." Mises, *Human Action*, p. 709.

[16]This has been suggested especially by Oscar Lange and Fred M. Taylor, *On the Economic Theory of Socialism* (New York: McGraw-Hill, 1956).

[17]Interestingly, another brilliant Austrian economist, Israel Kirzner, seems to commit the same fallacy. His mistake is a result of "confusing the category of entrepreneurship as it is defined in the imaginary construction of functional distribution with conditions in a living and operating economy." See Mises's argument on this, in *Human Action*, p. 306.

[18]For an application of this to modern corporation theory as it relates to insider trading, see Henry G. Manne, *Insider Trading and the Stock Market* (New York: The Free Press, 1966).

number, then it would be obvious who is, in fact, making the assessment. It is exactly the same case in "competition" between the managers, as they all have one ultimate boss. The central planner appoints the managers; the central planner decides about wages. The central planner decides about structure of industries, about which part is to be controlled by the manager and how particular inventories can be affected. Surely, he is the one who ultimately decides, although he might transfer some of his duties to his subordinates. This, however, does not change the fact that the whole system is subjected to one will acting.[19] There is no capital market, no land and real estate market, no asset market, nor any market for corporate control. Similarly, although managers in capitalism control resources to some extent (which creates a possibility for agency problems), ultimately owners still control the assets.

5. *Socialist prices are supposed to be accounting prices balancing quantity demanded and quantity supplied*

This proposition was to be mixed with the previous one; however, we will deal with separately. Specifically, Taylor, and then Lange after him, suggested that prices are supposed to be indicators responding to physical quantities.[20] If hammers are piling up in a warehouse, the central planner is supposed to lower the price. If a delivery is late, then the planner should raise the price. However, the problem noted earlier still remains: decisions about all industrial structures, employment, and possible actions are set up from the beginning by the central planner. Nothing, in this regard, is a result of the competitive process. He, of course, must instruct his subordinates how to act using his invented "price system." Instructions to the managers about what rules to follow are given by the planner himself. These two decisions will cause surpluses and shortages somewhere, and so the central planner will have to continually adjust his ratios to arrive at the accounting, which equalizes the quantity demanded with the quantity supplied. But

---

[19]Again see on this Cole, *Economic Planning*; Eucken and Hutchinson, "On the Theory of the Centrally Administrated Economy" (Parts I & II); and Bornstein, "The Soviet Price System."

[20]Fred Taylor, "The Guidance of Production in a Socialist State," *American Economic Review* 19, no. 1 (1929).

what does *this* mean exactly? Isn't each factor at a factory subjected to central planner's decision? Every factor is already put in the central plan—what then is a "surplus" or "shortage" supposed to mean? The planner decides when and how the prices are supposed to change—he then bounds himself and adjusts his decisions to his own decisions (in the capitalist system, a pricing mechanism for one entrepreneur is a mechanism of adjusting his actions to actions of others in the area of intellectual division of labor).

Apart from this, there are no real "bankruptcies" as we see them in the capitalist system. "Losses" in capitalism are linked to a rearrangement of ownership, for costs which are higher than prices cause "liquidation"—a transfer of assets between different parties. None of this is present in socialism, since one owner makes all decisions concerning officially administered prices, factor distribution, and alternative employment. We see then that everything is a derivative of the central planner's ultimate decision making. Apart from that, it is useful to point out that a process of production is not instantaneous. In other words, just because some factors or goods are stored for a certain time, not employed at every single moment, *it does not mean that such storage is uneconomical*. Under capitalism, such storage is under the boundary of the intellectual division of labor. Under socialism, it is a product of authoritative use of aggressive force. Or to put it differently, categories of shortages and surpluses are not simple accounting and physical categories, but complex economic phenomena judged by entrepreneurs within the framework of monetary appraisement.

CONCLUSION

The argument about the economic chaos resulting from the establishment of socialism (understood as one compulsory owner) was restated in this article. It was shown that socialism's economic deficiency does not result from the lack of a numerical system; rather, it flows from essential characteristics of socialism. Socialism means dictatorship, necessarily survives as dictatorship, and no centrally produced accounting ratios will change that fact. As such, competition is literally impossible under socialism, and this cannot be changed by the introduction of centrally administered accounting ratios. ॐ

34

A Theory of Socialism and Capitalism

Mark Thornton

I n the wake of the downfall of the Berlin Wall, the breakup of the Soviet Union, and the emergence of capitalism in China, I was asked to teach the comparative economic systems class at Auburn University for the summer term in 1989. My only exposure to the topic had been as an undergraduate student, where my teacher was a Cold-War-era professor who concentrated almost exclusively on the Soviet Union. His implicit message was to fear the Soviet Union, which would soon come to smother the American dream.

My assignment came at the last minute, so there would be no reviewing of textbooks and preparations of lectures in advance. I spent the summer term preparing lectures on the fly and staying one chapter ahead of the students. Also, I had to choose a textbook somehow, even though I wasn't familiar with my options, which meant I didn't know what political punch-line the author would deliver at the end. My unorthodox choice was the recently published *A Theory of Socialism and Capitalism* by Hans-Hermann Hoppe.[1]

Mark Thornton (mthornton@mises.org) is a Senior Fellow at the Ludwig von Mises Institute and Book Review Editor of the *Quarterly Journal of Austrian Economics*.

[1]Hans-Hermann Hoppe, *A Theory of Socialism and Capitalism: Economics, Politics, and Ethics* (Boston: Kluwer Academic Publishers, 1989).

My first exposure to Hans was at a public lecture he delivered to the economics faculty at Auburn University. As I remember, his topic was the theory of public goods.[2] His German accent was particularly thick at this time and he read his manuscript as only Hans can—with precision and authority.

Public goods theory was, and largely still is, sacred ground for most economists, and at the time it had not been subjected to many Austrian criticisms. I remember being impressed by Hans's detailed critique, but even more than that, the utter shock and surprise on the faces of the members of the economics departments. When the lecture was completed you could have heard a pin drop. The economics department was largely "free market" and "Austrian friendly," but questioning the validity of public goods theory was apparently a sort of desecration of Holy Scripture. Afterwards, and for several days, I defended Hans and debated his position. I would win over concession after concession in these debates with my professors, but failed to win a single convert.

The book arrived in the bookstore in time for my class, but it looked nothing like a textbook. In fact, the production values of the book were the worst I had ever seen. Neither of these factors mattered to me, but I do note them here to indicate that the deck was stacked against me the first day I walked into class. Plus the class was completely full of students who had little or no interest in comparative economic systems, but simply needed an elective of some type.

To my great surprise, the class went much better than I had hoped and was one of the most gratifying teaching experiences in my career. Free-market-oriented economics students seemed to revel in the complete and utter devastation of socialism that would follow, but even outright socialist students and more unbiased minds appeared to have a certain respect for the material presented in class. Much of the credit for this success I attribute to *A*

---

[2]See Hans-Hermann Hoppe, "Capitalist Production and the Problem of Public Goods," in idem, *A Theory of Socialism and Capitalism*; idem, "Fallacies of the Public Goods Theory and the Production of Security," in idem, *The Economics and Ethics of Private Property: Studies in Political Economy and Philosophy*, 2nd ed. (Auburn, Ala.: Ludwig von Mises Institute, 2006 [1993]).

Theory of Socialism and Capitalism, because more than three-quarters of class time relied specifically on the book.

The success of the book in reaching the students rests first on that fact that it is a theoretical rather than empirical treatise which provides a clear, unambiguous analytical framework to understand any particular economy that a student might face. Second, the book analyzes and debunks, or rather reconstructs, the two major "exceptions" of mainstream economics, monopoly and public goods theory, and therefore presents economic theory as a unified whole. Third, the moral and ethical aspects of economics and economic policy are introduced in an integrated and scientific fashion, and fourth, the book provides an understanding of economic and social change. Although this latter point may not have been a primary aim of the author, it sure was handy to answer questions regarding why socialism was imploding—especially given that most other professors on campus were teaching that socialism and redistributionism of all kinds were the panacea for social ills.

In addition to all these positive traits of the book, long time readers of Professor Hoppe will clearly recognize the consistency of his writings over time. Beginning in the Garden of Eden (so as to highlight the role of scarcity), he proceeds deductively to establish the concepts of property, contract, and aggression, and then to establish the meaning of pure capitalism as a social system based on property and the absence of coercion, while pure socialism is a system based on systemic violence and the absence of property rights. In addition, he shows how each system impacts the personality and prosperity of individuals living in those systems. From beginning to end, his argument is logically deduced and intuitively obvious. Throughout, Hans is always alerting the reader to possible misconceptions and weaknesses that he will address later in the text.

Beginning with the familiar case of Russian-style socialism, capitalism is shown to be superior to an economy run by caretaker-central planners. The absence of opportunity costs for the caretaker inevitably leads to reduced investment, misallocation, and overutilitzation of capital and labor. Added to this critique is the impact on the personal character and personality of individuals in a socialist society because efficient use of resources and catering to the consumer are no longer rewarded, and so people gravitate toward "political" action. Hoppe illustrates all this with a brief look at Russian-style economies and the natural experiment of East and West Germany, but modern westerners need only to take a close look at their own governments' bureaucracies to understand the impact of socialism on character and personality.

Russian-style socialism is the most obvious and recognizable form of socialism, but social-democracy is the most common and dominant form of socialism. Here, the democratic process substitutes for the central authority. Social-democratic socialism allows for some property rights to remain intact, although not immune from attack. It initiates a system of taxation that takes the property of producers and a system of redistribution to enrich non-producers. The system does solve some problems of soviet-style socialism and reduces others, but, in the end, it produces essentially the same type of results.

Conservative socialism is at the opposite end of social-democratic socialism, but both also have many similarities. Social democrats want "change," while conservatives oppose it. Social democrats want to redistribute property while conservatives want to enforce the status quo and "stay the course." Conservatives support price controls, regulations including antitrust policies, and behavioral controls like prohibitions. Hoppe shows how the reality of mixed economies and ideologies make empirical examinations complex but that his theoretical framework provides clarity to all conservative socialist systems such as feudalism, monarchies, Nazism, and the Republican Party. All lead to impoverishment just like social-democratic socialism.

Although most economists would not understand all the implications of these various types of socialism, many would now agree with Hoppe that Russian-style socialism is bad and that anything beyond moderate conservative or social democratic socialism is also bad for the economy.

After analyzing these forms of socialism, the book turns to more controversial matters and the case for social engineering, where economists and other academics would prefer to implement only policies that "work" rather than blindly following some ideology. Here, Hans embarks on an all-out onslaught on social engineering and its foundation in positivism. This section and the following digression on epistemology required extensive class coverage supplemented with examples and illustrations, but it was well worth the investment to undermine the so-called pragmatic notion that we should only implement "what works." Social engineering, with its scientific veneer, is in reality not scientific at all; in practice it is completely normative, and in the end is extremely dangerous.

The most controversial matter occurs in chapter seven: "The Ethical Justification of Capitalism and Why Socialism is Morally Indefensible," Hoppe's intriguing "argumentation ethics" defense of libertarian ethics.[3] The students found this interesting for many reasons, but the fact that it was an explicitly argued ethical position was something rather novel for them. I drove home Hans's core point where he demonstrates the moral superiority of capitalism over socialism in that "one cannot communicate and argue that one cannot communicate and argue" (which, by the way, is contained in a parenthetical statement). Some thought that this was some kind of trick, but most were willing to play along.

With the argument made, I told the students — for effect — that Hoppe's argument against socialism is completely undermined when you examine collective action that is completely voluntary. For example, Major League Baseball establishes and enforces all sorts of rules on its member teams; family units can adopt Russian-style socialism if they wish; homeowner associations can establish, change and enforce rules on how and when lawns will be mowed and garbage will be collected; fraternities can require that new members be spanked with wooden planks; and entrepreneurs can require that patrons wear shoes or not smoke on their premises. Anything that socialism claims to accomplish can be accomplished with voluntary agreements and much more. One bright, future economist in the class corrected me by pointing out that this really did not undermine Hans's argument, because it was actually an argument for capitalism. I think the fact that the "American way" is perceived to be more voluntary compared to other societies and

---

[3]See also Hoppe, *A Theory of Socialism and Capitalism*, ch. 2, and idem, *The Economics and Ethics of Private Property*, chaps. 11–13, 15, and "Appendix: Four Critical Replies."

that Hans was just taking volunteerism to its logical extreme helped win over many of the students to our position.[4]

Without efficiency or morality to back it, socialism is then revealed as merely a parasitic state using the carrot of political favors and the stick of violence to live off its host. Ultimately, the state uses propaganda of many forms to sustain an ideology that prevents the host from relieving itself of the parasite, and in class we had a wide-ranging discussion as to propaganda of the U.S. government.[5] Hoppe notes that the best system for achieving and sustaining the goals of the parasite is democratic-majority rule, which of course would be a major theme of his book *Democracy – The God that Failed*.[6] Ultimately, the state finds its strength in the immortal words of Franklin Roosevelt – "the only thing we have to fear is fear itself" – meaning everything will be fine as long as we have the state to take care of us.

The last two chapters of the book deal with the problems of monopoly and public goods.[7] Here, Hans aptly shows that monopoly is not a problem of the free market but is solely a problem of the government's own creation. He then demolishes the theory of public goods and explains how the market addresses the issues of public goods and externalities. This was all new information to the students, including the economics majors, and I employed several digressions using mainstream literature to back up Hans's points.

---

[4]At least none of the students complained to my department chairman or reported me to the dean's office.

[5]On the state's use of ideological propaganda, see Hans-Hermann Hoppe, "Banking, Nation States and International Politics: A Sociological Reconstruction of the Present Economic Order," *Review of Austrian Economics* 4 (1990): 62 *et seq.*; idem, "The Economics and Sociology of Taxation," in idem, *The Economics and Ethics of Private Property*, pp. 64–65; and idem, "Banking, Nation States, and International Politics: A Sociological Reconstruction of the Present Economic Order," in idem, *The Economics and Ethics of Private Property*, pp. 86–87.

[6]Hans-Hermann Hoppe, *Democracy – The God that Failed: The Economics and Politics of Monarchy, Democracy, and Natural Order* (New Brunswick, N.J.: Transaction Publishers, 2001).

[7]Hans-Hermann Hoppe, "Capitalist Production and the Problem of Monopoly," in idem, *A Theory of Socialism and Capitalism*; idem, "Capitalist Production and the Problem of Public Goods." See also note 2, above.

As I tightened the noose around the neck of the mainstream theories of monopoly and public goods using both deduction and illustrations, the students paid close attention and asked many questions. In the end, I think the students appreciated this new version of economics, where there were no exceptions to the rules of economics and where there was a way in which the moral and ethical implications of economic systems could be analyzed.

The success of the book in reaching my students was based on the fact that it helped explain the turbulent changes that were occurring in the world, such as the fall of the Berlin Wall, the breakup of the Soviet Union, and the acceptance of capitalism in China. In addition, the book presents economic analysis as a unified whole without the exceptions of monopoly and public goods. Furthermore, the book brings a moral and ethical analysis to comparative economic systems that is integrated into the economic analysis itself. In short, *A Theory of Socialism and Capitalism* is a treatise that is a "breath of fresh air" for student and teacher alike.

I believe that my experience supports an important point regarding strategy and the future of Austrian economics. Recall the reaction of my professors to the public lecture given by Hans Hoppe on public-goods theory. They were shocked into denial and beyond any attempt to logically debate the issues raised. Yes, public-goods theory could be criticized on any number of levels, but professional economists could not conceive of abandoning the concept in its entirety. On the other hand, undergraduate students who were probably leery of the concepts of natural monopoly and public-goods theory to begin with were open to Hoppe's criticisms, and many even accepted them. Indeed, I think that most of the students welcomed the opportunity to be exposed to this radical alternative, with several of them embracing it in its entirety.

The lesson here, I believe, is that Austrian economics should not proceed in a manner solely to gain acceptance among mainstream economists. That is not to say that Austrians should withdraw from debates and not engage with other economists—far from it. Lines of communication and debate should be maintained and discussions about commonalities and disagreements with other schools of economic thought should go forward, as is the great tradition of the Austrian School. However, my experience with students suggests that the most fruitful strategy is to spread the knowledge of the Austrian School to as wide an audience as possible, particularly amongst those with an open mind. The great practical advantage of the Austrian School is that it is a form of economic analysis that is founded in realism and helps us understand both progress and problems in the real world. Therefore, it is a useful tool for people in the real world, but is of little use, and indeed is a threat, to mainstream academic economists.

One final point I would like to make is that, in 1989 when Hans published *A Theory of Socialism and Capitalism*, every textbook in comparative economic systems was obsolete because of events surrounding the downfall of communism. In contrast, not only was Hans's book timely, but it has proven itself timeless in that it continues, twenty years later, to be as relevant as ever and a classic treatise on the subject. ❧

35

TPR, Entrepreneurial Component, and Corporate Governance

James D. Yohe and Scott A. Kjar

O
ne of Hans Hoppe's most important contributions concerns his application of time preference rates to monarchical (private) government and democratic (public) government. Hoppe lays out his position in his seminal "The Political Economy of Monarchy and Democracy, and the Idea of a Natural Order,"[1] and clarifies and extends it in pieces including "Time Preference, Government, and the Process of De-Civiliza-

James Yohe (jyohe@gadsdenstate.edu) and Scott Kjar (scottakjar@yahoo.com) both studied under Hans-Hermann Hoppe at the University of Nevada, Las Vegas, during the early 1990s, Kjar as a graduate student and Yohe as an undergraduate. They were regular members of Hoppe's weekly discussion of current events and political topics, affectionately (and descriptively) referred to as "drinking night" by its participants. Kjar and Yohe both subsequently earned their Ph.D.s in economics at Auburn University, with Hoppe serving on Yohe's dissertation committee. Yohe is currently Economics Instructor at Gadsden State College in Gadsden, Alabama. Kjar is currently Visiting Assistant Professor of Economics at the University of Dallas in Dallas, Texas. Thanks to Jeff Barr and Lee Iglody for comment and discussion on this topic.

[1]Hans-Hermann Hoppe, "The Political Economy of Monarchy and Democracy, and the Idea of a Natural Order." _Journal of Libertarian Studies_ 11, no. 2 (Summer 1995).

tion: From Monarchy to Democracy."[2] Hoppe argues that the time preference rates of private rulers (monarchs) will be lower than the time preference rates of democratic rulers, *ceteris paribus*. This difference is caused by each ruler's relationship with present income and the present capital values of their respective realms.

In this article, we extend Hoppe's argument to the corporate sector. We argue that Hoppe's analysis of short-term and long-term interests *vis-à-vis* owners and managers can be applied to entrepreneur-managers and non-entrepreneur corporate managers. Further, we add an entrepreneurial component to Hoppe's discussion of TPR to round out the differences between governments and corporations.

Private Rulers, Democratic Rulers, and the Time Preference Rate

Both private rulers and democratic rulers generate present income, whether from taxation, monetization, agricultural or industrial production from the realm's assets, or other sources. However, only the private ruler can accrue the present capital value of the realm, since only the private ruler possesses an ownership in the realm. A democratic ruler possesses the realm's assets only during a specified term of office after which the ruler faces the possibility of electoral defeat, removal from office due to term limits, or other restrictions on the ruler's temporal reign.

This implies that private rulers will tend to display lower discount rates in forming decisions regarding future endeavors. Their policies will encompass longer time horizons since the private ruler can expect to still rule at future times and can pass his realm on to his heir after death. By contrast, a democratic ruler will discount future benefits at a much higher rate that approaches infinity as the time horizon lengthens, both because of uncertainty over

---

[2]Hans-Hermann Hoppe, "Time Preference, Government and the Process of De-Civilization: From Monarchy to Democracy," in John V. Denson, ed., *The Costs of War: America's Pyrrhic Victories*, 2nd ed. (New Brunswick, N.J.: Transaction Publishers, 1999).

the ruler's tenure and also because of the ruler's inability to bequeath the realm to his heir.[3] Hoppe writes:

> The institution of private government ownership systematically shapes the incentive structure confronting the ruler and distinctly influences his conduct of government affairs. Assuming no more than self-interest, the ruler tries to maximize his total wealth, i.e., the present value of his estate *and* his current income. He would *not* want to increase current income at the expense of a more than proportional drop in the present value of his assets. Furthermore, because acts of current income acquisition invariably have repercussions on present asset values (reflecting the value of all future expected asset earnings discounted by the rate of time preference), private ownership, in and of itself, leads to economic calculation and thus promotes farsightedness.
>
> While this is true of private ownership generally, in the special case of private ownership of *government* it implies distinct moderation with respect to the ruler's drive to exploit his monopoly privilege of expropriation.[4]

---

[3]The fact that heirs sometimes get elected to the same position in no way negates this analysis. Further, such heirs are frequently temporally removed from their parents holding the same position. For example, John Adams did not bequeath the presidency to his son, John Quincy Adams. Rather, the son had to wait through the presidencies of Thomas Jefferson, James Madison, and James Monroe before he had his chance. Likewise, Richard J. Daley was Mayor of Chicago from 1955 to 1976, and his son, Richard M. Daley, has been Mayor of Chicago from 1989 to the present. Again, though, the elder Daley did not bequeath the position to his son, who had to wait through the mayoral regimes of Michael Blandic, Jane Byrne, Harold Washington, David Orr, and Eugene Sawyer before taking the position. George H.W. Bush did not bequeath the office of the president to his son, George W. Bush, and the latter had to wait through Bill Clinton's two terms. Clinton did not leave the office to his wife, Hillary, who unsuccessfully sought the position in 2008. In no case did the ruler bequeath even the office, much less the realm, to his heir.

[4]Hoppe, "Time Preference," p. 472; emphasis in original.

As Hoppe makes clear, wealth-maximizing private owners, whether of governments or of land and capital goods, will not consciously reduce the present value of their assets disproportionate to increases in current income. In fact, if an increase in current income was needed that would disproportionately affect the present value of the assets, a private owner would be better off selling those assets in whole or in part on the market to acquire the current income at a less-than-disproportionate reduction in his net wealth caused by misusing the asset.

Each incentive a private ruler has to increase current expropriation to increase current income is met by an incentive to decrease current expropriation in order to increase long-term income and capital value of the realm. However, the democratic ruler's incentives to increase current expropriation are *not* met by disincentives based on the realm's capital value. That leads the public ruler to discount future states more heavily.

All other things being equal, the heavier discounting that public rulers assess to future income results in a reduced present value of the realm. Because a public ruler cannot sell or pass on the realm, the only accumulations to his own wealth come through increases in current income via taxes and other confiscatory acts. Thus, the public ruler has greater incentives for such confiscatory actions and fewer incentives for long-term husbanding.

TPR AND CORPORATE GOVERNANCE

We now apply Hoppe's path-breaking analysis to corporate governance. After all, if the issues of present income and present capital value lead to different incentives for private rulers (owners) and public rulers (managers) of realms, it must follow that the same issues of present income and present capital value will lead to different incentives for entrepreneur-managers and non-owner corporate managers of businesses.

A private entrepreneur-manager faces a similar set of issues as does the private ruler. The entrepreneur-manager derives both the present income of a firm and the firm's present capital value based on its long-term income and asset value. This gives the private entrepreneur-manager incentives to engage in long planning horizons, thereby driving a low time preference rate.

By contrast, the corporate manager cannot accrue the capital value. The corporate manager cannot sell the corporation's assets for his own enrichment. Instead, the corporate manager's compensation is based on increasing the present income of the firm, from which he may generate an increased salary. Absent an increased present income for the firm, there is not likely to be an increased present income for the manager. The corporate manager's income is derived from his perceived benefit to the owners of the firm. It is through his usefulness in implementing the plans and policies of the corporate board that his employment and pay are based.

In the absence of certainty and neutral money, trust becomes an issue, as the board cannot be expected to possess the same information that the manager has. This includes the discount rate at which the manager discounts future earnings. Relative to the personal wealth of the entrepreneur-manager, the personal wealth of a corporate manager is less tied to the future earning of the firm, and thus less to the long-term capital value of the firm, than it would be if he were able to accrue the capital value as a private owner would.

Because the corporate manager is less tied to the future earnings, he has incentives to sell the firm's long-term assets and use the funds to acquire more present-income-oriented assets. As a manager, he cannot simply sell the assets and consume the cash; all he can do is rearrange their composition to produce greater amounts of income in the nearer future. More roundabout means of production are reversed toward less roundabout means in the interest of more current revenue, but at the expense of the firm's long-term capital value.

This leads to corporate managers attempting to maximize current income at a higher degree than they would as actual owners of a firm. This being the case, they also must discount future earnings at a higher rate relative to current income in the same manner as a democratic ruler would relative to a monarch.

UNCERTAINTY AND THE ERE

The Evenly Rotating Economy (ERE) is a fictitious system in which market prices always coincide with final prices. There are no price changes, and the same transactions are repeated day after day; tomorrow is no different from today, which itself is the same as yesterday. In the ERE, uncertainty regarding future prices and the available quantities of the production inputs are non-existent. The factors affecting the supply and demand for goods and services — the time preference rates of individuals — are known and do not change. Prices are stable in the ERE, and money is neutral, so there are no changes in the exchange ratio between goods and services caused by changes in the supply of money.[5]

In the ERE, because there is no uncertainty about the future, there is no role for entrepreneurs. Instead, natural resources, labor, and capital earn returns based on productivity and time preference. If the participants in an ERE economy have a high time preference rate, then the returns to factors of production will also be high at the margin; factors will not be utilized if their return is too low. If the participants in an ERE economy have a low time preference rate, then the returns to factors of production will be low at the margin because they will be utilized for low-returning projects.

In the ERE, the rate at which each factor of production is discounted over time is equal to the market rate of interest, and also to the originary rate of interest, which is derived from time preference. The originary rate of interest is

> the ratio of the value assigned to want-satisfaction in the immediate future and the value assigned to want-satisfaction in remoter periods of the future. It manifests itself in the market economy in the discount of future goods as against present goods. It is a ratio of commodity prices, not a price itself. There prevails a tendency toward the equalization of this ratio for all commodities. In the imaginary construction of the evenly rotating economy, the rate of originary interest is the same for all commodities.[6]

In the ERE, then, the role of the entrepreneur is strictly limited to the inter-temporal organizing of the factors of production. This

---

[5]See Ludwig von Mises, *Human Action: A Treatise on Economics*, Scholars Edition (Auburn, Ala.: Ludwig von Mises Institute, 1998), pp. 245–51.

[6]Ibid., p. 523.

is not an entrepreneur in the normal sense of the word, since real-world entrepreneurs not only organize factors but also bear the uncertainty of the future states. As Mises points out,

> Under the conditions of a market economy, the rate of originary interest is, provided the assumptions involved in the imaginary construction of the evenly rotating economy are present, equal to the ratio of a definite amount of money available today and the amount available at a later date which is considered its equivalent. The rate of originary interest directs the investment activities of the entrepreneurs. It determines the length of waiting time and of the period of production in every branch of industry.[7]

Thus, it is the rate of originary interest that ERE entrepreneurs use to compare future earnings, hence, present values with present earnings or income.

THE ROLE OF THE ENTREPRENEURIAL COMPONENT

However, in the real world, unlike the ERE, there is a substantial amount of uncertainty: uncertainty about future demand for goods and services, availability of factors of production, possible changes in the regulatory environment and the value of the currency, and much more. Such uncertainty leads to an important role for the entrepreneur.

The entrepreneur uses judgment to assess future changes and to prepare for them now. To the extent that he is successful in anticipating and adjusting for future changes, he is rewarded with economic profit. Economic profit is that received above the opportunity cost he bears. This entrepreneurial judgment extends not only to production but also to credit. As Mises notes, "The granting of credit is necessarily always an entrepreneurial speculation which can result in failure and the loss of a part or the total amount lent. Every interest stipulated and paid in loans includes not only originary interest but also entrepreneurial profit."[8]

---

[7]Ibid., p. 529.
[8]Ibid., p. 533.

Because all action, including production, takes time, all productive activities involve a transaction of present goods for future goods. The only way one can evaluate the exchange of present goods and future goods is through the use of an interest rate. As noted above, in the ERE, this rate is obtained purely through time preference rates and is found on the market through the rate of originary interest and the interactions between buyers and sellers of present money and future money. However, when we leave the ERE, we recognize the element of uncertainty regarding the exchange. Thus, we must add an entrepreneurial component to the interest rate that is used to discount future goods into present goods.

In essence, the capitalist-entrepreneur is present in both equity ownership and in the granting of loans. The capitalist-entrepreneur that purchases capital goods directly with his own resources must weight this decision against all other possible uses for his funds. In this case, the opportunity cost of his action, *ex ante*, is the next best opportunity available to him. For instance, if one could invest $100,000 in the production of a house that was expected to sell for $110,000 in one year, or to invest that same $100,000 into the production of a car that would sell for $108,000 in one year, the opportunity cost of investing in the house would be the $108,000 that could have been earned by producing the car. In the ERE, in the absence of uncertainty, the originary rate of interest is equal to the rate of return in all commodities. When we violate the certainty assumption of the ERE, we remove the certainty associated with every day becoming like the rest, and we remove the central point about which the ERE rotates.

In the presence of uncertainty, the capitalist-entrepreneur performs two functions. First, it is his savings that fund the production process. In this sense, he acts as a capitalist. He believes that his money will be returned to him with an additional premium: the gross market rate of interest. The gross market rate of interest includes the originary rate of interest, plus an entrepreneurial component.[9] As his repayment is uncertain, he must expect a

---

[9]The neutrality of money assumption leads to a convergence of the market rate of interest that reflects the underlying originary rate of interest in society. Capitalist entrepreneurs who possess higher originary rates (time preference

return that compensates him for the uncertainty he must deal with regarding the repayment of the loan.

> The market rates on loans are not pure interest rates. Among the components contributing to their determination there are also elements which are not interest. The money lender is always an entrepreneur. Every grant of credit is a speculative entrepreneurial venture, the success or failure of which is uncertain.[10]

Second, the entrepreneur takes on the additional task of dealing with several forms of uncertainty: the uncertainty associated with the completion of the project, the uncertainty regarding future prices in relation to the money costs of completing the project and the market, the uncertainty of the social and governmental conditions that are essential to the successful completion of the project, and the uncertainty of a return that exceeds the opportunity costs associated with the project. In choosing a project, an entrepreneur will evaluate future expected sales of his project and weigh them against the opportunity costs of the resources used to complete them. In this sense, the entrepreneur must discount future earnings to take into account their temporal distance from the present and the uncertainty that these revenues will occur at the prices expected by the entrepreneur in the future. In a world of money neutrality, the entrepreneur must form an interest rate based on this criteria by which he can discount future earnings. The rate at which he discounts future earnings includes an entrepreneurial component.

All of this is irrelevant to the corporate manager. The corporate manager, by not risking his own funds, has a very different relationship with future uncertainty. While the entrepreneur-manager (or capitalist-entrepreneur) puts up his own money and pays the

---

rates) will sell assets to capitalist-entrepreneurs with lower rates of originary interest. This sale would enable the higher-time preference capitalist-entrepreneur to increase his current income while not disproportionately decreasing the present value of the assets because it was sold to the entrepreneur with the lower time preference rate.

[10]Mises, *Human Action*, p. 536.

opportunity cost of foregoing other investments with it, the corporate manager risks nothing. To the corporate manager, then, the discounted future stream of revenues associated with an investment is important only insofar as it generates his income; he does not have to weigh that stream against the other possible revenue streams he could have generated with the money. Instead, because he cannot capitalize increases in the present value of the firm, his wealth can only be increased with increases in the present cash flows of the firm, either through increased salaries and bonuses to himself, or through increased spending by the firm on things of which he approves. His spending will be geared toward assets that increase his current income and cash flows for the firm at a higher degree than if he were a private owner of the firm. The certainty of gains from earnings in the future is lessened in contrast to those he could expect to earn if he owned the firm. Thus, the uncertainty of income from more distant projects is greater for the manager than if he were the actual owner. Future earnings must be discounted at a higher rate by a corporate manager than by a private owner. Less capital accumulation and less roundabout methods of production will be preferred by a corporate manager relative to a private owner, *ceteris paribus*.

CONCLUSION:
TPR, THE ENTREPRENEURIAL COMPONENT,
AND CORPORATE GOVERNANCE

We have demonstrated that Hoppe's path-breaking analysis of TPR and the distinction between monarchical (private) government and democratic (public) government can be applied to entrepreneurial (private) firms and corporate (public) firms. In both the government and the firm, the private owner, whether monarch or entrepreneur, benefits from both the present current income and the long-term capital value of the firm's assets. Likewise, in both the government and the firm, the non-owner manager, whether public official or corporate manager, is not entitled to the long-term capital value of the asset; all additions to the wealth of such individuals come from present earnings. This necessarily drives discount rates of such non-owner managers higher relative to what they would be for the otherwise similarly situated owner.

The uncertainty of benefiting from future earnings decreases the importance of such earnings to corporate managers. Removal from their position and other factors not present to owner-entrepreneurs make future earnings less certain for non-owner managers; such future earnings are thus discounted at a higher rate by corporate managers.[11] This leads to a greater degree of capital consumption, as managers cannot sell assets and add the revenues from such sales directly to their current income. Instead, managers will exchange more roundabout methods of production for less roundabout means. ❧

---

[11]We do not address the measures by which corporate equity owners can try to alleviate this problem. To do so would require the breaking of the assumption of the non-neutrality of money in the real world, which would lead to a further divergence of interests from owners and managers. Rather, we choose to focus exclusively on the rates at which owners and managers discount earnings, without discussing the relationship between managers and actual owners of their firm. This is a different relationship, and is the subject matter for continued work on this core issue of entrepreneurs versus managers.

Editors and Contributors

EDITORS

JÖRG GUIDO HÜLSMANN (jgh@guidohulsmann.com) is Professor of Economics at the Faculty of Law, Economics, and Management of the University of Angers, France; a Senior Fellow with the Ludwig von Mises Institute; and the author of *Mises: The Last Knight of Liberalism* (2007) and *The Ethics of Money Production* (2008).

STEPHAN KINSELLA (stephan@stephankinsella.com) is an attorney and libertarian writer in Houston, and Editor of *Libertarian Papers* (www.LibertarianPapers.org).

CONTRIBUTORS

ROLAND BAADER (M.Econ.; Roland-Baader@t-online.de) is a private scholar and major representative of the Austrian School in Germany, author of 15 books and hundreds of articles in newspapers, magazines, and scholarly journals.

PHILIPP BAGUS (philipp.bagus@web.de) is assistant professor of economics at the Universidad Rey Juan Carlos in Madrid.

JEFFREY BARR (BarrJ@cityofnorthlasvegas.com) practices law in Las Vegas, Nevada. He studied under Murray Rothbard and Hans Herman-Hoppe in the late 1980s and early 1990s.

LUIGI MARCO BASSANI (marco.bassani@unimi.it) is professor of History of Political Theory at the Università di Milan, Italy.

WALTER BLOCK (WalterBlock.com; wblock@loyno.edu), a long time friend and admirer of Hans Hoppe, is Harold E. Wirth Endowed

Chair and Prof. of Economics, College of Business, Loyola University New Orleans and a Senior Fellow of the Ludwig von Mises Institute.

HARDY BOUILLON (hardy.bouillon@publicpartners.de) teaches philosophy at the University of Trier; is Hayek Institute Endowed Guest Professor at the Vienna University of Economics and Business; and is a Fellow of the International Centre for Economic Research (ICER) in Turin. His books include *Government: Servant or Master?* (1993), *Libertarians and Liberalism* (1997), and *Ordered Anarchy* (2007).

JOHN V. DENSON (donna.moreman@alacourt.gov) is a Circuit Judge in Lee County, Alabama and has been closely connected with the Ludwig von Mises Institute since it was founded. He is the editor of two books, *The Costs of War* and *Reassessing the Presidency* and is the author of a third book *A Century of War*.

THOMAS J. DILORENZO (tdilo@aol.com) is professor of economics at Loyola University-Maryland, and a Senior Fellow of the Ludwig von Mises Institute.

DOUG FRENCH (douglasinvegas@gmail.com) received his Masters degree in economics from the University of Nevada Las Vegas under Murray Rothbard with Professor Hoppe serving on his thesis committee. He, along with Deanna Forbush, were the benefactors for the publication of the second edition of Hoppe's *The Economics and Ethics of Private Property*. French is the President of the Ludwig von Mises Institute in Auburn, Alabama.

MARTIN FRONĔK (fronek@libinst.cz) is a resident researcher at the Liberalni Institute, Prague, focusing on legal doctrines. He translated Bruno Leoni's Freedom and the Law into Czech.

SEAN GABB (sean@libertarian.co.uk), an English libertarian and conservative, is the director of the Libertarian Alliance, a British free market and civil liberties think-tank.

NIKOLAY GERTCHEV (ngertchev@gmail.com) is an economist with the European Commission, Brussels, Belgium.

DAVID GORDON (dgordon@mises.com) is a Senior Fellow at the Ludwig von Mises Institute, the author of numerous books, including *Resurrecting Marx, The Philosophical Origins of Austrian*

Economics, and *An Introduction to Economic Reasoning,* and editor of *The Mises Review.*

PAUL GOTTFRIED (gottfrpe@etown.edu) is Horace Raffensperger Professor of Humanities at Elizabethtown College and author of *Multiculturalism and the Politics of Guilt, The Strange Death of Marxism,* and *Conservatism in America: Making Sense of the American Right,* and his newly published autobiography, *Encounters: My Life with Nixon, Marcuse, and Other Friends and Teachers.*

JEFFREY M. HERBENER (jmherbener@gcc.edu) is professor of economics and chairman of the economics department at Grove City College. He is a Senior Fellow of the Ludwig von Mises Institute Institute and associate editor of *The Quarterly Journal of Austrian Economics.*

ROBERT HIGGS (RHiggs2377@aol.com) is a Senior Fellow in Political Economy for the Independent Institute and editor of *The Independent Review: A Journal of Political Economy.*

JESÚS HUERTA DE SOTO (huertadesoto@dimasoft.es) is Professor of Political Economy, Universidad Rey Juan Carlos, Madrid.

LEE IGLODY (leeiglody@yahoo.com), an attorney in Las Vegas, completed his Bachelor of Arts in Economics with honor under the guidance of Professors Murray N. Rothbard and Hans-Herman Hoppe at the University of Nevada, Las Vegas.

SCOTT A. KJAR (scottakjar@yahoo.com) is Visiting Assistant Professor of Economics at the University of Dallas. He did graduate work under Hans Hoppe and Murray Rothbard at the University of Nevada, Las Vegas.

PETER G. KLEIN (pklein@missouri.edu) is Associate Professor in the Division of Applied Social Sciences at the University of Missouri, Adjunct Professor at the Norwegian School of Economics and Business Administration, and a Senior Fellow of the Ludwig von Mises Institute.

CARLO LOTTIERI (lottieri@tiscalinet.it) is an Italian political philosopher with the University of Siena and Istituto Bruno Leoni whose main interests are in contemporary libertarian thought. Most recently he edited an anthology of writings by Bruno Leoni, *Law,*

Liberty and the Competitive Market (New Brunswick, N.J.: Transaction, 2009).

MATEUSZ MACHAJ (mateusz.machaj@mises.pl) is Instructor of economics at the University of Wroclaw in Poland.

YURI N. MALTSEV (maltsev.yuri@gmail.com) is Professor of Economics at Carthage College and a Senior Fellow of the Ludwig Von Mises Institute.

CHRISTIAN MICHEL (cmichel@cmichel.com) was born in Paris and is a financial consultant in London and Geneva. He is president of Libertarian International.

ROBERT NEF (robertnef@bluewin.ch) is Chairman of the Liberales Institut in Zurich, a classical liberal think tank.

LLEWELLYN H. ROCKWELL, JR., is founder and chairman of the board of the Ludwig von Mises Institute in Auburn, Alabama, and editor of LewRockwell.com.

JOSEPH T. SALERNO (salerno@mises.com) is the Academic Vice-President of the Ludwig von Mises Institute, a Professor of Economics (Chair) at the Lubin School of Business at Pace University, and editor of the *Quarterly Journal of Austrian Economics*.

EUGEN-MARIA SCHULAK (schulak@philosophische-praxis.at) is an entrepreneur serving as philosophical counselor in Vienna, Austria (www.philosophische-praxis.at). A university lecturer and author of six books, he is the director of the Department of Philosophy at the Siemens Academy of Life.

JOSEF ŠÍMA (sima@vse.cz) is a professor and chairman of the Department of Institutional Economics, University of Economics, Prague.

REMIGIJUS ŠIMAŠIUS (Remigijus@lrinka.lt) is Minister of Justice of the Republic of Lithuania. Prior to his appointment to this position in December 2008, he was President of the Lithuanian Free Market Institute.

EDWARD STRINGHAM (edward.stringham@trincoll.edu) is Shelby Cullom Davis Visiting Associate Professor at Trinity College.

MARK THORNTON is a Senior Fellow at the Ludwig von Mises Institute and Book Review Editor of the *Quarterly Journal of Austrian Economics.* mthornton@mises.org

JEFFREY A. TUCKER (tucker@mises.org) is Editorial Vice President of the Ludwig von Mises Institute.

FRANK VAN DUN (Frank.vanDun@Ugent.be) teaches philosophy of law at the University of Ghent. He is the author of *Het Fundamenteel Rechtsbeginsel* (1983, 2008), a Dutch-language book that uses argumentation ethics as the basis for a non-positivist, libertarian theory of law.

JAMES YOHE (jyohe@gadsdenstate.edu) is Economics Instructor at Gadsden State College in Gadsden, Alabama. He studied under Hans Hoppe and Murray Rothbard at the University of Nevada, Las Vegas. ❧

Index of Names

Index of Subjects

www.ingramcontent.com/pod-product-compliance
Lightning Source LLC
Chambersburg PA
CBHW071326280526
45787CB00001B/4